# THE LAW AND ECONOMI
## AGREEMI

Framework agreements have arisen in response to the well-documented high costs of public procurement procedures. The agreements have significant potential to improve procedural efficiency in public procurement, but they are complex to operate. Inadequate preparation and implementation can also frustrate their potential both to tackle waste, abuse and corruption and to enhance value for money. In this enlightening book, Gian Luigi Albano and Caroline Nicholas look at the key decisions required for designing and using framework agreements and address both legal and economic issues to give the reader a clear understanding of the planning, variables and flexibility needed for efficient implementation. This book will be of interest to policymakers, lawyers and public procurement practitioners who want to deepen their understanding of the legal and economic issues surrounding framework agreements.

GIAN LUIGI ALBANO is Head of Research at Consip Ltd, and Professor at the School of National Administration, Rome. He is also serving as Adjunct Professor (2015–16) in the Department of Economics at LUISS 'G. Carli', Rome, Italy.

CAROLINE NICHOLAS is Senior Legal Officer in the International Trade Law Division at the United Nations Office of Legal Affairs.

# THE LAW AND ECONOMICS OF FRAMEWORK AGREEMENTS

*Designing Flexible Solutions for Public Procurement*

GIAN LUIGI ALBANO

CAROLINE NICHOLAS

# CAMBRIDGE
## UNIVERSITY PRESS

University Printing House, Cambridge CB2 8BS, United Kingdom

One Liberty Plaza, 20th Floor, New York, NY 10006, USA

477 Williamstown Road, Port Melbourne, VIC 3207, Australia

314-321, 3rd Floor, Plot 3, Splendor Forum, Jasola District Centre, New Delhi - 110025, India

79 Anson Road, #06-04/06, Singapore 079906

Cambridge University Press is part of the University of Cambridge.

It furthers the University's mission by disseminating knowledge in the pursuit of education, learning and research at the highest international levels of excellence.

www.cambridge.org
Information on this title: www.cambridge.org/9781107434981

© Gian Luigi Albano and Caroline Nicholas 2016

This publication is in copyright. Subject to statutory exception and to the provisions of relevant collective licensing agreements, no reproduction of any part may take place without the written permission of Cambridge University Press.

First published 2016
First paperback edition 2018

*A catalogue record for this publication is available from the British Library*

*Library of Congress Cataloging in Publication data*
Albano, Gian Luigi author. | Nicholas, Caroline, author.
The law and economics of framework agreements : designing flexible solutions for public procurement / Gian Luigi Albano, Caroline Nicholas.
New York : Cambridge University Press, 2016.
LCCN 2015041409 | ISBN 9781107077966 (hardback)
LCSH: Public contracts. | Government purchasing – Law and legislation.
| BISAC: LAW / Commercial / International Trade.
LCC K884 .A95 2016 | DDC 342/.066–dc23
LC record available at http://lccn.loc.gov/2015041409

ISBN 978-1-107-07796-6 Hardback
ISBN 978-1-107-43498-1 Paperback

Cambridge University Press has no responsibility for the persistence or accuracy of URLs for external or third-party internet websites referred to in this publication, and does not guarantee that any content on such websites is, or will remain, accurate or appropriate.

*'To Iole, Gaia, Viola and Alice'*
*and*
*'To Ben, Tom and Charles'*

# Contents

| | |
|---|---|
| *List of figures* | *page* ix |
| *List of tables* | x |
| *Acknowledgements* | xi |

PART I  THE ESSENTIALS OF FRAMEWORK AGREEMENTS: BASIC DEFINITIONS, MAIN ECONOMIC FORCES AND INTERNATIONAL EXPERIENCE ... 1

1  Introduction ... 3

2  Description, taxonomy and motivations for using framework agreements ... 12

3  Some key economic dimensions in framework agreements ... 31

4  The economic analysis of framework agreements ... 50

5  International experience in framework agreements ... 84

6  International experience in centralised purchasing ... 124

PART II  FOSTERING COMPETITION AND PREVENTING COLLUSION IN FRAMEWORK AGREEMENTS ... 155

7  Promoting effective competition and enhancing outcomes in framework agreements ... 157

8  Integrity concerns in framework agreements ... 179

9  Addressing risks of collusion in framework agreements ... 212

PART III THE DESIGN OF FRAMEWORK AGREEMENTS         253

10  Essential issues in framework agreements for the individual
    buyer                                                        255
11  Framework agreements for centralised procurement             280
12  Legal and regulatory issues in framework agreements
    procedures                                                   305
    Conclusions                                                  324

*Glossary of commonly used terms that vary among systems*        331
*Index*                                                          332

# Figures

| | | |
|---|---|---|
| 2.1 | Models of framework agreements. | *page* 20 |
| 6.1 | Legal status of central purchasing bodies. | 127 |
| 6.2 | Number of items purchased through the Price Registration System as compared to the total number of items purchased by the Federal Government Procurement system. | 139 |
| 6.3 | Total confirmed value of purchases through the Price Registration System as compared to the value of all purchases by the Federal Government Procurement. | 139 |
| 6.4 | Number of government units purchasing through the Price Registration System as compared to the number of government units – Federal Government Procurement. | 140 |
| 6.5 | Share of public procurement by mechanism in Chile. | 141 |
| 10.1 | The choice of the appropriate family of framework agreements based on the main features of demand and supply | 262 |
| 10.2 | Balancing competition at the two stages of a framework agreement | 267 |
| 11.1 | Unbundling $n$ different services in a framework agreement | 295 |
| 11.2 | Geographical lots in a framework agreement for petrol and oil for heating | 296 |

# Tables

| | | |
|---|---|---|
| 3.1 | Consip's DPS for pharmaceutical products | *page* 48 |
| 4.1 | Sample of performance dimensions and measures of contract enforcement in Consip's National Framework Contracts (Italy) | 54 |
| 4.2 | An example of awardees' prices at the call-off stage of a multi-award Model 1 framework agreement | 63 |
| 6.1 | Role of central purchasing bodies in OECD countries | 125 |
| 6.2 | Value of purchases through Consip's framework agreements in 2014 | 129 |
| 6.3 | Number of products (SKU level) in ChileCompra's e-store | 142 |
| 6.4 | Value of purchasing orders in 2014 and 2015 through framework agreements awarded by Colombia Compra Eficiente | 143 |
| 6.5 | Oromiya framework contracts | 145 |
| 6.6 | Federal PPPDS framework contracts | 146 |
| 6.7 | Rate contracts versus maximum retail prices for six generic drugs bought by TNMSC | 150 |
| 8.1 | First-stage competition for entering a multi-award Model 2 framework agreement | 198 |
| 8.2 | Unit prices resulting from the first stage of competition in a multi-award Model 2 framework agreement | 202 |

# *Acknowledgements*

At a public procurement conference in Panama in 2012, the authors found themselves discussing some presentations on framework agreements as used in that region at some length. Our main conclusion was that the models of framework agreements presented were very far removed from those used in our own systems – in the European Union (EU) and as envisaged in the United Nations Commission on International Trade Law (UNCITRAL) Model Law respectively. The conversation started a journey that has, ultimately, led to this book. We were motivated by our experience to encourage more discussions across the world – we have found that there is much to be learned from those facing similar issues from outside our regions, whether that experience is positive or negative.

We would like to express our grateful thanks to all those who have assisted us in the preparation of this book. The list of colleagues and friends to whom we owe both a personal and an intellectual debt is so long that we will inevitably risk omission – but, to you all, you know who you are and we are immensely grateful.

From the economics side, the first and most deserved acknowledgement goes to Consip Ltd., a company that over the past fifteen years has become the pillar of the reform of the Italian public procurement system and remains a formidable laboratory for the design and implementation of innovative public procurement solutions.

We consequently also wish to thank the National School of Public Administration, Italy – and in particular Professor Giovanni Tria and Alberto Heimler – for offering Gian Luigi a position of part-time professor. At the School, he has had and still has the privilege of testing much of the book's content in training modules for procurement officials from all sectors of the Italian public administration.

From the legal side, there is an overwhelming debt of gratitude to the members of the UNCITRAL Working Group and Expert Groups who contributed so much to the development of the UNCITRAL Model Law on Public Procurement, and the education of its secretary, both in the field of public procurement law and policy and in the development of private international law.

Much of what we have learned about public procurement systems around the world is also the result of invitations to participate in and contribute to conferences, workshops, round tables and peer-review projects sponsored and organised by the European Commission, the European Parliament, the European Bank for Reconstruction and Development, the Inter-American Development Bank, the Organisation for Economic Co-operation and Development (OECD), the Organisation for Security and Co-operation (OSCE), the United Nations Office on Drugs and Crime (UNODC), the United Nations Development Programme (UNDP), the World Bank and the World Trade Organisation (WTO).

We are profoundly grateful to representatives of all these bodies and to other colleagues, including Rob Anderson, Elodie Beth, Janos Bertok, Peder Blomberg, Niall Bohan, Chenjerani Simon B. Chirwa, Ana Cristina Calderon Ramirez, Tomas Campero, David Drabkin, Gabriele Maria Del Monte, Julia Ferger, Michael Fruhmann, Felipe Goya, Jerome Grand D'Esnon, Cristina Gutiérrez, Leslie E. Harper, Shanker Lal, Knut Leipold, Marian Lemke, Ivo Locatelli, Paulo Magina, Eliza Niewadomska, Ana Rodrigues, Johannes Schnitzer, Peter Smith, Nikita Stampa, Don Wallace and Tore Wiwen-Nilsson.

During the drafting of the book, we have benefited from the generosity of many colleagues around the world, most notably Klenio Barbosa, Guillermo Burr, Anthony Butler, Trinidad Inostroza, Nicolás Penagos and María Margarita Zuleta. In spite of the continuous evolution of public procurement systems in virtually all continents, transactions-related data are often scant, and thus evidence-based policymaking exercises are all but an easy task. ChileCompra (Chile), Colombia Compra Eficiente (Colombia), the Federal and Oromiya Public Procurement and Property Disposal Services (the Republic of Ethiopia) provided crucial hints and first-hand figures which allowed this research endeavour to remain as close as possible to the real functioning of public procurement organisations.

'Economists are often considered as "intruders" – or, in the best cases, "new comers"' – in the academic world of public procurement, which is traditionally (and for sensible reasons) populated by legal scholars, and lawyers generally are unable to speak 'economics' even without the formulae. We have met many colleagues from each other's discipline in recent years that have assisted us in understanding our own and each other's disciplines, but it would be hard to exaggerate the positive influence exerted on our views in both fields by Professors Sue Arrowsmith, Daniel Gordon, Gabriella M. Racca, Roberto Cavallo Perin, Gustavo Piga, Alberto Sanchez Graells, Peter Trepte, Steven Schooner and Christopher R. Yukins.

A final and heartfelt 'thank you!' to our junior collaborators – Federico Antellini Russo, Angela Cipollone, Marco Sparro and Roberto Zampino – who have enthusiastically embraced our passion for bringing the logic of modern microeconomics into the wheels of a sophisticated public procurement 'engine' and allowed us to attempt to translate that logic into a policy and regulatory framework.

We would also like to acknowledge the support and encouragement we have received from Cambridge University Press for writing this book and the considerable patience shown during the process.

While we thank all mentioned above and others who have chosen to remain anonymous, the errors and omissions, of course, are all our own.

PART I

# The essentials of framework agreements
*Basic definitions, main economic forces and international experience*

CHAPTER I

## *Introduction*

Public procurement policy is commonly grounded in terms of promoting best value for money and avoiding corruption, waste and abuse.[1] Well-documented experience of failures in this regard, the enormous economic power of public procurement and the expansion of world trade and efforts to liberalise it have led to the development of formal rules governing public procurement at both the international and national levels.[2] Many of those rules, in addition to requiring that procurement officials follow open tendering (considered to be the most effective way of securing best value for the government), stipulate 'honesty and integrity in source selection, and equality of opportunity for would-be contractors',[3] together with requirements for internal controls, such as documenting decisions and formal approval processes.

---

[1] Preamble to the UNCITRAL Model Law (UNCITRAL Model Law on Public Procurement (2011)), *Official Records of the General Assembly, Sixty-sixth Session, Supplement No. 17* (UN document A/66/17). The text of the Model Law is available at www.uncitral.org/uncitral_texts/procurement_infrastructure.html. Hereafter, Model Law. See, also, Steven L. Schooner, Daniel I. Gordon and Jessica L. Clark, 'Public Procurement Systems: Unpacking Stakeholder Aspirations and Expectations', GWU Law School Public Law Research Paper 1133234 (2008), available at http://ssrn.com/abstract=1133234, p. 32.
[2] United Nations Convention against Corruption, UN General Assembly (hereafter, UNCAC), 31 October 2003, A/58/422, available at: www.refworld.org/docid/4374b9524.html, Article 9(1)(c); The World Trade Organisation Revised Agreement on Government Procurement available at www.wto.org/english/docs_e/legal_e/rev-gpr-94_01_e.htm. Hereafter, WTO GPA; Directive 2014/24/EU of the European Parliament and of the Council of 26 February 2014 on public procurement and repealing Directive 2004/18/EC Text with EEA relevance, OJ L 94, 28 March 2014, pp. 65–242, available at http://eur-lex.europa.eu/legal-content/EN/TXT/?uri=celex:32014L0024. Hereafter, the EU Directive; The UNCITRAL Model Law (UNCITRAL Model Law on Public Procurement (2011), *Official Records of the General Assembly, Sixty-sixth Session, Supplement No. 17* (UN document A/66/17). The text of the Model Law is available at www.uncitral.org/uncitral/uncitral_texts/procurement_infrastructure.html. Hereafter, the Model Law; Federal Acquisition Regulation (FAR), Code of Federal Regulations (CFR) Title 48. FAR 2005-83/07-02-2015, available at www.acquisition.gov/?q=browsefar.
[3] Joshua I. Schwartz, 'Katrina's Lessons for Ongoing US Procurement Reform Efforts', *Public Procurement Law Review*, 6 (2006): 362–373.

The introduction and growing use of framework agreements in many systems have coincided with three main policy developments in public procurement, which we present in broadly chronological order. The first is a growing focus on anti-corruption, reflected in the agreement of the United Nations Convention against Corruption, the relative speed at which it was ratified and came into force and in implementation activities;[4] the second is a near-universal attempt to reduce the cost of public procurement in national systems, given the impetus by what is generally referred to as the worldwide financial crisis starting in 2008;[5] and the third is the growing emphasis on 'sustainable procurement', which can include policies to support environmental, social and economic objectives in public procurement. Most public procurement systems seek to address all three policy areas – which can be expressed as objectives or constraints, depending on the reader's point of view – and, as has long been noted, they are not always mutually compatible.[6] Balancing the competing considerations – often described in terms of discretion versus efficiency – has been the focus of policy debate in public procurement for decades.

Framework agreements involve a two-stage procurement procedure to secure the supply of a good or service in the future, used primarily where the procuring entity does not know the exact quantities, nature or timing of its requirements over a given period. The first stage leads to the identification of one or more suppliers on the basis of a tender or similar offer and conclusion of a framework agreement (in essence, a master contract) for the future supply. At the second stage, when the need arises for the subject matter of the framework agreement, the procuring entity places an order or enters into a contract (in the European Union (EU), generally referred to as a 'call-off') for its need with the supplier or suppliers that have entered into the master or framework agreement.

Thus, the main potential benefit of framework agreements is that they can reduce transaction costs and time by aggregating purchases, so that some procedural steps, such as advertising and assessing qualifications or

---

[4] UNCAC, supra, note 2. For the Status of UNCAC, see www.unodc.org/unodc/en/treaties/CAC/signatories.html; for activities of the Conference of States Parties, see www.unodc.org/unodc/en/treaties/CAC/CAC-COSP.html.

[5] Providing a broader context: as procurement is 'politically less sensitive' than other government expenditure, it is a target for cost-controlling policies for governments – G. L. Albano and M. Sparro, 'Flexible Strategies for Centralized Public Procurement', *Review of Economics and Institutions*, 1, No. 2 (2010); retrieved from www.rei.unipg.it/rei/article/view/17, at p. 2.

[6] Joshua I. Schwartz, 'Regulation and Deregulation in Public Procurement Law Reform in the United States', in G. Piga and K. V. Thai (eds.), *Advancing Public Procurement: Practices, Innovation and Knowledge-Sharing* (Boca Raton, FL: PrAcademic Press, 2007), pp. 177–201.

tenders, are conducted once for the group of purchases, rather than individually for each purchase. The procedural costs concerned are aggregated over a series of purchases, and the time to issue purchase orders is generally far shorter than in traditional open and competitive procedures. Framework agreements and the procedures to conclude them are therefore primarily designed to improve procedural efficiency in public procurement,[7] resulting from, at least in part, a perception that anti-corruption measures had led to an overly complex, inefficient procurement process.[8] In addition, framework agreements are considered to have the potential to 'increase dramatically the freedom [given to] public officials to use their judgment in the procurement process' to enhance value-for-money outcomes, as the then head of the United States (US) Office of Federal Procurement Policy urged the procurement community to adopt back in 1990.[9]

From this perspective, framework agreements are particularly suitable for repeat purchases of relatively standard goods or services (office and simple information and communication technology [ICT] supplies, and simple services such as maintenance contracts), in which the procedural costs could also become disproportionate to the value of the procurement if conducted on a one-off basis. The savings of time mean, too, that framework agreements can be of assistance in circumstances that would otherwise justify less open and competitive procedures – such as emergencies and other urgent situations – where framework agreements have been concluded in advance. The aggregation of the purchases, so they are not undertaken through less open and competitive procedures, also offers potentially better outcomes in those procurements themselves. It is often assumed that framework agreements are used only for simple, standardised purchases but, as we shall see, the technique is of potentially much wider beneficial application.

Nonetheless, framework agreements are not always appropriate. Procedurally efficient procurement does not guarantee overall value for money. The second stage is considered to be more at risk from this perspective, as it may involve the use of considerable discretion and is not always fully transparent and competitive,[10] which may result in higher

---

[7] 'Efficiency' in this context refers to the administrative costs of engaging in a particular procurement process, rather than in the economic sense of allocating resources in an optimal way.
[8] 'Public Procurement Systems: Unpacking Stakeholder Aspirations and Expectations', note 1, supra.
[9] S. Kelman, *Procurement and Public Management: The Fear of Discretion and the Quality of Government Performance* (Washington, DC: The AEI Press, 1990), p. 90.
[10] It has been observed that 'once a master agreement is in place, an order for goods or services can be issued against that agreement with far less notice and process, often with little risk of accountability'.

prices exceeding administrative savings. In addition, the procedure as a whole can limit rather than expand market access. These potential risks also increase with framework agreements of longer duration.

In aggregating procurement, framework agreements also involve some complex design issues, so a robust planning process is required. For example, different structures of framework agreement will reflect whether the need for what is to be procured is narrowly defined or stable, and/or whether the relevant markets are volatile. Related questions include whether the offer that will best meet the needs of the procuring entity can be determined only when needs arise or at the first stage, the extent to which there is homogeneity of demand, and the extent to which standardisation can be imposed or encouraged. Clearly these issues need to be addressed as part of the planning process, so the first stage is a relatively complex one. On the other hand, the second stage is intended to be procedurally swift and straightforward, without complex assessments.

Consequently, and for the same reasons noted for public procurement systems as a whole, a consensus is emerging on the need for effective rules on the operation of framework agreements and the procedures to conclude them. This consensus is reflected in a trend towards express regulation of the technique, as noted in a study conducted by the United Nations Commission on International Trade Law (UNCITRAL) in 2006,[11] a process that is continuing at the national level. Formal rules for the use of framework agreements will reflect a series of key decisions, including regulating whether or not to use a framework agreement, how to ensure effective design and use, and providing for monitoring and *ex-post* controls.

The importance of the above considerations also means that the appropriate level of flexibility in any particular system needs to reflect the capacity of its participants, and the system may need a dynamic approach, as experience in the use of framework agreements may indicate a change in parameters. The different considerations for the two stages of the

---

See Christopher R. Yukins, 'Are ID/IQs Inefficient? Sharing lessons with European Framework Contracting', *Public Contract Law Journal*, 37, No. 3 (2008): 546–568.

[11] 'Possible revisions to the UNCITRAL Model Law on Procurement of Goods, Construction and Services – the use of framework agreements in public procurement', UN documents A/CN.9/WG.I/WP.44 and A/CN.9/WG.I/WP.44/Add 1, available at www.uncitral.org/uncitral/en/commission/working_groups/1Procurement.html. UNCITRAL Working Papers are designated by 'A/CN.9/WG', to represent a Working Group document under a General Assembly mandate, and then have a consecutive number assigned to the specific document (e.g. UN document A/CN.9/WG.I/WP.44, note 13, supra). Reports of the Working Groups do not have the 'WG' designation, as they are reports to UNCITRAL in plenary session (known as the Commission sessions), and so are, for example, A/CN.9/752.

procedure involve a dual approach from the policy perspective, so that the second stage in particular is not overburdened by procedural rules, though sufficient safeguards to protect transparency and competition are necessary.

This book seeks to tackle all these issues, drawing together the economic considerations underlying effective use of framework agreements and how those considerations should be reflected in the policy choices and rules implementing them. We will analyse the business case for the use of framework agreements procedures, and outline the policy considerations that their use raises, and then consider how the policy choices made can be best reflected in the regulatory rules and other tools and documents that will govern the system concerned, in the context of the system as a whole and as applied to a particular procurement procedure. A natural focus where rules are concerned is to discourage inappropriate use or misuse through procedural safeguards, but we shall also provide examples from practice designed to illustrate how the tool can be harnessed to support overall policy objectives in public procurement and to introduce innovation both in procedures and in what the government purchases. The regulatory rules enabling the use of framework agreements procedures should reflect an appropriate level of flexibility in rules and guidance by reference to existing capacity and levels of governance, and allow for development as experience in the use of framework agreements is acquired. We will make some recommendations, too, on how these policy objectives can be reflected and expressed in legal rules, guidance and other tools, with a view to maximising comprehensibility for those users and the bidders they are seeking to attract.

Framework agreements can be concluded by a procuring entity for its own use, by a 'buying club' of procuring entities for their collective use (generally with a lead procuring entity as the main contractor) or by an agency established for the purpose of procurement of goods and services for procuring entities (a 'centralised purchasing agency'). We will conduct the main analysis by reference to a procuring entity setting up a framework agreement for its own use, and subsequently consider additional issues where more than one procuring entity or a centralised purchasing agency sets up a framework agreement for other public bodies to use.

We will address the key decisions required for introducing, designing and using framework agreements: the decision whether or not to use a framework agreement; the need for effective planning; deciding among key variables in form, structure and other elements; monitoring; and implementing remedies for breaches of procedures. Designing the system for and setting up framework agreements, however, is only part of the question: data-gathering and empirical analysis of their operation in practice are crucial elements necessary to identify whether or not the potential benefits are materialising in practice.

Thus, we are addressing our thoughts to a wide audience, at the international as well as national level. We address both law and economics, with a view to ensuring that the use of framework agreements can be undertaken in as efficient and effective a manner as possible. In this regard, we ask how the legal rules on framework agreements and the procedures to procure using them can achieve the rather demanding objectives placed on the technique, and thus hope to provide comments of interest to those creating legal and regulatory frameworks. We also consider how the design and use of framework agreements in practice can contribute to (or compromise) the achievement of those objectives, and, in this regard, address our comments to public officials who are responsible for the organisation of public procurement, procurement officials and suppliers alike. This book is far from a comprehensive guidance to all legal issues arising, and still less an operational manual, though we identify the major issues concerned. We look at the individual framework agreement and the use of the technique for the aggregation of the needs of procuring entities through centralised purchasing.

The book is organised in three parts:

- Part I: *The essentials of framework agreements: Basic definitions, main economic forces and international experience*
- Part II: *Fostering competition and preventing collusion in framework agreements*
- Part III: *The design of framework agreements*

Part I introduces the reader to different families of framework agreements. While recognising that different approaches might be used to classify framework agreements, the book adopts a three-model approach: Model 1 comprises those arrangements whereby the master contract – that is, the framework agreement – contains all relevant clauses for awarding procurement contracts, and thus offers a straightforward purchase-order approach once the framework agreement is in place; Model 2 comprises those cases whereby the master contract is to some extent incomplete, hence a second round of competition is necessary for awarding procurement contracts. Moreover, both Models 1 and 2 are *closed* in that procurement contracts can be awarded only to those suppliers selected at the first stage of the process. Model 3, instead, is an *open* family of framework agreements, whereby new firms can enter the system at any time so they can then compete for each procurement contract thereafter.

Although aiming principally at enhancing process efficiency and at a better exploitation of economies of scale, the *practice* of framework agreements has gradually showed that such purchasing arrangements can be used to better guarantee readiness and security of supply especially for crucial products (e.g. medicines) and in emergency circumstances. Different objectives generate quite diverse economic forces that need to be pondered and anticipated in order to reap framework agreements' potential benefits.

The precise nature of the contract between the public purchaser and the seller(s) to the government concerned will depend on many elements, among which one of the most important is the extent to which the purchaser's need is stable over time (and, where there are multiple purchasers grouped together, the extent to which their needs vary). To this factor must be added the degree of concentration of the supply market, the extent to which the master contract is complete or incomplete, the nature of the award criteria and the number of awardees with which the framework agreement is concluded. Part I will flesh out a methodological approach not only to assess the impact of each of the above factors on the desired outcome but also to evaluate how they may interact (and potentially interfere) with each other.

In the last two chapters of Part I we shall examine international practice on framework agreements. We shall consider how the development of regulation and practice of framework agreements procedures in various systems has evolved over time, and identify some areas of concern of regulation and practice. For example, some aspects might be contributing to or detracting from the achievement of the potential benefits of framework agreements, and others to how they avoid, or fail to avoid, some common pitfalls. Our presentation of this international experience cannot rely on much data and formal analysis, beyond limited aggregate information from certain centralised purchasing agencies. Nonetheless, we have identified consistent elements of practice that emerge from existing systems, some positive and some less so.

Part II will be entirely devoted to the issue of anticompetitive conduct on the part of suppliers in the operation of framework agreements. A feature of framework agreements is that the *closed* varieties in particular can limit the market to a limited number of suppliers and so create a temporary shelter from competition from outside the framework agreement. This quasi-oligopolistic situation may facilitate collusion at either stage of the procedure, but the major concern arises at the second stage of some types of framework agreement (multi-supplier, Model 2 variants in particular). Some advances in the modern economic analysis of collusion are adapted in Part II of the book to highlight the extent to which different design solutions normally encountered in practice may raise the risk of collusion.

It is a widely held view that transparency of public procurement processes, while lowering the chances that an opaque relationship emerges between suppliers and procuring entities, may strengthen collusive agreements. The last chapter of Part II aims at opening up the black box of the 'transparency dilemma' by raising the following question: which pieces of information at what stages of the framework agreement procedure may have a pro-collusive impact on market conduct? While recognising that, in fact, cartels need very little information to implement collusive agreements, the analysis emphasises that procurement officials are in a position to withhold some pieces of information that are deemed to have an anti-competitive impact. Using discretion in this matter requires, needless to say, both a well-trained workforce and, perhaps more importantly, some explicit forms of cooperation between procurement organisations and antitrust authorities.

Part III of the book will lay down some 'nuts and bolts' for framework agreements design, both at the regulatory and operational levels. The main lesson coming from the earlier two parts of the book is that multiple layers of economic forces are at work in frameworks agreements, hence sound design requires: (i) a clear understanding of procuring entities' needs and of the main features of the relevant supply markets; (ii) a recognition that no 'free lunch' applies, either, in framework agreements markets, so that pursuing a specific objective may be feasible only to the extent that another goal is let go; (iii) the ability to assess, at least qualitatively, the magnitude of different economic forces that are likely to emerge from any feasible scenario; and (iv) a willingness to adopt a trial-and-error approach, which necessitates the recognition that there is no 'right' framework agreement solution. Avoiding over-ambition is vital, especially where framework agreements are used for ambitious projects of centralising public procurement, even in part.

Finally, we draw together the main conclusions that we have reached. Key among them is the need for a more coherent debate on economics in policymaking. We consider that economics and business practice should be the foundation of public procurement policy and how it feeds into the regulatory system, and – at the risk of proselytising – encourage all involved in policy, reform and operation to take up the mantle when implementing framework agreements in their systems.

The book was conceived to talk to as large an audience as possible: policymakers, lawyers, public procurement practitioners, academics and students who wish both to broaden and to deepen their understanding of the legal and economic subtleties of framework agreements. The discussion could make a contribution to the consideration of 'aggregation techniques' in advanced academic courses on the law and economics of framework agreements.

We sincerely hope that readers will find the journey through the book both intriguing and enlightening.

CHAPTER 2

# Description, taxonomy and motivations for using framework agreements

## 2.1 Introduction

The deceptively simple description of a framework agreement procedure set out in the introductory chapter belies a wide variation in the terms and use of the technique in practice. The term we have used as a common denominator, a 'framework agreement',[1] is also an umbrella term for a broad category of commercial arrangements. In a wide-ranging survey in 2006,[2] UNCITRAL identified the following additional English-language names for two-stage procurement techniques: indefinite-delivery/ indefinite quantity (ID/IQ) or task-order contracts in the United States, running and rate contracts in some countries in Africa and the Caribbean, as well as in India; supply arrangements and standing offers in Canada;[3] panel arrangements in Australia;[4] and periodic or recurrent purchase arrangements, periodic requirements arrangements, catalogue contracts, umbrella contracts and supply vehicles in the literature.[5] In the EU, a distinction is also drawn between 'framework agreements', 'framework

---

[1] The term 'framework agreement' is used in the European Union, in many countries in Africa and Asia that follow the British legal system, in Latin America and in some international financial institutions.

[2] 'Possible Revisions to the UNCITRAL Model Law on Procurement of Goods, Construction and Services – the Use of Framework Agreements in Public Procurement', UN documents A/CN.9/WG. I/WP.44 and A/CN.9/WG.I/WP.44/Add 1, available at www.uncitral.org/uncitral/en/commission/ working_groups/1Procurement.html. UNCITRAL Working Papers are designated by 'A/CN.9/ WG', to represent a Working Group document under a General Assembly mandate, and then have a consecutive number assigned to the specific document (e.g. UN document A/CN.9/WG.I/ WP.44, note 13, supra). Reports of the Working Groups do not have the 'WG' designation, as they are reports to UNCITRAL in plenary session (known as the Commission sessions), and so are, for example, A/CN.9/752.

[3] Ibid.

[4] According to the Department of Finance of the Government of Australia, a panel arrangement is a tool for the procurement of goods or services regularly acquired by procuring entities, concluded with a number of suppliers, and is to be contrasted with a multi-use list. See, further, www.finance .gov.au/procurement/procurement-policy-and-guidance/buying/procurement-practice/panel-and-mul/principles.html.

[5] A/CN.9/WG.I/WP.44, note 2, supra.

## Description, taxonomy and motivations for using framework agreements 13

contracts' and 'dynamic purchasing systems', which we will consider as variants of the framework agreements discussed in this book.

A key need therefore is to delineate the types of arrangement we shall analyse throughout this book and to exclude those not under consideration. We consider the following steps as necessary elements of a framework agreement procedure:

(a) an invitation to potential suppliers to present offers against a description of the procuring entity's needs;
(b) the selection of one or more suppliers on the basis of their responses to the invitation;
(c) the procuring entity and the selected supplier(s) entering into a framework agreement; and
(d) the subsequent placing of orders with the selected supplier(s) as particular requirements arise.

Steps (a)–(c) are the 'first stage' of the procedure. Step (d) is the 'second stage' of the procedure.

Framework agreements are qualitatively different from lists of suppliers, although the two techniques have been described as 'shades on a spectrum' in that both are designed to identify potential suppliers for future needs.[6] The difference between them is that a framework agreement sets the scope of future needs of the procuring entity, whereas a list of suppliers refers to generic types of procurement. Hence, an invitation to participate in a framework agreement procedure (step (a) above) contains a description of the procuring entity's needs and generally of other terms and conditions of the procurement, against which qualifications and responses are assessed. An invitation to register on a list of suppliers, on the other hand, need not describe a particular need, and the process need not require an assessment of the suppliers' status or qualifications, though suppliers may be screened in reference to their eligibility to participate in all public procurement or some types of procurement in a particular system.[7] Thus, the selection of the suppliers under a framework agreement procedure involves an assessment of their ability to respond to the identified needs

---

[6] Ibid.
[7] 'Possible Revisions to the UNCITRAL Model Law on Procurement of Goods, Construction and Services – Issues Arising from the Use of Suppliers' Lists'. Note by the Secretariat, UN document A/CN.9/WG.I/WP.45 and A/CN.9/WG.I/WP.45/Add.1, available at www.uncitral.org/uncitral/en/commission/working_groups/1Procurement.html. Information in some systems may be limited to basic data about suppliers (e.g. identification information, legal form, goods supplied, contact information), and in others eligibility for listing may extend to experience, technical, managerial and financial capacity, organisation and availability of equipment, staff and skills.

of a procuring entity whereas inclusion on a list of suppliers generally does not.

Consequently, not all of the techniques described are framework agreements for our purposes. The Canadian supply arrangements and standing offers referred to above are, under our analysis, more appropriately considered as lists of suppliers than as framework agreements, albeit to the extent that the scope of the procuring entity's needs is not defined in an invitation to participate and the second (award) stage is conducted through a full procurement procedure, though direct solicitation of identified suppliers is permissible.[8]

We shall refer to the salient characteristics of framework agreements and the procedures to conclude them mainly in reference to three legal systems, which define framework agreements procedures differently but consistently with the key elements we set out above. The definition in the EU Directive is as follows: 'A framework agreement means an agreement between one or more contracting authorities and one or more economic operators, the purpose of which is to establish the terms governing contracts to be awarded during a given period, in particular with regard to price and, where appropriate, the quantity envisaged'.[9]

The UNCITRAL Model Law has a similar definition: a framework agreement procedure is 'conducted in two stages: a first stage to select supplier (or suppliers) ... to be a party (or parties) to a framework agreement with a procuring entity, and a second stage to award a procurement contract under the framework agreement to a supplier ... party to the framework agreement'.[10] The purpose of the framework agreement itself is to establish 'the terms upon which purchases will be made (or [to establish] the main terms and a mechanism to be used to establish the remaining terms or refine the initially established terms)'.[11]

---

[8] A/CN.9/WG.I/WP.44, note 2, supra.
[9] Article 33(1), Directive 2014/24/EU of the European Parliament and of the Council of 26 February 2014 on public procurement and repealing Directive 2004/18/EC Text with EEA relevance, OJ L 94, 28.3.2014, pp. 65–242, available at http://eur-lex.europa.eu/legal-content/EN/TXT/?uri=celex:32014 L0024. Hereafter, the EU Directive.
[10] Article 2(e), UNCITRAL Model Law on Public Procurement (2011), *Official Records of the General Assembly, Sixty-sixth Session, Supplement No. 17* (UN document A/66/17). The text of the Model Law is available at www.uncitral.org/uncitral/uncitral_texts/procurement_infrastructure.html. Hereafter, Model Law.
[11] Para 2, p. 253, Introduction, chapter VII Introduction to Framework agreement procedures, Guide to Enactment of the UNCITRAL Model Law on Public Procurement (2012), *Official Records of the General Assembly, Sixty-seventh Session, Supplement No. 17* (para 46, UN document A/67/17). The text of the Guide to Enactment is available at www.uncitral.org/uncitral/uncitral_texts/procurement_in frastructure.html. Hereafter, Guide to Enactment.

*Description, taxonomy and motivations for using framework agreements* 15

The Federal Acquisition Regulation in the United States defines the equivalent procedure as follows: ' "Delivery-order contract" means a contract for supplies that does not procure or specify a firm quantity of supplies (other than a minimum or maximum quantity) and that provides for the issuance of orders for the delivery of supplies during the period of the contract. "Task-order contract" means a contract for services that does not procure or specify a firm quantity of services (other than a minimum or maximum quantity) and that provides for the issuance of orders for the performance of tasks during the period of the contract'.[12]

The terms 'framework agreements' and 'framework agreements procedures' will be used throughout this book for convenience, as they are the most common terms in English for this type of arrangement and are used by not only the European Union and UNCITRAL but also by the World Bank,[13] and are the most common translations of the terminology used in various national systems in Latin America. However, we are not referring to the procedures of any one system (save where mentioned); indeed, the significant differences between the procedures and requirements for framework agreements procedures under different regulatory regimes indicate that care is needed in transferring experience from one system to another.

Even within this relatively narrow notion of framework agreements, however, there remain many potential approaches. In essence, a two-stage process including steps (a)–(d) above can still encompass a range of procurement vehicles, from an identification of all willing and responsive suppliers in a particular market to the conclusion of a traditional procurement contract with a defined supplier, with defined terms and duration, for periodic deliveries within the duration of the contract itself (an arrangement that is called a 'term contract' in the United Kingdom and may be a 'framework contract' in the European Union).[14]

The structure of a framework agreement in practice will reflect the motivation(s) for using the technique, the market for the goods or services concerned and the interaction of a series of design considerations in the

---

[12] Federal Acquisition Regulation, Code of Federal Regulations (CFR) Title 48, Subpart 16.5–16.501-1, Definitions. FAR 2005-83/07-02-2015, available at www.acquisition.gov/?q=browsefar.

[13] See, for example, *The World Bank Group and Public Procurement: An Independent Evaluation* (World Bank, 2014).

[14] European Commission, Directorate General Internal Market and Services, Explanatory Note – Framework Agreements – Classic Directive (2005), CC2005/03_rev/ of 14 July 2005, available at http://ec.europa.eu/internal_market/publicprocurement/docs/explan-notes/classic-dir-framework_en.pdf; Procurement Lawyers Association, 'The Use of Framework Agreements in Public Procurement', March 2012, available at www.procurementlawyers.org/pdf/PLA%20paper%20on%20Fra-meworks%20PDF%20Mar%2012.pdf.

light of the motivations and market concerned. The remainder of this chapter will identify the three main models of framework agreements which will be the focus of the analysis of market and design considerations in later chapters; it will also summarise the motivations for using one or more types of framework agreement.

## 2.2 Taxonomy: three most common forms of framework agreement

The above discussion shows that the permutations of framework agreements are numerous. However, three main types of framework can be identified and discussed to assist policymakers in designing systems to permit the use of frameworks agreements procedures and users of framework agreements. Certain potential benefits and concerns will be more or less relevant to different types of framework agreement procedures, informing these decisions.

There follows, therefore, a taxonomy of the main models of framework agreements that we shall consider based on those seen in current practice. There are three main 'models' – the main categories of framework agreement – and within each model there are variations, which we shall call 'types'.

### 2.2.1 *Model 1 framework agreements – closed, complete, limited framework agreements without second-stage competition*

Model 1 framework agreements are concluded with a defined group of suppliers. We shall therefore refer to them as 'closed', in the sense that no new suppliers can become parties to the framework agreement after it is concluded.[15] Model 1 framework agreements may be single-award (made with one supplier only) or multiple-award (made with more than one supplier). Thus, Model 1 framework agreements include two types – single-supplier and multi-supplier framework agreements.

Model 1 framework agreements are all 'complete', in the sense that all terms and conditions for the supply of the goods or services concerned are established in the framework agreement, though the notion of 'completeness' is a pragmatic rather than a technical one, in that the

---

[15] Noting that in limited cases such as the bankruptcy of awardees or where the framework so stipulates, suppliers may be permitted to join the framework agreement and replace those that no longer participate. See, for example, Article 72, EU Directive, note 9, supra.

procuring entity can set final terms at the second stage, such as delivery times and locations and deadlines for provision of services.[16] Consequently, the procuring entity can simply issue a purchase order for the goods or services and no further arrangements with the supplier concerned are needed. For this reason, this class of framework agreement is also known as a 'framework contract' in the European Union.[17] Model 1 framework agreements do not require a further round of competition to identify the supplier that will be awarded a procurement contract under the terms of the framework agreement, which is a key difference between Model 1 framework agreements, on the one hand, and Models 2 and 3, on the other.

In order to allow the procuring entity to place purchase orders without further competition at the second stage, Model 1 framework agreements must involve a full examination of qualifications of suppliers and of the responsiveness of their offers; they must also carry out a competitive evaluation of those offers to identify the suppliers that will become the parties to the framework agreement – which we shall call 'awardees', recalling that the framework agreement is closed to other potential suppliers. The framework agreement's users are 'limited', in the sense that the procuring entities that can use the framework agreement must be identified at the outset and no other procuring entities can use them. From these two perspectives, Model 1 framework agreements are relatively close to traditional procurement contracts.

Under many systems offering Model 1 framework agreements, revised or improved offers from awardees during the term of the framework agreement are not permitted.[18] Model 1 framework agreements can consequently take the form of an e-catalogue, which is also a common format in Latin America.[19]

### 2.2.2 Model 2 framework agreements – incomplete, closed, limited framework agreements with second-stage competition

Model 2 framework agreements are a broadly encountered family of framework agreement in practice – examples being found in many national

---

[16] A/CN.9/WG.I/WP.44, note 2, supra.
[17] A type of agreement that may also include term contracts as described earlier in this chapter.
[18] An exception is found under Article 36(4) of the EU Directive: where the tender is an e-catalogue, it may be updated at the request of the procuring entity. See, further, Carina Risvig Hamer, 'Regular Purchases and Aggregated Procurement: The Changes in the New Public Procurement Directive Regarding Framework Agreements, Dynamic Purchasing Systems and Central Purchasing Bodies', *Public Procurement Law Review*, 4 (2014): 201–210.
[19] In most systems, e-catalogues are also open to new suppliers and are 'open' in the sense described in this chapter.

systems, as well as being provided for in the EU Directive, the Model Law and the US federal system and are envisaged in the World Bank's forthcoming new procurement system.[20] Most public procurement practitioners are inclined to think of Model 2 framework agreements as the archetypal framework agreement – indeed, they were identified by the European Commission as framework agreements *stricto sensu*.[21]

Model 2 framework agreements are closed, in the sense that no new suppliers can become parties to the framework agreement after it is concluded. They are incomplete, in the sense that not all conditions are established in the framework agreement, and so they do require a further round of competition to identify the supplier that will be awarded a contract under the terms of the framework agreement. Therefore, they must involve a full examination of supplier qualifications and their offers when the framework is concluded.

Some Model 2 framework agreements also involve a competitive comparison (or evaluation) of offers at the first stage, to identify a limited number of awardees (with the 'best' offers) that will become parties to the framework agreement. Where this takes place, the second round of competition can focus on a limited number of outstanding variables and a limited number of competing suppliers. In other cases, there is little or no competitive evaluation at the first stage, and so the second-stage competition can be extensive. Accordingly, there are two main types of Model 2 framework agreements from this perspective. In addition, and as we shall see in Chapter 4, there are consequential variations in the extent and scope of second-stage competition in Model 2 framework agreements.[22]

Most systems providing for Model 2 framework agreements – including the European Union and UNCITRAL's, but generally not the US federal system – require the procuring entities that can use the framework agreement to be identified at the outset, so that they are 'limited' in the sense described above. Model 2 framework agreements generally do not envisage

---

[20] The EU Directive, note 9, supra; Model Law, note 10, supra; FAR, note 12, supra. See, also, 'Procurement in World Bank Investment Project Finance, Phase Ii: Developing the Proposed New Procurement Framework', Framework paper for consultation, 8 July 2014, available at https://consultations.worldbank.org/Data/hub/files/consultation-template/procurement-policy-review-consultationsopenconsultationtemplate/phases/procurement_in_world_bank_investment_project_finance_-_phase_ii.pdf.

[21] Explanatory Note – Framework Agreements – Classic Directive (2005), note 14, supra.

[22] For example, the second-stage competition can take the form of a 'mini-tender', or it can be conducted using an electronic reverse auction. See, further, Chapter 4.

revised or improved offers from suppliers during the term of the framework agreement other than through the second-stage competition.

In practice, most systems that provide for both Model 1 and Model 2 framework agreements include in the governing law or other rules a maximum duration for those framework agreements – in the European Union, this is currently four years. The Model Law recommends a maximum duration of between three and five years. The US federal system contemplates varying time-frames for different types of ID/IQ.

### 2.2.3 *Model 3 framework agreements – open, incomplete framework agreements with second-stage competition*

Model 3 framework agreements are open, in the sense that new suppliers can become parties to the framework agreement after it is concluded. They are incomplete, in the sense that not all conditions are established in the framework agreement and so they always require a further round of competition to identify the supplier that will be awarded a procurement contract or purchase order under the terms of the framework agreement. Some Model 3 framework agreements are 'limited' in the sense described above; others are not.

Model 3 framework agreements are commonly encountered outside the European Union. The EU Directive provides for a 'dynamic purchasing system', which is in fact a Model 3 framework agreement as we describe the concept. This dynamic purchasing system was introduced in 2004 under Directive 2004/18/EC, but procedural restrictions meant it was very rarely used in practice.[23] These procedural restrictions have been relaxed in the 2014 EU Directive, and the take-up of the technique may therefore increase.

Unlike Model 1 and some Model 2 framework agreements, Model 3 framework agreements generally do not involve a competitive evaluation of offers when the framework is concluded. This is a logical consequence of the fact that new joiners are to be expected; there is little benefit to the ranking and exclusion of some suppliers that such an exercise would involve. While, in theory, Model 3 framework agreements involve an

---

[23] Sue Arrowsmith, 'Dynamic Purchasing Systems under the New EC Procurement Directives – A Not So Dynamic Concept?', *Public Procurement Law Review*, 14 (2006): pp. 16–29. Directive 2004/18/EC of the European Parliament and of the Council of 31 March 2004 on the coordination of procedures for the award of public works contracts, public supply contracts and public service contracts, OJ L 134, 30 April 2004, pp. 114–240, available at http://eur-lex.europa.eu/legal-content/en/ALL/?uri=CELEX:32004L0018.

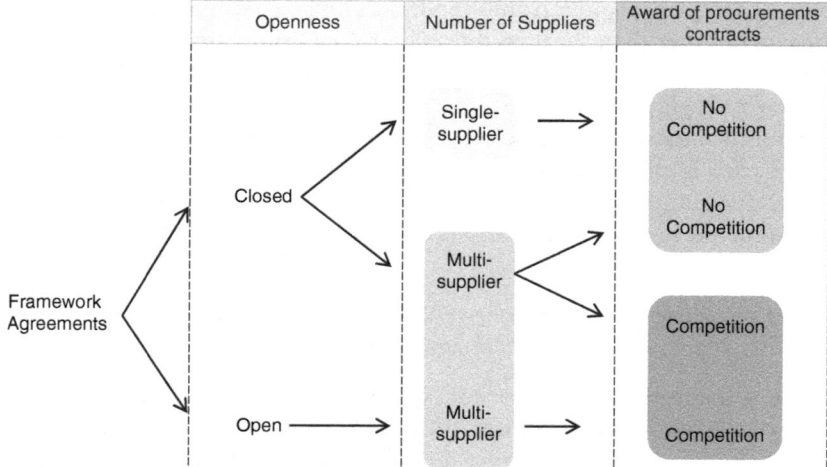

Figure 2.1 Models of framework agreements.

assessment of supplier qualifications and an examination of offers against the procuring entity's statement of needs, in practice in some types of Model 3 framework agreements offers are assessed only against a very broad expression of needs, so that the key distinguishing features from a list of suppliers described above may not always be present. As a general rule, competition takes place entirely at the second stage. Combining this feature with openness to new joiners, there is little risk of inequality of treatment and impeding market access, and so many systems permit suppliers to improve their offers at any time during the period when the framework agreement is in operation. Also, Model 3 frameworks are not always subject to a maximum duration (the Model Law and the EU Directive require a fixed duration only).

Model 3 framework agreements also involve two types – those that do not require the procuring entity or entities that can use the framework to be defined at the outset and those that require the users to be identified.

## 2.3 Common variables in framework agreements and framework agreements procedures

The three models of framework agreements mean that the type of arrangement ranges from – in essence – a traditional procurement contract, with more or less scheduled deliveries for individual purchases, to a list

*Description, taxonomy and motivations for using framework agreements* 21

of pre-qualified or short-listed suppliers for a fairly loosely defined need. In addition to the main models and types identified, some other common variations in the terms of the *framework agreements* include

- whether there is any restriction on the number of suppliers that are admitted to the framework agreement when it is concluded, whether as a matter of regulation or in practice;
- the extent to which the framework agreement is complete – that is, the extent of terms that remain to be settled at the second or call-off stage, and the extent to which variations in purchases are permitted;
- whether or not the use of the framework agreement is optional for procuring entities that are entitled to use it, or whether procuring entities that are parties to the agreement are bound to use it;
- whether or not the framework agreement contains a binding commitment from the procuring entity to purchase minimum or fixed quantities (in some cases, the agreement may commit the procuring entity or entities to purchase all their requirements for the product or service concerned); and
- whether suppliers are committed to fulfilling orders or call-offs under the framework agreement, or are committed to supplying quantities up to a defined maximum.[24]

Common variations in framework agreement *procedures* in addition to those described for the models and types above include

- whether awardees can be replaced or whether awardees can replace items they offer under the framework agreement during its term; and
- whether the criteria that are used to select suppliers to be parties to the framework agreement at the first stage are identical to those that will be used at the second or call-off stage.

In addition, and as we have seen, it is common for framework agreements to restrict (a) the maximum duration of the framework agreement,[25] (b) the extent to which purchase orders or call-offs can be placed towards the end of the framework agreement and (c) the extent to which the description,

---

[24] The legal implications of these contractual variations are discussed in Chapter 5: they include whether the framework agreement is treated as a procurement contract, or whether the awards under framework agreements are the procurement contracts.
[25] Most systems require that the duration of framework agreements be fixed at the outset. Some systems, such as the European Union and UNCITRAL's, also impose a statutory maximum duration. See, further, Chapter 5.

evaluation criteria and other terms of the framework agreement can be varied or amended over the course of its duration.[26]

The manner and level of detail in which the second stage of a framework agreement procedure is regulated (notably, as regards how competitive call-offs are awarded and what is treated as 'competition') vary significantly from system to system, and will be considered in Chapters 5 and 12.

## 2.4 Motivations for the use of framework agreements procedures

As set out below, the primary motivation for using framework agreements procedures is to increase administrative efficiency. From a policy standpoint, however, the pursuit of administrative efficiency is far from being the only objective in any public procurement system. Commonly accepted procurement system objectives include competition, transparency, integrity, objectivity and – perhaps most fundamentally – meeting the needs of the procuring entity itself.[27] Pursuing administrative efficiency can compromise these other policy objectives, as we discuss in Chapter 12. The policy choices in balancing different policy objectives involved can be complex and need to be based on rigorous analysis of motivations, needs, markets and design considerations, the subjects of the following sections and chapters.

### 2.4.1 Enhancing administrative efficiency

A common criticism of public procurement systems is that the rules generally involve 'a highly structured regime of organised competition [which], because of its rigidity, may at times impose costs that exceed its benefits'.[28] Most obviously, the regulatory system concerned, which covers the interaction of the procuring entity and potential suppliers, imposes costs through requirements for preparing solicitation documents, advertising, assessing qualifications and responsiveness, responding to questions and clarifications, perhaps holding pre-bid meetings, evaluating and comparing the tenders or bids, debriefings and challenges.[29] However, further

---

[26] The manner in which different systems address these issues is considered in Chapters 5 and 12.
[27] Steven L. Schooner, Daniel I. Gordon, and Jessica L. Clark, 'Public Procurement Systems: Unpacking Stakeholder Aspirations and Expectations', GWU Law School Public Law Research Paper 1133234 (2008), available at http://ssrn.com/abstract=1133234.
[28] Joshua I. Schwartz, 'Katrina's Lessons for Ongoing US Procurement Reform Efforts', *Public Procurement Law Review*, 6 (2006): 363–373.
[29] Guide to Enactment, chapter VII, Enactment Policy Considerations, para 4, p. 276.

administrative procedures and/or internal agency requirements may also be relevant, such as budgetary and prior approval requirements, hierarchical or internal oversight processes, requirements to compile and maintain records, transfer of information between the end user to procurement officials and other reporting requirements.

Many of these requirements are absent from private sector procurement, and, consequently, public procurement procedures are considered inefficient, costly and slow. According to a 2011 study for the European Commission, the average time taken for public procurement procedures in the European Union is 108 days (though with a spread of 180 days between the best and worst performers), at an average administrative cost of 1.4 per cent of contract value.[30] As a result, the potential for improvement in administrative efficiency (i.e. improving the ratio of the transaction costs and administrative time of each procurement procedure and its value)[31] is a main motivation in using framework agreements procedures.

The aggregation of what would otherwise be a series of procurement proceedings saves both administrative time and costs as a proportion of procurement spend (as many steps that would otherwise be taken for each of a series of procurements are undertaken once). These benefits may be particularly significant in the context of relatively low-value,[32] commonly used and simple purchases, such as standard office supplies, simple IT products and straightforward, small-scale services (e.g. maintenance and repair services), many of which are readily commercially available and need not be designed to the particular requirements of the procuring entity.

Nonetheless, administrative efficiency through aggregating procurement cannot be presumed: it is self-evident that the time and costs of running the two-stage procurement process that all framework agreements involve are, in most cases, likely to exceed those of running a one-stage process to procure the same goods or services if used only

---

[30] Public procurement in Europe. Cost and effectiveness. A study on procurement regulation. Prepared for the European Commission, PwC, London Economics and Ecorys, March 2011. Available at http://ec.europa.eu/internal_market/publicprocurement/docs/modernising_rules/cost-effectiveness_en.pdf

[31] '"Efficiency" in procurement means that relationship between the transaction costs and administrative time of each procurement procedure and its value are proportionate, [and] that the costs of the procurement system as a whole are also proportionate to the value of all procurement conducted through that system'. Guide to Enactment, Commentary on Objectives of the Model Law, 'Maximising Economy and Efficiency in Procurement', para 3 on p. 36. See, further, Caroline Nicholas, 'A Critical Evaluation of the Revised UNCITRAL Model Law Provisions on Regulating Framework Agreements', *Public Procurement Law Review*, 2 (2012): 19–46.

[32] Generally meaning procurement for contracts expected to fall below a threshold value.

once, particularly if a simplified procurement method is available. As we shall see, the planning process required prior to setting up a framework agreement and conducting the first stage of the procedure may involve costs that may be *more* significant and involve *more* time than a traditional procurement procedure for simple purchases. Consequently, framework agreements for repeat purchases are the most common variety of framework agreements in practice.

The planning process also requires certain assumptions to be made about the likely use of the framework agreement once established: the more the framework agreement is used, the better the amortisation of the additional time and costs of the two-stage process as compared with a traditional process.

In addition, framework agreements are not the only tool to offer administratively efficient solutions for frequently purchased goods and services. Increasing average contract size in a traditional (one-stage) procurement, for a defined (large) quantity of a product or service, with a one-off delivery[33] or as a series of deliveries in pre-arranged lots, could save both the time and costs of conducting a full procurement procedure for each lot or a framework agreement, and the time and costs of the procedures required for call-offs.[34]

Studies have shown that the rise in use of framework agreements has coincided with an increase in average contract size, likely to reflect the potential for economies of scale and the amortisation of administrative costs over a larger aggregate value. It can also be speculated that the reasons for this correlation also include that some of the administrative burden of administering larger single contracts can be alleviated through the use of framework agreements. Particularly, as compared with the case of single contracts with one-off deliveries, the operational costs of warehousing, inventory control and distribution, among others, can be avoided through a framework agreement procedure in which orders are placed as needs arise (using regular deliveries or a 'just-in-time' approach, allowing the procuring entity greater flexibility in scheduling). In addition, the costs of managing very large and consequently complex contracts for relatively simple needs can be avoided.

---

[33] These contracts might nonetheless offer good value for money where the arrangement leads to lower unit prices to reflect lower delivery costs on the part of the suppliers.
[34] This is the notion of a 'term contract' introduced above.

*Description, taxonomy and motivations for using framework agreements* 25

### 2.4.2 *Process efficiencies*

Framework agreements procedures, by aggregating procurement opportunities, can reduce transaction time and costs for both suppliers and procuring entities from the process efficiency perspective: 'efficiency often means more than quick delivery. Avoiding waste is also part of efficiency [which] might also be introduced, from the vendors' point of view, by providing a single point-of-entry for vendors interested in learning about upcoming procurements and ensuring that information provided to vendors is accurate and complete'.[35] Standardising approaches through framework agreements procedures can also allow standard training among procurement officials. The benefits of standardisation can include the issue of better-quality tender or bidding documents, higher uniformity in descriptions of needs among procuring entities and consequently better supplier understanding of those needs, which can then both encourage participation and improve the quality of offers from suppliers. It can even have an additional benefit in urgent or emergency situations – when unanticipated needs arise in response to a natural disaster in one part of the country, the government could more easily transfer procurement officials from other parts of the government into that region, where they could keep the procurement system moving efficiently.[36]

### 2.4.3 *Improving performance in urgent procurement and avoiding unnecessary use of urgent procurement methods in an emergency*

Framework agreements have the potential to reduce the common situation of excessively high prices and poor quality of food, water, shelter materials and medicines that governments need to procure from time to time within a short time span in urgent and emergency situations. Poor outcomes are commonly seen to arise from the use of procurement methods without competition, such as single-source procurement, in these cases.[37] If a framework agreement is already in place, the shorter times for awarding procurement contracts at the second stage compared with conducting a full procurement procedure can remove the justification for using single-source

---

[35] 'Public Procurement Systems: Unpacking Stakeholder Aspirations and Expectations', note 27, supra.
[36] 'Katrina's Lessons for Ongoing US Procurement Efforts', note 28, supra.
[37] Ibid., citing 'The Federal Response to Hurricane Katrina: Lessons Learned' (February 2006), pp. 44–45, available at www.whitehouse.gov/reports/katrina-reports-lessons-learned.pdf.

procurement and other relatively uncompetitive and non-transparent procedures designed for these situations.

As has been observed, emergencies will inevitably occur, without warning as to specific time and location (or at least without sufficient warning in the procurement context), there will be a need for an urgent response without the time to engage in standard procurement procedures, and there is a 'characteristic' and fairly predictable list of commonly required items to support initial rescue efforts. Here, using framework agreements procedures allows suppliers to be selected on a competitive basis *before* the advent of a disaster, so prices will be offered when the government is in a situation that is not influenced by immediate need, and those prices (assuming the framework agreement is so designed) will bind the suppliers even at the time when the emergency arises.[38]

### 2.4.4 Improving performance in simple and low-value procurement

The types of purchases for which framework agreements have proved themselves effective – standard office supplies, simple IT products and services and so on – are likely to be low-value items (i.e. procurement for contracts anticipated to fall below a threshold value).[39] Many may also be simple purchases, in the sense of being readily commercially available or off-the-shelf items. Open tendering is commonly accepted as the 'gold standard' for public procurement,[40] but it is not necessarily appropriate for

---

[38] Though as Schwartz ('Katrina's Lessons for Ongoing US Procurement Efforts', note 28, supra) also cautions, not all emergency items can be appropriately procured in this way – where demand is insufficiently predictable, or where the retainer or price to keep certain items available on appropriately short notice would be excessive. Other needs after the emergency, even of the type needed for the immediate relief effort such as reconstruction contracts, are not required with the same degree of urgency. The Guide to Enactment to the Model Law notes that 'only where there is an extreme degree of urgency can single-source procurement be justified: such as for the needs that arise in the immediate aftermath of the catastrophe (e.g. for clean water, emergency food and shelter or immediate medical needs). Other needs, which may still arise as a direct result of the catastrophe, involve a time-frame that allows the use of competitive negotiations rather than single-source procurement (and, the further in time from the catastrophe, the less likely it is that either of these methods remains available because there will be time to use other methods)', Guide to Enactment, commentary to Article 28, General rules applicable to the selection of a procurement method, note 11, supra.

[39] Many systems have rules on valuation and aggregation of contracts designed to prevent procurement officials splitting contracts artificially with the express purpose of avoiding procedural requirements, such as Article 12 of the Model Law, note 10, supra.

[40] Because it is the procurement method accepted as most likely to achieve the main system objectives as it insists on fully open competition throughout. The Guide to Enactment notes in the introductory commentary to chapter III, Open Tendering, that it 'is widely recognized as generally the

*Description, taxonomy and motivations for using framework agreements* 27

simple procurement. Relatively unstructured procurement methods – which are essentially less open, competitive and transparent than open tendering – may be available, such as request-for-quotations or shopping[41] and – in some cases – single-source procurement. Some systems also offer procedural exemptions below certain value thresholds – such as from the application of a standstill period and from the requirement for public notice of the contract award[42] – and available methods may involve direct solicitation. As a result, they may be flexible, but they are not always transparent and competitive, raising the possibility or likelihood of poorer outcomes in terms of meeting needs, value for money and integrity in simple procurement.[43]

In these cases, therefore, a primary motivation for using a framework agreement procedure can be to improve overall outcomes in simple procurement through aggregation and without imposing significant *additional* administrative burdens, rather than administrative efficiency per se: that is, a framework agreement procedure can offer a *more* transparent and competitive approach than the realistic alternatives, such request-for-quotations, and single-source procurement. Absent such aggregation, submitting simple procurement to the more stringent, generally applicable rules might enhance value for money and avoid abuse, but at a cost of a disproportionate administrative burden. The potential advantage of framework agreements, here, is that the aggregation itself brings the procurement above value thresholds and yet can reduce the administrative burden as a proportion of the amounts being purchased. Framework agreements procedures may also facilitate oversight of lower-value procurements for the same reasons. (Here, we are assuming that the rules on framework agreements and their operation in practice do in fact make framework agreements procedures more transparent and competitive than procurement methods designed for simple procurement.)

---

most effective method in promoting the objectives of the Model Law as set out in its Preamble', Guide to Enactment, chapter III, Open Tendering, Section A, Introduction, at p. 165. See, also, Jerry L. Marshaw, 'The Fear of Discretion in Government Procurement', Yale Law School, Faculty Scholarship Series Paper 1141 (1991), available at http://digitalcommons.law.yale.edu/fss_papers/1141; and Steven Kelman, *Procurement and Public Management: The Fear of Discretion and the Quality of Government Performance* (Washington, DC: The AEI Press, 1990).

[41] 'Shopping' is the World Bank term for request-for-quotations.
[42] See, for example, Model Law Articles 22(3)(b), 23(2), note 10, supra.
[43] A specific requirement under the Model Law (Article 28), note 11, supra. See, also, Sue Arrowsmith and Caroline Nicholas, 'Regulating Framework Agreements under the UNCITRAL Model Law', ch. 2, in Sue Arrowsmith (ed.), *Reform of the UNCITRAL Model Law on Procurement: Procurement Regulation for the 21st century* (West, 2009); 'A critical evaluation of the revised UNCITRAL Model Law provisions on regulating framework agreements', note 31, supra.

### 2.4.5 *Ensuring security of supply*

As they can bind a supplier to supply future requirements, framework agreements have been observed to be useful where security of supply is a concern, such as strategically important items for which there is an anticipated but fluctuating need (electricity or communications supplies, for example). Also, in the case of specialised items requiring a dedicated production line and/or items that need to be tailored to the needs of the procuring entity, where the need is identified but the time when the supply will be requested is unknown, framework agreements can secure the supply and its future terms.

In order to be effective in securing supply, the supplier will need to be bound to fulfil the procuring entity's requirements, for which a charge – such as a retainer or higher per-unit prices – will generally be levied. The security may be enhanced in practice if the agreement gives some expectation of future orders to the supplier(s), to allow for appropriate investment, and a maximum quantity can protect suppliers from unanticipated order levels and can allow procuring entities to procure elsewhere as appropriate.[44] While securing supply for repeat purchases will be the more common situation, the possibility exists to use a framework agreement for a one-off purchase from one supplier in the future,[45] though the additional cost may be disproportionate. A framework agreement can require the supplier to fulfil all orders placed and to keep a permanent stock of a product available even on the procuring entity's premises.[46]

As in the case of urgent procurement, this solution offers a potential benefit in the form of reductions in the time required to conclude a procurement contract as compared with conducting a full procurement procedure when the need arises. Where the product or service is not a standard one, however, it may not be practical for delivery to be effected in a very short time frame from the point of order because of the need for special design or manufacture, so the overall reductions in time to delivery should not be over-estimated. If delivery times need to be short, a higher retainer or higher per-unit prices may need to be factored in.

Single-supplier framework agreements are also useful to enhance security of supply to the extent that the supplier concerned is likely to be able to

---

[44] A/CN.9/WG.I/WP.44, note 2, supra.
[45] This situation is provided expressly for as a framework only in the Model Law, note 10, supra.
[46] A/CN.9/WG.I/WP.44, note 2, supra.

*Description, taxonomy and motivations for using framework agreements* 29

fulfil the total need.[47] Multi-supplier framework agreements are also suitable to secure the future supply of items, such as electricity and travel tickets, from more than one source when there are doubts about the capacity of a single supplier to meet all needs or where the market price may fluctuate and the best offer may not be known until the time of order.

### 2.4.6  Enhancing SME participation

Framework agreements could provide enhanced access to public procurement markets for small- and medium-sized enterprises SMEs, if the agreements allow for smaller orders that are more accessible to them than in a larger-scale traditional procurement contract. In practice, however, there is a trend towards larger-scale contracting through the use of framework agreements, which can favour larger suppliers. Improving SME access by disaggregating what might otherwise be larger (and perhaps more economically advantageous) contracts involves the interaction of social and longer-term economic objectives within governments as a whole, and this is addressed in Chapter 7.

### 2.4.7  Enhanced competition through aggregation

Aggregation of procurement can lead to better outcomes in terms of value for money as the effect of aggregation yields economies of scale. Suppliers may reduce prices without compromising quality in the anticipation of high-volume orders. Single-supplier agreements have the potential to maximise the benefits of aggregating demand in repeat purchasing,[48] especially as many terms are set at the first stage, so that bulk purchase discounts can be expected (provided that there is sufficient certainty as to future purchase quantities). On the other hand, in multi-supplier cases, where second-stage competition is part of the framework agreement procedure, successive competitive phases may allow a procuring entity to realise 'the benefits of an ongoing competitive environment throughout

---

[47] 'A critical evaluation of the revised UNCITRAL Model Law provisions on regulating framework agreements', note 31, supra. On the public policy implications as regards market access in both single- and multi-supplier frameworks, see Chapter 7.
[48] This point is emphasised in 'A critical evaluation of the revised UNCITRAL Model Law provisions on regulating framework agreements', note 31, supra, noting that otherwise, there is a tendency towards 'loose tailoring' of procurement contracts to the procuring entities' needs so that the efficiencies can be outweighed by lower value overall, in that the needs are not fully satisfied.

the duration of the contract',[49] and as suppliers reduce prices given the anticipated volume of orders.

Offering larger-scale contracts and using successive rounds of competition at the second stage, to match needs and bids at the detailed level, can improve overall competition and outcomes in terms of prices and quality.

It is self-evident that many of the above benefits can be further enhanced through aggregation across procuring entities, where centralised purchasing agencies or buying clubs operate framework agreements for a group of procuring entities. These benefits are discussed in Chapter 6.

## 2.5 Chapter summary

- Framework agreements comprise a wide array of purchasing arrangements consisting in two separate stages: the first ('conclusion') stage, and the second ('call-off') stage when procurement contracts are awarded.
- Three main dimensions are commonly used for classifying framework agreements: the degree of openness, the number of awardees and the modality for awarding procurement contracts. However, other features may come into play to further differentiate the different combinations of the main dimensions.
- The most relevant motivations for using framework agreements comprise enhancing administrative efficiency, improving performance in urgent procurement and avoiding unnecessary use of urgent procurement methods in an emergency; improving performance in simple and low-value procurement; ensuring security of supply; enhancing SMEs' participation in public procurement; and fostering competition through aggregation.

---

[49] U.S. Office of Management & Budget, Office of Federal Procurement Policy, 'Best Practices for Multiple Task and Delivery Contracting', 7 (Washington, D.C.: July 1997), available at www.acqnet.gov/Library/OFPP?/BestPractices/BestPMAT.html.

CHAPTER 3

# *Some key economic dimensions in framework agreements*

## 3.1 Introduction

Decision-making in public procurement requires *in primis* evaluating alternative (and legally authorised) solutions. Framework agreements are no exception to this general principle. *Sound* decisions generally stem from procurement specialists' ability reasonably to foresee the impact of procurement design on competing firms' choices; that is, on the content of their offers. As is evident from the discussions of each model in the previous chapter, framework agreements procedures can be very different in practice, and the type of purchase and market for which each model and type may be the most suitable will also vary widely.

The models, taken together with procurement methods available for the procurement of relatively simple, off-the-shelf or low-value products or services, can be considered as a toolbox from which the procuring entity should select the appropriate tool for the procurement concerned. Decisions on whether to use a framework agreement procedure and, if so, which type of framework agreement, will need to take into account the circumstances of the procurement concerned, the state of the market and how to structure the procedure to maximise competition and realise best value for money.[1] For example, monthly purchases of standard office stationery with differing quantities (a common-use item whose price is relatively stable), of cleaning services (charged for at hourly rates on the basis of defined square meterage) or of petrol (whose price is largely market determined) may indicate quite a different approach from irregular purchases, also in varying quantities, of fast-changing IT supplies (whose price and precise specifications vary). However, as we shall see, apparently

---

[1] The decisions concerned will also need to take account of the regulatory requirements in the procuring entity's own system, but this chapter will assume that there are no rules that would sway the decision away from the optimal one that reflects the type of purchase, the market and the maximisation of the economic benefits through competition.

'standard' purchases can hide variations in need that can have significant impact on the appropriate model and type of framework agreement and, indeed, whether a framework agreement procedure is a suitable tool at all.

This chapter will use stylised and highly simplified examples to demonstrate some key decisions involved.

## 3.2 The importance of competition in framework agreements procedures

Before turning to specific economic dimensions in framework agreements, it will be assumed that an overall goal is to maximise effective competition.[2] The extent of competition in procurement markets; that is, the process of rivalry between firms striving to gain sales and make profits, has a demonstrably clear relationship with the resulting performance:[3] the beneficial effects of rigorous competition include both reductions in costs and improvements in the quality of what is procured.[4] Public procurement systems consequently place a high premium on incentivising competition, effectively applying the experience gained in the private sector, whose businesses strive to improve competition in the markets in which they operate.[5]

The first goal is to remove – so far as possible – barriers to entry to procurement markets, on the basis that wide participation by bidders in those markets is a prerequisite for competition. Thus, the WTO GPA, EU Directive and UNCITRAL Model Law[6] all include provisions requiring

---

[2] Governments may pursue socio-economic policy goals through their procurement system, some of which may have the effect of reducing the competitive pool for a given procurement (such as a set-aside programme in favour of SMEs). The substantive discussion in this chapter assumes such policies are absent; see, however, Chapter 12.

[3] Paul Milgrom, 'Auctions and Bidding: A Primer', *Journal of Economic Perspectives*, 3, No. 3 (1989): 3–22; and Paul D. Klemperer (ed.), *The Economic Theory of Auctions* (Cheltenham, UK: Edward Elgar, 2000). See also R. I. Carr, 'Impact of the Number of Bidders on Competition', *Journal of Construction Engineering and Management*, 109, No. 1 (1983): 61–73; R. D. Anderson and W. E. Kovacic, 'Competition Policy and International Trade Liberalisation: Essential Complements to Ensure Good Performance in Public Procurement Markets', *Public Procurement Law Review*, 18 (2009): 67–101.

[4] With free entry and an absence of collusion, prices will be driven to marginal costs, and those costs will be minimised, as firms compete for survival; competition also serves as an important driver of innovation, and firms can learn from one another and improve their offers. Ibid. (Anderson and Kovacic, 'Competition Policy and International Trade Liberalisation: Essential Complements to Ensure Good Performance in Public Procurement Markets'), citing D. W. Carlton and J. M. Perloff, *Modern Industrial Organization* (Addison-Wesley, 2004).

[5] Ibid., citing D. N. Burt and R. L. Pinkerton, *A Purchasing Manager's Guide to Strategic, Proactive Procurement* (AMACOM, 2006).

[6] The World Trade Organisation Revised Agreement on Government Procurement (hereafter, WTO GPA, available at www.wto.org/english/docs_e/legal_e/rev-gpr-94_01_e.htm); Directive 2014/24/EU of the European Parliament and of the Council of 26 February 2014 on public procurement and repealing Directive 2004/18/EC Text with EEA relevance, OJ L 94, 28 March 2014, pp. 65–242,

open, international participation as a default requirement (though in the cases of the WTO GPA and EU Directive, 'international' refers to their membership rather than all countries), and discriminatory terms and conditions are prohibited. The second goal is to create the conditions in which competition can take place in practice. Transparency requirements are imposed to ensure that bidders can be confident that their offers will be treated in an objective and non-discriminatory manner, and that they have the information needed to allow them to submit their best offers. Consequently, the terms and conditions of the procurement and other relevant information must be publicised and provided to potential bidders at the outset, trade names are generally not permitted and award criteria must relate to the subject matter of the procurement, qualification criteria must be relevant and so on. In addition, the UNCITRAL Model Law requires the choice of procurement method (including framework agreements procedures) to be made with a view of maximising competition to the extent practicable.[7]

It should be emphasised that these measures do not create competition – they create the conditions in which competition can take place. Competition in public procurement needs to take account of the nature of public procurement markets, which is quite different from the norm in other markets, in which there is a push–pull relationship between price and quantities demanded and supplied in a market (elasticity of demand). The effect of a procurement procedure, on the other hand – say an open tendering process to select a supplier for the provision of $x$ quantity of petrol to the government – is to create a mini-market for that defined quantity of petrol. The quantity will not vary absent extraordinary circumstances that might justify the cancellation of the procurement contract concerned, though it can be assumed in the case of petrol purchases for a government that there will be a series of these mini-markets.

The effect on the procurement market for petrol regarding the procuring entity is to create incentives for bidders to bid aggressively for the first tender in the series, so that they can win lasting market dominance. Lasting market dominance can arise because switching suppliers during the period

---

available at http://eur-lex.europa.eu/legal-content/EN/TXT/?uri=celex:32014L0024. Hereafter, the EU Directive; UNCITRAL Model Law on Public Procurement (2011), *Official Records of the General Assembly, Sixty-sixth Session, Supplement No. 17* (UN document A/66/17). The text of the Model Law is available at www.uncitral.org/uncitral/uncitral_texts/procurement_infrastructure.html. Hereafter, Model Law.

[7] Article 28, Model Law, ibid.

of this series of tenders may involve costs (set-up costs, for example) for both the procuring entity and the potential new suppliers.[8] The effect is to create barriers to entry for new suppliers in repeated procurements – precisely the opposite of what procurement systems aim to do through the non-discrimination policies, and the associated requirements for transparency, competition and fairness in procedural rules described above.

This phenomenon can also be viewed as a parallel to the situation created by setting up a framework agreement. In a closed framework agreement, for example, there will be no switching of suppliers outside a small group that has achieved collectively 100 per cent market share for the series of mini-markets at issue. The same notion applies to open framework agreements in that awards under them at the second or call-off stage can be made only to parties to the framework agreement, but in these Model 3 framework agreements, new joiners are permitted so that the market is likely to include a larger number of suppliers at any time.

### 3.3 The main economic dimensions of setting up a framework agreement – demand and market analysis

The implication of this understanding of the procurement market is that the design of the first stage of the framework agreement procedure is critical: it will define the 'market'[9] and effectively set boundaries on the scope and extent of competition that can occur at both the stages of the procurement procedure. Grouping a bundle of procurement contracts under the same 'umbrella' agreement therefore requires a more comprehensive and meticulous *demand and market analysis* than the one that each procuring entity would carry out if it were to run a one-off procurement process for the types of goods and services that are normally the subject of framework agreements procedures.

In what follows, we shall describe the main economic dimensions from this perspective that are likely to enter procurement officials' reasoning when designing a framework agreement procedure, and that will influence

---

[8] See B. Tóth, M. Fazekas, Á. Czibik and I. J. Tóth, 'Toolkit for detecting collusive bidding in public procurement – With examples from Hungary', Corruption research Center Budapest (2015), available at www.crcb.eu/wp-content/uploads/2015/04/Toth-et-al_CRCB_WP_v2_150413.pdf.

[9] That is, the overall market for the series of procurement contracts envisaged under the framework agreement concerned. A more detailed discussion of market definition – which is a key consideration in competition policy, in general, and regarding risks to effective competition in framework agreements procedures, in particular – is found in Chapter 7.

competing bidders' behaviour.[10] In order to flesh out under what set of circumstances one type of framework agreement might be preferable to another (or, indeed, whether a framework agreement procedure is appropriate at all), we need to cast light on the rationales that competing firms adopt to formulate their bids.

### 3.3.1 *Efficiency*

At its simplest, an efficient allocation of a procurement contract requires the procuring entity to select the ablest contractor, that is, the firm with the lowest total cost for fulfilling the needs expressed in the contract. Take, for instance, a procurement contract for four-wheel drive cars, split into lots defined by the car's size, engine power and so on. Given that there will be minimal technical standards for each lot, the total costs of any bidder are mainly production and delivery costs. These costs may vary from bidder to bidder because of different production methods and labour costs, as well as each individual bidder's bargaining power with suppliers further up the supply chain and its own logistics.

Sometimes, though, production costs do not fully determine the price at which the bidder will submit its offer for the contract. The bidder may have ready-to-sell cars, possibly unsold in the private market, so that production costs are sunk.[11] The bidder's offer for the contract is therefore likely to reflect these sunk costs.

The bidder itself, when estimating the cost of performing a proposed contract, has to consider at least two different dimensions. The first dimension concerns its efficiency in performing a task (supply of a good or provision service) specified in the contract. Efficiency results from the interaction of the bidder's personnel's experience or know-how in similar tasks and, more generally, managerial skills. Combined with its production and delivery costs, the bidder's efficiency captures a *private* component in its production cost. It is private in that it is entirely firm-specific. When costs are firm-specific or internally determined in this sense, the concept of 'most efficient' or 'ablest' supplier is a meaningful one.

---

[10] We shall limit ourselves to consider the procurement process until the award stage of the procurement contract, without considering the likely impact of bidding behaviour on the subsequent buyer–seller relationship at the execution stage. This is an admittedly simplifying assumption that overlooks many real problems in real procurement markets, but it is instrumental to lay down the pillars of the decision-making process when designing framework agreements.
[11] A *sunk* cost is a cost that has been incurred and thus cannot be recovered.

There exist, however, other 'common components', which fall into two categories. The first includes dimensions of production costs that affect all suppliers equally, such as the prices of raw materials or intermediate goods such as oil, electricity and concrete. The second dimension concerns the bidder's ability to correctly estimate the mix of different elements that make up the task(s) in the contract and affects all participating bidders in a similar but not identical way. The differences reflect – for example – delivery locations. To see how the latter may affect firms' production costs, consider two slightly different procurement scenarios. In the first, a framework agreement is designed to bundle the needs for cleaning and (everyday) maintenance services of say, two departments of the same ministry, whose premises share exactly the same physical characteristics (i.e. two identical buildings) and that are very closely located from each other. In the second scenario, the two buildings have very different layouts because, say, one has open offices whereas the other does not.

Estimating production costs for each bidder requires, among other things, estimating (i) to what extent different layouts are going to affect the mix of production inputs, and (ii) the fraction of actual demand stemming from the two departments of the procuring entity (the ministry). Such a guessing exercise has very little impact in the first scenario, while it may have a profound impact on firms' business plans in the second scenario. Uncertainty affects all firms,[12] although some of them may have better information because of previous experience in similar procurement environments (an important distinguishing factor to which we will return later on in Chapters 4 and 8).

The main conclusion from this discussion is that the concept of (production) efficiency becomes slippery if not inapplicable when production costs need to reflect the different impact on bidders of variations in the procuring entity's needs, although the bidders may have imprecise information about those costs before bidding for the contract. In most real-world procurement processes, production costs will comprise both firm-specific and common components. However, when using the concept of (allocative) efficiency for present purposes, we shall emphasise the role played by the firm-specific ones and downplay the impact of the common components.

---

[12] Paul D. Klemperer, *Auctions: Theory and Practice* (Princeton University Press, 2004) and Paul Milgrom, *Putting Auction Theory to Work* (Cambridge University Press, 2004) provide extensive and analytically detailed treatments of several families of auctions as well as various applications in different markets.

### 3.3.2 The role of quality and price: product differentiation

In real-world markets, firms typically produce products or offer services that are not perfect substitutes for each other. Product differentiation, be it brand-driven or generated by different quality attributes, allows firms to compete less aggressively on price (perhaps yielding quasi-monopolistic profit, for example, in niche markets). In public procurement markets, firms can differentiate themselves even when they bid for supplying fairly homogenous goods, services or even construction items. Consider, for instance, a product that would be normally considered completely homogenous: we will choose once again the example of petrol. If a procuring entity wishes to set different delivery terms, then bidders will find themselves competing for a contract comprising a homogenous product dimension and a heterogeneous service dimension. Where this is the case, the nature of the competition will be different from a procurement in which they just compete on prices. Similarly, in construction procurement, some US Departments of Transportation have been using a procurement process called 'A+B' auctions[13] since 1990 for highway repair projects. 'A+B' auctions are competitive processes whereby firms submit their bids for labour and materials costs (A) and number of days to completion (B).[14] Again, in spite of the project being quite homogenous, firms can differentiate themselves by submitting different 'A+B' pairs.

Where quality and price are both variables that are being competed in a particular procurement, the consequences for competition are not clear-cut, largely because the competition consists of these two distinct dimensions. So, for instance, if the number of participating firms increases (the procuring entity may impose less stringent qualification requirements), as a general rule it will be hard to predict whether submitted prices will go down or the quality of the offers will be improved, or both. One would need to take into account additional information such as the procuring entity's relative quality-price weighting and the composition of the new set of competing firms.[15]

---

[13] In US parlance, the term 'auctions' does not refer to electronic reverse auctions or Dutch auctions, but a bidding procedure in which the procuring entity is permitted to select on a best-value rather than lowest-price basis, taking into account quality criteria.

[14] For an empirical assessment of the performance of 'A+B' auctions, the interested reader is referred to P. Bajari and G. Lewis, 'Procurement with Time Incentives: Theory and Evidence', *The Quarterly Journal of Economics*, 126, No. 3 (2011): 1173–1211.

[15] In the seminal theoretical work on quality-price tendering processes by Y.-K. Che, 'Design competition through multidimensional auctions', *RAND Journal of Economics*, 24, No. 4 (1993): 668–690, price competition becomes tougher when the number of competing bidders go up. From an empirical viewpoint, G. L. Albano, F. Dini and R. Zampino, 'Bidding for Complex Projects:

It would be fair to say that, by bundling different needs arising at different points in time under the same 'umbrella', framework agreements enhance the 'product differentiation effect' especially when firms compete at the first stage to be admitted to the framework agreement. The extent to which we can derive appropriate conclusions on the degree of competition at the first stage of a framework agreement will depend above all on how variable the call-offs or second-stage orders will be (such as the delivery locations, notice period before deliveries will be made and similar matters) – in other words, how consistent and predicable are the procuring entity's needs?

### 3.3.3 *The role and nature of information*

The concept of information in competitive procurement becomes a powerful tool for both positive and normative analysis: that is, provided that the information at issue means 'who knows what when'.

#### 3.3.3.1 *Information about demand characteristics (how the needs of the procuring entity are expressed)*

Demand characteristics include all procuring-entity-specific features that are likely to influence firms' bidding strategies: required quantities of a certain product or service, physical location and degree of technological lock-in (when buying, for instance, spare parts) are among the most common ones. The extent of a procuring entity's commitment to purchase through framework agreements is also a crucial dimension – a commitment might be expressed as a guaranteed minimum level of purchases, a percentage of its overall requirements or a guarantee that all purchases of item '$Z$' will be made through a framework agreement.

Consider, then, a simple framework agreement for purchasing repeat supplies of petrol and assume that only final quantities and places of delivery remain to be set at the call-off or second stage. One could safely embrace a two-stage design whereby firms compete on price only. The more the quantities ordered differ at the second stage and the more scattered the delivery locations, the more awarding prices will vary at the call-off stage. Since economies of scale will enter the pricing strategy at the call-off stage mainly through transportation costs, the more final quantities

---

Evidence from the Acquisition of IT Services by the Italian Ministry of Economy and Finance', in M. A. Wimmer, H. Jochen Scholl, M. Janssen, R. Traunmüller (eds.), *Electronic Government. 8th International Conference EGOV 2009* (Springer Verlag, 2009) find that the number of bidders is negatively correlated with awarding prices in the procurement of IT services where quality dimensions are subjectively evaluated by the procuring entity.

will vary, the more disperse the award prices. Rational – that is, profit-maximising – firms will duly take into account this competitive feature when bidding for the framework agreement. They will indeed have to figure out a pricing strategy at the first stage, making enough room for the possibility of both high and low prices at the second stage, as well as estimating the total sales volume over which uncertainties can be spread or amortised.

Uncertainty about this common component of production costs matters since the contractor may discover that the 'true' cost of performing the contract differs from its initial estimate. This may happen if the contractor submitted a bid on the basis of a too optimistic forecast of the common component (say, public entities' buildings are easily accessible). More generally, if a supplier does not take this possibility into account at the time of bidding for the contract, it may suffer from the 'Winner's Curse':[16] that is, it may realise that actual production costs are higher than estimated ones. On the one hand, the danger of running losses *ex post* may induce bidders to bid too cautiously for the contract: the situation calls for 'prudent' pricing at the first stage (i.e. higher than would be the case were all variables known). On the other hand, the bidder's inability to recognise the Winner's Curse may generate over-aggressive bidding that results in low awarding prices for the procuring entity, but may induce the supplier to cut production costs by lowering the quality of the performance in order to recoup losses or to raise profit. In the framework agreements context, the importance of this concern is that bidders that are admitted to the framework agreement at the first stage, but suffer the Winner's Curse will not participate at the call-off stage – either by failing to participate in second-stage competition or by failing to accept purchase orders if there is no competition at that call-off stage. Design solutions might be designed to mitigate the risk – for example, by making the framework agreement binding, so that bidders are legally required to fulfil orders – but it is evident that the solution is likely to be partially effective at best, and prevention is highly preferable.

Demand heterogeneity may further complicate firms' bidding strategies about how and on what terms to enter the agreement when mixed with other sources of uncertainty such as the degree of commitment of the procuring entity to purchase through the framework agreement itself. That is, will the procuring entity systematically compare quality-price conditions inside the agreement and those resulting from alternative purchasing

---

[16] The interested reader will find a thorough treatment of the 'Winner's Curse' problem in Richard H. Thaler, *The Winner's Curse: Paradoxes and Anomalies of Economic Life* (Princeton University Press, 1994). The author reveals many of the paradoxes that abound even in the most painstakingly constructed transactions.

arrangements before deciding to use the framework agreement, or has it committed to a certain level of purchases under it? Such an uncertainty translates into a sizeable amount of risk on the firms' side, thus adversely affecting both participation and competition when bidding to enter the framework agreement,[17] and is likely to be reflected in prices offered.

#### 3.3.3.2 Contract (in)completeness

Contract (in)completeness captures the extent to which contractual clauses are able to govern all possible contingencies that may arise when exchange between trading parties takes place.[18] Intuitively, contracts are always incomplete to some degree, as it would be impossible or prohibitively costly (and then inefficient for trading purposes) to describe *ex ante* all possible events that will affect the terms of the arrangement. In public procurement, the degree of incompleteness is often related to the complexity of the contract subject matter. A procurement contract for buying a desktop printer is intrinsically more complete than one for building complex infrastructure.

A higher degree of contract incompleteness may also become part of the design of the framework agreement itself, given the variations in demand from the procuring entity. In other words, while it would be feasible (i.e. not excessively costly) to set out the major terms governing second-stage procurement contracts in the framework agreement itself, the procuring entity might decide not to do so for some elements because it anticipates that its needs will vary over the duration of the framework agreement. Thus, contract incompleteness is in most cases the by-product of the demand heterogeneity discussed above.[19]

### 3.3.4 Transaction costs

In public procurement markets, transaction costs normally refer to all costs that need to be borne for the exchange between the seller and the

---

[17] While this is quite the usual situation for a public organisation setting up a framework agreement for its own use, the scenario may dramatically change when a framework agreement is concluded by central procurement agencies (CPAs) to aggregate other public bodies' demands for goods and services. Whether or not the latter are mandated to purchase through the agreement generates 'strategic' purchasing on the demand side as buyers might be tempted to adopt a 'wait-and-see' strategy. This issue will be dealt with more extensively in Chapter 11.

[18] A comprehensive introduction to the theory of incomplete contracts can be found in P. Bolton and M. Dewatripont, *Contract Theory* (MIT Press, 2004).

[19] As we shall see in Chapter 11, there may be genuine ignorance about procuring entities' preferences, a phenomenon that is far from being unrealistic when framework agreements are used by centralised procurement agencies.

buyer (bidder and procuring entity) to take place. They range from costs related to needs assessment to conducting the procurement process (sometimes called source selection), contract management and dispute resolution.[20] While different procurement arrangements generally bring about different levels of transaction costs, the introduction of framework agreements hinges on the notion that transaction costs can be reduced as a proportion of price or value of what is procured, so that a key motivating factor is to improve the administrative efficiency of procurement processes. At the same time, though, a naïve approach to framework agreements is to be avoided – they are not a panacea, and an excessive focus on administrative efficiency will not outweigh the consequences of, say, incorrect purchases planning or needs assessment, as is further discussed in Chapter 12.

Transaction costs are not borne by the procuring entity alone: the level of participation costs for bidders can negatively affect participation. Design solutions that envisage the collection and the analysis of data about probable demand at the second stage would reduce the impact of transaction costs for the public purchaser, and would enable the uncertainties noted above to be reduced, uncertainties that bidders might otherwise factor into their bids. Design considerations that can reduce participation costs for bidders are also addressed in Chapter 10.

We can conclude from the discussion carried out in this section that grouping a bundle of procurement contracts under the same 'umbrella' agreement requires a comprehensive and meticulous demand and market analysis, which is an input of the utmost importance for a sound design of the two stages of any framework agreement.[21]

### 3.4 Applying demand and market analysis to the design of the framework agreement procedure

*3.4.1 How to frame the procuring entity's needs*

An initial question is how precisely the needs of the procuring entity can be described. If the market for the type of product or service is a stable one,

---

[20] The so-called 'Transaction Costs Economics' is mainly linked to the work(s) of Oliver E. Williamson. See in particular 'Transaction Cost Economics', in R. Schmalensee and R. Willig (eds.), *Handbook of Industrial Organization* (Amsterdam: North Holland, 1989).
[21] Gathering information about procuring entities' different needs (i.e. 'drawing the picture' of demand heterogeneity) is time consuming and, particularly in the case of centralised procurement, requires specialised personnel, as we shall see in Chapter 11.

that is, it is not likely that the technical content or other features will vary during the life of the framework agreement, and the procuring entity's demand will equally not vary, a precise formulation of the procurement needs is possible and may be appropriate. A 'precise formulation' in this sense refers not only to the technical specifications for the product or service[22] but how often and where it is to be delivered, the best estimate of quantities and minimum and maximum purchase orders per delivery in total. As the explanations above make clear, a working assumption – for example – that a framework agreement for cleaning services involves a stable market and unvarying procuring entity demand may be unfounded.

Consequently, where a procuring entity can formulate the terms of the framework in this precise manner and the demand is indeed stable and unvarying, the suppliers can be encouraged to submit their best offers for a large overall contract on those fixed terms – a classic example of economies of scale. A Model 1 framework (i.e. without second-stage competition) therefore involves competition for the entire market to be contracted under the framework agreement and secures fixed terms of supply for the duration of the framework agreement itself. Thereafter, the winning supplier can be awarded the procurement contract at the second (or call-off) stage, simply by applying the terms of the framework agreement. The economies of scale can be assumed to be maximised the greater the scale of the framework agreement – so some procuring entities may decide to conclude what is known in the United States as a 'requirements contract'.[23] The logistical justification for a Model 1 framework agreement, therefore, is that an identified demand for product $X$ over period of time $Y$ may be contracted at the best possible price by procuring the entire demand in one procedure, rather than through a series of procedures as the particular needs arise.

There is no reason that this type of framework agreement should be limited to a single precisely formulated product or service. Where the product concerned is typically procured with complementary goods or services or there is a group of similar goods or services (such as office IT or

---

[22] It is likely that there may be a standard market terminology for the types of product or service being considered in this section, such as Regulation (EC) No 2195/2002 of the European Parliament and of the Council of 5 November 2002 on the Common Procurement Vocabulary (CPV), and the United Nations Standard Products and Services Code, available at www.unspsc.org.

[23] Defined in part 16 of the Federal Acquisition Regulation as contracts 'for filling all actual purchase requirements of designated Government activities for supplies or services during a specified contract period (from one contractor), with deliveries or performance to be scheduled by placing orders with the contractor'. Federal Acquisition Regulation, Code of Federal Regulations (CFR) Title 48, 16.503 – Requirements contracts, FAR 2005-83/07-02-2015, available at www.acquisition.gov/?q=browsefar.

> **Example 3.1 KONEPS e-Shopping Mall (Korea)**
>
> *KONEPS is the single-window e-procurement system established in 2002 in Korea. KONEPS e-Shopping Mall is an e-catalogue comprising 320,000 products from over 5,200 suppliers. In 2001, 860,000 transactions were carried out worth $11 billion.*
>
> *The e-shopping mall offers a one-click service for the public agencies to purchase pre-contracted items such as office supplies and construction materials, which are frequently purchased and commonly used by most public organisations. Unit-price contracts comprise also Multiple Award Schedules (MASs) concluded with more than three bidders by the Public Procurement Service (PPS), Korea's national procurement agency.*
>
> *Besides dramatically shortening the purchase cycle, the shopping mall enables suppliers to advertise and launch marketing efforts online, increasing the opportunities to participate in the public procurement market.*
> Source: http://www.g2b.go.kr/gov/koneps/pt/intro/file/4_KONEPS_eng.pdf

stationery supplies), a framework agreement that operates as a catalogue can further amortise the administrative costs of procuring the items concerned.

Where the need for certain items is grouped together, there can be limited variations such as place of delivery (as we saw in the cleaning services example above). In these cases, suppliers will require enough information to price their offers with precision, and where products or services will be combined in different ways, the best suppliers for each variation can be assessed as the procuring entity's needs arise. In such situations, too, suppliers can be permitted to bid for only part of the entire suite of needs – an approach that can also better accommodate SMEs, for example.[24]

However, there will come a stage at which the procuring entity's needs are sufficiently variable and diverse, and, as we have seen in the analysis above, the resulting uncertainty will be reflected through the use of 'prudent' pricing at that stage. Indeed, in extreme cases the uncertainty is so significant that a reduction in participation and competition is likely, unless suppliers are able to refine their offers at the time the procuring

---

[24] The Model Law, for example, contemplates partial submissions, which would allow this matrix approach to operate in a Model 1 framework agreement. See, also, the EU Directive (note 6, supra), which provides in recital 78 that '[p]ublic procurement should be adapted to the needs of SMEs. . . . to enhance competition, contracting authorities should in particular be encouraged to divide large contracts into lots. Such division could be done on a quantitative basis, making the size of the individual contracts better correspond to the capacity of SMEs, or on a qualitative basis, in accordance with the different trades and specialisations involved, to adapt the content of the individual contracts more closely to the specialised sectors of SMEs or in accordance with different subsequent project phases'.

entity's needs crystallise. In such cases, the logistical justification for a Model 1 framework may be absent, and a second round of bidding is a logical necessity.

In addition, it may be that one supplier is unlikely to be the best supplier for the goods and services that will be procured, or for all of the goods or services in combination and/or for all variations, so a second round of bidding to identify the best supplier for each purchase order might be the better course (indicating, again, that a Model 1 framework would not be the best course to take).

These stylised examples give a simple reflection of the basic proposition that the best offers will be encouraged at the point in time where the suppliers know the scope and extent of their commitment to supply. If the procuring entity's needs do not vary, or vary only to a limited extent, then there is benefit in engaging in rigorous competition at the first stage to identify the best potential suppliers: they are competing for a defined market, and as we have seen, the advantage of the Model 1 framework agreement is clear. This form of procedure is likely to be the most appropriate model of framework agreement for repeated, stable purchases, where most or all of the terms and conditions that will apply to the future call-offs can be fixed at the first stage of the framework agreement procedure. The economies of scale that such procedures can offer, together with administrative efficiencies, make them a valuable tool. As Chapter 6 shows, this model of framework agreements is commonly used in many systems – such as those in Australia,[25] European Union and Latin America.

### 3.4.2 Accommodating diverse needs on the part of the procuring entity

Model 1 framework agreements, as we have seen, are relatively inflexible and require a level of precise planning that may not be practicable: the procuring entity may often be faced with more variations than can appropriately be accommodated in a framework agreement with fixed terms, particularly where a group of procuring entities may wish to purchase collectively,[26] standardisation may not be appropriate or feasible (for technical or other reasons)[27] and the market itself may be evolving or

---

[25] In fact the framework type of arrangements used in Australia, known as 'panel contracts', may be a closed framework agreement (Model 1 or Model 2), but, occasionally, an open one (Model 3).
[26] Centralised purchasing is discussed in Chapter 11.
[27] Policy questions about standardisation are addressed in Chapter 12.

*Some key economic dimensions in framework agreements* 45

Unstable. Examples of these situations in practice are not difficult to find, as the discussion in the early sections of this chapter shows. These situations indicate that a second round of bidding is likely to be necessary so as to identify the best supplier at the times when the procuring entity's needs arise.

From a practical perspective, the question then becomes the extent of second-stage competition. In Model 2 framework agreements, the variations that will be subject to second-stage competition are limited: here, the main competition on most of the terms of the procurement is at the first stage, and some or most bidders are eliminated at that stage. Consequently, only a limited number of bidders are admitted to the framework agreement, who will compete at the second (call-off) stage on a limited number of variables or refined terms of the procurement. In Model 3 framework agreements (open framework agreements), as we shall see, there is effectively no competition at the first stage – all qualified and responsive suppliers compete at the call-off stage on all terms of the procurement that are not expressed as mandatory minimum requirements.

To consider Model 2 framework agreements first, several needs can be bundled together under one framework agreement, so as to provide flexibility for the procuring entity to finalise or refine its statement of needs when the needs arise, so that the competition is on the relevant components of the bundle. Overall, therefore, the framework agreement is less complete than in Model 1 framework agreements because certain terms of the procurement are set only at the call-off stage.

---

**Example 3.2 NHS Estate Procure 21**

In construction procurement framework agreement in the UK health sector, a key concern was the inability to offer consistent work to suppliers, which itself was acknowledged as a barrier to 'attracting the best suppliers'. Consequently, this health-care construction suffered from poor performance and quality (and consequently high running costs, among other things), in part because the construction contracts were awarded on the basis of price alone and each was individually tendered.

A case study on 'NHS Estate Procure 21', a programme that was, using our characterisation, a Model 2 framework agreement, found that in this programme benefits in terms of administrative and process efficiencies, innovation and enhanced competition were achieved. Some of the effects of the framework agreement's predictability in demand were satisfactory performance was

> **Example 3.2 (cont.)**
>
> rewarded with further contracts and agreed margins were said to increase stability, commitment and the ability to forward-plan; it yielded new forms of standardisation, variety reduction and modularisation that could reduce costs (such as the use of prefabricated modules, which also minimised construction-related disruption in health-care environments).
>
> The programme included a national database of performance, which allowed good ideas to be shared, and accurate data allowed meaningful price analysis (that could identify loss-leading, cross-subsidies and overcharging). The successor framework agreement, Procure21+, claims savings of 14.1 per cent for the United Kingdom's National Health Service, and an average estimated time saving of six months per contract. The relationships built with suppliers in this framework agreement, according to the published data, did not override objective award criteria.

If there is extensive variation in demand, diverse bundling and/or the market concerned is volatile or fast-changing, there may also be little benefit of engaging in rigorous competition at the first stage as a Model 2 framework agreement envisages – it would simply be repeated at the second stage (effectively defeating the administrative efficiency that is a main justification for framework agreements procedures). In these circumstances, assessing qualifications and responsiveness alone may be sufficient at the first stage. In a Model 3 framework agreement, which is an open framework agreement, all bidders whose offers are responsive (i.e. whose offers meet the procuring entity's needs and any minimum technical requirements) are admitted to the framework agreement unless they are not qualified for the procurement at issue. Further, the importance of the framework agreement being 'open' is that new suppliers are admitted at any time during the operation of the framework agreement, provided these conditions are met.

Consequently, all price and quality competition will take place at the second (call-off) stage in open framework agreements. This model of framework agreement can therefore be set up with a range of items that is relatively broad and with the caveat that procuring entities need to be able to assess bidders against one set of qualification and responsiveness criteria, which will limit the extent of the bundling that is appropriate.[28]

---

[28] It is assumed that the administrative complexity of assessing against a variation of criteria for different elements of the bundle is not efficient, so this possibility is discarded. As noted in Chapter 2, where an assessment of qualifications alone is undertaken, the result is a list of supplier and not a framework agreement.

If the framework agreement is so broad in scope that neither qualifications nor responsiveness can meaningfully be assessed at the first stage, an entire procurement procedure will be needed at the second stage, defeating the administrative benefit that framework agreements are intended to confer.

---

**Example 3.3 The dynamic purchasing system for pharmaceutical products managed by Consip (Italy)**

The Italian Regulation for the execution and implementation of the code of public contracts for works, services and supplies establishes that Consip – on behalf of the Ministry of Economy and Finance (MEF) – can set up dynamic purchasing systems (DPSs) and make them available to all public administrations. In 2011, Consip set up the first DPS in Italy, which was used for procuring pharmaceutical products. The system runs on the Italian MEF's e-procurement platform, which is managed by Consip. For any DPS, Consip publishes the contract notice, defines product characteristics and provides negotiation models and tender documentations.

Pharmaceutical products are standardised by using four dimensions: (i) the Anatomical Therapeutic Chemical (ATC) Classification System, controlled by the World Health Organization; (ii) the active ingredient; (iii) the dosage form; and (iv) the dose. Each procurement contract is always split to hundreds of lots, each consisting a specific combination of the four dimensions above. Table 3.1 reports the main features of procurement contracts awarded from January 2012 until June 2014.

Each call-off contract comprised on average 1,395 lots; in 50 per cent of cases the number of lots is exactly 1,231. Each lot received on average 2.8 offers, with a minimum of zero offers and a maximum of 24. In 50 per cent of all lots the number of submitted offers is at most equal to 2.

As of early 2015, the variety of active DPSs included: pharmaceutical products, IT products and (simple) services, foodstuff, assistive devices for persons with disabilities, products for health care (e.g. antiseptics, syringes and needles) and insurance services, which accounted for an overall estimated value approximately € 10 billion. In 2014, 21 procurement contracts were awarded accounting for an expenditure of € 1,383 billion.[29]

---

[29] Data retrieved for Consip 2015 annual report. The report is available at www.consip.it/opencms/export/sites/consip/press_room/bilanci/Documenti/Bilancio-2014.pdf.

**Example 3.3 (cont.)**

Table 3.1 *Consip's DPS for pharmaceutical products*

|  | Year | | |
| --- | --- | --- | --- |
|  | 2012 | 2013 | 2014 (1st semester) |
| No. of procurement contracts | 3 | 8 | 4 |
| No. of competing firms | 113 | 143 | 132 |
| Estimated value of contracts | €110 M | €2,500 M | €506 M |
| Weighted average rebate wrt the reserve price | 30% | 28% | 20% |

Note: Consip (Italy): DPS for pharmaceutical products
Source: Consip's dataware house (May 2015).

Model 2 and Model 3 framework agreements can therefore be described as existing on a sliding scale from framework agreements that are nearly complete procurement contracts to very loose arrangements indeed. Some Model 2 framework agreements approach the degree of certainty required for Model 1 framework agreements, so offers at the first stage are sufficiently predictive to allow for a rigorous selection of a limited number of bidders at the first stage that will compete for limited variations in demand at the call-off stage. For looser Model 2 frameworks and open frameworks, the additional benefits of extensive competition at the first stage are unlikely to exceed its costs. Nonetheless, in order to avoid the situation in which many marginal suppliers are admitted to an open framework agreement in particular, the minimum qualification requirements and minimum offer standards can be set at a level that accurately reflects the market from which the procuring entity wishes to fulfil its needs.

As this brief consideration of key economic dimensions of framework agreements procedures indicates, the tool may be appropriate for a wide range of needs and circumstances. Furthermore, the best results from framework agreements themselves will accrue where they are used to their fullest potential. Not only do these points demonstrate the importance of careful market and demand analysis within the planning process as a design consideration and in the context of relatively long-lasting procurement procedures, but they also underscore the importance of designing a process that provides for maximum competition at the appropriate point in

*Some key economic dimensions in framework agreements* 49

the procedure. In Chapters 6 and 8, we shall consider how to maximise competition in the framework agreements context and discuss issues that can impede or prevent fair and effective competition.

## 3.5 Chapter summary

- While pursuing the specific goals of enhancing administrative efficiency, facilitating demand aggregation and favouring supply diversifications, framework agreements have to meet the overarching objective of promoting participation and competition in public procurement markets.
- Different models of framework agreements are conceived to respond to different features of both demand and supply sides of the market.
- If a procuring entity's demand is stable and unvarying, bidders can be encouraged to submit their best offers for a large overall contract on those fixed terms, which would give rise to a Model 1 framework agreement.
- Demand heterogeneity needs to be handled with two stages of competition whereby only the common dimensions of procuring entities' needs will be part of the competition among firms to enter the agreement (Model 2). The resulting degree of 'contract incompleteness' at the first stage of the agreement does play a crucial role in determining the level of competition among participating firms.

CHAPTER 4

# The economic analysis of framework agreements

## 4.1 Introduction

In previous chapters, we have become acquainted with the two common traits in different types of framework agreements; namely, the aggregation of demand for goods, services and/or construction to be delivered or provided at different moments in time, and the two-stage process design. During the past decade, the evolution of international regulation has led procurement experts and scholars alike to classify framework agreements more meticulously, according to whether or not the agreement is open to entry of new suppliers after it is initially concluded; and, when closed to such entry, whether or not procurement contracts can be awarded directly, or whether a further round of competition is needed. This has led us to pin down three main families of agreements whose main characteristics have been painted in previous chapters.[1]

Clearly, there exist at least two additional (sub-)dimensions of framework agreements that play a non-trivial role in determining the nature and degree of competition and the extent to which procuring entities can appropriately satisfy their needs: the number of awardees, and whether or not procuring entities are required to use the framework agreement. In many cases, though, the main features of an

---

[1] In the European Union, the classification of framework agreements into four classes arose from an explanatory note from the European Commission: European Commission, Directorate General Internal Market and Services, Explanatory Note – Framework Agreements – Classic Directive (2005), CC2005/03_rev/ of 14 July 2005, available at http://ec.europa.eu/internal_market/publicprocurement/docs/explan-notes/classic-dir-framework_en.pdf. Hereafter, the Explanatory Note. The classification hinges on two dimensions only: the completeness/incompleteness of the framework agreement (i.e. whether or not a second round of competition is needed) and the number of awardees. The 2004 EU Directive considered in the Explanatory Note has been repealed by Directive 2014/24/EU of the European Parliament and of the Council of 26 February 2014 on public procurement and repealing Directive 2004/18/EC Text with EEA relevance, OJ L 94, 28 March 2014, pp. 65–242, available at http://eur-lex.europa.eu/legal-content/EN/TXT/?uri=celex:32014L0024. Hereafter, the EU Directive. Nonetheless, the provisions on framework agreements remain highly similar, save where noted in this chapter.

agreement are not 'genetically' hardwired at the outset. There exist, for instance, 'hybrid' families of framework agreements in which the number of awardees is not exogenously determined (i.e. set out in the solicitation documents), but depends upon the outcome of competition; framework agreements might also be characterised by fixed conditions or conditions that remain to be further specified at the second stage of the process.

This chapter will present a more in-depth analysis of the main economic forces at work in the three main classes of framework agreements, focusing particularly on Models 1 and 2, which raise the most pressing concerns in terms of how to ensure that the two-stage process design is suitable. We shall explore how the different features of framework agreements combine together to achieve the desired objectives, such as fostering competition through contract standardisation, while guaranteeing the appropriate degree of tailoring of the ultimate procurement contracts to each procuring entity's needs. We shall also emphasise how lack of attention to seemingly minor details of the framework agreement design may generate undesirable outcomes.

We shall proceed by assessing the main economic features of each family of framework agreement by benchmarking it in part against two alternative scenarios: a set of independently run procurement processes run by different public organisations ('multiple buyers or procuring entities'), and a set of procurement processes run by the same public organisation for satisfying its needs as they arise at different points in time ('single buyer or procuring entity'). The first case is meant to capture the situation whereby needs stemming from different public organisations are grouped into a framework agreement that may or may not be awarded by a different body (say, a centralised procurement agency). Thus, the design of a framework agreement will be instrumental in determining whether a move towards a higher degree of centralisation in the relevant procurement environment is feasible. The second case reflects the adoption of a framework by the same procuring entity for its own use. Hence, we shall assess qualitatively the performance of framework agreements relatively to a sequence of separate 'simple contracts'. Finally, along the same lines as previous chapters, we shall make the simplifying assumption that firms do not collude. Being one of the most relevant pathologies in public procurement markets, collusion will be the core subject of Chapters 7 and 8.

## 4.2 Model 1 framework agreements – closed and complete framework agreements

Model 1 framework agreements are characterised by (i) all contractual clauses governing the anticipated procurement contracts being laid down at the first stage of the process, and (ii) all awardees being selected at the first stage, and no entry of new suppliers being possible during the call-off stage. In what follows, we shall further distinguish two major dimensions; namely, whether the framework is concluded with one supplier or more suppliers.

### 4.2.1 Single-award framework agreement (also known as 'frame' or 'framework contracts')

It is worth starting our analysis with the case of a framework agreement concluded with one supplier and all conditions established in the framework agreement. This class of framework agreement, also known as a 'framework contract', is used either by a procuring entity for its own needs[2] or, alternatively, by (generally national) centralised purchasing agencies – in the European Union, including Consip in Italy, BBG in Austria and Hansel in Finland. Public bodies, both at a central and local level, are entitled to make purchase orders from the (often, nationwide) framework contract.[3] In some cases, national policymakers have foreseen the use of national framework contracts to be mandatory for procuring entities that are central government bodies.[4]

The main feature of a framework contract is that quality-price competition is entirely concentrated at the first stage, while the second ('call-off') stage involves simply issuing purchase orders. These features bear immediate consequences in terms of competition and process costs.

#### 4.2.1.1 Transaction costs

As we saw in Chapter 2, bundling separate procurement strategies into a single process or accommodating potentially different needs into a single

---

[2] In Chapter 6 we shall describe the evolution of the procurement strategy for IT services by the Italian Ministry of Economy and Finance from a frame contract towards a framework agreement approach.
[3] For instance, framework contracts awarded by Consip (Italy) establish both price and all the contractual clauses (but quantity and time of delivery of the single purchase orders). In addition, they never guarantee a minimum volume of purchases, as they only fix an upper bound (in terms of either volume or value of purchases). Thus the contractor bears all the uncertainty on the discrepancy between estimated and realised demand, although past purchases normally convey reliable information on actual demand.
[4] For more detailed institutional features, see Chapter 6.

contract not only is administratively efficient but also can improve the quality of tender documents, and so reduce the risk of litigation at any stage of the procurement cycle. There exists, however, an additional benefit that normally goes unnoticed, namely, a 'standardisation' of the procurement language, since different purchasing needs will be satisfied by relying on the same procedure. Standardisation also helps reduce barriers to entry into the procurement market, as firms will save on resources employed to check the differences in procurement strategies or documents adopted by distinct contracting authorities, even if the latter end up purchasing similar commodities. The potential drawback of awarding a single contract on behalf of many users is that more resources are needed in order to gather information on needs requirements before the procurement strategy is designed. Although this may sound a cumbersome task with the potential to slow down the procurement cycle, information gathering becomes less and less time- and resource-consuming over time, provided that purchasing patterns are stored and analysed as the process is repeated.

Less positively, there may be concerns about the effectiveness of contract enforcement. While a framework agreement does not seem to raise additional concerns with respect to the benchmark case of simple contracts awarded by a single buyer, contract enforcement of a framework agreement may become more costly and/or less effective than in the case of simple contracts awarded by multiple buyers. When different organisations' needs are merged into a single contract, instead, the awarding body is likely to be a separate organisation from those in charge of contract enforcement (i.e. a centralised purchasing agency rather than a procuring entity or final user). A central purchasing body may become less proactive at the contract execution stage as it has not taken an active part in selecting suppliers.

Evidence of ineffective contract enforcement in centralised procurement is provided by Albano and Zampino (2012),[5] who analysed data collected through the 'National Framework Contracts (NFCs) Monitoring System' that was put in place in 2006 by Consip – the national central purchasing body in Italy – to provide assistance to public administrations' efforts at the management stage of the NFCs. The system consists in sending inspectors and auditors all over the country to assess the performance of NFC awardees. The inspections are designed primarily to measure those

---

[5] G. L. Albano and R. Zampino, 'Strengthening the Integrity of Public Procurement Processes: What Do Data from the Italian National Framework Agreements Say?' in G. Piga and S. Treumer (eds.), *The Applied Law and Economics of Public Procurement* (Routledge, 2012).

Table 4.1 *Sample of performance dimensions and measures of contract enforcement in Consip's National Framework Contracts (Italy)*

| | |
|---|---|
| No. of cases of compliance | 1062 |
| No. of cases of compliance with remarks | 21 |
| No. of cases of low non-compliance | 41 |
| No. of cases of mild non-compliance | 39 |
| No. of cases of high non-compliance | 401 |
| Total no. of cases | 1564 |
| Total no. of cases of non-compliance (NC) | 481 |
| No. of enforced penalty clauses (PC) | 12 |

*Source:* G. L. Albano and R. Zampino (2012).

performance indicators related to objective quality dimensions concerning the execution of purchases or orders (before public buyers receive the item), and those related to other dimensions such as the delivered (intrinsic) quality of goods and post-purchase services (after public buyers have received the item). From a legal point of view, all evaluated quality dimensions are associated to contractually agreed penalty clauses that are to be applied when minimum levels of performance are not fulfilled (e.g. delivery time). Table 4.1 borrowed from Albano and Zampino (2012) suggests the coexistence of two seemingly conflicting circumstances: those situations whereby contract performance was almost close to perfect compliance (1083), and those in which (low) performance could or should have triggered the use of remedies (481). In spite of the high number of non-compliances (30.75%), figures show that contractual remedies were used only in 12 of out 481 cases (2.49%); see Table 4.1. This simple observation might be reinterpreted as a (low) probability that a bad-performing supplier (in relation to the agreed quality levels) will be caught and punished by the public buyer.

At least four, possibly coexisting, hypotheses might explain such stark evidence of ineffective contract enforcement:

- **Lack of knowledge.** If contracting officers purchasing through NFCs play no role in drafting the latter (Consip is in charge of drafting NFCs), they might not be as knowledgeable about all relevant contractual details as when the contract is drafted by the purchasing authority itself.

- **Lack of incentives.** Contracting officers have to pay a positive cost in enforcing the contract but do not foresee necessarily any concrete benefit accruing to the public authorities that employ them.
- **In-kind compensations.** Renegotiations between public buyers and suppliers, especially in case of more complex projects, might take place in that bad performance on one dimension might be compensated by the contractor's additional effort on another task.
- **Corruption.** Public officers might simply exert low effort in exchange for personal gains.

*4.2.1.2 Degree of competition*

When several simple contracts are merged into a single framework agreement, contractors may operate at lower unit (average) costs than the level that would be attainable when the overall value is split in possibly many separate contracts. This is normally due to economies of scale, which arise whenever production costs comprise a sizeable fraction of fixed costs; that is, of costs that are independent of the production scale. If this is the case, by increasing production, firms are able to operate at a lower unit cost.

Product standardisation seems to be almost a prerequisite for merging many simple contracts into a larger one. The dimension of product standardisation is, however, hard to disentangle from the degree of demand heterogeneity. To see this, consider a very simple case of procurement of petrol. This might be considered a highly standardised commodity, but final users may differ in their preferences about delivery conditions, time of payment, physical location, consumption profiles, contract management skills, degree of freedom in budget and accounting management. Thus, seemingly similar procurement contracts would end up being different 'objects' because of different contractual clauses. This implies that commodity standardisation – or, better, contract standardisation – should also be coupled with a low degree of demand heterogeneity for a framework agreement to deploy its full potential. When this is the case, demand aggregation generally allows firms to produce at a lower unit cost.

Lower production costs, however, may yield lower purchasing prices (or, more generally, better value for money) only if the buyer keeps intact or increases its bargaining power. In general, the degree of competition is usually expected to increase with the value of procurement contracts. In those markets where the public sector accounts for a relevant share of the total demand, moving from multiple independently awarded contracts to a single framework agreement can put the awardee in a position to significantly increase its market share. This strengthens the bargaining power of the public body awarding the framework agreement, thus leading the suppliers to compete more fiercely to offer lower price (and, possibly, better quality).

Nonetheless, two conflicting forces come into play. For a given number of competitors, demand aggregation leads to fiercer competition. However, as the size of contracts gets larger, smaller firms may find it impossible to participate in the competitive processes – because of more demanding economic and financial requisites – thus leading to a lower number of competitors if smaller firms decide not to participate (for which they may need to form joint ventures). Assuming that in most circumstances the lower participation effect is not overwhelming, demand aggregation usually leads to higher savings.

Standardisation of the subject matter of a framework agreement is necessary for triggering a higher level of competition than in the case of separate simple contracts. Thus, when the framework agreement is not used for buying commodities such as petrol, electricity, personal computers or printers, but rather to purchase a bundle of heterogeneous services, firms may react by adopting a more prudent bidding behaviour. This is the case, for instance, of a series of 'general purpose' framework agreements for IT services awarded by Consip on behalf of the Italian Ministry of Economy and Finance (MEF) over the period 1998–2008. Such framework agreements used to comprise a large variety of activities, from simple maintenance to developments of new applications, and from software customisation to integration of complex systems. Quality proposals consisted in providing effective and flexible teams of professionals and technological solutions to best meet the ministry's (fairly unpredictable) needs over the contract duration. Contractors were typically required to modify their working team to undertake a variety of tasks that would be precisely defined only after the 'master' contract had been awarded. These 'general purpose' framework agreements were often compared to a sort of 'Pandora's box' of heterogeneous services, which generated high uncertainty at the bidding stage.[6]

---

[6] In 2008, Consip and the MEF moved from a framework contract towards a full-fledged multi-award incomplete framework agreement approach. For more on this experience, see Chapter 6.

#### 4.2.1.3 Flexibility and 'adverse selection' among final users

By its very nature, virtually any framework agreement is at risk of becoming an inflexible purchasing tool that may not meet many procuring entities' needs. So the higher the degree of demand heterogeneity, the more difficult it becomes to squeeze several simple contracts into the same framework agreement. If demand aggregation is a bottom-up process, that is, if procuring entities explicitly delegate a third party (be it one of themselves or a centralised procurement body), then it should be possible, at least in principle, to determine in advance to what extent the same framework agreement meets procuring entities' needs. Should the framework agreement be designed as a top-down process – which may occur when a centralised procurement agency awards the framework agreement – then some of the positive effects of merging several simple contracts into a bigger one may be jeopardised if public bodies are not mandated to purchase through the same framework agreement. In other words, if procuring entities do have an 'outside option' to buy by themselves, competing firms run the risk of realised demand ending up being much lower than the pre-award conjectured level. High uncertainty makes firms raise prices, hence counterbalancing the positive effect on savings due to firms' ability to exploit economies of scale.

Another major drawback of framework agreements originates from the risk of *adverse selection*. It is well known since Akerlof's seminal contribution[7] that trade in markets may break down when buyers cannot distinguish between high- and low-quality goods. Since buyers' willingness to pay cannot exceed the value of the 'average' quality product, only sellers of low quality will be willing to trade. Anticipating this, (rational) buyers may refrain from buying altogether. A similar phenomenon may arise in a framework contract. Since the same contractual clauses apply to all subsequent purchases, and given that the framework agreement's final users differ from each other with respect to one or more dimensions that ultimately affect the contractor's profit, the latter is bound to make offers based on the final users' 'average' profile. Consequently, 'bad' final users are more likely to issue purchase orders. The potentially harmful consequences of adverse selection can be spelled out in a stylised framework agreement for car insurance described in Example 4.1.

---

[7] G. Akerlof, 'The Market for "Lemons": Quality Uncertainty and the Market Mechanism', *The Quarterly Journal of Economics*, 84, No. 3 (1970): 488–500.

> **Example 4.1 Adverse selection in a simple framework agreement for car insurance**
>
> Consider the following stylised framework agreement for car insurance to be awarded on behalf of two public bodies by using price-only competition. Suppose that the two public bodies – say, two ministries – differ from each other with respect to the risk of accident borne by employees using cars for accomplishing their duties. Ministry 'G' displays good accident records (low risk), whereas Ministry 'B' displays very poor records (high risk). Defining $p_G$ and $p_B$ the insurance premiums for low-risk and high-risk drivers respectively, an insurance company would set $p_G < p_B$ if it were able to make to distinguish low-risk from high-risk drivers and thus make two separate offers.
>
> Because of its fixed-condition nature, a framework agreement would determine *only one* insurance premium. How would firms set the average insurance premium $p_A$? The competitive level of $p_A$ is likely to depend, all else being equal, on whether the use of the framework contract is mandatory. Suppose first that the framework contract is mandatory and that firms correctly estimate the composition of the set of final users, say, 60 per cent of high-risk and 40 per cent of low-risk Ministries. Then competition would drive the premium to a level of $p_A = 0.6\, p_B + 0.4\, p_G$. The resulting purchase orders give rise to social inefficiency since the high-risk (respectively, low-risk) Ministry is paying too low a (respectively, too high a) insurance premium than the one that would emerge from insurance companies negotiating directly and separately with each ministry.
>
> If, instead, the use of the framework agreement is voluntary, then any 'average' insurance premium $p_A$ such that $p_G < p_A < p_B$, would cause low-risk public agencies to look for a better outside option. Rational profit-maximising firms will anticipate that only high-risk public agencies will purchase through the framework agreement, thereby setting $p_A = p_B$.

### 4.2.2 Multi-award framework agreements

While fixing all contractual conditions at the first stage of the process, this class of framework agreements makes room for multiple awardees. In what follows, we shall briefly explore the main logic underlying a purchasing arrangement which cannot be contractually modified at the call-off stage, but which allows procuring entities to select among several sources. We shall then focus on a potentially critical feature – both from a regulatory and economic viewpoint – namely, the method to be used for awarding procurement contracts at the second stage (call-offs in the EU system).

### 4.2.2.1 The economic rationales

Multiple sourcing coupled with a ready-to-use procurement contract may satisfy the need for supply diversification. There exist quite diverse reasons for pursuing supply diversification. First, awarding (a sizeable) procurement contract to one supplier only, as in the case of framework contracts, while maximising competition at the award stage, may dramatically increase the risk of supply interruptions as compared with having more suppliers ready to provide similar or identical products or services. Second, there might exist technological reasons for having more suppliers available at the same time. If, for instance, a procuring entity is concluding a framework agreement for the day-to-day maintenance of IT equipment, then service levels are likely to be the same for all different pieces of equipment, although there might exist a high degree of specialisation in maintenance services so that each brand would require specialised personnel. Consequently, more than one supplier of maintenance services is needed if the buyer owns different makes of the same IT equipment.

Multiple suppliers may be also necessary to ensure future security of supply for emergency situations. Swift action after a natural disaster would require ready-to-use contracts as well as the minimisation of the risk of lack of production capacity, which may otherwise arise if only one supplier were to be in charge of the contract(s). Moreover, supply diversification may be associated with suppliers being located in different geographical areas so that delivery costs or time are minimised if an adverse event occurs.

From a competitive viewpoint, it seems intuitively correct that, all else being equal, the degree of competition for a multi-supplier framework agreement with fixed conditions is lower than in the case of a single-supplier agreement (the so-called *framework contract*). The reason is that, unlike a framework agreement, more than one 'prize' (i.e. number of awardees) is to be awarded. Assuming that the number of prizes is exogenously given, then the higher the number of prizes, the lower the degree of competition when the framework agreement is concluded. This prediction may bring about additional efficiency properties. Supply diversification, say, for emergency purposes, is in fact equivalent to buying an insurance. Thus, the higher the number of prizes or awardees, the more 'complete' the insurance, which requires the purchasing entity or entities to pay a higher price caused by softer competition.

While yielding tangible benefits to procuring entities, supply diversification generally implies a certain degree of heterogeneity of the levels of value for money offered by selected firms. Suppose, for instance, that a framework agreement is concluded with the four highest-ranked firms by means of the most economically advantageous tender (MEAT) criterion. In this case, it is likely that the four highest-ranked firms will have submitted different quality-price schedules, thus yielding different levels of value for money. When the framework agreement is awarded by means of the lowest-price (LP) criterion, the case becomes even more compelling, since the awardees will be offering basically the same commodities or services at different prices. Consequently, the choice of the method to award procurement contracts at the second stage becomes a crucial decision.

*4.2.2.2 Awarding second-stage contracts*

From both a regulatory and economic perspective, one of the thorniest issues rests on how to award a procurement contract when more than one supplier has been selected and contractual clauses are completely specified. Generally, the selection process at the first stage will produce a list of awardees with different quality-price schedules if the framework agreement is concluded by means of the MEAT criterion, or different prices (or vectors of prices) if the award criterion is the LP criterion. In some systems, there are some hybrid approaches,[8] whereby a framework agreement with fixed conditions is concluded with multiple suppliers provided that suppliers other than the highest-ranked are asked to match the economic conditions of the highest-ranked. When one or more of them accepts this requirement, then multiple suppliers in fact offer identical goods and services at exactly the same prices. This is the case, for instance, of 'rate contracts' in India and 'framework contracts' in Ethiopia.

In the European Union, policymakers at the continental level have provided contracting authorities with some arguably rigid guidance for awarding procurement contracts. An 'Explanatory Note' from the European Commission in 2005 was designed to provide practical instructions concerning the call-off stage, as follows:

> One way of doing this is the '**cascade**' method, i.e. firstly contacting the economic operator[9] whose tender for the award of a framework agreement establishing all the terms (framework contract) was considered the best and turning to the second one where the first one is not capable of or interested in providing the goods, services or works in question.[10]

---

[8] For more on this issue, see Chapter 6.  [9] The term in the EU system for a supplier.
[10] Explanatory Note, note 1, supra. See, in particular, Section 3.2.

However, the cascade represents only one possible way of awarding each procurement contract. Indeed, footnote 24 provides that:

> A decision as to which economic operator a specific order is to be placed with may also be made according to other criteria, provided that they are *objective, transparent and non-discriminatory*.[11] Thus, let us imagine a large institution which, having photocopiers of different makes, has concluded framework agreements establishing all the terms for the maintenance and repair of this equipment with a series of economic operators so as to ensure the presence of at least one specialist for each make of photocopier in its machine pool. For the award of the framework agreements, the contracting authority has used award criteria such as price, speed of intervention, range of makes that can be catered for, etc. It is clear that an order to service e.g. a Rank Xerox machine may then be given to the specialist for this make even if the tender for Canons has been ranked first.

Although the Explanatory Note envisages alternative methods for awarding procurement contracts, the main text and the content of footnote 24 in fact depict quite diverse circumstances. The underlying, albeit unexpressed, assumption in the 'cascade' method is that the contents of awardees' respective tenders are (almost) perfect substitutes of each other. That being so, it would seem reasonable for a procuring entity to buy from the highest-ranked awardee subject to its capacity constraints or its ability to fulfil the purchasing order at the time when the procurement contract is awarded. The example in footnote 24 instead depicts a (rather extreme) case of specialisation among awardees, in that it is understandable that each make of photocopiers can require fairly specialised maintenance services. Consequently, a public buyer with a stock of different makes will be better-off by matching the service maintenance contract with the make of photocopiers. The procurement strategies in this case are appropriate, as the conclusion of a framework agreement with multiple suppliers responds to the logic of supply diversification given the heterogeneity in the stock of photocopiers. The 'brand-matching' criterion in this example seems to fulfil all requisites for objectivity, transparency and non-discrimination, hinging on a technological assumption that a maintenance service provided by a certain awardee best suits a machine with its offered make of photocopier. This is a case of complete lack of substitutability or perfect complementarity between maintenance service and the specific piece of office equipment.

---

[11] Emphasis added.

### 4.2.3 A closer look at the 'cascade' method

Consider now a somewhat different example; namely, a framework agreement for medical equipment such as ultrasound machines. A group of independent health-care facilities (say, hospitals), with a track record of purchases of similar, although not identical, machines, has decided to bundle its needs into a single procurement process and to adopt a multi-supplier framework agreement with fixed conditions. The choice of this specific type of framework agreement again appears to respond to the implicit goal of supply diversification. Suppose that tenders are evaluated according to quality characteristics such as software and ergonomic features (e.g. ease of transport, interface user friendliness, monitor resolution) and price, and that the value-for-money competition is such that the agreement is concluded with four awardees.

A straightforward application of the 'cascade' method in this case would require each hospital to conclude a procurement contract with the highest-ranked awardee. If, throughout the duration of the agreement, the latter is not affected by capacity constraints, it may be well the case that all hospitals in fact purchase the same machine. While from an *ex-ante* perspective the selected type of framework agreement was aimed at assuring supply diversification, from an *ex-post* perspective the 'cascade' method may concentrate all subsequent procurement contracts in the hands of the same firm, so that the framework agreement becomes *de facto* a single-supplier agreement.

This scenario, far from being a theoretical exercise, is likely to arise if procuring entities cannot find an alternative award method fulfilling the requirements of objectivity, transparency and non-discrimination. A closer examination may, however, reveal a potential source of complementarity between the machine's characteristics and the machine's final users (doctors). If the latter have accumulated over time expertise in and familiarity with using one particular brand, then each hospital might express 'preferences' over the composition of a bundle of (possible) different makes according to its own doctors' experience and expertise. Thus the result, at least in principle, would be that the relevant criterion for awarding the procurement contract should hinge on doctors' preferences rather than on the abstract measure of value for money. Needless to say, the hospitals' award criterion based on doctors' experience and practice-driven preferences would be virtually indistinguishable from preferences induced by opaque relationships between doctors and suppliers.

We are then led to a troublesome conclusion. The cascade method seems to be an adequate award criterion when tenders are almost perfect substitutes of each other. However, unless awardees are affected by severe capacity constraints, the highest-ranked supplier is likely to be awarded most of the procurement contracts. One is then left to wonder whether a *single-award* rather than a multi-award framework agreement would have been a more appropriate procurement strategy.

The cascade method usually suffers from an additional drawback. If the highest-ranked supplier is able or willing to sign all subsequent procurement contracts, then the other awardees would end up running losses since being party to a framework agreement requires each awardee to invest or freeze resources (e.g. financial guarantees), but does not receive any sales. This prospect might deter firms from bidding for future agreements as only the highest-ranked one ends up benefiting from the arrangement.

Sometimes, the cascade method need not have a straightforward interpretation. To see this consider the following stylised case of a framework agreement concluded with, say, three suppliers by using the lowest-price criterion. Suppliers are asked to submit prices for three items. Concretely, suppliers' ranking is determined by the lowest weighted-average price, where the price of item $i$ ($i$ = 1, 2, 3) is evaluated according to weight[12] $\alpha_i$, with $\alpha_1 + \alpha_2 + \alpha_3$ = 1. The awardees' resulting prices are indicated in Table 4.2.

Table 4.2 *An example of awardees' prices at the call-off stage of a multi-award Model 1 framework agreement*

|        | Unit price item 1 | Unit price item 2 | Unit price item 3 |
|--------|-------------------|-------------------|-------------------|
| Firm A | $p_1^A$           | $p_2^A$           | $p_3^A$           |
| Firm B | $p_1^B$           | $p_2^B$           | $p_3^B$           |
| Firm C | $p_1^C$           | $p_2^C$           | $p_3^C$           |

The cascade method could then be applied in two different ways:

- **Item by item**: The buyer purchases each item from whoever has set the lowest price for that particular item. For example, the vector of lowest prices might be ($p_1^A$, $p_2^B$, $p_3^C$), which implies that the identity of the

[12] The possible rationale for setting those weights will be dealt with in Chapter 10.

contractor at the call-off stage depends upon which item is to be purchased.
- **Lowest weighted-average price:** The award method at the call-off stage simply mimics the award criterion used to select suppliers at the first stage. However, the purchasing entity need not use the same weights adopted at the first stage. Each purchasing entity may have different preferences over the vector of $\alpha_i$'s, which reflect specific needs. Consequently, it may well be the case that the concrete application of the lowest weighted-average price method at the second stage leads to awarding a procurement contract to firm C rather than firm A, which was the highest-ranked at the first stage.

An immediate trade-off between savings and contract management costs arises. The item-by-item criterion ensures that procurement expenditure is minimised as procuring entities will always select the lowest standing price for each item. However, this might generate an administrative burden, as each purchasing decision might require signing a contract with a different contractor. The higher the number of items, the more administratively burdensome this solution. Alternatively, replicating at the call-off stage the same award criterion adopted at the first stage – that is, the lowest weighted-average price – would certainly minimise the procuring entities' administrative effort, since they would systematically address themselves to supplier A unless the latter is unable to serve the contract. Thus, the overall arrangement would suffer again from the drawback of having potentially one single supplier (firm A) selling at the call-off stage.

The choice of the specific award method at the second stage also feeds back into the nature of competition at the first stage. Suppose that the number of awardees had been exogenously determined by the procuring entity which concluded the framework agreement; that is, it was publicly announced that the three highest-ranked suppliers would be selected. If the award method at the second stage just reproduces the one at the first stage, it is reasonable to expect fairly tough competition among suppliers in order to achieve the highest rank. If, instead, procurement contracts are to be awarded by means of the item-by-item method, then competing firms will behave as 'niche' players;[13] namely, each of them will set

---

[13] A stylised model of framework agreement with firms behaving in a similar fashion is studied by G. L. Albano and M. Sparro, 'Flexible Strategies for Centralized Public Procurement', *Review of Economics and Institutions*, 1, No. 2 (2010), Article 4. The article can be downloaded from www.rei.unipg.it/rei/article/view/17.

prices as if each item were a market independent from all others subject to the constraint of offering a bundle whose weighted-average cost is not higher than the third lowest. Intuitively, competition at the first stage is likely to be softer if the award method at the call-off stage is driven by each item's price. So the average price of the bundle is likely to be higher than under the alternative award method. However, each firm is more likely to be aggressive on that (or those) item(s) – the 'niche' market(s) – for which it enjoys a competitive advantage, thus promoting *allocative efficiency*: each procurement contract is awarded to the supplier producing at the lowest cost (among those selected at the first stage). This situation is in fact reminiscent of a more general problem in procurement; that is, the potential tension between savings and allocative efficiency. A further stylised example will help clarify the problem (Example 4.2).

---

**Example 4.2 Bundling versus item-by-item award criterion**

Suppose two procurement contracts (coinciding with two geographical lots) for delivering foodstuff are awarded by using a *lowest-price* criterion. There are two potential participants: firm G and firm H. Firm G bears a distribution cost equal to €1 for lot 'North' and €10 for lot 'South'. Firm B, instead, bears a production cost of €9 and €4, respectively. Firms are long-run competitors in the market, so they know each other's distribution costs. Suppose that costs are additive; that is, the cost of serving the two lots for both firms is just the sum of the cost for each single lot, while production costs are assumed to be nought.

The bidding scenario can be illustrated by using the matrix below.

|                | lot 'North' | lot 'South' |
|----------------|-------------|-------------|
| Firm G's costs | €1          | €10         |
| Firm H's costs | €9          | €4          |

If the buyer were to bundle the two lots, then price competition would drive the awarding price down to (slightly below) €14 and the awardee will be firm G. If the buyer awards the lots separately, then competition would drive the price of lot 'North' down to (slightly below) €9 and the price of lot 'South' down to (slightly below) €10. In this case, firm G will be awarded lot 'North', while firm H will be awarded lot 'South'. The buyer's expenditure is €14 with the first strategy and €9 + €10 = €19 with the second strategy.

The example above highlights the tension between allocative efficiency and savings. The bundling strategy is to be preferred if the buyer wishes to minimise the purchasing price of the bundle. In doing so, however, she allocates lot 'South' to firm G although the latter bears a higher distribution cost than firm H (allocative *inefficiency* in the case of lot 'South').

### 4.2.4   On the 'rotation' method

We have argued above that the 'cascade' method tends to concentrate procurement contracts in the hands of a single supplier – the highest-ranked one – although the framework agreement itself has been concluded with more than one bidder or awardee. Thus, in order to raise the number of different contractors at the call-off stage, the 'rotation' method is advocated and foreseen in some regulatory frameworks, often at the level of secondary legislation. Rotating suppliers at the call-off stage does sound intuitive, but in fact raises concerns as to the concrete definition and implementation of the mechanism as well as evocates a quite common collusive scheme adopted by cartels.

Let us first investigate three possible ways of implementing the 'rotation' method.

### 4.2.4.1   Queuing

At the call-off stage, the contractor is determined by the temporal sequence of contracts starting from the highest-ranked and moving down the ranking as orders flow. That is, the first contract is awarded to the highest-ranked supplier, the second to the second-ranked and so forth. Although intuitively appealing in terms of objectivity, transparency and non-discrimination, this solution would not guarantee that the overall value of procurement contracts awarded to each supplier reflects its ranking in terms of value for money. Indeed, it may be the case that when the framework agreement expires, the highest-ranked supplier would find out that it has been allocated the smallest fraction (by value) of procurement contracts. From an *ex-post* perspective, the system as a whole – and, particularly, the set of procuring entities – would have been better-off had the contracts been reshuffled so as allocate a higher share to the first-ranked supplier.

### 4.2.4.2 Fixed shares

It may be foreseen that each supplier is to be awarded a predetermined share (in value) of procurement contracts. For instance, if four firms are selected at the first stage, then one could announce the following shares of procurement contracts: 40 per cent to the first-ranked, 30 per cent to the second-ranked, 20 per cent to the third-ranked and 10 per cent to the fourth-ranked.

The implementation problem, however, would not be solved as it remains unclear whether the shares have to be allocated on a sequential basis or in each single procurement contract. Fixed shares allocated sequentially would require a rather precise knowledge of the overall value of procurement contracts that will be awarded at the call-off stage. This seems practicable if the framework agreement is concluded by one single procuring entity for its own purchases, much less when, for instance, it is concluded by a centralised purchasing agency. Fixed shares within the same procurement contracts may result impracticable because of indivisibilities (how to allocate those shares if the procurement contract consists of purchasing four photocopiers?) or because the same purchasing entity cannot enter into a procurement contract simultaneously with four different suppliers because of different service levels agreements (say, janitorial services for the same building provided by different firms with different quality levels).

Besides the implementation difficulties, the 'rotation-through-fixed-shares' logic in awarding contracts seems rather at odds with the basic principle of competitive procurement. Defining a system that determines *ex-ante* contracts shares may solve one of the crucial problems in cartels. While postponing a more in-depth discussion to Chapter 7, where we shall explore the potentially anti-competitive features of framework agreements, suffice it here to say that the logic of rotating awardees in a framework agreement bears some resemblance with the one of lots design,[14] thus the same principles for promoting competition should inspire the design of a framework agreement. In Chapter 5, we also consider that some regulatory systems that require procurement contracts to be awarded to the lowest-price or most (economically) advantageous tender may not permit the use of the rotation method.

---

[14] See, for instance, V. Grimm, R. Pacini, G. Spagnolo and M. Zanza, 'Division into Lots and Competition in Procurement', in N. Dimitri, G. Piga and G. Spagnolo (eds.), *Handbook of Procurement* (Cambridge University Press, 2006).

### 4.2.5 Random allocation

Lotteries might in principle be used as an award mechanism. They are 'objective' in the sense that no discretion is left in the procuring entities' hands, but lotteries are also 'unpredictable' as it is impossible to say with certainty which awardee will be awarded any specific procurement contract. Lotteries at the call-off stage would simply assign a measure of likelihood (i.e. probability) that each awardee is assigned any procurement contract.

The practical and economically relevant dimension is the rationale for assigning a certain (level of) probability to each awardee. The simplest solution would be to assign equal chances to each firm. That is, if the number of the framework agreement holders is $N$, then each of them would have a $1/N$ chance of being selected at any time a procurement contract is to be awarded. Notice that this equal-chance mechanism resembles the equal-share mechanism described above. Indeed before any procurement contract is awarded the two mechanisms coincide, for each firm expects to get the same share of contracts. However, from *ex-post* perspective shares might turn out to be quite unequal under the equal-chance mechanism. So when the framework agreement expires, any of the firms might find itself with having been awarded no contract at all.

Although the layperson would consider this mechanism as 'fair', it does generate perverse incentives at the first stage of competition since competing firms would have no incentives in being ranked high given that this effort (in terms of submitted value for money) does not translate into a(n) (expected) high-value prize. In fact if, say, the number of awardees is $N$, then each competing firm at the first stage only has to beat the $(N+1)^{st}$ strongest competitor.

A more sophisticated version of the lottery might help provide 'correct' incentives at the first stage: probabilities assigned to awardees would have to be higher the higher each awardee's position is in the ranking. For instance, if firms A, B and C are ranked first, second and third respectively, then $p_A$ – the probability that firm A is awarded any procurement contract – should be greater than $p_B$, which, in turn, should be greater than $p_C$ (subject to the condition that $p_A + p_B + p_C = 1$). Providing the highest probability to the highest-ranked firm would become an effective incentive for any competing firm at the first stage to be the top-ranked firm. The question is then how to determine the values of those probabilities. Although we cannot report any real-case example, one might determine the probabilities so that the ratio between each pair of them is equal

*The economic analysis of framework agreements* 69

to the ratio between each pair of scores assigned at the first stage of competition. For instance, suppose that the first stage of competition has been carried out according to the MEAT criterion and that three selected firms – A, B and C – have been assigned scores equal to 80, 75 and 50 points (out of 100), respectively. Then $p_B$ would be equal to a fraction equal to 75/80 of $p_A$, while $p_C$ would be equal to a fraction 50/80 of $p_A$, which yields $p_A = 0.39$, $p_B = 0.37$ and $p_C = 0.24$.

The random method may also suffer from the same regulatory restriction as noted for the rotation method above.

## 4.3 Model 2 framework agreements – closed and incomplete framework agreements

Model 2 framework agreements raise further economic issues as firms will compete at the first stage without knowing all the terms of subsequent procurement contracts. Thus, the nature and the degree of competition at the first stage will depend both on the number of awardees to be selected and to the extent to which future needs have been accurately described.

### *4.3.1 Multi-award framework agreements*

Despite the formal classification into different 'families' sketched in Chapter 2, most public procurement practitioners are inclined to think about framework agreements by implicitly referring to incomplete framework agreements concluded with more than one bidder or awardee. It is unsurprising, then, that they were identified by the Explanatory Note[15] as framework agreements *stricto sensu*.

As discussed in Section 4.2, framework contracts allow public buyer(s) to reap most of the foreseeable benefits of aggregating potentially different needs into a single contract via tough competition, efficient use of specialisation and knowledge sharing among procurement specialists and minimisation of the effort and process cost of the purchasing unit(s). On the other hand, simple contracts concluded through separate awarding procedures, while giving up such benefits, provide the contracting authorities with the maximum flexibility and possibility of customisation and reduce the uncertainty faced by competitors. Ideally, simple contracts also ensure allocative efficiency, in the sense that each contract will likely be served by the supplier which is the most efficient to

---

[15] Explanatory Note, note 1, supra.

undertake the project given the buyer's preferences in terms of quality-price combinations.

If we were to rank different procurement strategies on the basis of the degree of standardisation of the master contract, multi-award incomplete framework agreements lie somewhere in between a framework contract and simple contracts. This suggests that the main purpose of framework agreements *stricto sensu* should be to address the trade-off between demand standardisation and process efficiency on the one hand and customisation, flexibility and allocative efficiency on the other.[16] In other words, the main goal of multi-award incomplete framework agreements is to streamline the process for repeated purchases by allocating a large amount of the overall required effort in the first selection round, while leaving some space for customisation and further competition at the second stage, when the actual procurement needs arise and their specific features (quantities, delivery conditions, specific tasks to be undertaken, customisations requested) become better known. Such a purchasing arrangement has proved itself to be an effective solution for centralised purchasing agencies that conclude the agreement in order to define the basic qualitative features, as well as those that set upper-bound price conditions for contracts to be awarded by different and heterogeneous procuring entities. This is the case, for instance, in the General Services Administration (GSA) system in the United States (accessible to all US federal government agencies, as we shall see in Chapter 5), and in framework agreements concluded by some of the most experienced central purchasing agencies in Europe such as Crown Commercial Service in the United Kingdom, BBG in Austria, SKI in Denmark and Hansel in Finland.

### 4.3.2 The nature of the two-stage competition

Where the needs and/or the preferences of the procuring entity are unknown to some extent, or heterogeneous with respect to relevant aspects of the contracts to be awarded, it is then optimal to let these aspects to be defined through a second round of selection (the so-called mini-competition at the call-off stage). As soon as actual

---

[16] The trade-off between competition and efficiency in multi-award incomplete framework agreements is analysed in a stylised two-stage model with horizontal differentiation by G. L. Albano and M. Sparro, 'A Simple Model of Framework Agreements: Competition and Efficiency', *Journal of Public Procurement*, 8, No. 3 (2008): 356–378.

needs arise, and uncertainty about the characteristics of a single specific contract is resolved the selection is reopened and the awardees are asked to precise and/or complete their first-stage offer. Thus, unlike the situation in framework contracts described above, the two-stage procurement process consists of two distinct rounds of competition.

More concretely, let us consider the case of a process based on the MEAT award criterion, whereby at both stages offers are evaluated on the basis of both price and technical sub-criteria, established in the documentation governing the framework agreement. Importantly, following the provisions in the EU Directive, let us assume that offers submitted at the first stage cannot be substantially modified at the second stage.[17] A possible practical interpretation of this principle is that 'core' or 'basic' technical features of the product or service have to be evaluated when concluding the framework agreement and may not be successively modified or better specified. Competition will instead have to be reopened with respect to optional items or services, customisations or further improved qualitative features. As regards the financial offers, a commonly adopted rule is that prices submitted at the first stage may only be lowered at the call-off stage.

Such a mechanism yields several strategic implications. First, at the first stage, suppliers may want to submit their best offers only with respect to those features of the contract that cannot be successively amended. To the contrary, they will possibly avoid competing too aggressively on price, so as to offer the highest price that allows them to be selected at the first stage. In fact, this could allow them to exploit a possible (technical) competitive advantage at the second stage and keep their profit high. Second, it is possible that some competitors aim at entering the agreement in order to serve one (or a few) specific contract only. This might induce them to submit a very aggressive bid at the first stage while leaving some call-off unanswered at the second one, thus distorting the first-stage competition and hampering the efficiency of the whole mechanism.[18]

---

[17] In particular, Article 33 of the EU Directive, note 1, supra, states that 'Contracts based on a framework agreement may under no circumstances entail substantial modifications to the terms laid down in that framework agreement'. A possible rationale for this provision is that 'substantial modifications' to the contracts at the call-off stage would represent a harmful distortion of the first-stage competition.

[18] Both features characterise the stylised model of framework agreements in Albano and Sparro, 'A Simple Model of Framework Agreements'.

### 4.3.3 Award and evaluation criteria

The nature of competition in a multi-award incomplete framework agreement depends crucially on the choice of the award and evaluation criteria at the two stages of the procedure. Although the decisions are often intertwined, for the sake of argument we shall first tackle the issue of the award criterion and then the one of the evaluation criteria.

International regulations (more or less explicitly) recognise that public authorities may adopt either the lowest-price or the most economically advantageous tender criterion at each stage of the procedure. For instance, the Guide to Enactment of the UNCITRAL Model Law on Public Procurement provides that:

> [t]he basis of the award will normally, but need not necessarily, be the same as that for the first stage; for example, the procuring entity may decide that among the highest-ranked suppliers or contractors at the first stage (chosen using the most advantageous submission), the lowest-priced responsive submission to the precise terms of the second-stage invitation to participate will be appropriate.[19]

Hence, at least in principle, there are four possible cases to consider, which are generated by the choice at each stage of either the lowest-price or the MEAT criterion. We shall consider each case in turn, highlighting the potential impacts on the nature of competition at each stage.

*Case 1: Lowest price at Stage 1, lowest price at Stage 2*   This is arguably the simplest case to handle in terms of degree of complexity of the whole procedure. Adopting the lowest-price criterion at the first stage implies that awardees are ranked according to a financial offer only (possibly a vector of prices) provided that the submitted technical dimensions fulfil minimal quality standards. Given that the same criterion is used to award procurement contracts, it seems reasonable to conclude that demand is quite homogenous among different procuring entities, although the latter may differ from each other in terms of quantity, physical location and other buyer-specific characteristics such as payment delays. These aspects provide incentives to select firms to 'tailor' prices when mini-competition rounds are carried out.

---

[19] Para 14, p. 280, Commentary on Article 59 – Requirements for closed framework agreements, Guide to Enactment of the UNCITRAL Model Law on Public Procurement (2012), *Official Records of the General Assembly, Sixty-seventh Session, Supplement No. 17* (para 46, UN document A/67/17). The text of the Guide to Enactment is available at www.uncitral.org/uncitral/uncitral_texts/procurement_infrastructure.html. Hereafter, Guide to Enactment.

The assumption made earlier in this section that prices at the second stage cannot be higher than at the first stage leads us to the conclusion that prices at the first stage will implicitly represent the highest possible terms of trade that awardees are willing to offer given their expectations on the features of the stream of procurement contracts. This also implies that procuring entities may lower but cannot raise minimal quality standards when reopening competition at the call-off stage.

*Case 2: MEAT at Stage 1, MEAT at Stage 2*   In this scenario, competition at both stages takes place both on quality and financial aspects. At least two sets of questions arise:

a) the relationship between the evaluation criteria at the two different stages of the procedure
b) the choice of the methods used at each stage to evaluate tenders, particularly financial offers

Competition among firms based on both quality and financial aspects may have a rather more sophisticated nature than price competition only. Firms do offer not only differentiated goods and services but rather a *set* of differentiated goods and services, depending on the degree of incompleteness of the master contract (i.e. the framework agreement). The nature of competition at both stages of the procedure is then determined, all else being equal, by the relative weights on quality and price as well as by the relative sub-weights on quality (and possibly financial) dimensions.

There is a widely accepted view that the choice of weights and sub-weights at the call-off stage needs to be coherent with the one made for selecting suppliers at the first stage. In this respect, the Guide to Enactment is explicit in acknowledging that varying weights or sub-weights at the second stage would reflect each procuring entity's characteristics, but at the same time leaving those decisions completely in the procuring entity's hands would raise the risk of manipulation and abuse.[20]

Example 4.3 will help clarify the potential problems explained above.

Case 3 and Case 4 do not seem to have an immediate appeal in terms of practical use, and thus deserve a special attention.

*Case 3: MEAT at Stage 1, LP at Stage 2*   In order to explore its main economic properties, we amend Example 4.3 by assuming that all

---

[20] Guide to Enactment, p. 212 (15).

**Example 4.3 Using MEAT criterion at both stages of a multi-award incomplete framework agreement**

Suppose a framework agreement for maintenance services has been concluded with three awardees – A, B and C – by means of the MEAT criterion with a quality-price ratio equal to 60/40. Assume the highest possible technical score to be $TS_{max} = 60$ and the highest possible financial score $FS_{max} = 40$. Moreover, two technical sub-dimensions, 1 and 2, are evaluated according to (sub-)weights $TS^1_{max} = 40$ and $TS^2_{max} = 20$. Then $TS_{max} = TS^1_{max} + TS^2_{max}$. Firms have been ranked as follows:

|        | $TS^1$ | $TS^2$ | $FS$ | Total Score |
|--------|--------|--------|------|-------------|
| Firm A | 40     | 5      | 20   | 65          |
| Firm B | 10     | 20     | 25   | 55          |
| Firm C | 5      | 5      | 35   | 45          |

For each firm the table reports the technical score assigned to the two technical sub-dimension, the financial score and the total score, which is simply the sum of the technical score(s) and financial score. It appears that firm A enjoys a competitive advantage over firm B on Sub-dimension 1, whereas the latter overcomes the former on Sub-dimension 2. On the other hand, firm C has an overall lower technical proposal than the other two competitors, but submitted the best financial conditions.

At the call-off stage,[21] if a procuring entity were to have, say, a *positive bias* towards firm B's initial proposal, it might consider inverting the relative weight between Dimensions 1 and 2; namely, to change it from the initial $TS^1_{max} / TS^2_{max} = 40/20 = 2$ to $20/40 = 1/2$. This would in principle give Firm 2 much higher chances, albeit no certainty, to be awarded the procurement contract. A procuring entity might have, instead, a *positive bias* towards firm C. In this case, it should consider giving a much higher weight to the financial dimension by changing the ratio $TS_{max} / FS_{max}$ from 60/40 to, say, 35/65.

In principle, a positive bias towards any firm's tender proposal might reflect the procuring entity's preferences or needs, but, absent any constraint on the choice-of-evaluation criteria at the call-off stage, abuse and favouritism would be more likely to overwhelm efficiency considerations.

---

[21] For sake of simplicity, we are ignoring the logic underlying the relationship between evaluation criteria at the first and second stage of competition. This issue will be dealt with in more depth in Chapter 10.

procurement contracts at the call-off stage are to be awarded by using the lowest-price criterion.[22] The initial ranking depicts a scenario in which firm C made the lowest investment in quality (above some minimal thresholds), thus enjoying a competitive advantage with respect to firms A and B at the call-off stage.

The question then becomes whether firms would have any incentive at all in submitting higher-than-minimum quality levels at the first stage. In other words, would the MEAT criterion provide any incentive to firms to commit to higher-than-minimum quality levels when the framework agreement is concluded? The answer is not necessarily a negative one as it depends on whether firms' commitment to a certain quality level depends upon an investment made in the past (which is sunk when competition takes place) or rather on an amount of effort to be deployed in the future. If, for instance, evaluation criteria refer to quality dimensions which are linked some commodities' characteristics (e.g. the screen definition of a type of medical equipment or the emission of toxic substances by a vehicle), then quality is likely to be given before competition takes place the first stage. If, instead, the framework agreement is a contract for a service (or a bundle of services), then quality-related costs will mostly depend on firms' offers. That is, the higher the service levels promised at the first stage, the higher the costs when procurement contracts are awarded at the call-off stage.

When quality investment costs are sunk, then it is not necessarily the case that high-quality firms will be competitively disadvantaged at the call-off stage with respect to low-quality competitors. This may be the case when a product comes closer to its life cycle so that quality-related (fixed) costs are likely to have been recovered by the hitherto realised sales. As high-quality firms are willing to sell at marginal cost at the second stage, they are not necessarily in a disadvantaged position vis-à-vis low-quality competitors. In the second scenario, quality-related costs depend on the content of tenders. Higher quality provides a more concrete chance to be ranked high at the first stage, but it does not yield an additional benefit at the call-off stage when low(er)-quality firms may benefit from a

---

[22] A caveat is in order here. When the first stage of the framework agreement is carried out by using the MEAT criterion, awardees are likely to be differentiated with respect to the quality dimensions of the submitted tenders. Thus although the second stage may be carried out on a price-only basis, rankings for awarding procurement contracts will have to take into account the technical score assigned at the first stage. As a consequence, strictly speaking, price-only competition at the call-off stage does not imply that the award criterion is the lowest-price criterion. For ease of exposition we shall, however, abstract away from this caveat in the discussion.

competitive advantage. This effect, in turn, feeds back into a low(er) incentive to promise high quality at the first stage.

*Case 4: LP at Stage 1, MEAT at Stage 2*  Two broad sets of circumstances may be compatible with this sequence of awarding criteria: (a) purchasing entities greatly differ with respect to their preferences over quality characteristics, thus the evaluation of the latter becomes meaningful only at the call-off stage; (b) the framework agreement consists of a bundle of different goods or services, some of which become part of the evaluation at the first stage while some others are evaluated at the second stage.

Under scenario (a) firms competing at the first stage have to anticipate correctly that procurement contracts will be awarded eventually by evaluating some additional quality characteristics; thus, bids at the first stage have to be set so as to cover the most 'expensive' configuration in any of the procurement contracts. Under scenario (b) one or more goods and services become part of the evaluation process only when a procurement contract is awarded at the call-off stage. For instance, those aspects evaluated at the first stage may represent the 'essential' elements of a bundle of services and thus common to every procurement contract; some other elements are, instead, only 'ancillary'; that is, they may or may not be included in a procurement contract according to purchasing entities' needs.

Providing appropriate incentives to firms participating at the fist-stage competition would require: in case (a) to provide competitors with precise and detailed information about the additional characteristics to be evaluated at the call-off stage and to give the latter a relatively low sub-weight, lest competition be distorted towards dimensions that had not been evaluated at the first stage, and in case (b) to give the 'ancillary' dimensions a lower weight than the 'essential' aspects of the contract.

### 4.3.4  Single-award incomplete framework agreements

When the framework agreement is incomplete and only one supplier is selected at the first stage, an immediate question rises about which mechanism is used to award procurement contracts. Reopening competition is not possible in this environment, as only the top-ranked supplier at the first stage becomes the framework-agreement awardee. The main consequence is that procurement contracts have to be concluded by means of different kinds of interaction between the buyer and the seller in which the latter enjoys a possibly strong bargaining power.

*The economic analysis of framework agreements*

> **Example 4.4 Purchase of a standardised good with unspecified delivery place or time**
>
> Firms are asked to submit a vector of $K > 2$ prices where the first component indicates the price of a specific commodity, while all other $K$-1 components indicate the delivery prices for $K$-1 different locations (where demand arises). The single awardee is selected on the basis of the lowest weighted average of all $K$ prices. However, which delivery price is to be included in the procurement contracts' clauses depends upon the exact place where demand arises.

> **Example 4.5 Purchase of chemical reagents**
>
> Firms are asked to submit a vector of $K > 2$ prices where each of them indicates the unit price of a specific chemical reagent. The framework awardee is selected on the basis of the lowest weighted average of all prices. At the call-off stage, each procuring entity (say, a hospital) will specify how many units of each reagent it needs. Thus the contract price is simply the product of each reagent price, determined at the first stage, multiplied by the number of units purchased.

Examples 4.4 and 4.5 illustrate two different circumstances where this family of framework agreements might be used.

The examples above share some similarities. The nature of repeated purchases is such that spurring competition – and thus selecting only one firm – seems a sensible choice. The kind of heterogeneity among purchasing units refers to 'location' (Example 4.4) or the composition of the bundle (Example 4.5) does not provide ground for the choice of supply diversification (or multi-award) in the framework agreement. At the same time, uncertainty as to the delivery place and number of units of each reagent will resolve only when demand arises, which in turn determines the exact procurement contract value.

## 4.4 Model 3 framework agreements – open and incomplete framework agreements

When a framework agreement is signed with some of (possibly all) the bidders in the market, a new market emerges. The degree of competition in this 'downstream' market is affected by the extent to which the set of incumbents may be challenged by outsiders. For a given profile of call-offs, an open framework agreement may foster competition as new entrants will find it possible to compete for all contracts although they had not been selected when the agreement was initially concluded. Thus, openness exerts a competitive pressure on incumbents as it introduces uncertainty on the number and main characteristics of those firms that will compete at the call-off stage. Conversely, closed framework agreements provide a safe harbour to those firms with whom the agreement has been initially concluded, raising potential concerns as to the level of competition for call-offs.

International regulations such as the UNCITRAL Model Law and the EU Directive[23] have adopted a virtually identical approach in identifying the conditions under which framework agreements can be either closed or open: openness is related to the entirely electronic nature of the procedure. This does not rule out *per se* that a closed framework cannot be designed including some electronic phases. However, only an entirely electronic system can allow for new bidders to (quickly) enter and compete for contracts after the system has been set up.

As discussed in Chapter 3, a two-stage fully electronic system is suited for products or services whose main technical specifications can be objectively described in a standardised way. Moreover, because entry of new competitors is possible every time a procurement contract is to be awarded at the call-off stage, the terms against which tenders are evaluated for firms to be admitted into the system need to be loose or light. In other words, keeping the door open to new entrants at the call-off stage would seem to go hand in hand with a very incomplete framework agreement. We can then safely borrow from the economic logic used in the previous section and conclude that, in many cases, open framework agreements are likely to resemble a list of suppliers where awardees have proven their ability or capacity to supply a set (or a subset) of goods and services fulfilling some minimal quality levels. As a consequence, competition is entirely concentrated at the call-off stage when procuring entities fully express their needs.

There are cases of open framework agreements that are not required to operate through a completely electronic system, such as Multiple Award Schedules (MAS) contracts awarded by the GSA in the United States and 'panel contracts' used in South Australia.[24] Unlike what is provided for in

---

[23] Note 1, supra.
[24] We shall touch on the main features of MAS contracts in Chapter 5 and on those of 'panel contracts' in Chapter 6.

the UNCITRAL Model Law and the EU Directive,[25] the award of procurement contracts at the call-off stage need not be conducted through a competitive process in that direct awards remain possible. Given this, entering the system would require assessing suppliers' bids according to more stringent and better specified evaluation criteria so as to avoid, for instance, that the definition of contract clauses is left to a bilateral, possibly opaque, relationship between a procuring entity and one specific supplier.

## 4.5 Hybrid models of framework agreements

Under the label 'hybrid system', we collect those families of framework agreements whereby features such as contractual conditions and/or the number of awardees may depend upon the outcome of the competitive process at the first stage. Alternatively, whether or not a second round of competition takes place at the call-off stage depends upon the occurrence of one or more additional conditions. In what follows, we shall consider two cases of hybrid framework agreements: the first one, known as 'rate contracts', are commonly used especially in South Asia; the second one is provided for by the EU Directive.[26]

### 4.5.1 Rate contracts

Rate contracts, as we have seen, are a form of multi-award framework agreement with fixed conditions. Unlike the class of framework agreements analysed in Section 2.2, financial conditions are generally driven by the most competitive bid; that is, purchasing authorities face the same prices (and technical conditions) at the call-off stage. Specific applications of rate contracts are found in South Asia[27] and Latin America. Technically there are often separate arrangements with each supplier, giving rise to the notion of parallel rate contracts. The intention here is to benchmark prices in the framework to that of the most efficient provider.

Although quality-price conditions are meant to be fixed after the first stage of competition, procuring entities may in fact use rate contracts as a starting point for their own rate contracts and commonly report that they get lower prices despite the use of 'no-undercutting' clauses in the initial contract. The logic of rate contracts seems, then, to hinge on providing a

---

[25] Note 1, supra.   [26] Note 1, supra.
[27] Some concrete examples of 'rate contracts' in India will be described in Chapter 6.

panel of suppliers with very similar, if not identical, value-for-money offers to procuring entities. This is consistent with the objectives of providing purchasing entities with 'equal treatment' in terms of quality-price ratio, while reducing the risk that public demand is concentrated in the hands of a few suppliers. However, the practice of rate contracts raises several concerns. First, lack of commitment on volumes together with the multi-supplier feature implies that each competing supplier is expected to bear a considerable level of risk (i.e. uncertainty about the extent of economies of scale and inventory planning), which translates into a risk premium in the price. Second, by definition, a rate is struck that is held constant for a period of time, typically 6–12 months. This means that if supply costs may be adversely affected by uncontrollable factors such as oil prices or interest rates, the supplier needs to build in this risk for the period from the commencement time for the contract, even if these risks do not come about. Thus, the government contract essentially provides the supplier with insurance for cost inflation.

Competition concerns are further heightened by the feature that the rate contact is determined by a first stage of competition, but the lowest bidder – which will determine the rate contract's price – effectively receives no preference in the placement of the subsequent purchase orders. Thus there is no effective incentive in competing for being the lowest bidder. The only (apparent) incentive is to enter the 'panel' and be in a position to match the lowest bid. Consequently, a cartel can exploit this feature and have each member bid a high price that any other cartel member can match.[28]

Where fixed technical specifications and fixed prices are appropriate, it seems unclear what is the advantage of establishing a multi-award rather than a single-award framework agreement unless the single source cannot be relied upon to deliver. If this is the case, the multi-award solution weakens the suppliers' incentive to invest in expanding their capacities. Such a mechanism would also be inappropriate in conditions of rapid innovation.

### 4.5.2  *Complete-but-amendable framework agreements*

The EU Directive introduced a hybrid family of framework agreements that was absent in the earlier Directive in 2004.[29] The new provision

---

[28] This striking anti-competitive feature of rate contracts is further explored in Chapter 8.
[29] Art. 33.3(b), EU Directive, note 1, supra, cf. Directive 2004/18/EC of the European Parliament and of the Council of 31 March 2004 on the coordination of procedures for the award of public works contracts, public supply contracts and public service contracts, OJ L 134, 30 April 2004, pp. 114–240, available at http://eur-lex.europa.eu/legal-content/en/ALL/?uri=CELEX:32004L0018.

describes a hybrid type of framework agreement combining the main features of the multi-award class with complete and incomplete contractual conditions. More precisely,

> 'where the framework agreement sets out all the terms governing the provision of the works, services and supplies concerned,' purchases can be made 'partly without reopening competition following the terms and conditions of the framework agreement...' and 'partly with reopening of competition amongst the economic operators parties to the framework agreement'.

The provision above seems to embrace a combination of different circumstances. First is the recognition that some of the purchases can be realised according to the clauses governing the framework agreement. Thus, the latter has to contain all the necessary clauses for procurement contracts to be awarded without any new round of competition. Yet the multi-award nature of this family raises the same problems at the award stage that were discussed in Section 4.2.2. Second is the possibility of reopening competition for awarding some procurement contracts according to the logic described in Section 4.3.1. Hence, while containing *ab initio* all the necessary clauses for procurement contracts to be awarded, the framework agreement could be supplemented by additional clauses that would then require a second stage of competition. Alternatively, the same clauses or a subset of them might be the object of a new round of competition when a particular circumstance occurs.

At least two broad sets of circumstances might justify the use of this hybrid class, as illustrated in Examples 4.6 and 4.7.

While real-world procurement processes will provide far more cases in which this class of framework agreement suits public buyers' needs, the fundamental economic feature is immediate. 'Complete-but-amendable' framework agreements are meant to provide a ready-to-use contract for future purchases while guaranteeing at least a minimal degree of tailoring – should the relevant circumstances occur – be it only a price renegotiation due to very large demands. Intuitively, the level of competition at the first stage depends crucially on the fraction of purchases that will be realised according to the conditions set in the framework agreement. The higher this fraction, the more a 'complete-but-amendable' framework agreement will resemble a 'framework contract'. Uncertainty over this fraction will call for firms' to use a cautious bidding strategy at the first stage, thus lowering the level of competition.

> **Example 4.6 A complete-and-amendable framework agreement for photocopying machines**
>
> A procuring entity owns a large set of photocopying machines of different makes distributed over several offices. The machines have reached quite different stages of their life cycle. For 'young' machines the buyer only needs day-to-day maintenance services, while for 'old' machines the buyer needs both maintenance and decommissioning services. Thus procurement contracts for the maintenance of 'young' machines could be awarded by using the multi-award nature of the framework agreement without reopening competition. For 'old' machines, instead, the framework agreement holders will have to compete on the decommissioning service part of the contract that was not evaluated at the first stage of competition.

> **Example 4.7 A complete-and-amendable framework agreement for laptops**
>
> A central purchasing body aggregates the demand for laptops from different central government bodies (say, ministries). Procurement contracts at the call-off stage are awarded according to the following 'threshold rule': if a ministry needs a number of machines below a certain threshold, the contract will be awarded according to the 'cascade method'; that is, to the highest-ranked holder of the framework agreement); if demand is above the same threshold, then the holders of the framework agreement are invited to a second round of price competition.

## 4.6 Chapter summary

- A two-stage procurement arrangement raises novel economic dimensions compared to a stream of independently run procurement processes. This observation is striking particularly in multi-award Model 2 framework agreements. The more procuring entities attempt to achieve a certain degree of contract standardisation while preserving some room for customisation, the more complex the interaction between the first and the second stage of competition.
- The nature of competition is not entirely predictable even in the seemingly less complex family of framework agreements; namely, the single-supplier framework agreements (the so-called framework

contracts). Additional sources of complexity, such as some persisting dimensions of heterogeneity among procuring entities, may adversely affect the pro-competitive force generated by demand-aggregation-driven economies of scale. The resulting extra amount of uncertainty may substantially hurt the level of competition.

- From an economic viewpoint, the method for awarding contracts in multi-award Model 1 framework agreements remains a major 'procurement puzzle'. The 'cascade' method, although appealing at a first sight, may turn out to be rewarding only for a subset of selected awardees, possibly only for the highest-ranked. This contradicts, at least to some extent, the purpose of supply diversification. A second commonly used method, known as 'rotation', does not seem to have a clear-cut interpretation, though. Three alternative concrete implementations of the 'rotation' method have been discussed, each of them suffering from non-negligible drawbacks.

- In Model 2 framework agreements concluded with more than one awardee, varying the award criterion between the two stages of the procedure may generate misleading incentives to competing firms. Using the lowest-price at the first stage and the MEAT criterion at the second may cause firms not to correctly anticipate the cost of additional quality dimensions that will be evaluated at the call-off stage; using the MEAT at the first stage and the lowest-price at the second may cause firms not to provide quality levels above minimum standards when the framework agreement is to be concluded.

CHAPTER 5

# International experience in framework agreements

## 5.1 Introduction

Much long-standing experience with framework agreements procedures is found in the European Union (notably in France, the Nordic countries and the United Kingdom)[1] and in the United States. In earlier chapters, we examined the potential benefits and some disadvantages of framework agreements, and highlighted the essential economic considerations. In this chapter, we will consider how some of those issues have played out in rules and practice.

Systematic analysis of experience in the European Union in particular is hampered by a paucity of data and of empirical analysis of outcomes under framework agreements, beyond analyses conducted by some centralised purchasing agencies (and which are presented in the next chapter). As the Organisation for Economic Co-operation and Development (OECD) reported in 2013, the scale of public procurement is such that an in-depth review would be appropriate: public procurement accounts for 12.8 per cent of GDP on average across OECD countries and represents on average 29 per cent of their total general government expenditure, ranging from 12 per cent in Greece to 45 per cent in the Netherlands in 2011.

In addition, as the OECD continued in its report, while 97 per cent of OECD countries use framework agreements to achieve economies of scale, and although the number of framework agreements in the European Union increased by almost four times between 2006 and 2009,[2] 'only

---

[1] Over two-thirds of the total use of framework agreements in the European Union is accounted for by United Kingdom (the largest user), France, Germany and Denmark (2006 findings): see Europe Economics, Evaluation of Public Procurement Directives Markt/2004/10/D, Executive Summary (2006), available at http://ec.europa.eu/internal_market/publicprocurement/docs/summary_en.pdf, and Evaluation of Public Procurement Directives, Markt/2004/10/D, Europe Economics (2006), available at http://ec.europa.eu/internal_market/publicprocurement/docs/final_report_en.pdf.

[2] In 2009 over 25,000 framework agreements notices were published in the OJEU, representing 11 per cent by volume and 17 per cent by value. See www.ec.europa.eu/internal_market/publicprocurement/docs/modernising_rules/executive-summary_en.pdf, and Public procurement in Europe: cost

*International experience in framework agreements* 85

about half of the OECD countries calculate the savings resulting from the use of these mechanisms to verify whether economies of scale were achieved'.[3] The notable exception of Chile aside, the OECD notes that the main reason for this situation is a lack of data, beyond aggregates at the national level that can be derived from national accounts.[4] In the United States, on the other hand, the US General Services Administration (GSA) issues an annual report of its performance,[5] and the US Government Accountability Office (GAO) issues regular reports of aspects of the federal procurement system, under its mandate to audit the performance of that system, which includes policy analysis and hearing 'bid protests' (the US term for review of or challenge to procurement decisions).[6] Further and perhaps equally surprising, there is relatively little academic research on framework agreements.[7]

In this chapter, we will consider the development of regulation and practice of framework agreements procedures in various systems, and identify some areas in which further development is indicated. For example, while some developments have contributed to the achievement of the potential benefits of framework agreements, others have done so to a lesser degree, if at all. Similarly, not all have avoided the potential pitfalls. Our presentation of this international experience in the use of framework agreements procedures is, given significant lack of data and formal analysis, necessarily ad hoc and largely qualitative. Nonetheless, there is a certain level of consistency in findings as regards how framework agreements, once set up, are used – and, in some cases, misused. Most of the concerns relate to the second stage of the procedures, but the first stage is not entirely exempt from concerns.

---

and effectiveness, a study on procurement regulation. Prepared for the European Commission, PwC, London Economics and Ecorys, March 2011, available at http://ec.europa.eu/internal_market/pub licprocurement/docs/modernising_rules/cost-effectiveness_en.pdf.

[3] Ibid., citing, as regards the four-fold increase, European Commission (2011), Evaluation Report: Impact and Effectiveness of EU Public Procurement Legislation, part 1, Commission Staff Working Paper SEC(2011), 853 final, Brussels.

[4] Other commentators have noted a similar paucity of empirical evidence regarding public procurement more generally: see, for example, Cernat, Lucian and Zornitsa Kutlina-Dimitrova. International public procurement: from scant facts to hard data. No. 2015–1. Directorate General for Trade, European Commission, 2015.

[5] See, for 2014 report, the Summary of Performance and Financial Information, US General Services Administration, available at www.gsa.gov/portal/category/26851.

[6] As further explained by the US Government Accountability Office: www.gao.gov/about/index.html.

[7] Exceptions would comprise G. L. Albano and M. Sparro, 'A Simple Model of Framework Agreements: Competition and Efficiency', *Journal of Public Procurement*, 8, No. 356 (2008): 378; Y. Gur, L. Lu and G. Y. Weintraub, 'Framework Agreements in Procurement: An Auction Model and Design Recommendations,' Columbia Business School Working Paper (2013), available at www.columbia.edu/~gyw2105/GYW/GabrielWeintraub_files/PaperFA20130426-post.pdf.

Consequently, we shall focus on some key areas of risk that we earlier identified in the operation of framework agreements, including the consequences where the rules governing them are not clear, issues arising in ensuring effective competition and whether framework agreements are used as intended (i.e. neither over- nor under-used).

## 5.2 Development of the existing regulatory systems for framework agreements

### 5.2.1 Early use of framework agreements

Early experience in the use of framework agreements was seen in such countries as France (originating with 'purchase order contracts' without specific legal regulation in the 1930s, though regulation of 'marchés à commande' and 'marchés de clientele' commenced in the 1950s);[8] in the Nordic countries in the 1970s;[9] the United Kingdom (such as in the construction sector in the early 1990s,[10] again in the absence of special regulation);[11] and the United States (where task and delivery order or indefinite delivery indefinite quantity (ID/IQ) contracts – then called 'call contracts' – were found as early as the 1950s).[12]

---

[8] L. Folliot-Lalliot, 'The French Approach to Regulating Frameworks under the New EC Directives', chapter 4, in S. Arrowsmith (ed.), *Public Procurement Regulation in the 21st Century: Reform of the UNCITRAL Model Law on Procurement* (Eagan, MN: West, 2009). See, also, UNCITRAL Model Law on Public Procurement (2011), *Official Records of the General Assembly, Sixty-sixth Session, Supplement No. 17* (UN document A/66/17). The text of the Model Law is available at www.uncitral.org/uncitral/uncitral_texts/procurement_infrastructure.html. Hereafter, Model Law.

[9] Particularly Denmark and Sweden. See OECD, 'Centralised Purchasing Systems in the European Union', *SIGMA Papers* No. 47 (Paris: OECD Publishing, 2011), p. 36, available at http://dx.doi.org/10.1787/5kgkgqv703xw-en.

[10] K. Potts, 'From Heathrow Express to Heathrow Terminal 5: BAA'S Development of Supply Chain Management', in chapter 8, S. Pryke (ed.), *Construction Supply Chain Management Concepts and Case Studies* (Oxford: Wiley-Blackwell, 2009), pp. 160–181, doi: 10.1002/9781444320916; S. Tennant and S. Fernie, 'A Contemporary Examination of Framework Agreements', 26th Annual ARCOM Conference, 6–8 September 2010 (Leeds Metropolitan University, Leeds: Association of Researchers in Construction Management, 2010), Vol. 1, pp. 685–694.

[11] By implication, in these countries, it was considered that framework agreements were permitted under the then EU Directives, a point that led to the threat of infringement proceedings against the United Kingdom by the Commission, which took a different view: see, further, S. Arrowsmith, and C. Nicholas, 'Regulating Framework Agreements under the UNCITRAL Model Law', chapter 2, in *Public Procurement Regulation in the 21st Century* (2009) Model Law, note 8, supra.

[12] Daniel I. Gordon and Jonathan L. Kang, 'Task-Order Contracting in the U.S. Federal System: The Current System and Its Historical Context', chapter 5, ibid. As their names indicate, indefinite delivery contracts leave delivery times flexible; indefinite quantity contracts permit volume fluctuations within defined parameters, but the two are commonly combined.

*International experience in framework agreements* 87

In a 2006 survey, UNCITRAL found that more than two-thirds of the systems it surveyed made provision for framework agreements,[13] including countries in Africa and Latin America, as well as in Europe and the United States. Consistent with the OECD findings noted above, the trend towards use of framework agreements appears to be increasing,[14] and increasingly that use takes place under express regulation. Spending at the subcentral (state or local) level of government comprises 55 per cent of public procurement spend on average across OECD countries, rising to 76 per cent among its federal countries,[15] which may offer significant opportunities for aggregated purchasing, and indicating that lessons learned from national systems should be considered when using framework agreements at the subcentral level.

### 5.2.2 Framework agreements and dynamic purchasing systems in the European Union

#### 5.2.2.1 Development of the regulatory framework and the picture in 2015

Formal regulation of framework agreements in the European Union is currently contained in Directive 2014/24/EU (notably, Article 33),[16] which updates equivalent provisions in the Public Sector Directive 2004/18/EC.[17]

---

[13] 'Possible revisions to the UNCITRAL Model Law on Procurement of Goods, Construction and Services – the Use of Framework Agreements in Public Procurement', UN documents A/CN.9/WG.I/WP.44 and A/CN.9/WG.I/WP.44/Add 1. The working papers used by UNCITRAL when drafting the Model Law and reports of the conclusions are available www.uncitral.org/uncitral/en/commission/working_groups/1Procurement.html. UNCITRAL Working Papers are designated by 'A/CN.9/WG', to represent a Working Group document under a General Assembly mandate, and then have a consecutive number assigned to the specific document (e.g. UN document A/CN.9/WG.I/WP.44). Reports of the Working Groups do not have the 'WG' designation, as they are reports to UNCITRAL in plenary session (known as the Commission sessions), and so are, for example, A/CN.9/752.

[14] See, further, www.ec.europa.eu/internal_market/publicprocurement/docs/modernising_rules/executive-summary_en.pdf, and Public procurement in Europe: cost and effectiveness, a study on procurement regulation. Prepared for the European Commission, note 2, supra.

[15] Public Procurement Spending, Government at a Glance 2013: Procurement Data, Organisation for Cooperation and Development, Public Governance and Territorial Development Directorate, Public Governance Committee, 23 January 2013, GOV/PGC/ETH(2013)2, available at www.oecd.org/gov/ethics/Government%20at%20a%20Glance%202013_Procurement%20Data%20GOV_PGC_ETH_2013_2.pdf.

[16] Directive 2014/24/EU of the European Parliament and of the Council of 26 February 2014 on public procurement and repealing Directive 2004/18/EC Text with EEA relevance, OJ L 94, 28 March 2014, pp. 65–242, available at http://eur-lex.europa.eu/legal-content/EN/TXT/?uri=celex:32014L0024. Hereafter, the EU Directive.

[17] Directive 2004/18/EC of the European Parliament and of the Council of 31 March 2004 on the coordination of procedures for the award of public works contracts, public supply contracts and public service contracts, OJ L 134, 30 April 2004, pp. 114–240, available at http://eur-lex.europa.eu/legal-content/en/ALL/?uri=CELEX:32004L0018. Framework agreements (known as 'framework

(References in this chapter to the EU Directive are to the 2014 Directive, unless indicated otherwise.) The EU Directive leaves most of the provisions of the 2004 Directive unchanged,[18] which allows a consideration of how framework agreements are regulated and operate in practice in the European Union to be undertaken by reference to experience with the earlier Directive, as well as through early commentary on the 2014 provisions.[19] A 2014 survey of EU member states indicated that there were no available texts that indicated implementing provisions going beyond the provisions of the EU Directive.[20]

As we saw in Chapter 2, a framework agreement in the EU system is defined as 'an agreement between one or more contracting authorities and one or more economic operators, the purpose of which is to establish the terms governing contracts to be awarded during a given period, in particular with regard to price and, where appropriate, the quantity envisaged'. Explicit provisions to regulate framework agreements procedures were introduced following a consultation process in the European Union, at the end of which it was concluded that concerns about long-term contracts posing a threat to competition were such that precise rules should be set for the use of framework agreements. Particular areas of focus were the provision of appropriate transparency and mitigation of the anti-competitive potential, for which a combination of limitations on the duration of framework agreements and ensuring that they remained 'open' to new suppliers (as we have described for Model 3 framework agreements) was suggested.[21]

contract arrangements') were permitted under earlier rules on utilities procurement and are now regulated under Art. 51 of Directive 2014/25/EU of the European Parliament and of the Council of 26 February 2014 on procurement by entities operating in the water, energy, transport and postal services sectors and repealing Directive 2004/17/EC Text with EEA relevance, OJ L 94, 28 March 2014, pp. 243–374, available at http://eur-lex.europa.eu/legal-content/EN/TXT/?uri=celex:32014L0025.

[18] See, further, Recital 60 to the EU Directive (2014/24/EU, ibid.).

[19] As at the time of writing, only the United Kingdom has implemented the EU Directive at the national level – in the Public Contracts Regulations 2015, available at www.legislation.gov.uk/uksi/2015/102/contents/made. According to the European Commission, EU member states have until April 2016 to transpose the new rules into their national law (except with regard to e-procurement, for which the deadline is September 2018).

[20] 'The transposition of the new EU public procurement directives in the member States', Department of European Union Policies of the Presidency of the Council of Ministers and National Anti-Corruption Authority, Italian Presidency of the European Commission, study into planned implementation of the new rules and on the different transposition options through the Public Procurement Network, at page 39, available at www.publicprocurementnetwork.org/docs/ItalianPresidency/documento%206.pdf.

[21] See (1998) Public Procurement in the European Union – Communication from the Commission. Follow up to the Green Paper. COM (98) 143 final, 11 March 1998.

In the EU system as it now stands, framework agreements can take the form of Model 1 or Model 2 framework agreements as described in Chapter 2. Model 3 framework agreements are regulated separately under the title 'dynamic purchasing systems'.[22] The theoretical difference between the two concepts is that framework agreements are 'closed', whereas dynamic purchasing systems are 'open', but in practice many of the policy issues arising in the call-off procedure are related. Closed framework agreements identify a limited number of best-ranking offers subject to possible finalisation of certain terms and conditions at the second, or call-off, stage, whereas open framework agreements identify as many qualified, responsive suppliers as may wish to sell to the government. Most experiences in the European Union relate to closed framework agreements, because the procedures in the 2004 Directive on the use of dynamic purchasing systems operated as a major disincentive to their use, though the 2014 Directive has eliminated some of the procedures concerned.[23]

The main motivations for introducing formal rules on the operation of framework agreements procedures – aside from yielding to the reality that the technique was being used in a number of member states – were grounded in their potential administrative efficiency in the sense that we have discussed in earlier chapters,[24] and in facilitating aggregation of demand.[25]

---

[22] Article 34(1) of the EU Directive states, 'For commonly used purchases the characteristics of which, as generally available on the market, meet the requirements of the contracting authorities, contracting authorities may use a dynamic purchasing system. The dynamic purchasing system shall be operated as a completely electronic process, and shall be open throughout the period of validity of the purchasing system to any economic operator that satisfies the selection criteria. It may be divided into categories of products, works or services that are objectively defined on the basis of characteristics of the procurement to be undertaken under the category concerned. Such characteristics may include reference to the maximum allowable size of the subsequent specific contracts or to a specific geographic area in which subsequent specific contracts will be performed.'

[23] Including requirements for a simplified contract notice to all interested suppliers seeking an indicative tender and review of responses prior to initiating a call-off. See, further, S. Arrowsmith, 'Dynamic Purchasing Systems under the New EC Procurement Directives – a Not So Dynamic Concept?', *Public Procurement Law Review*, 14 (2005): 16–29.

[24] Such arguments were voiced as early as 1993: see S. Arrowsmith, 'Framework purchasing and qualification lists under the European procurement Directives: Part 1', *Public Procurement Law Review*, 3 (1999): 115. Cf. Nicholas, Caroline, 'A Critical Evaluation of the Revised UNCITRAL Model Law Provisions on Regulating Framework Agreements', *Public Procurement Law Review* 2 (2012): 19–46; Marta Andrecka, 'Framework Agreements', *EU Procurement Law and the Practice*, No. 2 (2015): 127, Upphandlingsrättslig Tidskrift, available at www.urt.cc/?q=oa_papers.

[25] Recital 59 to the EU Directive, note 17, supra.

*5.2.2.2 Scope of the provisions applicable to framework agreements procedures*
Which provisions of the EU Directive apply to framework agreements procedures?

An initial issue is to understand the scope of procedural rules applicable to framework agreements procedures under the Directive. This is less straightforward a process than might be imagined. A framework agreement, concluded to 'establish the terms' of future (procurement) contracts, is regulated by Article 33 of the Directive. The scope of the Directive as a whole 'establishes rules on the procedures for procurement by contracting authorities with respect to public contracts' (and design contests).[26] A public contract is 'a contract for pecuniary interest ... for the purchase of [goods, services, etc.] by a contracting authority [...] or for the hire of goods by a contracting authority'.[27] (The reference to pecuniary interest means, in essence, that the contract is a legally binding one.)

The European Commission discussed the overlap between these two definitions in an Explanatory Note accompanying the 2004 Directive.[28] The Explanatory Note states that 'framework agreements that establish all the terms (framework contracts) are "traditional" public contracts and that their use was possible under the [EU Directives prior to 2004]'. Consequently, the European Commission considered that they were subject to all the procedures of the 2004 Directive, such as those regulating award criteria (now found in Article 67, then in Article 53), and that call-offs could be placed under them without requiring further agreement between the parties (so that they were pragmatically 'complete' in the sense described in Chapter 2).[29] That being so, the logical conclusion is that call-offs under framework contracts are exempt from procedures other than as addressed specifically in Article 33, which as regards single-supplier framework agreements means making an award within the limits of the framework agreement (though the procuring entity may request a supplier to 'supplement its tender as necessary'), and as regards multi-supplier

---

[26] Article 1(1). EU Directive, ibid.
[27] Article 1(5), EU Directive, ibid., 'Public contract' is the term used for a procurement contract under the directives.
[28] European Commission Explanatory Note 'Framework Agreements – Classic Directive' (CC2005/03_rev/of 14 July 2005), available at http://ec.europa.eu/internal_market/publicprocurement/docs/explan-notes/classic-dir-framework_en.pdf.
[29] Article 33(4)(a), EU Directive, note 17, supra, describing the concept as setting out 'all the terms governing the provision of the works, services and supplies concerned and the objective conditions for determining which of the economic operators, party to the framework agreement, shall perform them'. On the other hand, as the Explanatory Note continues, a framework agreement *stricto sensu* is not 'complete' in that certain terms are either not binding or need to be finalised through further agreement between the parties.

*International experience in framework agreements* 91

framework agreements means 'following the terms and conditions of the framework agreement, without reopening competition'.

A framework contract, in the sense described, is also capable of being a framework agreement as defined in Article 33. In addition, but as has been observed, describing a 'framework contract' as if it is a public contract 'seems to confuse the establishment of terms for the delivery of works, services or supplies with an obligation to provide, receive and pay for those works, services or supplies':[30] only framework contracts that are legally binding are, it is considered, 'public contracts'.

Framework agreements are, however, public contracts for the purposes of the rules restricting variations and amendments to public contracts under the EU Directive and for the purposes of the EU Remedies Directive,[31] so breaches of the procedures to award them can be challenged.[32] This raises the question of the procedures stipulated to conclude framework agreements. Article 33 provides that the conclusion of framework agreements must follow the 'procedures provided for in this Directive', though it is not clear whether this is intended to amend substantively the 2004 provisions (which stated that the award of framework agreements 'shall follow the rules of procedure referred to in this Directive for all phases up to the award of contracts based on that framework agreement', adding that the 'parties to the framework agreement shall be chosen by applying the award criteria set in accordance with Article 53').

This issue is more than an exercise in legal semantics: several provisions in the Directive and other applicable regulations apply differently to framework agreements and public contracts. For example, should the Directive's procedural rules also apply to call-offs? Commentators' views have differed on this matter.[33] Also, there are rules to limit the duration of framework agreements to four years under the Directive (absent exceptional circumstances). Would this apply to public contracts that provide for future deliveries (which could be classified as framework contracts) as well as to framework agreements?

---

[30] Procurement Lawyers Association, 'The use of framework agreements in public procurement', March 2012, available at www.procurementlawyers.org/pdf/PLA%20paper%20on%20Fra-meworks%20PDF%20Mar%202012.pdf.
[31] Article 72, the EU Directive, note 17, supra, discussed further below.
[32] Framework agreements, EU procurement law and the practice, note 24, supra.
[33] S. Arrowsmith, 'Methods for Purchasing on-going Requirements: The System of Framework Agreements and Dynamic Purchasing Systems under the EC Directives and UK Procurement Regulations', in S. Arrowsmith (ed.), *Public Procurement Regulation in the 21st Century: Reform of the UNCITRAL Model Law on Procurement* (2009), pp. 167–168, note 8, supra.

A practical example of a contract for which this question is particularly apposite is a 'term contract'. Term contracts have long been used in the United Kingdom, and are generally concluded between a single procuring entity and a single supplier, involving 'discrete items of work or services ... initiated by orders placed under the contract in question',[34] that is, in accordance with the provisions of the term contract, which is a legally binding agreement. Each order determines the nature, quantity and terms of delivery goods or services to be provided. For example, in the social housing and highways sectors, an order is issued whenever a tenant requests a repair to his or her property, or a hole in the road needs to be repaired; alternatively, the term contract may state that the supplier is to 'deal with all responsive repair requests that are made' over the period to which the order relates.[35] The Statens Indkøb (SKI) in Denmark and the NPS in Wales use framework agreements that include commitments by the procuring entity to purchase under the agreements concerned,[36] treating them as framework agreements despite their binding nature. Since term contracts are often concluded for a duration exceeding four years, there would be a breach of the Directive's term limits if they are classified as framework agreements.[37] On the other hand, Article 46 encourages procuring entities to split contracts into lots, which would indicate that staged deliveries by themselves would not definitively indicate a framework agreement.

This legal confusion does not appear to have been rectified in national procurement legislation implementing the EU Directive. UNCITRAL's Model Law, as set out below, offers a solution that would clarify the situation – a framework agreement is defined in terms that state it is *not* a procurement contract (though it may be a legally binding contract in accordance with national law), and consequently second-stage awards constitute the awards of the procurement contract.

---

[34] The use of framework agreements in public procurement, note 30, supra.   [35] Ibid.
[36] In 2011, the Danish government and local government bodies agreed to establish 15–20 binding framework agreements by 2015, to be operated by SKI on behalf of the municipalities concerned. As at 2015, the SKI has established twelve such framework agreements, and six more are in the making, and the programme will be extended after 2015. See, further, framework agreements, *EU Procurement Law and the Practice*, note 24, supra.
[37] Ibid. It is explained that most of the industry standard-form term contracts include provisions to the effect that: (a) the employer (contracting authority) does not guarantee that any particular volume of orders will be issued to the contractor; and (b) any variation of the amount of work ordered from that anticipated does not lead to an entitlement for the contractor to claim extra costs. The inclusion of such clauses could turn what would otherwise be a public contract into a framework agreement. If there is no obligation (explicit or implied) on the employer to place any orders under the contract, it is hard to escape the conclusion that such a contract is, indeed, a framework agreement.

*International experience in framework agreements* 93

As regards exceptions to the four-year limit, the recitals to the Directive give one example in which a longer duration might be justified:[38] where suppliers need to make equipment available at any time over the entire duration of the framework agreement, and whose amortisation period is longer than four years. There is, otherwise, little guidance on the matter. While the recitals clarify that a call-off can be awarded that will last longer than the framework agreement,[39] there is no guidance on how much longer that period could be. When assessing the motives for longer call-offs, it is interesting to note that the legal statement in the 2004 Directive that 'Contracting authorities may not use framework agreements improperly or in such a way as to prevent, restrict or distort competition' has been relegated to the recitals of the 2014 Directive.

#### 5.2.2.3 *Main procedures in the EU Directive – Article 33*

The Directive applies only above a defined valuation threshold, so that when that threshold is reached, its procedures for the award of pubic contracts, including advertising in the *Official Journal of the European Union* (OJEU), must be followed. Aggregation rules for the purposes of framework agreements procedures are therefore needed as they are generally concluded for an undefined total quantity. The Directive provides that the 'value to be taken into consideration shall be the maximum estimated value ... of all the contracts envisaged for the total term of the framework agreement or the dynamic purchasing system'.[40]

Aggregation is relatively straightforward in the case of single-user framework agreements, but more complex for multi-user ones, where the scale of future purchases may be difficult to estimate. The importance of accurate estimates such as a range of contract prices for this purpose is a more complex question than can be answered by erring on the safe side and advertising in the OJEU, including what may turn out to be an overestimate of the aggregate value. The policy goal is (or should be) to ensure that potentially interested suppliers are provided with the best information available to encourage them to participate where they are capable of doing so (in the EU context, the OJEU advertisement is to facilitate cross-border participation) and to submit their best offers. From this perspective, inaccurate estimates can also operate as a disincentive to participate where, for example, they indicate call-off volumes that exceed a supplier's capacity, and may consequently compromise offer quality, as we discuss

---

[38] Recital 62 to the EU Directive, note 17, supra.  [39] Ibid.
[40] Article 5(5), the EU Directive, note 17, supra.

further in Chapter 10. (Other inaccuracies in the prospective terms advertised can operate likewise.)

In addition, where the framework covers a bundle of related goods and services, there may in fact be little cross-border interest where each component is of a relatively low value, but the aggregate of the purchases of all elements under the framework agreement requires the full EU procedures to be followed. As has been noted, if all suppliers are likely to be capable of fulfilling the entire agreement, then the aggregated value is meaningful to a potential bidder. If a combination of suppliers will be required, then aggregation does not provide an accurate estimate of the possible value of the contract to individual providers, and whether cross-border interest would exist is questionable. While a procuring entity may therefore consider splitting the requirements across different framework agreements, there is a risk of running foul of the Directive's provisions that forbid splitting contracts for the purpose of avoiding the Directive's requirements.[41]

A multi-supplier framework agreement can be concluded with two or more suppliers (a change from the 2004 requirements for at least three awardees), and a further new provision (which may enhance use in practice) is that awardees can be replaced in some situations, such as insolvency, provided that the right to do so has been reserved in the solicitation documents (a so-called 'review clause'), or the change is required for technical or economic reasons, or where there are other exceptional situations that would otherwise involve excessive inconvenience.[42] A further caveat is that the incoming suppliers must meet the qualification requirements, and the effect of the change may not constitute a substantive modification to the framework agreement.

A common criticism of framework agreements is that they do not reflect changes in the market, and the Directive has introduced flexibility in this regard, by allowing substitutions, subject to similar caveats as noted immediately above: that is, subject to express reservation in the solicitation documents and provided that there is no substantive modification to the framework agreement, or where additional goods or services have become necessary.[43] Limited consequential price increases are also permitted.

These limitations, which are far more restrictive than the situation in the United States, indicate that a dynamic purchasing system may be useful in

---

[41] The EU Directive also states, 'A procurement shall not be subdivided with the effect of preventing it from falling within the scope of this Directive, unless justified by objective reasons' (Article 5(3)), ibid.
[42] Article 72, ibid.   [43] Ibid.

more volatile markets (see the description of these systems in the following section). From a more general policy perspective, some of the concerns observed in the US system might emerge if attempts are made to avoid these rules through issuing broad and flexible specifications, and as a matter of design, the resulting offers may be less responsive and offer poorer value than if more accurate terms are provided (as we saw in the previous Chapter).

*First stage of the procedure* As noted above, the general rule is that the Directive's normal procedures for award of the framework agreement need to be followed, though there may be some uncertainty about some provisions (Such as whether a framework agreement must be awarded as a public contract to the most economically advantageous tender under Article 67 is unclear, though most commentators assume that it must). This uncertainty is heightened in that some provisions explicitly refer to framework agreements, raising the question of which others might *not* apply: for example, the rules on contract award notices state that '[n]ot later than 30 days after the conclusion of a contract or of a framework agreement, following the decision to award or conclude it, contracting authorities shall send a contract award notice on the results of the procurement procedure'.[44] For practical purposes, the safer course is to follow the Directive's rules in full, and it would be helpful to clarify the position explicitly in national legislation. The consequence for practice is that, as a general rule, open and competitive procedures will be required, with the normal transparency obligations.

The Directive requires that the identity of the procuring entities that can use the framework agreement be disclosed at the advertisement stage, as the recitals explain, either by name or 'by other means, such as a reference to a given category of contracting authorities within a clearly delimited geographical area, so that the contracting authorities concerned can be easily and unequivocally identified'.[45] The rules also prohibit other procuring entities from using the framework agreement (save as mentioned below), so the question has practical importance. The explanation in the recitals is not a definition, but an explanation, which leaves some area of doubt, though the principle is clear enough. Nonetheless, it can be argued that centralised purchasing agencies (and perhaps particularly those operating on a commercial fee-paying basis) may have an incentive to include very broad categories of users to maximise the potential users: this information may

---

[44] Article 50(1), the EU Directive, note 17, supra.  [45] Recital 60, ibid.

be inaccurate, and, if so, it may operate as a disincentive to participating suppliers over the long term.

*Second stage of the procedure*[46]   The basis of the procedure was set out in the introductory comments above. As regards Model 1 framework agreements, the procedure is clear and simple – the terms of the framework are applied. For Model 2 framework agreements, the procedures in Article 33 require that all awardees that are capable of performing the call-off be 'consulted' in writing for every contract to be awarded, and the deadline for submission of offers must be sufficiently long to allow awardees to respond in the circumstances of the call-off concerned. Offers must be in writing, and may not be opened until after the submission deadline. There is no guidance on the meaning of 'consult' – it is assumed that the intention is that capable awardees must be invited to participate, but there is some room for doubt.

Whether the call-offs need to be awarded to the most economically advantageous tender (MEAT) under Article 67 is also not entirely clear.[47] To the extent that the call-offs constitute a public contract – that is, after a mini-competition – the answer should be yes (though Article 33 rather undermines this simplicity by stating that the award is to the 'best tender',[48] identified 'on the basis of the award criteria set out in the procurement documents for the framework agreement', which could allow any criteria that do not offend the Treaty principles). To the extent that the award of the original framework agreement was the award of the public contract – that is, in a Model 1 framework agreement – the call-off is not itself a public contract and the terms of the procurement documents and framework agreement will govern the award.

Various approaches have been postulated and used in practice. They include the 'cascade' method (awarding to the best awardee, and then the second-best if the first is not capable of or not interested in providing the goods or services in question);[49] the 'cab-rank' method (acceptance of any given order); rotation between suppliers; percentage allocation; alphabetical rotation; and random selection.[50] The legality of these methods other than the cascade method is not clear, in that they cannot clearly be identified as the best tender or MEAT,[51] though given that the EU

[46] Framework agreements, EU procurement law and the practice, note 24, supra.   [47] Ibid.
[48] A term that may or may not be synonymous with 'MEAT'.
[49] Explanatory Note, at 3.2, note 28, supra.
[50] The use of framework agreements in public procurement, note 30, supra.
[51] The Model Law (note 8, supra) also has difficulties in this regard, as further explained below.

Treaty obligations will apply, the awards must follow the general principles of equal treatment, transparency and so on.

In addition, it is permitted that, in a multi-supplier framework agreement, both 'direct award' and 'mini-competition' may be used as a method of awarding call-off contracts, as long as objective criteria for the choice of the method are provided at the stage of establishing the framework agreement.[52] The flexibility in this provision is recognised as a welcome development, as it allows – for example, and as recent UK government advice has noted – a hybrid approach. Thus, a direct award could be made for orders for delivery to a specific region, and a mini competition could be held where:

(a) the contract exceeds a set financial threshold;
(b) the quantity of products required is over a certain level; and
(c) the contract has particularly complex requirements.

The objective criteria governing the option to be exercised are required to be set out in the framework agreement.[53]

*5.2.2.4 Experience in the use of framework agreements in the European Union*

Chapter 6 discusses the experience in the use of centralised purchasing agency-led framework agreements in the European Union. Despite the paucity of published data, there are also limited reports of benefits of single-supplier framework agreements in practice in the literature, including savings resulting from Model 1 framework agreements, reflecting the security of large-scale future orders.[54] In addition, single-user framework agreements, apart from being seen as simpler and cheaper, may allow for better control of decentralised procurement, and using the framework is less administratively burdensome.[55]

Some concerns have been expressed about risks to transparency and competition at the call-off stage in the EU system, in addition to risks arising from the uncertainties noted above. Recalling the general principle

---

[52] Article 33, the EU Directive, note 17, supra. See also Carina Risvig Hamer, 'Regular Purchases and Aggregated Procurement: The Changes in the New Public Procurement Directive Regarding Framework Agreements, Dynamic Purchasing Systems and Central Purchasing Bodies', *Public Procurement Law Review*, 4 (2014): 201–210.

[53] See 'The Public Contracts Regulations 2015: Guidance on Framework Agreements', Crown Commercial Service, available at https://www.gov.uk/government/uploads/system/uploads/attachment_data/file/430313/public-contracts-regulations-guidance.pdf.

[54] Framework agreements, EU procurement law and the practice, note 24, supra. [55] Ibid.

of transparency in the Directive,[56] it is perhaps surprising that there are few checks and balances on how the requirement to invite all 'capable' awardees to participate in a call-off will be applied in practice. There is no obligation to inform awardees about a call-off where they are not to be invited to participate; there is no requirement for any *ex-ante* public notice of forthcoming call-offs; and there is no mandatory individual award notice after the call-off is awarded.[57] While there may be a theoretical right to challenge an award under the Remedies Directive, the aggrieved supplier may only learn about the award if the procuring entity decides to issue a grouped notice of awards under the framework agreement.[58] On the other hand, the rules for a dynamic purchasing system are more robust: grouped quarterly notices, at a minimum, are required (see, further, below).[59]

Of the EU member states surveyed in 2014 about their intentions on implementing Article 51 of the Directive, Estonia, Slovakia and the United Kingdom indicated that they would follow the provisions in the article,[60] and Norway and Cyprus added that they did not plan to add more detailed procedural rules on either stage of the procedure, to allow for flexibility provided that the equal treatment rules were followed.[61] Thus, it appears that the uncertainties noted above will be reflected in national legislation in member states. In Chapter 12, we make some suggestions about possible approaches to filling these uncertainties.

The dynamic purchasing system (DPS, a Model 3 framework agreement) is provided for under Article 34 of the Directive, and operates under procedures similar to those applicable to framework agreements. The objective is to allow the contracting authority to have access to a 'particularly broad range of tenders and hence to ensure optimum use of public funds through broad competition in respect of commonly used or

---

[56] Article 18, the EU Directive, note 17, supra.
[57] Marta Andrecka, 'Framework Agreements: Transparency in the Call-off Award Process', *European Procurement & Public Private Partnership Law Review*, 10, No. 4 (2015): 227–238.
[58] These are optional under Article 50(2), the EU Directive, note 17, supra: 'contracting authorities shall not be bound to send a notice of the results of the procurement procedure for each contract based on that agreement. Member States may provide that contracting authorities shall group notices of the results of the procurement procedure for contracts based on the framework agreement on a quarterly basis. In that case, contracting authorities shall send the grouped notices within 30 days of the end of each quarter'.
[59] Article 50(3), ibid.: 'Contracting authorities shall send a contract award notice within 30 days after the award of each contract based on a dynamic purchasing system. They may, however, group such notices on a quarterly basis. In that case, they shall send the grouped notices within 30 days of the end of each quarter'.
[60] A stance confirmed in the Public Contracts Regulations 2015, note 19, supra.
[61] The transposition of the new EU public procurement directives in the member states, note 19, supra.

off-the-shelf products, works or services which are generally available on the market'.[62]

The system is to be initiated by the use of a restricted procedure, and all suppliers that meet the selection criteria and are not otherwise excluded under specified grounds for exclusion are admitted to the DPS, so that there can be no quantitative limitation on participation. The system remains open so that potential suppliers can at any time request admission to the DPS through an indication of interest and submission of an indicative tender, and requests to participate must be examined within ten days of receipt (fifteen days in exceptional circumstances), and until they have been evaluated, no tenders can be awarded. The suppliers must be notified of the result promptly.

The DPS is time-limited, and the duration must be set out in the initial contract notice – though they can, in effect, be extended through what is in effect a new contract notice without terminating the DPS itself. The DPS must be operated as a completely electronic process (so that, for example, all communications are to be made by electronic means only), and access must be free of charge to suppliers. The contract notice must set out that the procurement concerned will operate as a DPS and describe the purchase's expected and envisaged quantities or values under the DPS. It must provide essential information concerning the operation of the DPS (which must state the Internet address where documents can be consulted and will remain available electronically throughout the duration of the DPS, and the DPS must offer unrestricted, direct access to the system for the period of its operation). If any division into categories of goods or services is intended, it must be included.

At the call-off stage, all suppliers must be invited to participate (or, where relevant, all suppliers admitted for any predefined categories), and the contracting authority must set a time limit for submission of their tenders. The award is to be made on the basis of MEAT and the award criteria for the DPS (though they can be formulated more precisely in the invitation to tender for the specific contract).

As noted above, there are more stringent transparency requirements for a DPS than for a framework agreement. All participating suppliers must be advised of the proposed award decision, though the use of a standstill period at the call-off stage is optional, there is a mandatory contract award notice (individual or grouped), and any supplier is entitled to a debriefing, which must be provided within fifteen days of the request. It has also been observed that dynamic nature of the DPS, its duration and time limits involved do not

---

[62] Recital 63 to the EU Directive, note 17, supra.

seem to be a source of competition distortions, of purchases in excess of the needs (actual or reasonably estimated) of the contracting authority or of the excessively broad specifications or terms of the procurement that are an acknowledged risk of framework agreements more generally.[63]

### 5.2.3 Indefinite delivery/indefinite quantity contracts (ID/IQs) in the US federal system[64]

#### 5.2.3.1 The evolution of the regulatory framework

The US federal system presents a plethora of concepts and acronyms unfamiliar to the outsider, which we shall attempt to explain in describing the development of the main legislative framework for ID/IQs.

The starting point is that the US federal procurement is required to be conducted using full and open competition, as required by the 1984 Competition in Contracting Act (CICA).[65] Full and open competition requires that any 'responsible sources' be permitted to participate.[66] Certain exemptions from this requirement for some types of ID/IQs that had existed for decades were permitted when CICA was passed,[67] provided that the purchase offered the lowest overall cost alternative to the procuring entity (called 'agency' in US terminology, a term that we shall adopt for the purposes of this section).[68] From 1984 until the next series of reforms in 1994, it became clear that the federal system was excessively bureaucratic, its procedures were time-consuming[69] and that it was particularly unsuited to

---

[63] Albert Sanchez-Graells, *Public Procurement and the EU Competition Rules*, 2nd ed. (Oxford: Hart, 2015), at pp. 363–366.
[64] For a more detailed discussion of the US system, see Daniel I. Gordon and Jonathan L. Kang, 'Task-Order Contracting in the U.S. Federal System: The Current System and Its Historical Context', chapter 5, in S. Arrowsmith (ed.), *Public Procurement Regulation in the 21st Century: Reform of the UNCITRAL Model Law on Procurement*, note 8, supra.
[65] Competition in Contracting Act of 1984, 10 U.S.C. ss2304 (2000). See, also, R. J. Sherry, G. M. Koehl and S. A. Armstrong, 'Competition Requirements in General Services Administration Schedule Contracts', *Public Contract Law Journal*, 37, No. 3, (2008): 467–487.
[66] Federal Acquisition Regulation (FAR), Code of Federal Regulations (CFR) Title 48, part 2 (2.101) and 9. FAR 2005-83/07-02-2015, available at www.acquisition.gov/?q=browsefar. The term 'responsible sources' in this sense means, broadly, that the supplier is both capable of fulfilling the agency's need, and meets government eligibility requirements.
[67] The Federal Supply Schedules, discussed below.
[68] 'Task-Order Contracting in the U.S. Federal System: The Current System and Its Historical Context', note 64, supra.
[69] Streamlining Defense Acquisition Laws: Report of the Acquisition Law Advisory Panel to the United States Congress, cited in 'Competition Requirements in General Services Administration Schedule Contracts', ibid., and Christopher R. Yukins, Discussion Draft, 'Assessing Framework Agreements under the WTO's Government Procurement Agreement: A Comparative Review of the US Experience', Materials Presented at Colloquium at George Washington University

the burgeoning need for IT equipment – the two-to-three-year lead time for purchases was considered intolerable.[70] The delays in concluding contracts were exacerbated by rising levels of protests and successful protests.[71]

The consequences included a major change in procurement regulation, starting with the Federal Acquisition Streamlining Act (FASA) of 1994, as implemented by the Federal Acquisition Regulation (FAR). Also at that time, the policy goals of the Office of Federal Procurement Policy were restated to give procurement officials increased discretion and to encourage the use of commercial judgement.

The main objectives of the reforms put in place through FASA were to shorten the time and costs involved in US federal procurement and to promote more commercial purchasing (allowing, among other things, greater flexibility in identifying the best value offer rather than requiring acceptance of the lowest-cost responsive bid).[72] The reforms to improve administrative efficiency were designed to

> reduce paperwork burdens, facilitate the acquisition of commercial products, enhance the use of simplified procedures for small purchases, clarify protest procedures, eliminate unnecessary statutory impediments to efficient and expeditious acquisition, achieve uniformity in the acquisition practices of federal agencies, and increase the efficiency and effectiveness of the laws governing the manner in which the government obtains goods and services.[73]

Among the reforms was the codification of ID/IQ contracts.[74] An ID/IQ is a contract that provides for the issue of task or delivery orders up to a defined maximum value,[75] but does not commit the procuring entity to purchase more than a (generally small) minimum quantity of the goods

---

Law School 67, No. 48 (2005), available at http://docs.law.gwu.edu/facweb/sschooner/GWUFrameworksProgram, Materials_Final.pdf.

[70] 'Task-Order Contracting in the U.S. Federal System: The Current System and Its Historical Context', note 64, supra.

[71] Ibid. CICA had placed Government Accountability Office protests on a statutory basis, but a second forum for IT contracts had a far higher success rate.

[72] Ibid. Professor Steven Kelman, the then head of the Office of Federal Procurement Policy: 'promoted best value decisions and consideration of contractor's past performance, as well as expanded use of Indefinite Delivery – Indefinite Quantity (ID/IQ) contracts and task and delivery orders under them, all of which tipped the scales in favor of efficiency because of, at least in part, a perception that concerns about integrity had led to an overly complex, inefficient procurement process'. 'Public Procurement Systems: Unpacking Stakeholder Aspirations and Expectations', Steven L. Schooner, Daniel I. Gordon and Jessica L. Clark, GWU Law School Public Law Research Paper 1133234 (2008), available at http://ssrn.com/abstract=1133234, at p. 11.

[73] See S. REP. 103–258, 1994 U.S.C.C.A.N. at 2562 (providing a summary and describing the purpose of the reform).

[74] FAR Subpart 16.5, note 66, supra.    [75] FAR Subpart 8.404(b)(3), ibid.

and services concerned.[76] The solicitation must also set out the period of the contract (including any option periods) and a statement of the work to be performed. The award of an ID/IQ (in terms of our analysis, the first stage of the procedure) was treated as the issue of the procurement contract for the purposes of CICA, so that purchasing through existing ID/IQs (the second stage of the procedure) is considered as fulfilling the CICA competition requirements, provided it follows FAR procedures.

The 1994 reforms also promoted multi-supplier ID/IQs to several suppliers, known as multiple awards, so that a statutory preference was established in favour of awarding, 'to the maximum extent practicable, multiple task or delivery order contracts for the same or similar services or property [goods]'.[77] Multiple awards imply, in turn, that the procurement official will select a contract holder for a task or delivery order from many available and responsible bidders (reflecting that the generally low minimum-order requirement allows the procurement official a wide choice of bidders). These procedural flexibilities, together with (from the European perspective) flexible rules defining best value, imply the use of significant discretion, which has attracted criticism particularly in light of the fact that FASA was considered to exempt task orders that emerge from this streamlined process from protests, with limited exceptions.[78] Over time, multi-user ID/IQs have become the norm, and procuring entities (called 'user agencies') using them have been said to operate 'below the radar' given few transparency obligations. FASA also exempts micro-purchases (in 1994, those under $2,500, currently those under $3,000) from all procedural requirements, and permits substantial relaxations of competition requirements for purchases between the micro-purchase threshold and $100,000. A further procedural simplification is that the federal Small Business Administration set-aside programme is generally not mandatory for many centralised ID/IQs.[79]

---

[76] This minimum quantity is a legal requirement, designed to provide consideration so that the ID/IQ is a binding contract. See 'Task-Order Contracting in the U.S. Federal System: The Current System and Its Historical Context', note 64, supra, at pp. 217–218 & case cited.

[77] The Federal Acquisition Streamlining Act of October 13, 1994, Public Law No. 103–355, Sec. 1004, § 2304a.

[78] Unless the orders were beyond the scope, period or maximum value of the ID/IQ. This restriction was a response to a significant rise in protests during the previous decade. FASA did require, however, the creation of an ombudsman function within individual procuring entities (termed 'agencies' in the US system) as an alternative. Subsequently, GAO decided that it did have the competence to hear protests under the Federal Supply Schedules (see below), as they were treated separately under FAR. See, further, 'Task-Order Contracting in the U.S. Federal System: The Current System and Its Historical Context', chapter 5, in *Public Procurement Regulation in the 21st Century*, at section 5.5, note 8, supra.

[79] FAR part 19, note 66, supra.

The second element of the reform (to encourage a more commercial approach) included encouraging the government to move away from issuing its own specifications for common purchases to purchasing items without bespoke specifications, in an attempt 'to break [government's] longstanding habit of demanding that firms create government-unique versions of goods and services available in the commercial marketplace'.[80] There was much criticism and some ridicule of long and complex specifications for everyday items.[81] The policy approach took into consideration that there would be an available pricing benchmark in the market, which would obviate the need for traditional procurement procedures and audits and for cost-reimbursement contracting. 'Commercial' items include both those available in the market and items modified or sold exclusively to the government, provided that they are similar to commercial items widely available.[82]

This process was extended in 1996, when the 'Clinger-Cohen Act'[83] introduced 'commercial-off-the-shelf items (COTS)', as a subset of commercial items. COTS items comprise 'commercial items' that are both sold in substantial quantities in the commercial marketplace; and sold to the government 'without modification'.[84] Commentators have

---

[80] S. L. Schooner, 'Commercial Purchasing: The Chasm between the United States Government's Evolving Policy and Practice' (19 May 2011), chapter 8, in S. Arrowsmith and M. Trybus (eds.), *Public Procurement: The Continuing Revolution* (2003); GWU Law School, Public Law Research Paper No. 25. Available at SSRN: http://ssrn.com/abstract=285536 or http://dx.doi.org/10.2139/ssrn.285536, at p. 6.

[81] For example, a much-vaunted twenty six-page specification for oatmeal cookies and chocolate brownies for the Department of Defense, available at http://liw.iki.fi/liw/misc/MIL-C-44072C.pdf. See also, 'Commercial Purchasing: The Chasm between the United States Government's Evolving Policy and Practice', ibid.

[82] 'Commercial items' include:

- Products that are 'of a type' customarily used by the general public or by non-governmental entities for purposes other than governmental purposes, and that have been (1) sold, leased, or licensed to the general public; or (2) offered for sale, lease, or license to the general public;
- Products derived from commercial technology and expected to soon be in the commercial marketplace;
- Products that fit one of the two categories described immediately above and have been modified in either minor, insignificant, or commercially-standard ways;
- Products and services that fit any of the above-described categories and have been combined in such a way as to be customarily combined and sold in combination to the general public;
- Services that are designed to service or maintain a commercial product;
- Services that are offered and sold competitively in substantial quantities in the commercial marketplace based on established market prices; and
- Certain non-developmental items that are sold in substantial quantities on a competitive basis to multiple State and local governments.

See U.S. Code (U.S.C): Title 41 – Public Contracts, section 403.

[83] National Defense Authorization Act for Fiscal Year 1996, Pub. L. No. 104–106, §186 (1996).

[84] See 41 U.S.C., note 81, supra, section 431.

noted that these definitions are vague and the system allows procurement officials to decide whether purchases are of commercial items in this sense, which has led to the predictable criticism that they stretch the concept to avoid otherwise cumbersome procedures.[85] The reforms were also designed to encourage more potential suppliers into the government procurement market (an issue of particular relevance to encouraging effective competition in the framework agreements context, as we shall see in Chapter 7).

*5.2.3.2 Centralised purchasing: the General Service Administration Multiple Award Schedule contracts, Federal Supply Schedules contracts and Government-Wide Acquisition contracts*

As we noted earlier in this Chapter, ID/IQs have operated for decades, and they allow federal procuring entities (as user agencies) to use ID/IQs established by other agencies. In addition, there are three systems for government-wide ID/IQs, as follows.

The US GSA established the Federal Supply Schedule (FSS) programme in 1949 to facilitate federal agencies purchase common-user items from commercial firms through 'schedule contracts', which comprise a form of supplier catalogues. The Multiple Award Schedules (MAS) programme, the largest available FSS programme, was designed and implemented to provide agencies, via 'MAS contracts', with varying quantities of a wide range of commercially available goods and services, originally comprising largely office furniture and supplies, but now extending to personal computers, scientific equipment, professional services and network support.[86] User agencies can purchase the goods and services from the GSA online catalogue or from suppliers directly.[87]

Government Wide Acquisition Contracts (GWACs) were introduced in 1996 for IT purchases, and are available to any federal agency. However, they are set up by an agency itself, rather than by GSA, though in practice they operate similarly. The agency that establishes a GWAC can also charge other agencies an administrative fee when the latter issue an order under the GWAC.[88]

---

[85] 'Commercial Purchasing: The Chasm between the United States Government's Evolving Policy and Practice', note 80, supra.
[86] FAR 8.402, note 66, supra.   [87] The catalogue is available at www.gsaadvantage.gov.
[88] As noted in 'Task-Order Contracting in the U.S. Federal System: The Current System and Its Historical Context', note 64, supra, the flexibility for agencies to provide services to other agencies had previously existed, and so some ID/IQ that operate like GWACs in practice operate without the oversight that the GWACs system is intended to provide through the Office of Management and budget.

The US federal system, therefore, appears markedly different from the European one in terms of scale and structure. The GSA schedules, of which there are many, may themselves have thousands of suppliers with parallel framework agreements with the government (in 2009, GSA schedule 70 was reported to have more than 5,000 contract holders, for contracts for general-purpose commercial IT equipment, software and related services).[89] There are many thousands of MAS contracts open for use by any federal user agency. In terms of the models of framework agreements described in Chapter 2, they are akin to Model 3 framework agreements in that they are always open to new suppliers, but they are significantly different in that the competitive phase is frequently undertaken at the first stage alone. The MAS contracts themselves can exceed ten years' duration (the general contract period being five years, with an optional extension of another five years and exceptional extensions theoretically possible thereafter).

The procedure for concluding and using ID/IQs also requires some explanation, in that they are based on the concept of multiple fixed-price offers for a catalogue of goods and services regularly purchased by agencies, reflecting prices discounted from those commercially offered by suppliers rather than a simulation of competition designed to set a fair price. For simplicity's sake, we shall describe the processes for the MAS contracts that are regulated under FAR Subpart 8.4.

*First-stage procedures* To become a MAS contractor, any responsible supplier must submit an offer in response to a MAS solicitation, publicised on the portal FedBizOpps.gov.[90] Contracts are awarded to responsible suppliers offering commercial items for goods and services that fall within

---

[89] 'Task-Order Contracting in the U.S. Federal System: The Current System and Its Historical Context', ibid.

[90] There are three parties to a MAS Schedule contract: the GSA contracting officer, the contractor and the authorised ordering agency. Their respective roles and responsibilities can be summarised as follows: The *GSA contracting officer* (i) evaluates proposals from commercial contractors; (ii) negotiates discounts and contract-specific terms and conditions, thus determining fair and reasonable prices by relying on market research, commercial sales practices and audits; and (iii) awards and administers resulting ID/IQ contracts. The *contractor* (i) attends GSA training such as 'Pathway to Success' on the MAS programme, (ii) submits proposals that comply with the solicitation provisions, (iii) discloses to the schedule contracting officer its commercial sales practices as required by the contract, (iv) adheres to the terms and conditions of its MAS contract, and (v) keeps its offerings current. The *authorised ordering agency* (i) relies upon and complies with the terms and conditions of the MAS contract; (ii) solicits quotes for specific commercially available requirements; (iii) seeks additional discounts, if appropriate; (iv) negotiates requirement-specific terms and conditions that are within the scope of an MAS contract; and (v) makes best value award based on quotations received.

the broad scope of the MAS solicitation and whose prices are 'fair and reasonable'. In determining whether prices are fair and reasonable, the GSA officer (a) conducts, a price analysis using market research, sale histories, invoices and references and (b) perhaps, more importantly, requires the supplier to disclose its commercial sales practices per the instructions and format found in the GSA Acquisition Manual (GSAM).[91] On this basis, by requiring the suppliers to offer discounts on their prices in the commercial market, GSA negotiates the best price given to any customer (so it is the 'most favoured customer'), while also benchmarking government prices against those available in the commercial market.

The determination that the prices are 'fair and reasonable' fulfils the CICA competition requirements and allows a simplified ordering process at the second stage, as described below. Since prices that agencies pay for schedule products and services are the result of these negotiations between GSA and individual firms, this negotiated pricing process – rather than a traditional competitive bid – is the key factor for making sure that the government obtains 'fair and reasonable' prices in practice. Nonetheless, in practice, GSA admits thousands of responsible suppliers to the schedules, which are described as having the opportunity to compete akin to a 'hunting licence', so that there is no selection of the comparatively 'best' offers at the first stage, contrary to the approach in our Models 1 and 2 framework agreements.

*Second-stage procedures – placing orders under MAS contracts*[92] Where MAS contracts are in place, a procurement official wishing to purchase from them is not required to make any further assessment of whether prices are fair and reasonable and need not engage in any further competition, unless the value of the order exceeds certain thresholds. As we noted above, there are no procedural requirements for micro-purchases, though procurement officials are encouraged to spread orders around suppliers; for those above that threshold but below $100,000, the official must survey at least three relevant MAS contracts,[93] and determine which offers the best value and meets the agency's needs at the lowest overall cost. He then places an order with the supplier concerned.[94] For those purchases above $100,000 (the 'simplified acquisition threshold' [SAT]), 'Simplified Acquisition Procedures' (SAP) require the procurement official to

---

[91] At Section 515.408. The GSAM is available at www.acquisition.gov/?q=browsegsam.
[92] For a more comprehensive explanation, see 'Competition Requirements in General Services Administration Schedule Contracts', note 65, supra.
[93] Using the GSA online ordering system – GSA Advantage!, found at www.gsaadvantage.gov.
[94] FAR 8.405–1(c)(1), note 66, supra.

consider more than three suppliers' offers and seek additional discounts (though suppliers are not obliged to discount further). While the procedures are relatively informal (allowing, for example, the use of oral quotations) and do not involve public notices, there are record requirements to facilitate oversight.

There are slightly more complex procedures when the procurement official issues a request-for-quotation (RFQ) containing a Statement of Work (SOW),[95] which enables suppliers to identify from among the goods or services under their MAS contract those that they wish the procurement official to consider (as opposed to the general situation in which the procurement official himself or herself identifies the goods or services to survey). These procedures, broadly speaking, resemble the RFQs or shopping in that limited statements of needs and criteria are required and bring the approach similar to Models 2 and 3 framework agreements (i.e. with second-stage competition). In addition, the GAO has also held that the RFQ must provide for fair and equitable competition where a technical evaluation and selection decision are needed (the agency must apply procedures similar to those for other procurement using a best-value approach).[96]

The MAS programme also permits 'Contractor Team Arrangements' (CTAs), which allow what are effectively joint ventures between MAS suppliers, and 'Blanket Purchase Agreements' (BPAs), which are larger-scale MAS awards for a user agency's repeat needs that can be called off without further competition at the order stage, though they are generally limited to five years' duration and are subject to annual review.[97] BPAs, which again resemble EU-style framework agreements with second-stage competition, have been considered useful 'where the agency wants to standardize on a set of products for interoperability and integration. Instead of conducting a competition for each purchase, the agency can conduct a one-time BPA competition'.[98]

---

[95] A SOW is required, in very broad terms, for purchases other than simple contracted goods and fixed-price services for a specific task, such as installation, maintenance and repair (FAR 8.405–2, ibid.).

[96] 'Competition Requirements in General Services Administration Schedule Contracts', note 92, supra.

[97] FAR 8.405–3, note 66, supra. For a more detailed discussion of CTAs and BPAs, see 'Competition Requirements in General Services Administration Schedule Contracts', ibid., and 'Assessing Framework Agreements under the WTO's Government Procurement Agreement: A Comparative Review of the US Experience', note 69, supra.

[98] General Services Administration, White Paper: Acquisition Sources and Alternatives (August 1998) (hereafter GSA, White Paper), available at www.itpolicy.gsa.gov/mke/acqwp.htm, cited in 'Commercial Purchasing: The Chasm between the United States Government's Evolving Policy and Practice', at p. 29, note 80, supra.

Further, the MAS programme also permits the purchase of what are colloquially referred to as 'open market items' from MAS suppliers. These items are *not* included on the supplier's MAS schedule, but in limited quantity may be procured alongside contract items on conditions established under the FAR.[99] Restrictions on the use of 'open market items' may also encourage the use of CTAs in practice, where combined suppliers can complete a task order.

GSA can also make use of two tools that are specifically designed to protect the government from overpricing: pre-award and post-award audits. Pre-award audits enable the contracting officer to verify that firm-provided pricing information is accurate and complete before awarding the contract. Post-award audits are used as a deterrent to overpricing and as a primary tool for recovering supplier overcharges. Nonetheless, and despite the importance of ensuring fair and reasonable prices, the Government Accountability Office (GAO) has repeatedly reported that GSA has not consistently made good use of findings in pre-award and post-award audit reports to the effect that the prices inside the MAS programme were not demonstrably below those in the marketplace,[100] raising concrete concerns as to the extent to which the award phase of GSA schedules could be considered competitive in reality.

*5.2.3.3 Observations on the operation of ID/IQs in practice – failures of competition and transparency despite procedural advantages*[101]
The positive effects of the reforms to the US federal system are commonly put in the context of some well-voiced criticisms. To start with the benefits, ID/IQs (GSA schedules, GWACs and user-agency ID/IQs) are considered to have streamlined the acquisition process by allowing US agencies to

---
[99] FAR 8.40, note 66, supra. These conditions include additional competition and transparency requirements, a determination that the prices are fair and reasonable, the items are clearly labelled as outside the scope of the MAS schedule and the order records all terms applicable to the open-market items. In the 1990s, unconditional purchases of 'incidental' amounts of open-market items were common, but both GAO and the courts rejected the practice as inconsistent with CICA. See, further, 'Competition Requirements in General Services Administration Schedule Contracts', at p. 479, note 65, supra.
[100] See GAO-05-911T 'Contract Management – Opportunities Continue for GSA to Improve Pricing of Multiple Award Schedules Contract', cited in 'Commercial Purchasing: The Chasm between the United States Government's Evolving Policy and Practice', note 80, supra, p. 32.
[101] For more detailed assessments of ID/IQs in the US federal system, see 'Task-Order Contracting in the U.S. Federal System: The Current System and Its Historical Context', chapter 5, in *Public Procurement Regulation in the 21st Century*, note 8, supra, and 'Are ID/IQs Inefficient? Sharing Lessons with European Framework Contracting'; Christopher R. Yukins, *Public Contract Law Journal*, 37, No. 3, Spring (2008): 546–568, at page 552, and 'Competition Requirements in General Services Administration Schedule Contracts', note 65, supra.

## International experience in framework agreements

avoid 'delays associated with awarding several individual contracts for each requirement and conducting recompetitions',[102] to enable reduced inventory costs, allow shipments to be sent directly to government end users, enable better scheduling of delivery requirements and, through reducing administrative time frames, 'allow the government to access much more current commercial technology'.[103] Considerable savings (16.7 per cent annually) to the US Department of Justice were also reported.[104] Thus there are incidences of the main motivations set out in Chapter 2 arising in practice.

The authority for procedure-free procurement below the micro-purchase threshold gave additional impetus for the use of purchase cards that were widely introduced in the 1990s. Thus combined, they allowed commercial purchasing behaviour in circumstances in which the procedural costs of procurement procedures would otherwise outweigh their benefits.[105] However, it was indicated that procurement officials deliberately split their purchases to remain below the micro-purchasing threshold, and that the negative effects in aggregate might be significant (in fiscal year (FY) 2000, estimated at 5 per cent of the entire federal procurement spend).[106] The GAO found in an internal report that its own staff use of purchase cards required improvement.[107] Indeed, the SAPs have not always led to fair and reasonable prices: GAO found that the lack of public notice may have been a significant contributor to this failure.[108]

---

[102] U.S. Office of Management & Budget, Office of Federal Procurement Policy, Best Practices for Multiple Task and Delivery Contracting 7 (Washington, D.C.: July 1997), www.acqnet.gov/Library/OFPP?/BestPractices/BestPMAT.html, as cited in 'Assessing Framework Agreements under the WTO's Government Procurement Agreement: A Comparative Review of the U.S. Experience', note 69, supra.

[103] 'Are ID/IQs Inefficient? Sharing Lessons with European Framework Contracting', note 101, supra, citing FAR 16.501–2(b).

[104] U.S. Office of Management & Budget, Office of Federal Procurement Policy, Best Practices for Multiple Task and Delivery Contracting (Washington, DC: July, 1997), www.acqnet.gov/Library/OFPP?/BestPractices/BestPMAT.html, as cited in 'Are ID/IQs Inefficient? Sharing Lessons with European Framework Contracting', ibid.

[105] Commercial Purchasing: The Chasm between the United States Government's Evolving Policy and Practice, note 80, supra, at p. 23.

[106] Ibid., at p. 24.

[107] U.S. Government Accountability Office Report: Financial Management: Actions Needed to Strengthen GAO's Purchase Card Program Controls, Financial Management: Actions Needed to Strengthen GAO's Purchase Card Program Controls, number OIG-15-2, dated 5 May 2015, finding that more effective internal controls for preventing, detecting and responding to potential misuse, waste and abuse of GAO purchase cards were indicated.

[108] GAO, Report GAO-01-517, Contract Management: Benefits of Simplified Acquisition Test Procedures Not Clearly Demonstrated (20 April 2001), available at www.gao.gov.

An in-depth academic review of GAO reports and Department of Defense Inspector General reports in 2005 highlighted multiple failures of competition in practice.[109] GAO found that there were regular breaches of competition requirements – in 1999, 66 of the 124 (53 per cent) studied task orders were awarded on a sole-source or directed-source basis, and only eight correctly justified the lack of competition with one of the permissible exceptions; in 2001, sole-source awards had increased to 72 per cent (304 out of 403 task orders, of which only 40 were correctly justified).[110] Furthermore, GAO found that exceptions to allow for 'follow-on' orders intended to permit technical compatibility had been abused, including uncovering two follow-on orders that were together forty-six times greater than the original (also non-competitively awarded) order.[111] In part these failures might be attributable to the ability of ID/IQ contract holders to 'market their services directly to individual agencies, those agencies – affected by considerations including speed, convenience, personal preference, and human nature – frequently obtain those services on a sole source or non-competitive basis from those possessing these hunting licenses. As a result, legitimate competition infrequently occurs'.[112] In addition, instances are cited of agencies that award ID/IQs seeking to accommodate the preferences of their (fee-paying) customer agencies by failing to notify ID/IQ holders of task-order opportunities, distorting specifications and technical requirements and/or failing to assess offers or other rules, in order to favour the customer agency's favoured supplier.[113]

Furthermore, an incumbency problem appeared significant – GAO also found that many task orders received only one quotation – nine out of ten cases examined received offers from incumbents alone.[114] Procurement officials were reported to award ID/IQs to targeted groups of suppliers, among which collusion or non-compete agreements appeared to be in existence, so that the ultimate orders could be directed to a favoured

---

[109] 'Assessing Framework Agreements under the WTO's Government Procurement Agreement: A Comparative Review of the US Experience', note 69, supra.

[110] Comparative Review of the U.S. Experience, note 109, supra, at p. 16, citing GAO, U.S. Government Accountability Office, Civilian Agency Compliance with Task and Delivery Order Contracts, Report No. GAO 03-983 (August 2003), also listing many studies with similar findings available through the Services Acquisition Advisory Panel, at www.acqnet.gov/aap/doc uments/Sources%20for%20Interagency%20Contracting%20Group.pdf.

[111] Ibid., at page 17, citing GAO, United States Government Accountability Office, Few Competing Proposals for Large DOD Information Technology Orders, Report No. GAO/NSIAD-00-56, 8–9 (March 2000).

[112] See generally GEN. ACCT. OFF., REPT. NO. GAO/NSIAD-00-56 at 4, Contract Management: Few Competing Proposals for Large DOD Information Technology Orders (20 March 2000).

[113] Comparative Review of the U.S. Experience, note 109, supra, at p. 20.   [114] Ibid., at p. 18.

*International experience in framework agreements* 111

supplier.[115] This overall review included the statement that the 'vast majority of opportunities were not properly competed among the awardees' of a Navy Space and Warfare Systems Command ID/IQ,[116] a finding that the reports overall might apply elsewhere.

Other problems in ID/IQ awards related to overuse or misuse of the ID/IQs themselves.[117] Once holding a schedule contract, suppliers could supplement their offers with additional goods and services, meaning that assessing whether orders were within the scope of the original schedule award was 'sometimes a murky question'.[118] The fee-paying relationship between the ID/IQ awarding agencies and their customer agencies and the relative procedural freedom of ID/IQ awards (arguably distorting decisions on which would be the appropriate tool for a particular purchase)[119] may also have contributed to a relaxed attitude in considering whether task orders were properly 'within scope', even where the purchase of 'open market items' had been restricted,[120] and recipient suppliers were also unlikely to object to orders placed with them. The scope issue was also observed to play out through facilitative writing of excessively broad requirements and interpretation of those requirements, of which the most egregious example may be the now-notorious example of an FSS

---

[115] Indeed, an audit report revealed that two-thirds of the contracting organisations reviewed 'awarded task orders on a directed-source basis because the program offices preferred to work with a specific contractor', Yukins, ibid., at p. 18, citing e.g. Thomas F. Burke and Stanley C. Dees, 'Feature Comment: The Impact of Multiple-Award Contracts on the Underlying Values of the Federal Procurement System', 44 GOV. CONTRACTOR ¶ 431 (6 November 2002) (citing U.S. Department of Defense, Office of Inspector General, Multiple Award Contracts for Services, Report No. D-2001-189 (30 September 2001)).
[116] Audit report, ibid.
[117] For example, procuring entities may procure through an existing framework agreement that does not quite meet their needs, to avoid having to draft their own specifications and terms and conditions, to issue a procurement notice, to examine the qualifications of suppliers, to evaluate full tenders and so on. The end result may be a cheaper procurement in terms of administrative costs, but the purchase may not offer optimal value for money. See, further, 'A Critical Evaluation of the Revised UNCITRAL Model Law Provisions on Regulating Framework Agreements', note 24, supra.
[118] 'Task-Order Contracting in the U.S. Federal System: The Current System and Its Historical Context', chapter 5, in *Public Procurement Regulation in the 21st Century*, at section 5.5, note 8, supra, referring to the 1990s in particular.
[119] Noting that 'once a master agreement is in place, an order for goods or services can be issued against that agreement with far less notice and process, often with little risk of accountability', the consequent risks of failing to meet needs effectively and compromising value for money have also been raised: see, for example, 'Regulating Framework Agreements under the UNCITRAL Model Law', chapter 2 in *Public Procurement Regulation in the 21st Century*, note 8, supra.
[120] 'Task-Order Contracting in the U.S. Federal System: The Current System and Its Historical Context', chapter 5, in *Public Procurement Regulation in the 21st Century*, at section 5.5, note 8, supra.

contract for IT services that was used to hire interrogators for Abu Ghraib.[121]

#### 5.2.3.4 Reforms post-1994

Recurrent reports of failures in ID/IQs (some of which may be inadvertent and reflect the differing competition requirements for GSA schedules and other ID/IQ contracts of various sizes, as well as the issues above)[122] have led to a series of reforms. In the early 1990s, both civilian and Defense Department panels were established to review the federal procurement process. In particular, task-order contracts, although conceived to serve legitimate interests, were placed under close scrutiny as their use had expanded significantly and they had occasionally been (mis)used to avoid competition. The result was a series of reforms to the regulatory framework, starting in the 1990s. First, FASA was amended to require that any awardee is to be afforded a 'fair opportunity to be considered' for each task or delivery order under the ID/IQ, though the phrase is not defined.[123]

Throughout the period 2000–2011 the FAR was revised, among other things, so as to provide guidance to agencies on the appropriate use of task and delivery order contracts.[124] In 2000, a requirement for a statement of work in each task order or delivery order issued that clearly specified all tasks to be performed or property to be delivered under the order was introduced.

In 1996, the Clinger-Cohen Act had introduced measures to limit protests, but the GAO ruled in 1997 that it did have jurisdiction over

---

[121] Ibid., at section 5.6.
[122] Christopher R. Yukins and Steven L. Schooner, 'Incrementalism: Eroding the Impediments to a Global Public Procurement Market', *Georgetown Journal of International Law*, 38 (2007): 529–576; GWU Legal Studies Research Paper No. 320; GWU Law School Public Law Research Paper No. 320. Available at SSRN: http://ssrn.com/abstract=1002446.
[123] As set out in FAR 16.505(b). However, the then head of the Office of Federal Procurement Policy Professor Steven Kelman explained that this did not require agencies to compete each order, noting that '[u]nder multiple award ID/IQ contracts for COTS products, prices are typically set forth in price sheets and are often available electronically ... for customers to select the products that best satisfy their needs. As long as the contracting officer or customer can easily compare the various prices and products being offered under these contracts, awardees will have been given a fair opportunity to be considered ... Negotiations with each awardee prior to awarding a delivery order should not be necessary, unless the contracting officer believes that the information provided on the price sheets is insufficient to make an award in the best interest of the government', as cited in 'Are ID/IQs Inefficient? Sharing Lessons with European Framework Contracting', at p. 560, note 101, supra.
[124] National Defense Authorization Act for Fiscal Year 2000, Pub. L. No. 106–165, §804, 113 Stat. 512 (1999).

FSS schedule awards.[125] In 2007, the federal court ruled that FASA's restriction on protest competence in the federal courts did *not* extend to GSA schedule contracts (i.e. only agency-led ID/IQs were prevented from protest in that forum),[126] a situation subsequently confirmed in legislation.[127]

The annual National Defense Authorization Act has become a vehicle for procurement reform for both defence and non-defence agencies. In 2002 and 2008, rules for defence procurement were amended to provide that the orders for services over $100,000 be awarded on a competitive basis, where the latter meant that all multiple-award contract holders offering those services had to be notified of the government's intent to purchase, a description of the work to be purchased and the basis for selection.[128] Thus the amendments were largely aimed at increasing the scope for a competitive allocation of orders at the task-order stage.

In 2008 further amendments were adopted so as to foster competition at the order stage, so that task and delivery order contracts in excess of $100,000,000 were required to be multiple awards, unless the head of the agency generated a written determination that an exception applied.[129] Notably, Section 843 of the National Defense Authorization Act (NDAA) for FY 2008 imposed additional competition requirements for orders in excess of $5,000,000, whereby each contract holder had to be provided with a fair opportunity to compete, which consisted in (i) issuing a notice of the task or delivery order that includes a clear statement of the agency's requirements; (ii) a reasonable period of time to provide a proposal in response to the notice; and (iii) a disclosure of the significant factors and subfactors, including cost or price, that the agency expects to consider in evaluating such proposals, and their relative importance.[130]

---

[125] 'Task-Order Contracting in the U.S. Federal System: The Current System and Its Historical Context', chapter 5, in *Public Procurement Regulation in the 21st Century*, at p. 227, note 8, supra.
[126] 'This limitation on protests only applies to orders issued under the newly authorized 'task order contracts' or 'delivery order contracts' (i.e., contracts authorized under 41 U.S.C. § 253h or 253i), see 41 U.S.C. § 253f, not orders placed against GSA schedule contracts'. Decision of the Court of Federal Claims, Data Management Services JV *v.* United States, No. 07-597C (24 September 2007), at note 4, available at www.uscfc.uscourts.gov/sites/default/files/opinions/BRUGGINK.DATA092407.pdf.
[127] National Defense Authorization Act for Fiscal Year 2009.
[128] National Defense Authorization Act for Fiscal Year 2002, Pub. L. No. 107–107, §803, 115 Stat. 1012 (2001).
[129] National Defense Authorization Act for Fiscal Year 2008, Pub. L. No. 110–181, §843 (2008).
[130] Ibid.

In 2009, the Congress broadened the 2002 reforms, and extended their scope beyond the Department of Defense. Competition required by all executive agencies was enhanced for orders under multiple-award contracts. In particular, Section 863 of the NDAA for FY 2009 required that the orders for services over the simplified acquisition threshold be awarded on a competitive basis (with limited exceptions). Moreover, it was required that all sole-source task or delivery orders in excess of the SAT that are placed against multiple-award contracts be published on FedBizOpps within fourteen days of order placement (unless certain conditions apply).[131] The NDAA also reintroduced GAO competence to hear protests of awards over $10,000,000.

The Small Business Jobs Act in 2010 required guidance to be published giving agencies the discretion to (i) set aside part or parts of a multiple-award contract for small business concerns, including subcategories of small business; (ii) notwithstanding fair opportunity requirements, place set-aside orders against multiple-award contracts for small business; and (iii) reserve contract awards for small business concerns under full and open multiple award procurements.[132]

### 5.2.4  UNCITRAL – provisions in the Model Law

The UNCITRAL Model Law's provisions were drafted starting in 2006,[133] and therefore UNCITRAL had the benefit of being able to consider early experience in the use of the EU provisions introduced in 2004, and the US experience above.

As noted above, the Model Law distinguishes procurement contracts from framework agreements through definitions of relevant terms, which make it clear that a framework agreement results at the end of the first stage of the procedure, and a procurement contract at the second,[134] irrespective of whether a framework agreement may be an enforceable contract in

---

[131] National Defense Authorization Act for Fiscal Year 2009, Pub. L. No. 110–417, §863 (2009).
[132] Small business Jobs Act of 2010, Pub. L. No. 111–240 §1331 (2010).
[133] Revisions to the UNCITRAL Model Law were negotiated from 2004 to 2011.
[134] Article 2 of the Model Law, note 8, supra. A 'framework agreement procedure' is a 'procedure conducted in two stages: a first stage to select a supplier (or suppliers) or a contractor (or contractors) to be a party (or parties) to a framework agreement with a procuring entity, and a second stage to award a procurement contract under the framework agreement to a supplier or contractor party to the framework agreement'. A framework agreement itself is defined as an 'agreement between the procuring entity and the selected supplier (or suppliers) or contractor (or contractors) concluded upon completion of the first stage of the framework agreement procedure', and a 'procurement contract' as a 'contract concluded between the procuring entity and a supplier (or suppliers) or a contractor (or contractors) at the end of the procurement proceedings'.

enacting states.[135] Consequently, all procedural safeguards apply throughout both stages of a framework agreement procedure, unless they are varied expressly (such as for the contents of solicitation documents, and for award notices and standstill provisions).[136] Where requirements might otherwise apply to procurement contracts alone, such as regarding the rules on assessing responsiveness, evaluation criteria and standstill provisions, there are express inclusions of framework agreements within the scope of the provisions concerned.[137]

The Model Law provides for the three models of framework agreements set out in Chapter 2,[138] with a maximum duration for closed framework agreements.[139] Unlike the European Union, however, the Model Law does

---

[135] It should be noted, however, that the definition does not discuss whether or not a framework agreement procedure is a procurement method or not, which does raise some uncertainty about open framework agreements procedures, which operate as stand-alone technique (closed framework agreements, however, are concluded using a procurement method under chapters III–V of the Model Law). Whether or not obligations to maximise competition in the circumstances of the procurement applies is uncertain. In light of UNCITRAL's policy objectives, this is a surprising omission; it was drawn to the Working Group's attention, but was not corrected. See 'A Critical Evaluation of the Revised UNCITRAL Model Law Provisions on Regulating Framework Agreements', note 24, supra, in which it is recommended that states considering adopting the Model Law should include an open framework agreement procedure as a procurement method under the national legislation concerned.

[136] Under Articles 58, 22 and 23, Model Law, note 8, supra.

[137] Articles 10, 11 and 23, note 8, supra, though there are limited exceptions for awards under the general thresholds provided for in those articles and for second-stage awards without competition (see, further, Chapter 9).

[138] See Article 2(e) (i)–(v), Model Law, note 8, supra. The Model Law does not provide for the type of framework under which suppliers can unilaterally improve their offers. The policy reason this exclusion that there would be no mechanism for preventing the procuring entity from passing information to favoured suppliers to assist them in improving their relative position, or for monitoring improved offers, and so it was considered that the risks to competition, transparency and integrity would outweigh any possible benefits from the use of this type of framework agreement. Other commentators consider that there are mitigating steps that can reduce the risks, such as through online publication of the current terms offered by the suppliers (although not necessarily their identity). See, for example, Sue Arrowsmith, 'Public Procurement: An Appraisal of the UNCITRAL Model Law as a Global Standard', *International and Comparative Law Quarterly* 53 (2004): 17–46, at p. 18.

[139] However, the maximum duration itself is deferred to enacting states as it was considered that there was no single appropriate duration (experience indicated a wide variety in practice, reflecting rules designed to provide a period long enough to allow repeat purchases and administrative efficiency, to accommodate administrative requirements and to set a limit that would not exceed the period during which the market would remain relatively stable). Consequently, a three-to-five-year maximum duration is recommended in the Guide to Enactment of the UNCITRAL Model Law on Public Procurement (2012), Official Records of the General Assembly, Sixty-seventh Session, Supplement No. 17 (para 46, UN document A/67/17). The text of the Guide to Enactment is available at www.uncitral.org/uncitral/uncitral_texts/procurement_infrastructure.html. Hereafter, Guide to Enactment. The Guide to Enactment also emphasises that a maximum duration should not be taken as an indication of an appropriate duration, which should be considered on a case-by-case basis.

not envisage extensions to concluded framework agreements or exemptions from the prescribed maximum duration, though the Guide to Enactment notes that enacting states may wish to do so. It adds that enacting states should ensure that any exceptions are limited, such as to the situations in which single-source procurement might be an alternative – emergency situations, for example. On the other hand, and as is the case for dynamic purchasing systems under the 2014 Directive, there is no maximum duration for open framework agreements (though they must be concluded for a fixed duration).[140]

The Model Law (unlike the EU Directive) is not subject to a general *de minimis* threshold, so the rules on aggregation are more flexible and are designed to ensure that potential suppliers are presented with the best information available.[141] The solicitation documents are not required to include minimum or maximum aggregate values unless they are in fact known at that stage.

As in the European Union, UNCITRAL was concerned about the issue of a lengthy or sizeable purchase order or procurement contract towards the end of the validity of the framework agreement, not only to avoid abuse but also to ensure that procuring entities are not purchasing outdated or excessively priced items. However (perhaps conveniently), it was decided that the question could not appropriately be addressed in primary legislation, but should be handled through other rules and guidance by enacting states.

Emphasizing transparency requirements, the Model Law requires the procuring entities that can use a multi-user framework agreement to be identified at the outset (so that new users cannot later join or purchase through the framework agreement, contrary to the position in the United States but similar to that in the European Union), that only parties to the framework agreement can be awarded procurement contracts under the framework agreement[142] and that the framework agreement be concluded in writing. The framework agreement itself is required to set out the rules and all the terms for second-stage competition, including the envisaged frequency of the competition, and anticipated time frame for presenting second-stage bids – though this information is not binding on the

---

[140] Article 62(1)(a), Model Law, note 8, supra.
[141] They are given practical effect by rules on valuation of the procurement in Article 12, which prevents artificial splitting of contracts to avoid procedural requirements, and requires the value of all envisaged call-offs to be aggregated.
[142] This rule applies to both open and closed framework agreements. In the case of open framework agreements, it is therefore necessary that there are clear procedures to ensure swift assessment of submissions to become a party to the open framework agreement, which are set out in the Model Law and discussed in Chapter 12.

procuring entity.[143] Finally, and in order to protect the integrity of the process, the Model Law prohibits changes to the description of the subject matter (other changes are allowed only in so far as they are envisaged in the framework agreement).[144]

As set out in the following subsections, the Model Law regulates both stages of the procedure in some detail. The first procedural requirement is expressed in permitting the use of framework agreements in certain conditions only: this requirement does not have an equivalent in the EU or US systems. The overall objective is to ensure that the procuring entity considers whether or not the use of a framework agreement is appropriate and plans accordingly.[145]

The first stage is regulated in the manner that all procurement methods are provided for in the Model Law (as explained below), with separate provisions for closed and open framework agreements. The second stage of Model 2 and Model 3 framework agreements, both of which involve competition, is addressed under common provisions and Model 1 framework agreements that have a non-competitive second stage are regulated separately. The decisions and actions taken during both stages are all subject to challenge under Chapter VIII of the Model Law.

This overall summary points to a relatively high level of detail in the provisions regulating framework agreements procedures. The Model Law is unusual in regulating the second stage in detail, and so the concerns about risks to transparency and competition raised in the EU and US systems above are therefore addressed. The Guide to Enactment explains that appropriate planning and design can avoid unnecessary procedural complexity — for example, ensuring that the two stages do not simply repeat rounds of competition between the same or reduced numbers of suppliers in a multi-supplier framework agreement. In addition, many procedural steps are designed to regulate how the framework agreement is itself designed and structured and to ensure appropriate participation and competition, and appropriate planning should allow a streamlined and straightforward call-off stage, as is further discussed in Chapter 12.

*First stage of the procedure* As regards closed framework agreements, and following the EU system, the main requirement is that the procuring entity must follow the rules of Chapter II of the Model Law on choice of

---

[143] This information may include technical issues for accessing online framework agreements, for example.
[144] Article 63, Model Law, note 8, supra.   [145] See, further, Chapter 12.

procurement method and solicitation, so the Model Law's normal transparency and competition safeguards apply.[146] In practical terms, the requirement means that the first stage must be concluded using open tendering unless the relevant conditions for use of another procurement method apply – relevant circumstances include specialised and complex procurement, urgent procurement and low-value and simple procurement. As these situations are only exceptionally likely to arise in framework agreements procedures, this flexibility may simply add to the complexity of the planning process and mandating open tendering would be an overall more straightforward approach, with fewer risks of abuse in limiting competition for a procedure that will already close the market to full competition for the duration of the framework agreement.

Flexibility in the solicitation documents as compared with open tendering is permitted, so that certain information normally issued (such as precise quantities) can be omitted in favour of estimates,[147] and evaluation criteria can be set out in a more flexible manner. There can be different evaluation criteria and relative weighting at the first and second stages, provided that they are disclosed in advance,[148] but both the framework agreement and the call-off (i.e. procurement contract) must be made to the lowest-priced or most advantageous bid.[149] Where there is to be a second stage of competition, the relative weight of the evaluation criteria can also vary within a predetermined range if it is disclosed in the solicitation

---

[146] In particular, Article 28 requires the decision on the procurement method to take account of the circumstances of the procurement and to maximise competition; the default rule under section II of chapter II requires open solicitation. In the European Union, as noted in Methods for purchasing on-going requirements: the system of framework agreements and dynamic purchasing systems under the EC Directive and UK procurement regulations, note 33, supra at p. 137, one of the normal four procurement methods must be used to award the framework (Article 32(2) of Directive 2004/EC/18).

[147] Subject to a general rule that estimates are required if there are terms that cannot be definitively established at that stage (Article 59(2)(c)), Model Law, note 8, supra. Where the goods or services concerned may be subject to price or currency fluctuations, or the combination of service providers may vary, it may be counter-productive to try to set a contract price at this stage. A common criticism of framework agreements of this type is that there is a tendency towards contract prices at hourly rates that are generally relatively expensive, and task-based or project-based pricing can alternatively be considered therefore, where appropriate.

[148] The basis of the award will normally, but need not necessarily, be the same at both stages; for example, the procuring entity may decide that from the highest-ranked suppliers at the first stage, the lowest-priced responsive bid at the second stage will be taken.

[149] The possible flexibility to allow for rotation or cab-rank awards in the European Union is therefore not permitted. Where longer-term competition is a concern, however, evaluation criteria under Article 11 (Model Law, note 8, supra) can include criteria designed to pursue socio-economic policies that do not need to relate to the subject matter of the contract. There are no reports that states have sought to use this flexibility in practice as at the date of writing, however.

documents.[150] This flexibility allows the procuring entity to set the relative weights and their precise needs only at the second stage (important in longer-term procurement and when centralised purchasing agencies or groups of procuring entities are operating the framework agreement). The prior publication of the predetermined range is intended to promote transparency and integrity (preventing the use of vague and broad criteria to favour certain suppliers or contractors, or abusive changes to them).[151] A further caveat is that the use of such a range may not lead to a change in the description of the subject matter of the procurement.[152]

*Second stage of the procedure* There are relatively limited provisions for the second stage of Model 1 and Model 2 framework agreements without second-stage competition. The solicitation documents at the first stage are required to set out 'the manner in which the procurement contract will be awarded' at the second stage which, cumulatively with the requirements on evaluation criteria, should ensure that the terms and conditions are determined and available in advance (this information is also required to be repeated in the framework agreement itself). The aim is to ensure transparency, but call-offs without second-stage competition are exempted from otherwise generally applicable requirements (a) for *ex-ante* notifications to all suppliers that are parties to a multi-supplier framework agreement prior to a call-off and (b) for a standstill period, so that the protections from abuse in practice may not have more impact than their equivalents in the EU system.

The second stage (mini-competition) under Model 2 and Model 3 framework agreements is regulated in more detail.[153] The call-off must be made in accordance with the procedures set out in Article 62, and also as set out in the framework agreement. The transparency protections, here, include that alternative evaluation criteria cannot be introduced, and that only parties to the framework agreement can be awarded a procurement contract.[154] The procedures for the mini-competitions are based on those governing open tendering in Chapter III of the Model Law, including rules on the contents of the invitation to a call-off, a standstill

---

[150] This approach was designed to balance the need for flexibility and transparency, and can also have benefits where collusion is a potential problem: see, further, Chapter 9.
[151] Oversight of the use of framework agreements can be useful to identify, for example, if the range set out in the framework agreement is so wide as to make the safeguard meaningless in practice.
[152] Article 63, Model Law, note 8, supra.   [153] Article 62, ibid.
[154] Article 62(2), ibid. This rule has to be borne in mind if the procuring entity wishes to use an electronic reverse auction within an open framework, in which normally the procuring entity is able to assess qualifications and responsiveness after the auction.

period[155] and individual award notices unless the call-offs fall below a *de minimis* threshold. In such cases, a cumulative notice is required of all call-offs under a framework agreement, at least once a year. Consequently, as a general rule, the full safeguards of the Model Law's procedures apply to the award of the procurement contract itself at the end of the mini-competition.

A consequence of this latter point is that reference needs to be made to the general rules set out in Chapter 1. Some of the concerns about the incumbency advantage discussed in the context of the US system may be alleviated by the cross-application of provisions requiring the submission deadline to 'allow sufficient time' for suppliers to prepare their bids in the circumstances of the relevant procurement.[156] Unlike the EU Directive, there is no stipulated minimum time period, allowing enacting states to provide specific time limits in their regulations or other rules should they so choose (noting that so doing would enhance certainty and transparency).

As is the case in the European Union and the United States, a key issue is identifying the suppliers that will be invited to participate in the mini-competition, and UNCITRAL took the concerns raised by the US experience, described above, into account.[157] Practical issues so considered included that the additional costs of sending a notice to all rather than some suppliers were negligible in electronic systems; that, in other frameworks, and as the number of suppliers was likely to be small, those costs should not dictate the policy; and that there was a risk that large numbers of unresponsive bids might need to be evaluated, and a compromise solution was agreed. As a result, the default rule is that all parties to the framework agreement must be invited to participate in the call-off, with a limited exception. The exception as originally conceived was based on the 204 EU Directive (which provided that all 'capable' suppliers should be invited). Concerns were raised in particular about ensuring objectivity in the assessment of 'capability',[158] so the compromise solution is that either

---

[155] However, if there is a single minimum standstill period in the national law concerned (as the Model Law indicates, despite suggestions that a shorter period for most call-offs would be appropriate), the impact would be that the call-off procedure is unnecessarily delayed.

[156] Article 14 (3), Model Law, note 8, supra.

[157] A/66/17, para 133, and A/CN.9/WG.I/WP.44/Add.1, note 13, supra, which described that US experience.

[158] In A/CN.9/731/Add.9, at para 7 under the guidance to Article 61(now 62), it is noted that the assessment should be objective, because the framework agreement should set out the main parameters as to whether individual suppliers can fulfil the requirement concerned (by reference to quantities, particular combinations of requirements, etc.).

*all* suppliers must be invited or only 'capable' suppliers can be invited, but in the latter situation, a prior notice of the call-off must be provided to all suppliers, who can then request participation.[159] Some commentators have suggested that this requirement is cumbersome in the same way as the first iteration of the EU's dynamic purchasing system,[160] but the Guide to Enactment notes that the notification process can be automated, and there is no requirement to wait for a period of time to elapse before the mini-competition itself is held.[161] In addition, the Guide notes that that second-stage competitions in open frameworks should be publicised on the website operating the framework agreement as a matter of best practice.

## 5.3 Consistent issues arising among the systems considered

It was observed in the US system that the reasons for failures of competition in ID/IQs are not limited to a lack of regulation: a 'noticeable rift between policy and practice' was observed,[162] though many scholars[163] and commentators have emphasised the need for further regulations requiring competition and transparency at the second stage of ID/IQ contracts. Although the US system is now considered to favour second-stage competitive awards as a general proposition for larger task orders, the system may still be considered both to remain 'grossly uneven' in terms of transparency, and still to labour under 'uncertain competition'.[164]

Competition and transparency requirements at the call-off stage are features that characterise framework agreements practices in the European Union and the Model Law and they are more rigorous participation rules and transparency standards for call-offs, prohibiting material changes in awarded framework agreements, limiting end-of-term call-offs and extending review competence.

---

[159] A/66/17, paras 130–133, the provision added being 'only to each of those parties of the framework agreement then capable of meeting the needs of that procuring entity in the subject matter of the procurement, provided that, at the same time, notice of the second-stage competition is given to all parties to the framework agreement so that they have the opportunity to participate in the second-stage competition'. It was also noted that the Guide to Enactment would address the risks of challenges if such an approach were not followed and would advise on the manner of fulfilling the notice requirement (e.g. through electronic means, to minimise the administrative burden).
[160] Framework agreements, EU procurement law and the practice, note 24, supra.
[161] A/CN.9/731/Add.9, note 13, supra, Guidance to Article 61 (now 62), para 6.
[162] Commercial Purchasing: The Chasm between the United States Government's Evolving Policy and Practice, note 80, supra, at p. 6.
[163] For a critical assessment of the ID/IQ contract system, see 'Are ID/IQs Inefficient? Sharing Lessons with European Framework Contracting', note 69, supra.
[164] 'Are ID/IQs Inefficient? Sharing Lessons with European Framework Contracting', note 101, supra, at p. 561.

Nonetheless, concerns that full competition and transparency requirements would dilute the administrative efficiency that framework agreements are designed to offer mean that individual call-offs are exempted from some significant protections. Chief among these are standstill periods, *ex-ante* notices of many call-offs (the rules, as we have seen, are different in the EU and UNCITRAL systems, but some exemptions apply in both cases) and exemptions for award notices, though the requirements for DPSs are more robust. The US experience also demonstrates the importance of practical and institutional measures to support requirements for competition – transparency measures in reasonable time and permitting reviews or protests of second-stage awards being among the most important. Given the mandatory use of e-procurement systems in the EU system, and their encouragement in the Model Law, and the rules on open framework agreements procedures including those for DPSs, some of the procedural exemptions in these systems appear difficult to justify. Furthermore, if national systems do not undertake in-depth evaluation of data, procedures and outcomes, the difference between policy and practice noted for the US system may appear in these systems, too.

In the context of dynamic markets and e-procurement systems, the US 'most-favoured customer' approach could also be harnessed to avoid unnecessary procedural steps such as a competitive call-off in favour of a discounted e-catalogue approach where commercial items are being procured, as has been recognised as potentially beneficial in the European Union.[165] This approach, when combined with the Model Law's transparency requirements to issue public electronic *ex-ante* notices of call-offs,[166] should ensure that offers can be considered – to adopt the US term – 'fair and reasonable'.

Encouraging the use of commercial items to benefit from discounted commercial prices to reflect economies of scale when selling to the government is a welcome innovation, but whether better prices will be realised will largely depend on the behaviour of procuring entities. As we have seen in Chapter 4, if required to discount from commercial prices, suppliers will participate only where they can still make reasonable profit, which means if the costs of doing business with the government significantly exceed that of doing business in the private sector and likely economies of scale, they may choose not to participate at all. The suggested approach, therefore,

---

[165] Abby Semple, *A Practical Guide to Public Procurement* (Oxford University Press, 2015), at p. 125.
[166] Recommended as a manner of providing notice to awardees in open framework agreements under the UNCITRAL Model Law (Model Law, note 8, supra).

presupposes genuinely commercial behaviour on the part of procuring entities – behaviour that, as we have seen, may be difficult to achieve in practice while following the general tenor of public procurement rules.

The policy choices required to balance procedural efficiency, competition, transparency and accountability are complex, and there is no one-size-fits-all solution, as we shall explain in Chapter 12. Finally, the business model of centralised purchasing agencies and the organisational conflicts of interest that fee-for-use types can encourage are further policy issues, which we address in Chapter 11.

## 5.4 Chapter summary

International experience demonstrates that the following areas require more stringent requirements in almost all systems:

- More robust transparency and competition at the second stage, which currently operates to variable degrees 'under the radar', are needed, notably as regards prior notifications at the call-off stage and award notices.
- Concerns that imposing those requirements will necessarily undermine the administrative efficiency of the entire procedure appear to be unfounded, as practical examples from the DPS in the EU and the Model Law's procedures also indicate.
- In the US system, there are significant efforts towards reform in these areas, but they are not universally applicable.
- There is a critical exemption from practical measures to enforce transparency and competition requirements – both the standstill and review or challenge mechanisms, to varying degrees. The US system now permits larger call-offs to be protested, and the EU debriefing requirements for DPSs are welcome improvements, but exemptions from any scrutiny of non-competitive call-offs are troublesome.
- Self-financing centralised purchasing agencies may increase the risk of distortions in the market.

Policy responses to the transparency and competition issues raised are discussed in Chapters 11 and 12.

CHAPTER 6

# International experience in centralised purchasing

## 6.1 Introduction

In the preceding chapter, we examined the development of regulation and practice in framework agreements, and highlighted some of the concerns that have arisen. In this chapter, we shall have a closer look at some concrete experiences in the use of framework agreements for demand aggregation through centralised purchasing agencies (CPAs), using examples from selected countries in several geographical regions. Collecting data, even at an aggregate level, from single procuring entities concluding framework agreements for their own purchases is always a challenging task and, as we have seen, is not commonly undertaken. For this reason, we shall present some evidence on the use of framework agreements for *centralised* procurement; that is, those awarded by CPAs[1] in different countries on behalf of other public bodies.

Before providing the details concerning the activities of specific CPAs, it is quite instructive to summarise the result of a survey carried out by the OECD in 2014.[2] In most of the OECD member countries surveyed, CPAs act as a contracting authority aggregating demand and purchasing (81 per cent), and as manager of the system for awarding framework agreements or other consolidated instruments, from which contracting authorities then order (78 per cent). In fewer countries, though, CPAs coordinate training for public officials in charge of public procurement (33 per cent) and establish policies for contracting authorities (30 per cent). CPBs in Greece, Ireland, Switzerland, the United Kingdom and the United States exercise all the above-mentioned functions, whereas CPBs in nine OECD member countries (33 per cent) perform a single role. Table 6.1 reports the details of the role carried out by CPAs in different countries.

---

[1] The main challenges of designing framework agreements for centralised procurement are dealt in Chapter 11.
[2] The results of the survey will become part of the 2015 OECD report 'Government at a Glance 2014'.

Table 6.1 *Role of central purchasing bodies in OECD countries*

| | CPBs act as a contracting authority aggregating demand and purchasing | CPBs act as manager of the national system awarding framework agreements or other consolidated instruments, from which contracting authorities then order | CPBs coordinate training for public officials in charge of public procurement | CPBs establish policies for contracting authorities |
|---|---|---|---|---|
| Austria | X | X | | |
| Belgium | | X | | |
| Canada | X | X | | |
| Chile | | X | X | X |
| Denmark | | X | | X |
| Estonia | | X | | |
| Finland | X | X | | |
| France | X | X | X | |
| Germany | X | | | |
| Greece | X | X | X | X |
| Hungary | X | X | | |
| Ireland | X | X | X | X |
| Italy | X | X | | |
| Korea | X | X | X | |
| Luxembourg | X | | | |
| New Zealand | X | X | X | |
| Norway | X | | | |
| Poland | X | | | |

Table 6.1 (*cont.*)

| | CPBs act as a contracting authority aggregating demand and purchasing | CPBs act as manager of the national system awarding framework agreements or other consolidated instruments, from which contracting authorities then order | CPBs coordinate training for public officials in charge of public procurement | CPBs establish policies for contracting authorities |
|---|---|---|---|---|
| Portugal | X | X | | |
| Slovak Republic | X | | | |
| Slovenia | X | X | | |
| Spain | X | X | | X |
| Sweden | X | X | | |
| Switzerland | X | X | X | X |
| Turkey | X | | | |
| United Kingdom | X | X | X | X |
| United States | X | X | X | X |
| Brazil | X | | X | X |
| Colombia | | X | X | X |
| OECD 27 | 22 | 21 | 9 | 8 |

*Source:* 2014 OECD Survey on Public Procurement.

*International experience in centralised purchasing* 127

Among the OECD member countries where CPAs are present, almost all of them have one or more CPA(s) at the central level, while almost half of them also have CPA(s) at the regional level (48 per cent). With regard to their legal status, in some OECD member countries, CPAs are state-owned enterprises (19 per cent), as evidenced by those in Finland, Italy and Turkey, whereas the majority of CPAs either operate under a line ministry (33 per cent) or function as a government agency (48 per cent). In some countries, as in Ireland, a preliminary discussion on the appropriate degree of independence of the CPB is taking place. Figure 6.1 provides the details on the CPAs' legal status in each country.

The OECD survey is also instructive as regards the reasons surveyed countries adduced for creating CPAs. These include better prices of goods and services (100 per cent); lower transaction costs (96 per cent); improved capacity and expertise (81 per cent); increased legal, technical, economic and contractual certainty (81 per cent); and greater simplicity and usability (77 per cent). Additionally, CPAs are increasingly playing an important

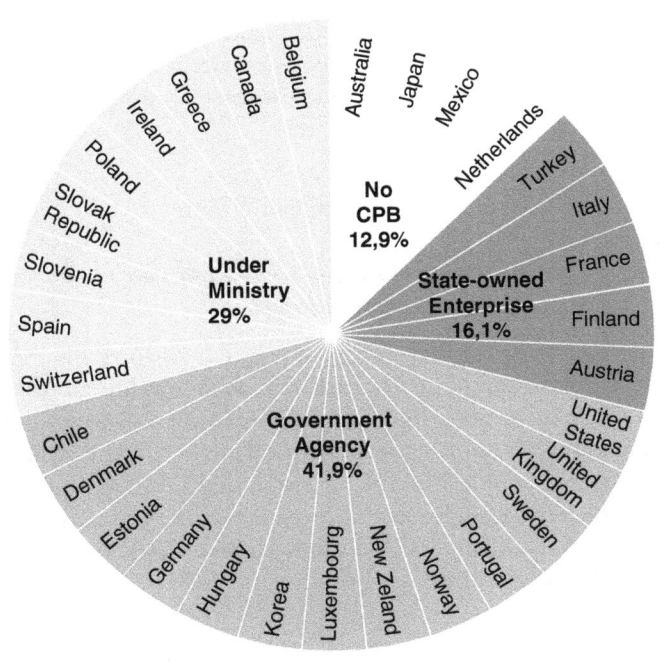

Figure 6.1 Legal status of central purchasing bodies.
Source: 2014 OECD Survey on Public Procurement.

role in the implementation of secondary (or horizontal) policy objectives. More precisely, 58 per cent of the CPAs in the OECD member countries surveyed include environmental considerations as award criteria in more than half of the cases, and smaller numbers of CPAs (28 per cent) include support to SMEs in their awarding criteria for more than half of the cases, while 36 per cent infrequently do so.

CPAs most commonly establish framework agreements for standardised products and services. Typically, they focus on office equipment (mainly ICT and essential services), office furniture and supply, telecommunications and energy. Some CPAs have also established framework agreements covering more advanced services, including architectural and engineering consultancies, management and audit services, or when purchasing sophisticated goods such as helicopters.[3] Construction, defence-related purchases and some health services are often excluded from the remit of national CPAs[4] and are often entrusted to sectorial CPAs.

The examples given underscore – as we noted in Chapter 5 – that the mechanisms and procedures used for aggregating procurement vary widely. While this variety once again demonstrates the flexibility of the tool, it also offers a challenge to the policymaker, as the lessons to improve practice that can be drawn from any one system may not transfer to another. The main practical and policy issues arising in centralised purchasing will be considered in Chapter 11.

## 6.2 The European Union

### 6.2.1 *Italy – The experience of Consip Ltd.: the national central purchasing body*

Created in 1997 as a private company entirely owned by the Italian Ministry of Economy and Finance (MEF), Consip was initially established to operate complex projects in the fields of information technology with the ultimate aim of promoting technological change in the Italian public administration and, more broadly, of sustaining the development of an information society through the dissemination of the use of ICT. Because of its expertise in the field of ICT, in 1999 Consip was also entrusted with the mission of implementing, on behalf of the MEF, the Programme for

---

[3] Fact Sheet on main Features and Characteristics of Central Purchasing Bodies, April 2014, 2nd edition, paper prepared by the CPB Network for the Lisbon meeting.

[4] In the defence sector, procurement is normally centralised by the Ministry of Defence itself and thus purchase fragmentation is virtually non-existent.

Table 6.2 *Value of purchases through Consip's framework agreements in 2014*

| Framework agreements categories | Value of purchases through active framework agreements in 2014 (€M) |
|---|---|
| Common-use goods and services | 611 |
| Energy (e.g. petrol, gas, electricity) | 1,810 |
| IT (goods and services) | 127 |
| Health care (goods and services) | 17 |
| Real estate (buildings maintenance) | 755 |
| Telecommunication (e.g. Internet services, telephone services) | 138 |
| Total value of purchases | 3,457 |

*Source:* Consip's dataware house (June 2015).

the Rationalisation of Public Expenditure in Goods and Services through the use of information technologies, innovative purchasing tools and centralised procurement initiatives.

Since 2000, Consip has been using framework agreements on behalf of central and local government. In the overwhelming majority of cases, Consip relies on single-supplier Model 1 framework agreements. Table 6.2 reports the value of purchases carried out by Italian public bodies through Consip's active framework agreements during 2014. Purchases are aggregated in seven macro-categories.

### 6.2.2 The first multi-award Model 2 framework agreement for IT services in Italy

Throughout its sixteen years of projects management for the MEF,[5] Consip's activities were split into three main groups:

(a) optimisation of the organisational and functional processes of the MEF's departments. These projects were characterised by a fairly low level of IT complexity and included the digitalisation and automation of administrative procedures as well as the enhancement of

---

[5] Consip's engagement in complex IT projects lasted until 2013, when its entire IT activities (and associated human resources) were assigned to another private MEF-owned company, Sogei S.p.A.

knowledge tools for the departments' day-to-day operations, and the creation of top-level decision-making support tools;
(b) improvement of access to and circulation of information, both within and beyond the ministry;
(c) rationalisation and coordination of the IT expenditure and management of the technical IT infrastructure of the MEF.

The span of activities ranged from process optimisation and adoption of modern management technologies and methodologies to rationalisation and coordination of expenditure on IT items and tools. Consip also provided consultancy and project support covering all the software life-cycle phases, from needs and requirements codification to software delivery, maintenance and process integration in the ministry's organisational structure.

At the outset of Consip's IT mission in 1997, both the dimensions and the features of the technological projects were such that awarding (simple) contracts for acquiring well-defined products and services was probably the most appropriate strategy. Indeed, this approach guaranteed a focus on specific projects without limiting the possibility of adopting innovative solutions. The nature and size of such contracts were usually best suited to SMEs, and the project activities themselves were typically allocated to the contractor, rather than to Consip's internal resources.

The main drawback of this approach was that it hinged on a high number of lengthy procurement processes, thus delaying the time needed for a complete solution to become operational. In addition, activating of more than one contract with more than one contractor at the same time raised process and transaction costs considerably, thus triggering complaints by the MEF's final users.

Over the years, Consip moved towards an 'all-purpose frame contracts' (APFC) approach. Such contracts were typically of much larger value and longer duration than simple contracts. A typical APFC was, for instance, a contract for the outsourcing of a data centre or the development of a very large software project, such as a software for the management of EU structural funds. Due to the broad scope of these projects, the actual tasks and activities to be carried out were fully defined at the second stage. This is because the tender documentation was written and the contract was awarded when the project was at the very early stage of its life cycle. Hence, an APFC set guidelines and general service conditions about tasks which would be pinned down at a later stage, once the contractor had been selected on the basis of a series of project-based but broad requirements. The perceived benefits from APFCs typically included a reduction of transaction costs, a more secure continuity of the contractor's involvement which favoured a better learning (of the final users' evolving needs) and productivity improvements in the adapted technological solutions. As a consequence, a more solid customer–contractor relationship was perceived to emerge which, among other things, provided the contractor with 'informal' incentives to commit to tasks in areas which were consequential to, albeit not explicitly included in, the original scope of the APFC itself.

However, APFCs, while solving many of the problems stemming from simple contracts, suffered from other kinds of drawbacks. First, the procurement process became overstretched, and thus IT solutions were sometimes obsolete before being fully available.[6] Second, the sizeable value of the average APFC constituted a concrete barrier to entry for SMEs, a particularly unwelcome development given that SMEs in the ICT market are considered more flexible and innovative than bigger operators. Third, it became clear that uncertainty about the nature of individual tasks to be performed shifted competition from quality to price at the award stage. This hurt suppliers' profit margins and negatively affected quality at the delivery or execution stage.

In 2009, the quest for the appropriate compromise between 'simple contracts' and APFCs led Consip to design the first multi-supplier incomplete framework agreement for IT services in Italy. The inspiration behind the idea was to strike a balance between flexibility and timeliness of technological solutions, aggregating the procurement of similar, albeit non-identical, projects, and ensuring effective price competition for well-defined tasks. A multi-supplier incomplete framework agreement was considered the appropriate solution for the following reasons:

1. The higher number of awardees (with respect to an APFC approach) selected at the first stage of the framework agreement was expected to soften price competition at that stage, when specific needs and requirements were yet to be defined. The awardees were those firms that were best qualified and most responsive in fulfilling a broad set of needs, mainly defined in terms of technical or qualitative criteria and time optimisation.

---

[6] This situation, as we saw in the previous chapter, was a significant impetus for the reforms to the US FAR in 1994, and which led to a huge increase in ID/IQs for IT procurement in the US federal system.

2. Price competition was to become more relevant at the call-off stage when awardees would 'learn' the details of each single project to be implemented. This approach was considered to reduce the risk of 'Winner's Curse',[7] typical of competitive tenders taking place in conditions of relevant uncertainty. In addition, the reduced value of the individual procurement contract (relative to an APFC) was meant to complement the other structures designed to limit price competition at the first stage.
3. The adoption of the MEAT award criterion at the call-off stage made it possible for Consip to tailor concrete technical solutions to specific requirements. This was expected to enhance competition on the quality dimension at the call-off stage.

It was expected, however, that the design might encounter three main drawbacks. The first concerned the potentially excessive time period between the conclusion of the framework agreement and the implementation of any specific project, so that managing the call-off stage still required additional time and effort (for designing and running the bidding process and for assessment of offers). The second was a heightened risk of collusion at the call-off stage when the awardees (five out of the nine suppliers that had participated at the first stage) were sheltered from competition (i.e. from outside the framework agreement). Finally, lower-ranked awardees would find it very difficult to win any procurement contract. This was due to the asymmetric nature of competition at the call-off stage: awardees inherited a fraction of the score assigned at the first stage. As a consequence, despite the intention of softening price competition, bidders appear to have found it profitable to submit very low prices as the only way to compensate for their technical-score disadvantage.

## 6.3 The United States: The General Services Administration in the US federal system

As we saw in the previous chapter, the US Federal Acquisition Regulation (FAR) provides for a purchasing arrangement known as indefinite delivery/indefinite quantity (ID/IQ) contracts. The US General Service Administration (GSA) was established in 1949 under the Truman

---

[7] The 'Winner's Curse' refers to the circumstance whereby a bidder may not take into proper account that being awarded the procurement contract reveals that he or she held too optimistic beliefs about the contract's costs. See further Section 8.4.2.4.

administration to improve the administrative services of the federal government. GSA engages in constructing, managing and preserving government buildings by leasing and managing commercial real estate. GSA's acquisition solutions offer private sector professional services, equipment, supplies, telecommunications and information technology to government organisations and the military. GSA policies also aim at promoting management best practices and efficient government operations.[8]

GSA established the Federal Supply Schedule (FSS) programme in 1949 to facilitate federal agencies' purchase common-user items from commercial firms through schedule contracts. The Multiple-Award Schedules (MAS) programme, the largest available FSS programme, was designed and implemented to provide agencies with varying quantities of a wide range of commercially available products such as office furniture and supplies, personal computers, scientific equipment, professional services and network support.[9]

In FY 2008 federal agencies spent $45.7 billion through the MAS programme; the estimated figure for 2013 was in the region of $35 billion.[10] These figures give an idea of the extent of the responsibility that GSA has in ensuring that the government fully benefits from its bargaining power (using the negotiated procedure we have seen, which is designed to ensure that the government obtains 'fair and reasonable' prices), and of the enormous scale of the US federal programme as compared with its European and other regional counterparts. The White House in 2012 stated that GWACs for office supplies[11] had since 2010 'saved over $140 million by offering lower prices than any single agency could negotiate on its own. Similar vehicles for domestic delivery services saved over $31 million in FY 2011 over what agencies were paying under previous agreements'.[12]

The largest single MAS schedule is Schedule 70 – General Purpose Commercial Information Technology Equipment, Software, and Services,[13]

---

[8] http://gsa.gov/portal/category/100000.
[9] Federal Acquisition Regulation (FAR), Code of Federal Regulations (CFR) Title 48, 8.402. FAR 2005-83/07-02-2015, available at www.acquisition.gov/?q=browsefar.
[10] www.gsa.gov/portal/mediaId/201491/fileName/GSA2014AFR_InspectorGeneralsAssessment.action.
[11] Described in Section 5.2.3.2.
[12] Memorandum for the Heads of Executive Departments and Agencies, Executive Office of the President, Office of Management and Budget, 5 December 2012, 'Improving Acquisition through Strategic Sourcing', available at www.whitehouse.gov/sites/default/files/omb/memoranda/2013/m-13-02_0.pdf.
[13] http://gsa.gov/portal/content/104506.

which has more than 5,000 MAS contract holders. The main categories of Schedule 70 are as follows:

- Cloud IT Services
- Computer and Networking Hardware
- Cyber Security
- Data Center and Storage
- IT Mandates and Initiatives
- Satellite Services
- SmartBuy: Commercial Software Solutions
- Software and Applications
- Sustainability
- Systems Life Cycles Integration
- Telecommunications, Wireless and Mobility
- Telepresence

As a further indication of the scale of Schedule 70, a subcategory of Computer and Networking Hardware, 'Purchase of New Equipment', has 1,005 contractors, most of which have their products listed as e-catalogues under the GSA Advantage! online system. GSA claims, on the basis of its own review of 700 non-GSA government contracts covering Schedule 70 goods and services, that 'the time it takes a government entity to award its own full and open contract, using products and services readily available from GSA ... [is] 25 months to complete on average. This timeframe is well over the average of IT Schedule 70 contacts. Further, in 77 percent of the 700 contracts examined, contract awards were ultimately made to vendors that already hold existing IT contracts'.[14] However, savings in time, even if of wider application than this limited survey, may not be matched by other performance criteria. The GSA's inspector-general concluded in 2013 that, as regards MAS contracts:

> The majority of vendors provided information that was not current, accurate, and/or complete to support their proposed prices. Nearly half of the vendors had minimal or no non-federal commercial customers, making it impossible to use non-governmental commercial sales as a basis for determining price reasonableness. Over a quarter of the vendors ... audited

---

[14] Special Report into GSA Schedule 70, commissioned by the Content Solutions unit, an independent editorial arm of 1105 Government Information Group, available at http://fcw.com/microsites/2011/gsa-schedule/index.aspx.

supplied labour that did not meet the minimum educational and/or experience qualifications required by the contracts.[15]

GSA's Strategic Plan for 2014–2018 states that GSA will improve in areas identified as weak, and will, for example, save $255 million ($111 million during FY 2014 and $144 million during FY 2015) through the use of the Federal Strategic Sourcing initiative, which – among other things – seeks to improve the information available through data sources to negotiate better prices.[16]

The MAS programme itself is funded through a fee-per-service approach, known as 'Program Industrial Funding Fee' (IFF), which is a small percentage (0.75 per cent) of reported sales under MAS contracts, and therefore considered simple and transparent. It was reported in 2012 that, nonetheless, the IFF was set at a level that 'consistently generates net operating revenue in excess of amounts required to recover MAS Program costs, make MAS Program investments and maintain a risk mitigating buffer'.[17] Since the IFF is included in the price of items, the indication is that this may be one contributing factor, albeit a small one, to findings that MAS prices were not lower than commercial prices,[18] but, more significantly, might be operating to reduce the uptake of aggregating purchasing approaches ('strategic sourcing') that could potentially increase value for money.

## 6.4 Latin America

### 6.4.1 The system of Price Registration: the Brazilian approach to framework agreements

The Brazilian system of Price Registration (PR) is a pooled procurement system whereby several public agencies and entities group together to carry out a joint competitive bidding to purchase goods and services at uniform

---

[15] Major Issues from Multiple Award Schedule Pre-award Audits, Audit Memorandum Number A120050-3, available at www.gsaig.gov/?LinkServID=F4D7B876-D9EA-4133-898D063ACE C15999&showMeta=0. Pre-award audits are designed to ensure 'fair and reasonable' contract prices, and are undertaken before an initial MAS award and during any renewal of a MAS contract. The aim is to improve the GDA's negotiating position.
[16] USA GSA FY 2014–2018 Strategic Plan, at page SP-5, available at www.gsa.gov/portal/mediaId/187599/fileName/GSA_FY14-18_GSA_Strategic_Plan.action.
[17] Report of the Audit of the MAS Program IFF (Report Number A090256/Q/A/P12003), by the US General Services Administration, Office of Inspector General, 3 February 2012, available at www.gsaig.gov/?LinkServID=47A49706-9720-35B7-193A7E6FF2A3353C&showMeta=0.
[18] See Section 5.2.3.3.

prices and terms.[19] Those public entities joining the PR system may contract the awardee[20] to provide goods and services and order shipments of various sizes at their own convenience and without a predetermined frequency within a period of twelve months.[21] As in the remainder of the Brazilian public procurement system, the procuring entity must specify the reserve price; that is, its maximum willingness to pay for the goods or services. The reserve price is normally determined through a market-wide survey.

The procurement transactions in the Price Registration System must rely on an open competitive bidding, open hybrid or electronic competitive bidding. Lowest price is the only award criterion allowed in PR.[22] According to the Brazilian law, the PR system should be employed when a set of off-the-shelf goods or services are acquired by more than one agency, entity or government programme during one year and when, by the nature of the goods, it is not possible to stipulate precisely the extent of demand for them.[23]

#### 6.4.1.1 *Institutions and assignments*

There are basically two types of institutions in the Brazilian PR system: buyers (public bodies and entities) and sellers (suppliers). Within the PR pool, buyers are classified into three different classes: 'manager-participant', 'no-manager-participant' and 'free rider'. The manager-participant is the public entity responsible for the procurement procedures in the PR (i.e. invitation of suppliers for competitive bidding, market

---

[19] This approach has historically also been common in the United Kingdom – see, for example, www.schoolsbuyingclub.com/.
[20] The Brazilian Procurement Act also allows for more than one supplier to be selected. This normally happens if a public body makes use of either the open hybrid or electronic competitive bidding procedures (see further note 22).
[21] The Brazilian System of Price Registration is regulated by Decree 3.931/01 and 4.342/02.
[22] Brazilian government's bodies may use the following forms of procurement for goods, works and services: (i) open competitive bidding (a lowest-price sealed-bid auction in which any supplier is allowed to submit a bid), (ii) pre-qualified Bidding (a lowest-price sealed-bid auction in which only suppliers with a solid track record of providing good for the government are allowed to bid), (iii) invited bidding (a lowest-price sealed-bid auction in which only invited bidders are allowed to bid), (iv) open hybrid competitive bidding (a lowest-price sealed-bid auction followed by a reverse English auction in which any supplier is allowed to submit a bid) and (v) open electronic competitive bidding (an electronic reverse English auction in which any supplier is allowed to submit a bid. There are two other formats, which are used for other purposes: contest and standard open ascending price auction. Contest, for example, is used to award technical studies, scientific or art works, while standard auction is used for selling public assets.
[23] The existence of prices recorded in a certain price registration system does not require the members to sign contracts with the suppliers of the goods and services registered in the system.

research, specification of the demanded goods and quantities, definition of the reserve price and handling of the competitive procedure), and also for managing all information in the procurement transactions. A no-manager-participant is a public entity purchasing from the PR system and helping the manager organise the procurement procedure. A free rider, by contrast, does not participate in the procurement process, but it can apply for the acquisition of goods and services at prices and terms convened between the original pool and the awarded supplier at a later stage. Suppliers are all companies who apply for the contracts of supply of goods and services to be awarded through a PR-pooled procurement. Any firm that meets the requirements set by the managing agency may apply to be admitted as a new awardee of the PR minutes, the document that certifies the convened price; that is the price resulting from the competitive process.[24]

*6.4.1.2 Empirical evidence on the Price Registration benefits and inefficiencies*

There is a growing attention also among academics on both potential benefits and drawbacks of the Brazilian PR system.[25] However, almost no empirical investigation has been carried out, with the sole exception of a piece of research[26] whose findings are summarised in the following description.

Data were extracted from the ComprasNet data warehouse and contain information on all purchases by the federal government made either through a PR system or through a standard bidding between 2002 and 2009. This database also includes all purchases made by state and city governments through a PR system concluded by the federal government or to which the latter adhered.

The scope of the analysis was limited to procurement of health-related products since these products are described, standardised and coded according to the Materials and Services Code Catalogue. Such

---

[24] The winning supplier can opt out provision for the free rider.
[25] E. Fiuza, 'Um Diagnóstico Preliminar sobre as Compras Publicas Federais: Linhas de Ação e de Pesquisa para o seu Aperfeiçoamento' [in Portuguese], IPEA, mimeo, 2007; E. Fiuza, 'Desenho Institucional em Compras Públicas, Aperfeiçoando a Qualidade Regulatória' [in Portuguese], VI Jornada de Estudos da Regulação, IPEA, 2010; K. Barbosa, 'Brazilian Price Registration System: Virtues and Defects in the Light of Economic Theory', Final Report IPEA-PNPD Program, 2010.
[26] K. Barbosa and E. Fiuza, 'Demand Aggregation and Credit Risk Effects in Pooled Procurement: Evidence from the Brazilian Purchases of Pharmaceutical and Medical Supplies', EESP-FGV, mimeo, 2011.

standardisation enables a more rigorous comparison between prices of products purchased through different regimes.[27]

The database contains information on the procurement of 8,511 different items products. Products vary a great deal from drugs and medicines to medical-hospital furnishings and equipment. The products analysed are within the Classes 6,505 (drugs and medicines), 6,510 (surgical materials for dressings), 6,515 (medical and surgical instruments and supplies), 6,530 (hospital furnishings, equipment, utensils), 6,532 (hospital and surgical clothing or apparel and correlated items) and 6,545 (medical sets and assemblies) of the classification of the Federal Government Materials and Services Code Catalogue. For each product, the database provides detailed information about price, technical description and classification, year of purchase, the level of the reserve price used for the competitive procedure, estimated quantities, purchases quantities, number of bidders and buyers' identities.

Figures 6.2–6.4 depict the evolution of use of the Price Registration System by public bodies and entities of the Brazilian federal government. Such evolution is broken down by type of product according to the Federal Government Materials and Services Code Catalogue. All figures show that the Brazilian government has favoured the use of the PR system over the standard individual procurement in procuring medical-hospital products. Such migration from purchases under standard individual procurement to Price Registration is consistent with the theoretical works[28] claiming that the Price Registration enhanced the public procurement system in Brazil.

### 6.4.2 Chile

ChileCompra is Chile's procurement authority in charge of the creation and maintenance of framework agreements[29] through which public entities purchase products and services. ChileCompra (jointly with a

---

[27] The standardisation of description, coding and supply units of purchased items-products was carried out for the creation of the Health Prices Database of the Ministry of Health. The purpose was the integration of data in order to standardise and unify the language by favouring the comparisons of product prices.

[28] See note 23, supra.

[29] Framework agreements are provided for by the Public Procurement Law (no. 19.886) and related bylaw. The English version can be downloaded from www.chilecompra.cl/index.php?option=com_phocadownload&view=category&id=10&Itemid=548.

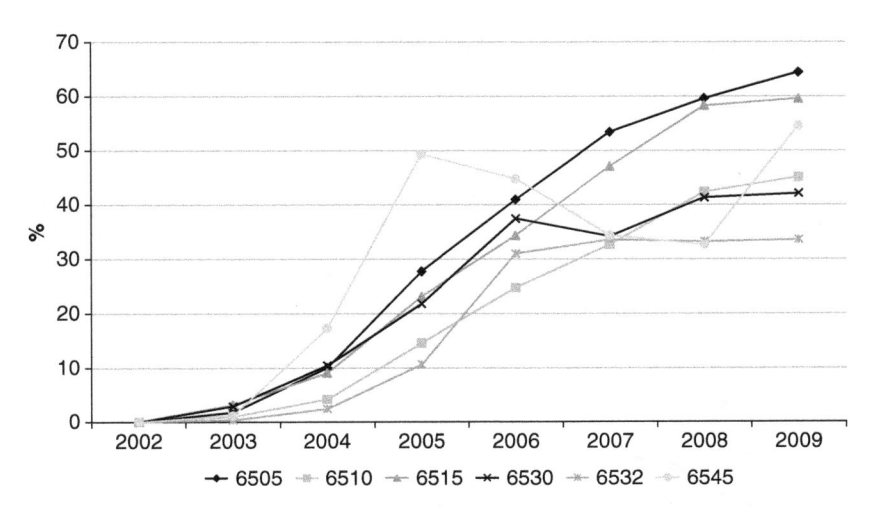

Figure 6.2 Number of items purchased through the Price Registration System as compared to the total number of items purchased by the Federal Government Procurement system.
Source: Compras Net.
*Note:* The above classes refer to the following items: 6,505 (drugs and medicines), 6,510 (surgical materials for dressings), 6,515 (medical and surgical instruments and supplies), 6,530 (hospital furnishings, equipment and utensils), 6,532 (hospital / surgical clothing/apparel and correlated items) and 6,545 (medical sets and assemblies) of the classification of the Federal Government Materials and Services Code Catalogue.

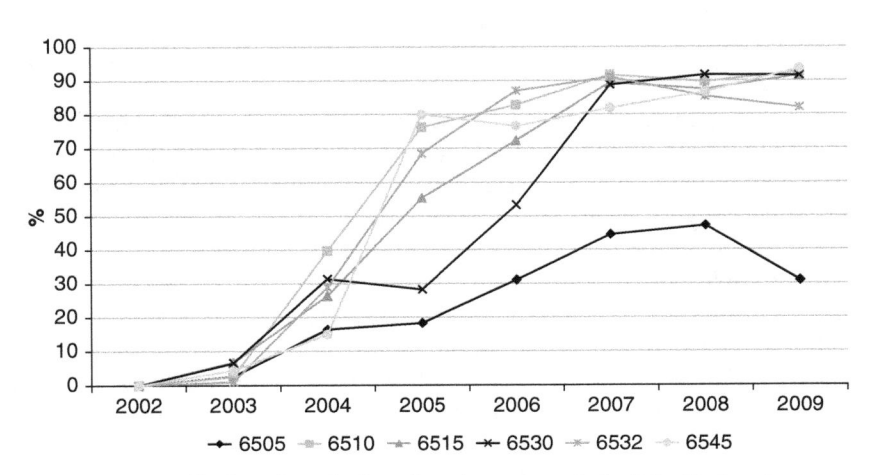

Figure 6.3 Total confirmed value of purchases through the Price Registration System as compared to the value of all purchases by the Federal Government Procurement.
Source: Compras Net.
*Note:* The above classes refer to the following items: 6,505 (drugs and medicines), 6,510 (surgical materials for dressings), 6,515 (medical and surgical instruments and supplies), 6,530 (hospital furnishings, equipment and utensils), 6,532 (hospital/ surgical clothing/apparel and correlated items) and 6,545 (medical sets and assemblies) of the classification of the Federal Government Materials and Services Code Catalogue.

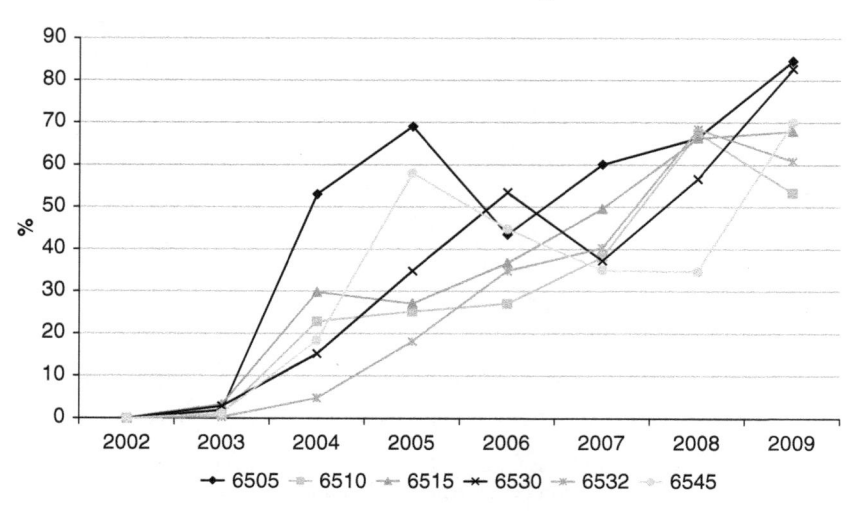

Figure 6.4 Number of government units purchasing through the Price Registration System as compared to the number of government units – Federal Government Procurement.
Source: Compras Net.
*Note:* The above classes refer to the following items: 6,505 (drugs and medicines), 6,510 (surgical materials for dressings), 6,515 (medical and surgical instruments and supplies), 6,530 (hospital furnishings, equipment and utensils), 6,532 (hospital/surgical clothing/apparel and correlated items) and 6,545 (medical sets and assemblies) of the classification of the Federal Government Materials and Services Code Catalogue.

supporting partner)[30] specifies a broad product category (e.g. PCs), possibly comprising thousands of needed products (at a Stock Keeping Unit [SKU] level)[31]. Suppliers are allowed to submit bids for any item of a macro-category of products, while an auction-type mechanism is carried out to select a group of products with unit and volume prices.

Once ChileCompra selects the winning bids (e.g. 'bid-product'-tuples),[32] public entities purchase their most preferred product at the agreed price and conditions as needed, without undergoing any additional public tendering process, unless the amount of the purchases exceeds $80,000. In this case, a new round of competition – carried out on either a price-only or

---

[30] Depending on the nature of the framework agreement. In some cases, they are required by a different authority from ChileCompra; in some other cases, the supporting partner is required due to the technical nature of the products to be tendered.
[31] The Stock Keeping Unit is the product/service identification code.
[32] That is, a vector of bid-product pairs.

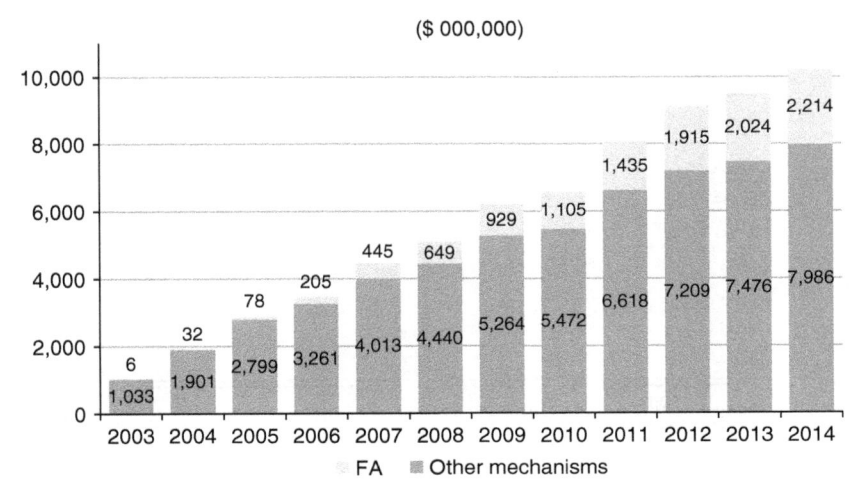

*International experience in centralised purchasing* 141

Figure 6.5 Share of public procurement by mechanism in Chile.
Source: ChileCompra (June 2015).

best-value-for-money basis – takes place among the framework awardees according to the same conditions set at the first stage. Once a framework agreement is awarded, supplier's products are loaded on the e-catalogue[33] where the buyers select the items they need and all transactions are made (e-ordering).

Figure 6.5 shows the evolution of the value of transactions through framework agreements since 2003 as well as of transactions through other procurement mechanisms (as expressed in US dollars, including taxes). In 2014, the overall amount of procurement transactions managed by ChileCompra was approximately 3.5 per cent of Chile's GDP, while framework agreements accounted for almost 0.85 per cent of the GDP.

Table 6.3 contains the number of products available in the e-store per year at an SKU level. Since 2010, the e-store (*Tienda de convenios marco*) is bigger than most business-to-consumer (B2C) stores in Chile (in terms of SKU) and has matched the value of the whole electronic commerce in Chile, according to a 2014 study by the Santiago Chamber of Commerce.

---

[33] The e-catalogue is completely open and can be consulted through the following link: www.mercadopublico.cl/Portal/Modules/Site/TiendaPublica/TiendaPublica.aspx.

Table 6.3 *Number of products (SKU level) in ChileCompra's e-store*

| Year | Increase of different products (SKU level) |
|---|---|
| 2008 | 25,788 |
| 2009 | 45,205 |
| 2010 | 48,601 |
| 2011 | 63,821 |
| 2012 | 65,723 |
| 2013 | 72,880 |
| 2014 | 75,155 |

*Source:* ChileCompra (June 2015).

### 6.4.3 Colombia

Framework agreements were introduced in the 2007 Law n. 1150. Nevertheless, framework agreements remained unused due to the fact that there was no institution which could conclude and manage them, until Colombia Compra Eficiente, the national procurement agency, was established. Colombia Compra Eficiente (CCE) is entrusted with designing and concluding framework agreements for the use of procuring entities at various levels of government. National-level entities that belong to the executive branch and use the General Statute for Public Procurement are obliged to use framework agreements. Other entities may use them if they so wish.

Framework agreements are further regulated by Decree 1510 of 2013, which requires framework agreements to be awarded through an open tender. Once awarded, the agreement is closed and no other suppliers may be included during its period of operation.

Framework agreements are structured by the business unit of CCE, where a team of economists, engineers and mathematicians study supply and demand in order to structure optimal selection processes. The first framework agreements were signed in late 2013, for the procurement of fuel in the city of Bogota and car liability insurance. Both of these have regulated prices, and the suppliers were asked to bid with discounts from these reference prices.

In early 2015, ten framework agreements were active (among which two – private cloud and connectivity services – were included in

Table 6.4 *Value of purchasing orders in 2014 and 2015 through framework agreements awarded by Colombia Compra Eficiente*

|  | 2014 | | 2015 (until June 11) | |
|---|---|---|---|---|
|  | Value of purchasing orders (COP'000)[1] | Number of purchasing orders | Value of purchasing orders (COP'000) | Number of purchase orders |
| Janitorial services | 44,195,947.277 | 85 | 124,020,731.989 | 376 |
| Contact center | 129,080,742.618 | 3 | 44,376,554.405 | 25 |
| Data center | 10,041,559.156 | 12 | 579,055.161 | N.A. |
| Fuel (Bogotá) | 45,726,588.466 | 488 | 21,540,027.963 | 284 |
| Fuel (National) |  |  | 5,552,933.135 | 17 |
| Connectivity | 33,604,258.662 | 28 | 27,347,736.086 | 68 |
| Clothing |  |  | 23,730,596.047 | 374 |
| Retailers | 1,155,185.797 | 89 | 799,470.787 | 80 |
| Government intranet | 10,838,600.433 | 2 | 882,761.103 | 6 |
| Private cloud |  |  | 8,298,872.525 | 18 |
| Public cloud | 4,131,823.950 | 1 | 537,977.373 | 6 |
| Stationery | 11,492,418.989 | 86 | 11,844,290.348 | 207 |
| Oracle services |  |  | 23,408,814.674 | 21 |
| Mandatory car insurance | 13,469,568.330 | 153 | 17,904,551.685 | 132 |
| Vehicles | 90,305,324.564 | 188 | 34,068,482.981 | 82 |
| Total value | 394,042,018.242 | 1,135 | 344,892,856.260 | 1,696 |

*Source:* Colombia Compra Eficiente (June 2015).
[1] Colombian Peso (COP) = 0.00035 euro.

the same process). Some framework agreements have only one competitive stage, such as fuel and purchase of office supplies, which are therefore multi-supplier Model 1 framework agreements. All other foresee a second round of competition whereby procuring entities specify needed quantities and awardees engage in a price-only mini-competition, and so are Model 2 framework agreement in terms of our overall classification. Table 6.4 provides 2014 and 2015 data on purchasing orders through framework agreements.

## 6.5 Africa: framework agreements in Ethiopia[34]

Ethiopia is governed as a federal system, with nine regions and two city administrations. At the federal level, Ethiopia has a public procurement law modelled on the UNCITRAL Model Law, and this law is followed in delegated legislation at the regional level. Though there are some differences, the main elements of the law are essentially similar. Following a series of independent audits in 2011, which underlined that 68 per cent of procurement transactions (for the promotion of basic services) were at substantial risk, the government responded by implementing substantial capacity-building activities targeted at federal, regional and local (Woreda) levels.[35] At the federal and regional levels, the government has also initiated the use of 'framework contracts' under the Public Procurement and Property Administration Agency (FPPA)[36] in order to improve transparency and efficiency in procurement of common user goods.

Since 2011 the scope of goods procured under these framework contracts has included office supplies, vehicles, office equipment and IT equipment. Framework contracts at the federal level are procured and managed by the Public Procurement and Property Disposal Services (PPPDS) under the Ministry of Finance and Economic Development (MoFED) and similar organisations under the Bureau of Finance and Economic Development at regional level, most notably the Oromiya PPPDS. Other entities such as Pharmaceutical Fund and Supply Agency (PFSA), which handles procurement of health sector goods, have shown interest in introducing framework agreements.

The degree of demand aggregation at both the federal and Oromiya regional level is approaching 100 per cent. Although centralised solutions for goods and services are becoming more and more widespread (particularly in many OECD countries and the United States), it is rarely the case the whole demand for a particular commodity by central government's bodies is handled by a single purchasing organisation.

At the federal level, the number of items procured through framework contracts has increased from around twenty to more than fifty items in three years. Tables 6.5 and 6.6 provide a picture of the nature or value of

---

[34] This section borrows almost entirely from a report prepared in September 2014 by G. L. Albano for the World Bank.
[35] Third-level administrative division in Ethiopia.
[36] In the Ethiopian relevant regulations 'framework contracts' and 'framework agreements' are used almost interchangeably, although the use of the latter is prevalent given that the 'Proclamation', namely the Act that introduced the major public procurement reform, provides for the use of 'framework contracts'. In this section, we will then adopt the label 'framework contracts'.

Table 6.5 *Oromiya framework contracts*

| I/no. | Framework contract description | Number of participating firms | Number of awardees | Total contract size/amount (ETB) |
|---|---|---|---|---|
| \multicolumn{5}{l}{Framework contracts in 2012/2013 (2005 Ethiopian calendar)} |
| 1 | Procurement of different types of stationary materials, IT equipment & office equipment | | | |
| | 1.1 Procurement of different types of stationeries | 7 | 5 | 6,494,164.14 |
| | 1.2 Procurement of IT equipment | 9 | 3 | 10,357,420.08 |
| | 1.3 Procurement of office equipment | 8 | 2 | 2,074,011.60 |
| 2 | Procurement of different types of vehicles | 13 | 6 | 85,208,345.80 |
| 3 | Procurement of IT equipment | 7 | 2 | 1,615,066.25 |
| 4 | Procurement of different types of civil servant working clothes | 5 | 4 | 2,816,421.06 |
| | | | Total 2005 (ETB) | 108,565,428.93 |
| \multicolumn{5}{l}{Framework contracts in 2013/2014 (2006 Ethiopian calendar)} |
| 1 | Procurement of different types of toners | 9 | 6 | 6,742,457.98 |
| 2 | Procurements of IT equipment | 12 | 6 | 18,582,882.20 |
| 3 | Procurement of different types of office equipment | 5 | 3 | 9,534,574.35 |
| 4 | Procurement of different types of stationery materials | 5 | 3 | 10,138,972.45 |
| | | | Total 2006 (ETB) | 44,998,886.98 |

framework contracts awarded by Oromiya and Federal PPPDS as well as the number of participating firms and awardees.

Part VI of the Directive of the MoFED provides the procedures that procuring entities must follow. In particular, three features are noteworthy: (i) framework contracts are to be used for common user items; (ii) all public bodies (both at the federal and at each regional states level) are

Table 6.6 Federal PPPDS framework contracts

| l/ no. | Framework contract description | Number of participating firms | Number of awardees | Total contract size/ amount (ETB) | Additional explanations |
|---|---|---|---|---|---|
| Framework contracts in 2011/2012 (2004 E.C.) | | | | | |
| 1 | Procurement of different types of stationary materials, A4 & A3 size paper, notebooks | 4 | 2 | 28,173,094.00 | The number of FC signed is 2 with the two awardees. |
| | | | Total 2004 (ETB) | ETB 28,173,094.00 | |
| Framework contracts in 2012/2013 (2005 E.C.) | | | | | |
| 1 | Procurement of different types of office equipment, supplies and stationery materials, (heavy-, medium-, light-duty machines, laptops, desktops, printer toners A4 & A3 size paper, notebooks etc.) | 34 | 9 | ETB 323,766,000.46 | The number of FC signed is 11. In this case, more than one supply contracts (lot) have been signed with a single supplier. |
| Framework contracts in 2013/2014 (2006 E.C.) | | | | | |
| 2 | Procurement of different types of office equipment, supplies and stationery materials, (heavy-, medium-, light-duty machines, laptops, desktops, printer toners A4 & A3 size paper, notebooks etc.) | 42 | 11 | ETB 636,278,152.02 | The number of FCs signed is 21. In this case, more than one supply contracts (lot) have been signed with a single supplier. |

mandated to purchase through the framework contracts concluded by their respective central procurement bodies; and (iii) whenever a framework contract is concluded with more than one supplier, the share of the contract awarded to highest-ranked firm cannot be less than 60 per cent of the total procurement value, although this share may slightly differ at the regional level. The mechanism could be thought of as a 'multi-award lowest-price technically acceptable' (MALPTA) award criterion whereby the central procurement body gives an option to some of the non-winning bidders to match the lowest bidder's financial offer. If they accept, they are given an equal share of the remaining 40 per cent of the framework contracts. According to Federal PPPDS officials, virtually all framework contracts are awarded to either two or three bidders, which means that either the second-ranked bidder only or the second- and third-ranked bidders are offered the option of matching the highest-ranked bidder. In the first case, the lowest bidder is awarded 60 per cent of the framework contract, while the second awardee (that matched the lowest bidder's offer) gets the remaining 40 per cent; in the second case, the other two bidders get 20 per cent each.[37]

The maximum number of awardees is made explicit in the bidding documents. The unit price resulting from the competitive process is then benchmarked against a 'reference market price' provided by the Central Statistics Agency (CSA), although the methodology used by the CSA to estimate the 'reference price' is neither transparent nor publicly available.

## 6.6 Asia: 'rate contracts' in India

Framework agreements have been used in India for many decades and are normally referred as 'rate contracts'. The system of rate contracts enables the procuring entity to place orders directly with suppliers without going through a tendering procedure, and is thus procedurally efficient. In addition, the rate contract system promotes decentralisation, while maintaining uniformity of prices in the procurement made by different purchasing units. It may also enhance outcomes in smaller procurements, by allowing economies of scale even to procuring entities buying in small quantities.

A rate contract is an agreement between the purchaser(s) and the supplier(s) to supply goods at a specified rate during a fixed agreed period

---

[37] This is in fact a special kind of Model 1 framework agreement where the single- rather than the multi-award nature is not exogenously determined by the procuring entity.

called the rate contract period. The contractor is bound to execute the supply orders placed during the currency of the rate contract. The rate contract is in the nature of a standing offer, and a legal contract comes into existence the moment an individual supply order is placed. Thus, each supply order becomes a separate procurement contract. A supply order can be placed up to the last date of the currency of the rate contract. Being a standing offer, the rate contract can be revoked at any time by either party, but orders placed before such revocations are binding. Neither is any quantity mentioned in the rate contract nor is any minimum purchase guaranteed.

Rate contracts are concluded for repeat purchases of common user items, items with well-defined and generalised standard specifications (e.g. using those of the Bureau of Indian Standards), and preferably for items for which rates are likely to be stable and not subject to significant market fluctuations, although rate contracts can contain price variation clauses.

### 6.6.1 Federal-level framework agreements: rate contracts of the Directorate General of Supplies and Disposal

The Directorate General of Supplies and Disposal (DGS&D) is working under the Ministry of Commerce and its main business is setting up rate contracts, which may be used by any government agency in India. While there is no federal public procurement law, chapter 6 of the Ministry of Finance's General Financial Rules addresses the applicable procedures, and the DGS&D maintains a website with details of all items available through rate contracts. The procedures involve a mandatory prior registration for suppliers (open to national and some foreign suppliers) and a tender process, itself conducted electronically. Awards are made with price as a major determinant.

The DGS&D e-procurement platform is an end-to-end solution beginning with the identification of new items for bringing on rate contracts, consultative meetings to finalise deletion or addition of items, formulation of governing specifications, creation and invitation of tender, receiving and opening of bids through a secured e-tendering platform, generation of comparative and ranking statements, information regarding dispatch of supplies and receipt by the consignee, e-payments and debit adjustments.

Normally DGS&D enters into parallel rate contracts with at least three firms, which in any case cannot be less than two by considering (a) the capacity of the tendering firms; (b) the quantity committed against the existing rate contracts; (c) the estimated annual requirement; and (d) reasonable price range so as to include products of established and reputed manufacturers and also items produced by different sectors so that buying departments have wider choice. To enable signing of rate contracts with multiple firms, DGS&D counter-offers the rates quoted by lowest bidder to other qualified firms. Thus, DGS&D enters into parallel contracts with whoever matches the lowest rate.[38]

All the government departments (federal and provincial) and the state-owned enterprises (SOE) are entitled to use the DGS&D rate contracts, but their use is not mandatory.

Normally rate contracts are concluded for a period of one year, which can exceptionally be extended but in no case beyond a period of three years. In early 2014, DGS&D rate contracts covered 302 items. The total value of the items procured (where purchase orders were routed through DGS&D) through the rate contracts during 2010–2011 was INR 78400 million (approximately $1.2 billion). It may be noted that a much larger volume is procured by government agencies directly (without involving DGS&D) using these rate contracts.

If the purchase order is routed through DGS&D, the contractual conditions are strictly adhered to. However, a large percentage of purchase orders are placed directly by the users, and, in these cases, it may be possible to renegotiate some of the conditions (understood not to include price, but other elements such as delivery terms).

### 6.6.2 State-level framework agreements: rate contracts of Tamil Nadu Medical Services Corporation Ltd.

The Tamil Nadu Medical Services Corporation Ltd. (TNMSC) was set up with the primary objective of ensuring availability of all essential drugs and medicines in the government medical institutions throughout the state of Tamil Nadu in India. TNMSC procures and supplies 268 types of drugs and medicines, eighty-four varieties of suture items and sixty-three surgical items to various government hospitals, primary health centres, and through them, to the health subcentres throughout Tamil Nadu every year. There are about 11,000 users of the rate contracts, but the purchase orders are placed only through TNMSC, which is introducing an e-procurement system.

---

[38] This is again a hybrid system mixing the features of single- and multi-award Model 1 framework agreements.

Table 6.7 *Rate contracts versus maximum retail prices for six generic drugs bought by TNMSC*

| Generic name of drug | Unit | MRP printed on pack/strip (Rs.) | TNMSC prices 2010–2011 (Rs) |
|---|---|---|---|
| Albendazole Tab IP 400 mg | 10 tablets | 250.00 | 4.62 |
| Alprazolam Tab IP 0.5 mg | 10 tablets | 14.00 | 0.45 |
| Cetrizine 10 mg | 10 tablets | 35.00 | 0.50 |
| Diclofenac Tab IP 50 mg | 10 tablets | 25.00 | 0.63 |
| Diazepam Tab IP 5 mg | 10 tablets | 29.40 | 0.47 |
| Amikacin 500 mg | 1 injection | 70.00 | 6.78 |

The tendering process includes price negotiations with the bidder who has submitted the lowest financial bid, should the latter be higher than estimate(s). Other technically qualified bidders are then invited to match the rates negotiated with the lowest-rate bidder. Purchasing orders are placed only with the original lowest-rate bidder, while other bidders that matched the lowest rate are used if the original lowest-rate bidder fails to supply. TNMSC has recently started using e-procurement system.

The price-related performance of the rate contracting system of TNMSC is reflected in Table 6.7, where the rate contracts prices of some generic drugs achieved by TNMSC are compared with maximum retail prices.

### 6.6.3 Project-level framework agreements: the World Bank-funded National Dairy Support Project

The World Bank Procurement Guidelines[39] allow the use of framework agreements in projects financed by the World Bank. The National Dairy Support Project (NDSP) was approved by the bank in March 2012 (loan amount being $352 million). The Indian National Dairy Development Board (NDDB) is the counterpart of the bank, and the project is being implemented by about 100 end-implementing agencies (EIAs) scattered over the entire country. As each EIA communicated the need of some standard items, the NDDB proposed using a framework agreement

---

[39] World Bank (2011), accessible through http://go.worldbank.org/RPHUYoRFI0.

solution for procuring such items. The World Bank also supported NDDB/EIAs in developing documents for setting up framework agreements. Two models of framework agreements are being used in this project.

*Open framework agreements with a second stage of price competition (Model 3 framework agreements)* These framework agreements have a maximum duration of three years (initial duration one year, extendable by further two years). Proposals are invited for multiple items, and firms are free to submit an offer for one or more items. The first stage involves an assessment of qualifications and responsiveness, but there is no selection of the best-performing bids.

At the second stage, each procurement contract is signed with the awardee that offers the lowest price and complies with the delivery requirements required by the relevant EIAs. Unlike the Model Law's provisions and the EU DPS, these framework agreements use a traditional manual procurement system.

*Closed framework agreement with a single stage of competition (Model 1 framework agreements)* These framework agreements operate as single-supplier framework agreements. EIAs issue purchase orders directly to the awardee during the validity of the framework agreement, indicating details such as quantity, delivery location, delivery schedule and so on. Other features are similar to open framework agreements discussed above. By the end of 2013 the NDDB had concluded framework agreements with a cumulative value of about INR 1.40 billion (about $22 million).

## 6.7 Australia

According to the Guidelines issued by the Government of South Australia' State Procurement Board, a *panel contract* (also referred to as panel arrangement) is a 'contractual arrangement established with at least two suppliers for the anticipated provision of goods and services as and when required over a specified period of time. The panel contract contains standard terms and conditions under which the goods and services will be provided by panel members'.[40]

---

[40] Government of South Australia – State Procurement Board, 'Panel Contracts Guidelines', April 2014. Available at www.spb.sa.gov.au. In New Zealand, a similar purchasing arrangement is known under the name of 'standing arrangements': www.oag.govt.nz/2008/procurement-guide/docs/procurement-guide.pdf.

A panel contract, which may be either mandatory or voluntary for those public entities covered by the agreement, may be established at a public authority level as well as across government levels. The scope and nature of panel contracts normally vary in terms of their product and service offerings and in the level of detail. Some panel contracts may include a set price or schedule or rates. Sometimes details may have to be negotiated between the panel member and the public authority at the call-off stage.[41] The selection of supplier through 'secondary procurement process' will normally depend upon the complexity and the value profile of the procuring entity's acquisition. The Guidelines list the following examples of supplier selection methods at the second stage:

- non-competitive (e.g. directly obtaining a quote from any one panel member);
- competitive (e.g. obtaining a quote or assessing technical/commercial characteristics from several or all panel members);
- equal division of work;
- monetary (e.g. obtaining three quotes for higher-level values);
- rotational;
- geographical; and
- preferred supplier (e.g. one supplier is give the opportunity to undertake the procurement first; then other suppliers are approached only if required).

Procuring entities have significant awarding flexibility at the second stage of any panel contract, some of which raise integrity concerns (e.g. the 'preferred supplier' and the 'equal division of work'), and thus require close scrutiny and performance assessment.

Interestingly, a panel contract may be either open or closed. It may stipulate the right to add suppliers where appropriate – for instance, in the case of 'changing circumstances, demographics, obsolescence or increased service requirements'[42] – although, generally, no entry of new suppliers is permitted until the expiration of the framework agreement. New candidates are evaluated using exactly the same process as for the original suppliers.

A panel contract differs from a prequalified list (also known as multi-use list – MUL). MULs are mechanisms for prequalification of suppliers, and the Commonwealth Procurement Rules (CPRs) provide that the

---

[41] The call-off stage is defined 'secondary procurement process' in the Guidelines.
[42] See the Guidelines, note 25, supra, p. 7.

'conditions for participation' must be limited to those that will ensure that a potential supplier has the legal, commercial, technical and financial abilities to fulfil the requirements of the related procurement. Practically, a MUL

- contains nothing that can be interpreted as a contract between a public authority and suppliers on the list;
- does not have a finite number of suppliers who may qualify for inclusion;
- is updated on either a continuous or annual basis, adding new suppliers who meet the prequalification criteria; and
- is used as a basis for undertaking further open or selective procurement processes (including establishing a panel contract).

A recent report by the Australian National Audit Office highlighted that in some cases, MULs have become more similar to a two-stage procurement arrangement. As the report relates, in relation to the MUL for legal services (LSMUL):

> The request documentation developed by (the Attorney-General's Department) for the LSMUL included conditions for participation, guidance material for applications, a legal services MUL deed and the application for inclusion. The conditions of participation set out in the application for inclusion required potential suppliers to:
>
> - provide list rates and innovative fee arrangements;
> - have public liability insurance and professional indemnity insurance for an amount not less than $10 million (AUD) per event per policy;
> - provide two duly completed and executed LSMUL Deeds; and
> - demonstrate understanding and capacity to meet the requirements of the Legal Service Directions 2005, including commitment to pro-bono legal work.

The report goes on, however, to explain this anomaly as follows:

> When considered against Finance guidance and the CPRs, the conditions for inclusion on the LSMUL included conditions that could be considered to be additional to the minimum required to ascertain whether the supplier had the legal, commercial, technical and financial ability to fulfill the requirements of the procurement. This may have resulted in a more onerous and costly application process for suppliers[;] however, the inclusion of these conditions reflected that the LSMUL was a whole-of-government arrangement and sought to streamline the later procurement processes for both suppliers and agencies.

It then appears to have been a substantial use of the MUL vehicle to create *quasi-frameworks* from which users may source services with little regard to their obligations to seek competitive offers from registrants. The auditor-general has, however, emphasised in his report the need to promote competition in the future.

### 6.8 Chapter summary

- A wide array of procurement practices is inspired by the framework agreement's logic of the two-stage process. Examples of the two-stage process for centralisation purposes abound in different regulatory environments, possibly paving the way for further developments in the use of framework agreements at a global level.
- Many experiences, particularly in developing countries, seem to indicate that framework agreements are used to provide procuring entities with supply diversification at similar, if not identical, value-for-money conditions. This would also guarantee quite a high degree of standardisation in purchasing patterns.
- In more developed countries such as the United States and Australia, framework-like arrangements have been traditionally used to streamline procuring entities' purchases, sometimes at the expense of transparency and competition at the call-off stage. While in recent years the US regulation has gradually raised competition requirements, in Australia multi-use supplier lists have come under close scrutiny by oversight authorities as they have been used as substitutes for framework-like arrangements.

# PART II
# *Fostering competition and preventing collusion in framework agreements*

CHAPTER 7

# *Promoting effective competition and enhancing outcomes in framework agreements*

## 7.1 Introduction

Effective competition – the process of rivalry between firms striving to achieve sales and to make profits[1] – is 'not automatic, and can be harmed by inappropriate government policies and legislation, and by the anti-competitive conduct of firms'.[2] In this chapter, we shall look at the aspects of framework agreements design that can maximise the potential for competition at both stages of the procedure, and achieve the best possible outcomes for the public purse. In Chapters 8 and 9, we will identify some examples of collusion in public procurement, consider general observations about anti-competitive conduct on the part of bidders and suppliers in the procurement process and address the particular context of framework agreements.

Private sector businesses strive to improve competition in the markets in which they operate, providing instructive examples for governments in the public procurement context.[3] The economic benefits of competition in procurement may be simple in economic terms – better quality and/or lower prices[4] – but the commonly accepted reasons for the proposition bear restatement:

---

[1] 'Why Is Competition Important for Growth and Poverty Reduction?', Department for International Development, London, paper produced to the OECD Global Forum on Investment, March 2008, available at www.oecd.org/investment/globalforum/40315399.pdf. See, also, R. D. Anderson and W. E. Kovacic, 'Competition Policy and International Trade Liberalisation: Essential Complements to Ensure Good Performance in Public Procurement Markets', *Public Procurement Law Review*, 18, No. 2 (2009): 67–101, at p. 68.
[2] 'Why Is Competition Important for Growth and Poverty Reduction?', ibid.
[3] Ibid., citing D. N. Burt and R. L. Pinkerton, *A Purchasing Manager's Guide to Strategic, Proactive Procurement* (AMACOM, 2006).
[4] P. Milgrom, 'Auctions and Bidding: A Primer', *Journal of Economic Perspectives*, 3, No. 3 (1989): 3–22; and P. D. Klemperer (ed.), *The Economic Theory of Auctions* (Cheltenham, UK: Edward Elgar, 2000). See also R. I. Carr, 'Impact of the Number of Bidders on Competition', *Journal of Construction Engineering and Management*, 109, No. 1 (1983): 61; R. D. Anderson and W. E. Kovacic, 'Competition Policy and International Trade Liberalisation: Essential Complements to Ensure

[f]irst, with free entry and an absence of collusion, prices will be driven to marginal costs. Secondly, costs themselves will be minimised, as firms compete for survival. Thirdly, competition serves as an important driver of innovation. Fourthly, competition enables the participating firms to learn from one another and thereby to continuously improve their products in addition to their marketing, production and managerial techniques.[5]

Case studies of public procurement reforms that have increased competition for government contracts demonstrate improved economic benefits.[6]

## 7.2 Concerns about competition in framework agreements procedures

Even before Directive 2004/EC/18 was issued in 2004[7] – which first authorised the use of framework agreements in the European Union – concerns were raised about whether effective competition could be achieved in what are now framework agreements procedures. The European Commission in its 1998 Communication had already stated that long-term contracts, including framework agreements, might 'pose a threat to competition in that they could cause positions to become entrenched and certain firms to be shut out'.[8] Subsequent reviews of the implementation and use of the authorisation to use framework agreements in the European Union indicated that concerns about competition had

---

Good Performance in Public Procurement Markets', *Public Procurement Law Review*, 18 (2009): 67–101.
[5] 'Competition Policy and International Trade Liberalization: Essential Complements to Ensure Good Performance in Public Procurement Markets', note 1, supra.
[6] OECD, Transparency in Government Procurement: The Benefits of Efficient Governance (TD/TC/WP/(2002)31/Rev2/14 April 2003), available at www.oecd.org/officialdocuments/publicdisplaydocumentpdf/?doclanguage=en&cote=td/tc/wp(2002)31/final, and Europe Economics, Evaluation of Public Procurement Directives, Markt/2004/10/D, September 2006, available at http://ec.europa.eu/internal market/publicprocurement/docs/final report en.pdf. Also cited in 'Competition Policy and International Trade Liberalization: Essential Complements to Ensure Good Performance in Public Procurement Markets', note 1, supra.
[7] Directive 2004/18/EC of the European Parliament and of the Council of 31 March 2004 on the coordination of procedures for the award of public works contracts, public supply contracts and public service contracts, OJ L 134, 30 April 2004, pp. 114–240, available at http://eur-lex.europa.eu/legal-content/en/ALL/?uri=CELEX:32004L0018, Article 32.
[8] Commission Communication COM (1998) 143 final, 3 November 1998, available at http://ec.europa.eu/internal_market/publicprocurement/docs/green-papers/com-98–143_en.pdf. This paper was issued as a follow-up to the 1996 Green Paper 'Public Procurement in the European Union: Exploring the Way Forward', COM (1996) 583, final 27 November 1996, available at http://europa.eu/documents/comm/green_papers/pdf/com-96–583_en.pdf. For a more detailed discussion of this point, see Procurement Lawyers' Association, the Use of Framework Agreements in Public Procurement, March 2012, available at www.procurementlawyers.org/pdf/PLA%20paper%20on%20Frameworks%20PDF%20Mar%2012.pdf, page 8.

indeed emerged. A 2006 European study reported that centralised purchasing agencies conducting framework agreements procedures – intended to be the key drivers of a more centralised and efficient system – were viewed as 'less transparent, less fair, and more bureaucratic than other public procurement bodies',[9] an issue we will return to in Chapter 11.

Similar commentary appeared in the United States, even though the procedures for framework agreements ID/IQ in the federal public procurement system are rather different from those in the European Union.[10] In the US federal system, second-stage competition is designed to be ensured through a legal requirement that bidders must be afforded a 'fair opportunity' to be considered at the call-off stage, but concerns have arisen about procuring entities flouting the requirement,[11] and about the tension between seeking to enhance competition and efficiency in a single system.[12]

---

[9] A. Sanchez-Graells, *Public Procurement and the EU Competition Rules*, 2nd ed. (Oxford: Hart, 2015), at pp. 298–299; Europe Economics, 'Evaluation of Public Procurement Directives – Markt/2004/10/D', (September 2006), sections 5.7–5.28, available at http://ec.europa.eu/internal_market/publicprocurement/docs/final_report_en.pdf.

[10] See, further, Chapter 5 and, for example, Steven L. Schooner, 2001, 'Fear of Oversight: The Fundamental Failure of Businesslike Government', 50 AM. U. L. REV. 627. A 1999 audit conducted in the United States found that 53 per cent of purchase orders were awarded without competition and only 12 per cent of those orders would justify a lack of competition; a subsequent audit found that the non-competitive awards increased to 72 per cent. See also Christopher R. Yukins, Discussion Draft, 'Assessing Framework Agreements under the WTO's Government Procurement Agreement: A Comparative Review of the US Experience', Materials Presented at Colloquium at George Washington University Law School 67, No. 48 (2005), available at http://docs.law.gwu.edu/facweb/sschooner/GWUFrameworksProgramMaterials_Final.pdf, at p. 16, citing U.S. Department of Defense, Office of Inspector General, DOD Use of Multiple Award Contracts, Report No. 99–16, 14 (2 April 1999) and Office of Inspector General, Multiple Award Contracts for Services, Report No. D-2001–189 (28 September 2001); Acquisition Advisory Panel, Report of the Acquisition Advisory Panel to the Office of Federal Procurement Policy and the U.S. Congress 67–72 (2007), available at www.acquisition.gov/comp/aap/24102_GSA.pdf (citing reports and legislation mandating stronger competition among holders of standing ID/IQ contracts); U.S. Government Accountability Office, GAO-08–160, Federal Acquisition: Oversight Plan Needed to Help Implement Acquisition Advisory Panel Recommendations (2007), available at www.gao.gov/new.items/d08160.pdf (supporting panel recommendations).

[11] Daniel I. Gordon and Jonathan L. Kang, 'Task-Order Contracting in the U.S. Federal System: The Current System and Its Historical Context', chapter 5, in S. Arrowsmith, (ed.), *Public Procurement Regulation in the 21st Century: Reform of the UNCITRAL Model Law on Procurement* (Eagan, MN: West, 2009), at p. 237. See, also, C. R. Yukins, Feature Comment: The Gathering Winds of Reform— Congress Mandates Sweeping Transparency for Federal Grants and Contracts, 48 Gov't Contractor at para. 318 (2006), in which the author examines large ID/IQ being used to prevent access other than to a 'few vendors that hold standing agreements with the Government'.

[12] Competition is often at odds with, or at least perceived to be at odds with, efficiency, because generally, the competition process slows things down. Acquisition Advisory Panel, Report to the Office of Federal Procurement Policy and the United States Congress, at 93 (January 2007), available at www.acqnet.gov/comp/aap/24102_GSA.pdf, in which it was reported that the 'Use of task and delivery order contracts by agencies for the acquisition of complex services on a best value basis has

This concern may reflect a lack of clarity about the scope of the legal requirement itself (which one commentator described as 'a motley disaster, by any reasonable measure, a twisted set of compromises which likely reflects, in part, the procurement community's quiet resistance to bringing more competition, and more transparency, to ID/IQ contracting', and an 'enormously complicated system, with grossly uneven transparency and uncertain competition').[13] However, reports also demonstrate intentional non-compliance (see Section 7.4). In consequence it may not be surprising that the US General Accountability Office (GAO) has reported on failure to seek competition at all, and has concluded that even where competition was sought, its extent was limited and probably not in compliance with the requirements.[14]

It may be queried, therefore, why the European Commission has recently concluded that framework agreements may be *more* competitive than some other procurement techniques – finding that 'framework agreements and joint purchasing attract more bids' than average.[15] The answer is that the reference in this recent evaluation is to competition *at the first stage* – when the framework agreement is concluded – whereas the concerns voiced in the preceding paragraph relate to the *second, or call-off, stage* of the procedure.[16] In effect, what is being recognised is that the first stage of the procedure, when future purchases are aggregated into one procedure, is likely to be relatively attractive to bidders for the same reasons that it is desirable for procuring entities: transaction costs per unit of sales or purchase should be lower than in other procurements of the same items. In addition, the 'typical' framework agreement procedure is undertaken for repeated purchases of relatively straightforward goods and services, as we saw in Chapter 2, which generally

---

been increasing'. See, further, Steven L. Schooner, Daniel I. Gordon and Jessica L. Clark, 'Public Procurement Systems: Unpacking Stakeholder Aspirations And Expectations', GWU Law School Public Law Research Paper 1133234 (2008), available at http://ssrn.com/abstract=1133234.

[13] Christopher R. Yukins, 'Are ID/IQs Inefficient? Sharing Lessons with European Framework Contracting', *Public Contract Law Journal*, 37, No. 3 (Spring 2008), noting that part of the confusion came from the then head of the Office of Federal Procurement Policy, who encouraged purchasing agencies not to engage in second-stage competition when ordering commercial off-the-shelf (COTS) items.

[14] See, also, Nicholas, Caroline. 'A Critical Evaluation of the Revised UNCITRAL Model Law Provisions on Regulating Framework Agreements', *Public Procurement Law Review*, 21, No. 2 (2012): 19–46.

[15] EU Public Procurement Legislation: Delivering Results Summary of Evaluation Report (2011), available at http://ec.europa.eu/internal_market/publicprocurement/docs/modernising_rules/executive-summary_en.pdf, at p. 13.

[16] As Section 7.4 explains, the second stage is often not regulated in any detail, whereas the first stage may be required to follow fully open and competitive procedures as in any 'traditional' procurement.

operate in markets that are relatively competitive. A conclusion that there are more than average bids for framework agreements at the first stage appears justified from this theoretical perspective.

Public procurement policies (and regulatory regimes) place a high premium on incentivising competition to improve outcomes, but the general rules vary in the extent to which they accommodate framework agreements procedures. In this context, the procuring entity needs to select the models of framework agreements and among options within for conducting the procedures concerned as a way of promoting a competitive market. We consider this aspect of framework agreements design in Chapter 10. We will now turn to promoting effective competition at both stages of the procedure, and some obstacles that may be encountered.

### 7.3 Wide participation as a prerequisite for effective competition − first stage of a framework agreements procedure

#### 7.3.1 Barriers to entry

A key objective is to create the conditions in which rigorous competition can take place. A first relevant requirement is to remove − so far as possible − barriers to entry to procurement markets, on the basis that wide participation by bidders is a prerequisite for competition and, in the context of recent findings, that framework agreements procedures can limit rather than promote market access.[17]

The WTO GPA, EU Directive and UNCITRAL Model Law[18] all include provisions requiring open, international participation as a default requirement (though in the cases of the GPA and EU Directive, 'international' refers to their membership rather than to all countries). Transparency measures (to the effect that all potential bidders are informed of the terms of an intended procurement), prohibitions on discriminatory terms and conditions (such as

---

[17] Section 1.9, Commissioning and competition in the public sector, UK Office of Fair Trading, available at www.oft.gov.uk/shared_oft/reports/comp_policy/OFT1314.pdf.
[18] The World Trade Organisation Revised Agreement on Government Procurement available at www.wto.org/english/docs_e/legal_e/rev-gpr-94_01_e.htm (hereafter, WTO GPA); Directive 2014/24/EU of the European Parliament and of the Council of 26 February 2014 on public procurement and repealing Directive 2004/18/EC Text with EEA relevance, OJ L 94, 28 March 2014, pp. 65–242, available at http://eur-lex.europa.eu/legal-content/EN/TXT/?uri=celex:32014L0024 (hereafter, the EU Directive); UNCITRAL Model Law (UNCITRAL Model Law on Public Procurement (2011), *Official Records of the General Assembly, Sixty-sixth Session, Supplement No. 17* (UN document A/66/17). The text of the Model Law is available at www.uncitral.org/uncitral/uncitral_texts/procurement_infrastructure.html. Hereafter, Model Law

bans on the use of trade names unless there is no satisfactory alternative), rules requiring award criteria to relate to the subject matter of the procurement, qualification criteria to be relevant and so on are designed to prevent discrimination more generally. In addition, the Model Law, for example, requires the choice of procurement method to be taken with a view to maximising competition to the extent practicable.[19]

As noted in the introduction to this chapter, government policies and legislation have the potential to support market access or to present impediments to broad participation. In the framework agreements context, securing SMEs' participation – given the nature of the purchases and common scope of call-offs – may be a desirable outcome. However, the very aggregation and bundling that framework agreements procedures involve can operate as a significant disincentive to SMEs to participate (at least at the small enterprise level).[20] Recent examinations into legal and procedural requirements that indicate why SMEs under-participate in public procurement markets have yielded conclusions that may also be instructive in improving participation from bidders of all sizes in the framework agreements' context. The main conclusions are as follows:[21]

---

[19] Article 28, Model Law, ibid.
[20] Recent research suggests that the value threshold above which the statistics indicate that SMEs underperform is in the range of €300,000 to €1million, and that the median contract size (above EU thresholds) may be as high as €928,000 (EU, 2009). Even by 2003, the US equivalent of framework agreements accounted for nearly 30 per cent of federal public procurement; the value of one type of framework agreement alone rose from $4 billion in 1992 to $32.5 billion in 2004. See, further, 'Task-Order Contracting in the U.S. Federal System: The Current System and Its Historical Context', note 11, supra.
[21] This section draws, in particular, on Caroline Nicholas and Michael Fruhmann, 'Small and Medium-Sized Enterprises Policies in Public Procurement: Time For a Rethink?' *Journal of Public Procurement*, 14, No. 3 (2014): 328–360; R. Fee, A. Erridge, and S. Hennigan, 'SMEs and Government Purchasing in Northern Ireland: Problems And Opportunities', *European Business Review*, 14, No. 5 (2002): 326–334; E. Mishory, 'Leveling Asymmetry: The Information-Leveling Model of Transparency in Government Procurement' (2013) [Online]. Available at http://papers.ssrn.com/sol3/papers.cfm?abstract_id =id=2365092; K. Karjalainen and K. Kemppainen, 'The Involvement of Small- and Medium-Sized Enterprises in Public Procurement: Impact of Resource Perceptions, Electronic Systems and Enterprise Size', *Journal of Purchasing and Management*, 14, No. 4 (2008): 230–240 [Online]. Available at www.sciencedirect.com/science/article/pii/S1478409208 000642; L. Georghiou, J. Edler, E. Uyarra and J. Yeow (2013) 'Policy Instruments for Public Procurement of Innovation: Choice, Design and Assessment, Technological Forecasting & Social Change' [Online]. Available at www.sciencedirect.com; European Union (2009): Evaluation of SMEs' Access to Public Procurement Markets in the EU: Final Report [Online]. Available at http://ec.europa.eu/enterprise/policies/sme/business environ ment/files/smes_access_to_public_procurement_final_report_2 010_en.pdf. European Union (2014). 'Small and Medium-Sized Enterprises (SMEs)' [Online]. Available at http://epp.eurostat.ec.europa.eu/portal/page/portal/european_business/special_sbs_topics/small_medium_sized_enterprises_SMEs [Online]. Available at http://ec.europa.eu/enterprise/policies/sme/ index _en.htm.

(a) SMEs do not realise the benefits of participating in the public procurement market, perhaps as a result of inadequate information. The European Union has identified poor information about procurement opportunities, about tenders themselves (ambiguous requirements, late information and a lack of debriefing), and about procurement regulations and procedural requirements more generally. These observations serve to highlight the importance of pre-procurement publicity, outreach and advertising – aspects of which are further considered in Section 7.3.2.

(b) SMEs are disproportionately affected by the costs of participating in public procurement, which are noted as being 10–50 per cent higher than for comparable projects in the private sector. The costs include requirements for tender securities, performance bonds, licences, fees and the costs of complying with detailed procedural requirements (registration, provision of detailed tender information), particularly when combined with unnecessary qualification requirements. In the framework agreements context, some requirements that would generally apply to contracts of the value of the framework agreement as a whole may be excessive for second-stage contracts, and tender securities are unlikely to be available at the first stage in any event (banks may decline to provide guarantees given the uncertainties involved). Technical, health and safety, sustainability, equality and diversity policies when implemented in framework agreements procurement can effectively put the contracts beyond SMEs, as can stringent qualification requirements aimed at mitigating reputational risk and attempts to reduce the work involved in assessing marginal bids. (In addition, excessive qualification requirements may be evidence of attempts to ensure that only favoured suppliers are qualified.)

(c) SMEs may offer innovative solutions, but may suffer from risk aversion on the part of procurement officials. From a design perspective, ensuring that excessive 'standard' requirements are avoided and setting this out clearly in the initial publicity may assist in enhancing interest from SME bidders. The EU Directive[22] introduces new measures to address some such concerns: first, self-declarations in qualification, and, second, the evidence of financial capacity of the supplier that can be required is to be

---

[22] EU Directive, note 18, supra.

limited (e.g. turnover requirements may not exceed a maximum of twice the estimated value of the contract).

(d) Seeking to maximise participation requires (i) balancing the benefits of a broad and flexible framework agreement with a greater potential disincentive to participate on the part of some potential bidders as a result of significant bundling and/or excessive estimates of quantities to be purchased through the framework agreement, unless call-off sizes and frequencies are designed to allow smaller bidders to participate; and (ii) deciding on whether or not to use lots to reflect different delivery locations and combinations or ranges of items under the framework agreement. Disaggregating in this way and/or scaling the size and frequency of anticipated call-offs to reflect the size and scale of market-players can have a significant impact on the types and numbers of bidders that may participate. Very broad and large-scale requirements, for example, may be accessible only to diversified operators. A further design issue is that the use of functional rather than technical specifications may also encourage bidders (see, further, below).

(e) SMEs are less experienced bidders: allowing them sufficient time to bid in new opportunities and engaging in outreach to build capacity in how to draft and present a bid may also yield benefits. SME weaknesses in terms of technical and financial capacity can be addressed by allowing joint bidders to fulfil requirements. For example, SMEs may combine to gain size or to be able to offer complementary components. However, a careful approach to joint bidding is required, because temporary consortia between rivals may be a tool for enforcing a cartel or collusive agreement.

More generally, while it has long been accepted that, as a general rule, fully unrestricted participation is likely to generate the most rigorous competition; there will be circumstances in which competition is best assured by limiting the number of participants. This situation may arise if the costs of participating in the procedure are high, such as in the procurement of highly complex, large and/or specialised products or services – unless the suppliers consider their chances of winning the ultimate contract are reasonable, they may be unwilling to participate at all. This situation may arise in the framework agreements context if the disclosed terms for the second stage indicate that certain groups of suppliers are likely to be disadvantaged. In the United States, a GAO report found that practical considerations often made it impossible for non-incumbent awardees to respond in time to an invitation to take part at the call-off stage,[23] a lesson with clear relevance to long-standing open framework agreements in other systems.

### 7.3.2 Disclosure of terms and conditions of the procurement

A clear implication of the above issues is that the terms and conditions of the procurement and other relevant information should be proportionate and publicised in advance. Combined with non-discrimination measures, the effect should be to allow bidders of all sizes to assess whether they can and wish to participate and to submit their best offers. There follows a summary of how general principles on the question of disclosure of prior information can be applied to a framework agreement procedure at the practical level.

The general principle common to all regimes, including UNCITRAL's, is that descriptions of what is to be procured should be clear, sufficiently precise, complete and objective.[24] A vague or ill-defined description poses particular difficulties in a framework agreements procedure, because changes to the description raise a risk of abuse (e.g. deliberate 'refinement' of broad criteria could be used to divert awards to favoured suppliers); there may be 'loose tailoring' of procurement contracts to the procuring entities' needs (so that administrative efficiencies are outweighed by lower value for money overall); and where second-stage competition may be reduced or distorted where potentially responsive bidders are excluded at the first stage, or decide not to participate, as a result of such a description.[25]

The UNCITRAL Model Law, in common with the EU Directive,[26] consequently prohibits changes to the description of the subject matter of the framework agreement itself throughout its operation.[27] On the other

---

[23] 'Assessing Framework Agreements under the WTO's Government Procurement Agreement: A Comparative Review of the US Experience', note 10, supra, at p. 17, citing US GAO, Few Competing Proposals for Large DOD Information Technology Orders, Report No. GAO/NSIAD-00-56, 8-9 (March 2000).

[24] Guide to Enactment of the UNCITRAL Model Law on Public Procurement (2012), commentary to Article 10. Official Records of the General Assembly, Sixty-seventh Session, Supplement No. 17 (para 46, UN document A/67/17). The text of the Guide to Enactment is available at www.uncitral.org/uncitral/uncitral_texts/procurement_infrastructure.html. Hereafter, Guide to Enactment.

[25] 'A Critical Evaluation of the Revised UNCITRAL Model Law Provisions on Regulating Framework Agreements', note 14, supra, at p. 27.

[26] Article 33(2), EU Directive, note 18, supra: 'Contracts based on a framework agreement may under no circumstances entail substantial modifications to the terms laid down in that framework agreement'.

[27] Article 63, Model Law, note 18, supra.

hand, changes to other terms of the procurement (including to the evaluation criteria) are permitted and necessary, in order to provide appropriate flexibility to the extent that they are envisaged in the framework agreement itself. Thus refinements at the second stage, to allow for competition for call-offs, or to select among call-off options in the framework agreement, are permitted if they are provided for in the framework agreement.[28] The terms of second-stage competition and any variation in evaluation criteria at the second stage must also be disclosed in advance and set out in the framework agreement (as discussed in more detail in Chapter 8).

The flexibility is nonetheless limited: the general provisions applicable to all procurement under the Model Law apply to framework agreements, and include a requirement for a re-advertisement of the procurement (i.e. the procedure will have to start afresh) where the solicitation or bidding documents are modified to the extent that original advertisement then contains a material inaccuracy. These documents will remain applicable throughout a framework agreement procedure.[29]

Where descriptions are input-based, the risk of limiting access to or restricting participation in the framework agreement procedure is more likely to arise (as noted above, and may also raise a greater risk of collusion, an issue we shall consider in Chapter 8). Consequently, the Model Law provides that descriptions should be objective, functional and generic to the extent practicable.[30] While such descriptions may include both technical and quality characteristics, output-based or functional descriptions permit substitute goods, and so can encourage innovative design solutions (and may encourage SMEs, which may have a comparative advantage from this perspective, to participate). In addition, they can enhance the efficacy of framework agreements as they allow for technological development (product modifications and technology substitutions) and can more easily accommodate refinements or variations to suit the procuring entity's actual needs at the second (call-off) stage. They thus address, albeit not completely, a common disadvantage of framework agreements – that they are not responsive to market changes.

---

[28] Examples of permissible variations include estimates of terms for firm commitments are not available, or an explanation of why estimates are not possible (e.g. where emergency procurement is concerned); the applicable range of evaluation criteria at the call-off stage, under Article 58(1)(d). When drafting these provisions, UNCITRAL considered that complete flexibility regarding relative weights of evaluation criteria at the call-off stage could be abused. Guide to Enactment, note 24, supra, commentary to Article 58. The EU Directive in Article 33 is slightly more flexible, note 18, supra.

[29] Article 15(3), Model Law, note 18, supra.

[30] In the sense of avoiding reference to trademarks or other proprietary terms.

Nonetheless, procuring entities should be able to include technical requirements (including quality and performance standards) where appropriate, including through the use of input-based or technical specifications. In the context of framework agreements (a) a precise and technical description can enhance first-stage participation and competition where no second-stage competition is to take place; that is, where the procuring entity will use a Model 1 framework because its needs and the market are not expected to vary; (b) the nature of the procurement market may be such that swift comparisons at the second stage will be needed – perhaps to be undertaken electronically – which in turn will require simple comparison techniques, such as a formulaic approach to evaluation, and so will preclude complex assessments of relative technical merit;[31] and (c) technical requirements may be necessary to allow the goods or services to be procured to be compatible or integrate with existing supplies or equipment.

Although trademarks and similar IP restrictions are generally proscribed, the use of a brand name or a trademark instead of a very long and technical description may improve bidders' understanding of the procuring entity's needs. If it is permitted, however, it should be accompanied with the words 'or equivalent', and guidance on how bidders should demonstrate equivalence will be important to avoid the use of trademarks as a real barrier to participation.[32] Standardising documents and terminology, such as through use of the EU common procurement vocabulary (CPV, adopted by Regulation (EC) No. 213/2008), and the United Nations Standard Products and Services Code ('UNSPSC'), can assist in enhancing understanding statements of need and technical requirements, but may also prevent innovative solutions by limiting the manner in which those needs and requirements can be met.

Where what is to be procured under the framework agreement indicates that a Model 1 framework agreement is the appropriate model (i.e. without second-stage competition), the procedure resembles a 'traditional' procurement in that all terms are competed at the first stage. Consequently, the procurement contracts themselves are awarded as lots, without further competition, though with refinements or combinations of items or services, and with determined quantities and other delivery conditions, as determined in accordance with the framework agreement itself.[33] Firms

---

[31] This approach, however, may restrict participation for the reasons noted above.
[32] Article 10, Model Law, note 18, supra.
[33] Article 59, Model Law, ibid. The article requires that the framework agreement set out its duration, all terms and conditions (or estimates for those unknown at the time the framework is concluded). This information includes, regarding call-offs, all terms for the call-offs themselves (what is to be competed, award criteria, anticipated time frame for call-offs, procedural requirements and so

will have little opportunity to improve their offers at the call-off stage, so they have an incentive to submit their best offers at the first stage. The offers, however, can reflect only the information issued by the procuring entity at the outset of the procedure, which should consequently be as accurate as it can be, including the terms and conditions of the call-offs.

Issuing the best-available information may also reduce the risks of abnormally low first-stage offers (the 'Winner's Curse' referred to in Chapter 8). Consequences of abnormally low bids include that bidders may withdraw from participating in the framework agreement or reduce the quality of their offer at the call-off stage; similarly, bidders may submit a highly competitive first-stage offer, intending to compete for only a few call-offs (a higher possibility where the scope and description of the procuring entity's needs is broad). Such behaviour distorts the first-stage competition, and potentially compromises effective competition and value for money at the call-off stage.

## 7.4 Ensuring effective competition at the second stage of a framework agreement procedure (Model 2 and Model 3 framework agreements)

As noted in the introduction to this chapter, concerns have been expressed that framework agreements procedures operate – particularly at the call-off stage – with significantly reduced transparency and competition compared with 'traditional' procurement methods. Many systems, however, do not regulate the second stage in detail (and perhaps partly provide a cause of this situation). For example, in the United States, it is the award of the framework agreement itself (ID/IQ) that is the award of the contract for the purpose of its 'full and open competition' requirement under the FAR, so orders under the ID/IQ are generally exempt from more requirements than that noted above for bidders to be afforded a 'fair opportunity' to be considered at the call-off stage.[34] The provisions of the EU Directive do not provide detailed guidance on the call-off stage.[35]

---

forth). However, UNCITRAL has exempted call-offs where there has been no second-stage competition from standstill notices and periods, as further discussed in Chapter 12.

[34] A statutory preference for multiple-award contracts for identical or similar supplies or services is intended to ensure competition at the second stage, with streamlined procedures, so that orders are to be awarded on a 'fair opportunity to be considered' basis (though that notion is not defined). Further, exemptions from the bid protest (review or challenge) system also limit the oversight of compliance with these rules.

[35] See, further, Chapter 5. Recital 61 to the EU Directive, note 18, supra, provides, 'Contracting authorities should be given additional flexibility when procuring under framework agreements,

A main design constraint for procuring entities is that terms of the second stage must be set prior to the commencement of the entire procedure, which will be more challenging the more variations that they seek to accommodate in the framework agreement.[36] Relevant issues include the appropriate extent of second-stage competition. Limiting second-stage competition to few elements and to a limited number of awardees will generally simplify the process and minimise its administrative time and cost, but offers less flexibility and allows for fewer variations to be accommodated. However, engaging in competition on significant terms of the procurement at both stages of the procedure may defeat the administrative efficiency that underlies many of the benefits of a framework agreement procedure in the first place, as well as distort the relevant market if some bidders that would be able to offer good terms of supply at the call-off stage are eliminated at the first stage. An open framework agreement (Model 3) can more easily allow for larger numbers of participating suppliers, more variations and a changing marketplace than other models, and (as explained in Chapter 2) there is little competition at the first stage, so there is less duplication of competition at both stages. The US federal system has encouraged the use of open framework agreements also as a way of promoting second-stage competition.[37]

This point acquires additional significance as there are legal restrictions that prevent procuring entities from reducing the participants in competitions at the call-off stage. The general rule in both the Model Law and the EU Directive is that all awardees of the framework agreement must be

---

which are concluded with more than one economic operator and which set out all the terms. In such cases, contracting authorities should be allowed to obtain specific works, supplies or services, that are covered by the framework agreement, either by requiring them from one of the economic operators, determined in accordance with objective criteria and on the terms already set out, or by awarding a specific contract for the works, supplies or services concerned following a mini-competition among the economic operators parties to the framework agreement. To ensure transparency and equal treatment, contracting authorities should indicate in the procurement documents for the framework agreement the objective criteria that will govern the choice between those two methods of performing the framework agreement. Such criteria could for instance relate to the quantity, value or characteristics of the works, supplies or services concerned, including the need for a higher degree of service or an increased security level, or to developments in price levels compared to a predetermined price index. Framework agreements should not be used improperly or in such a way as to prevent, restrict or distort competition.'

[36] For a consideration of aggregated procurement and framework agreements operated by centralised purchasing agencies, in which this issue is at its most acute, see Chapter 11.

[37] 'Are ID/IQs Inefficient? Sharing Lessons with European Framework Contracting', note 13, supra, at p. 558; citing Federal Acquisition Regulation (FAR), Code of Federal Regulations (CFR) Title 48, 16.500. FAR 2005-83/07-02-2015, available at www.acquisition.gov/?q=browsefar ('This subpart prescribes policies and procedures for making awards of indefinite-delivery contracts and establishes a preference for making multiple awards of indefinite-quantity contracts'.)

invited to participate at the call-off stage, with a limited exception that all 'capable' suppliers could be invited.[38]

A new flexibility to allow a combination of Models 1 and 2 framework agreements has been introduced in Article 33 (4)(b) of the EU Directive, so that a procuring entity may choose whether or not to use competition at the call-off stage.[39] In other words, the choice of applying the terms laid down in the framework agreement (i.e. based on the terms of original tenders) or to re-open competition in a mini-tender can be left until the second stage. The rules require the use of this hybrid approach to be disclosed in advance; where the procuring entity does so, the effect may be to elicit better offers at the first stage as bidders seek the highest-ranking in case the second stage is not competitive, and yet still allow the procuring entity the flexibility to tailor its needs at the second stage, where necessary. Views differed regarding whether this hybrid approach was permitted previously, and so the majority of countries did not allow for it. Consequently, empirical evidence on whether the potential benefits of a hybrid approach have arisen in practice is as yet unavailable.

The UNCITRAL Model Law, unlike the EU and US systems, contains dedicated procedures for the second-stage competition that apply to both Model 2 and 3 framework agreements (closed and open respectively).[40] The provisions are modelled on UNCITRAL's open-tendering procurement method (though are designed to operate more speedily and simply), and provide the limited flexibility in refining terms and conditions and the general requirement, noted above, to invite all awardees to participate. They impose transparency requirements – so that only awardees can take part in the call-off competition,[41] no new award criteria can be introduced, the invitation to participate must contain the same type of information

---

[38] For a discussion of the notion of 'capable' in this context, see Section 5.2.4. The provisions are slightly expanded for open framework agreements – a notification of the call-off is provided to all awardees, but there is no requirement to wait for a period of time to elapse before the second-stage competition.

[39] The provision reads, in full, 'where the framework agreement sets out all the terms governing the provision of the works, services and supplies concerned, partly without reopening of competition in accordance with point (a) and partly with reopening of competition amongst the economic operators parties to the framework agreement in accordance with point (c), where this possibility has been stipulated by the contracting authorities in the procurement documents for the framework agreement. The choice of whether specific works, supplies or services shall be acquired following a reopening of competition or directly on the terms set out in the framework agreement shall be made pursuant to objective criteria, which shall be set out in the procurement documents for the framework agreement. These procurement documents shall also specify which terms may be subject to reopening of competition'.

[40] See, further, Section 5.2.4.

[41] The provisions are designed to allow new joiners to open framework agreements to be admitted speedily.

*Promoting effective competition* 171

that is normally found in solicitation documents; defined submission deadlines is needed; and a standstill notice and period are required.[42]

The invitation process for the call-off stage can be automated, which may make the time and marginal costs of inviting all 'capable' awardees negligible in practical terms but the issue of ensuring efficiency in assessing responsiveness may be more significant given a wider pool of participants (unless the bids can be assessed automatically, as noted above).

The US federal system has taken a different approach to ensuring second-stage competition for some ID/IQs:[43] its US General Services Administration (GSA) Multiple Award Schedule (MAS) contracts, which are essentially open framework agreements available for the use of any US federal procuring agency, require awardees to provide discounts to their benchmark commercial prices (known as the 'most-favoured customer' approach).[44] For other ID/IQs there has been a move towards requiring second-stage competition in the way described above,[45] both for GSA/MAS contracts,[46] particularly when used by agencies of the US Defense Department, which is the largest user of these contracts.[47]

It is important to note that compliance with procedural provisions will not guarantee effective competition – it should ensure the widest appropriate participation. Examples from the US federal system (which has much longer-standing experience with framework agreements) indicate that 'multiple-award framework agreements had been used on at least one occasion to create an illusion of competition, when in reality the customer agency had already selected a preferred contractor or knew that two contractors had agreed not to compete against each other', because call-offs were 'a logical follow-on' from earlier call-offs (in one case, the follow-on call-offs were forty-six times the size of the original),[48] and because the program officers 'preferred to work with a specific contractor'.[49]

---

[42] There is, however, a general threshold below which there is no standstill/notice requirement in Article 22 of the Model Law, which may apply to many call-offs.
[43] Noting that not all ID/IQs are subject to the same requirements under the FAR, note 37, supra.
[44] 'Are ID/IQs Inefficient? Sharing lessons with European framework contracting', note 13, supra, at p. 558.
[45] Ibid., at p. 561.   [46] FAR, note 37, supra, 8.405–1 and 8.405–2.
[47] Defense Federal Acquisition Regulation Supplement (DFARS) 208.404 *et seq.*, 48 C.F.R. § 208.404 *et seq.*, available at http://farsite.hill.af.mil as cited in 'Assessing Framework Agreements under the WTO's Government Procurement Agreement: A Comparative Review of the US Experience', note 10, supra, at p. 12.
[48] 'Assessing Framework Agreements under the WTO's Government Procurement Agreement: A Comparative Review of the US Experience', note 10, supra, at p. 18.
[49] Ibid, citing, for example, T. F. Burke and S. C. Dees, 'Feature Comment: The Impact of Multiple-Award Contracts on the Underlying Values of the Federal Procurement System', 44 Gov't

Again from the United States, examples of how procedural safeguards have been abused are instructive. The procuring entity may fail to notify other awardees of a call-off, may provide inadequate notice,[50] may fail to provide useful descriptions/specifications, may impose biased technical requirements, may allow a slanted evaluation of offers and may ignore the many other rules meant to ensure vigorous, transparent competition. As one commentator noted, the

> Inspector General for the Department of Defense reported that contracting officials did not comply with the Federal Acquisition Regulation or the General Service Administration Special Procedures in 71 of 73 (97 per cent) of orders examined. As a result, the inspector general concluded that the government had been severely affected its ability to receive reasonable prices or the best value on these orders.[51]

In part, the ability to side-step procedural safeguards arises from a lack of transparency and accountability, indicating that the more robust approach in the Model Law to procedural requirements is both appropriate and necessary, including the requirements to issue award notices,[52] and that the award of framework agreements and of call-offs are open to challenge. Nonetheless, the call-off stage will need to be the subject of ongoing oversight.

## 7.5 Enhancing outcomes in framework agreements procedures

The above analysis focused on competition as a key driver for achieving value for money in framework agreements procedures. It was also noted in the introduction that competition can also be a spur for innovation,

---

Contractor Para 431 (6 November 2002), and U.S. Department of Defense, Office of Inspector General, Multiple Award Contracts for Services, Report No. D-2001-189 (30 September 2001).

[50] As the discussion above notes, in the federal system in the United States, task orders under a master contract need not be publicised for competition or award. Similarly, under the EU Directive, once a framework agreement is in place, the 'mini-competitions' among multiple awardees for the follow-on contracts need not be publicised – see Article 12 of the EU Directive, note 18, supra. Guidance published by the UK Office of Government Commerce (OGC) indicates that, if the original agreement is publicised in the *Official Journal of the European Communities*, subsequent contracts competed ('called off', in the British vernacular) under that agreement need not be advertised. See www.gov.uk/government/uploads/system/uploads/attachment_data/file/62063/ogc-guidance-framework-agreements-sept08.pdf.

[51] 'Assessing Framework Agreements under the WTO's Government Procurement Agreement: A Comparative Review of the US Experience', note 10, supra, at p. 19.

[52] Though with some exceptions, as discussed in Chapter 12.

as bidders seek to distinguish themselves from the pool of potential suppliers.[53] In the context of framework agreements, the relatively long-term nature of the relationship between suppliers and the procuring entity can operate to build sufficient trust to allow for an innovative response to the procuring entity's needs. However, two conditions will be needed for this possibility to materialise (assuming it is a desirable one) – first, the statement of needs in the solicitation or procurement documents will need to be sufficiently flexible for technological innovation. In terms of framework agreements design, functionally based statements of needs may also mitigate a common criticism of framework agreements procedures themselves – that they are not sufficiently responsive in practice to technological change and dynamic markets, though technical specifications may be appropriate for other reasons. Consequently, allowing for technological innovation may not always be feasible.

The second condition is a need for lower risk aversion generally evident among the procurement community. The reasons for such risk aversion have been well ventilated in the literature,[54] and it may suffice for present purposes to note the difficulty in encouraging 'the exercise of reasonable judgment and less risk aversion',[55] while bearing in mind the '[absence of a] change ... in existing rights and obligations concerning fraud and corruption',[56] including the full transparency requirements discussed in Chapter 8. It has recently been observed that procurement officials may be reluctant to retreat from the tried-and-tested, 'safe' solutions, specifications and suppliers and that the 'nobody ever got

---

[53] Some observers, however, consider that procurement regulation and the pursuit of efficiency in public procurement act as a barrier to innovation – see, for example, J. Potts, 'The Innovation Deficit in Public Services: The Curious Problem of Too Much Efficiency and Not Enough Waste and Failure', *Innovation: Management, Policy & Practice*, 11, No. 1 (2009): 34–43 (especially p. 36); E. Uyarra and K. Flanagan, 'Understanding the Innovation Impacts of Public Procurement', *European Planning Studies*, 18, No. 1 (2010): 123–143.

[54] An early and significant work on the topic was 'Procurement and Public Management: The Fear of Discretion and the Quality of Government Performance', S. Kelman (Washington, DC: The AEI Press, 1990); others include 'An Analytical Framework for the Management and Reform of Public Procurement', P. R. Schapper, J. V. Malta and D. L. Gilbert, 'An Analytical Framework for the Management and Reform of Public Procurement', *Journal of Public Procurement*, 6, No. 1/2 (2006): 1–26; J. Gutman, 'Is There Room for Discretion? Reforming Public Procurement in a Compliance-Oriented World', Global Economy and Development Working Paper 74 (2014), Brookings. Available at http://www.brookings.edu/research/papers/2014/05/29-reforming-public-procurement-gutman.

[55] The World Bank and Public Procurement—An Independent Evaluation, *Overview* (Vol. 1, p. 1). Independent Evaluation Group, available at http://ieg.worldbankgroup.org/evaluations/world-bank-group-and-public-procurement.

[56] Ibid., p. 2.

fired for choosing IBM' rationale remains a real barrier, particularly in the SME context.[57]

A related topic is the question of past performance in the assessment of suppliers, which remains a thorny issue in public procurement, though largely from a theoretical and policy perspective as empirical research into the benefits and possible costs of allowing past performance to figure in award decisions is limited. Framework agreements could offer the opportunity to reward suppliers for good performance or better-than-others performance,[58] but commentary on framework agreements procedures in this context (as in procurement more generally) focuses on the risks of past performance evaluations, such as that call-offs may be made on the basis of developing relationships between procuring entities and awardees. Even in the US federal system, where assessment of past performance is required in award decisions and encouraged as a matter of policy (and which can either upgrade or downgrade bidder ratings),[59] concerns have been expressed about errors, subjectivity and abuse.[60]

Commentary on the goal of assessing past performance is therefore commonly couched in terms of risk management, both in the United States and the European Union. For example, the Green Paper preceding the issue of the 2014 EU Directive noted that while most respondents to the consultations undertaken by the European Commission had voiced the opinion that past performance should be a permissible award criterion, nonetheless those respondents were

> aware of the risks and drawbacks of such a suggestion: some critical answers are cautioning against the danger of favouritism and discrimination while others are proposing safeguards to ensure a fair and objective assessment, such as the requirement of a measurable and objective performance control system (to avoid subjective blacklisting), judicial protection and possibly a

---

[57] 'Small and medium-sized enterprises policies in public procurement: time for a rethink?', note 21, supra.

[58] Which some observers consider would be a highly positive development in enhancing outcomes in public procurement – see, for example, G. Spagnolo, 'Reputation, Competition, and Entry in Procurement', *International Journal of Industrial Organization*, 30, No. 3(2012): 291–296.

[59] FAR, note 37, supra, Section 41.1201, states, 'Past performance information is relevant information, for future source selection purposes, regarding a contractor's actions under previously awarded contracts. It includes, for example, ... of reasonable and cooperative behaviour and commitment to customer satisfaction; and generally, the contractor's business-like concern for the interest of the customer'. See, also, G. Spagnolo, supra, and D. D. Gransberg and M. A. Ellicott 'Best-value Contracting Criteria', *Best-Value Contracting Criteria*, 39, No. 6 (1997): 31–34. Available at: http://works.bepress.com/douglas_gransberg/8.

[60] K. V. Thai, ed., *International Handbook of Public Procurement* (CRC Press, 2008), at p. 614.

cap for the weighting of the relevant criterion, to keep the market open for newcomers.[61]

Unsurprisingly given the prior policy approach to constrain the use of past performance information, the provisions in the EU Directive allow procuring entities to penalise for poor performance, though with safeguards, and do not, for example, contemplate rewarding good performance.[62]

Another element of past performance in public procurement that remains under-researched is the impact of managing procurement risk by continuing to contract with a supplier whose past performance has been satisfactory.[63] Further, a study has (unsurprisingly) found that 'the most important incentive [to do high-quality work] that an owner has is the promise of repeat work'.[64] Given the concerns noted above, safeguards and systems would clearly be necessary and imposed before positive past performance criteria were permitted to allow future call-offs to take earlier performance into account, so that performance is evaluated in an objective fashion. From an administrative perspective, too, care would be needed not to require exhaustive evaluation of poor performance (which would impose a disproportionate burden where an alternative may be not to award future call-offs to an underperforming awardee).[65] Such systems can allow 'good working relationships and cosy relationships' between procuring entities and suppliers to be distinguished through safeguards such as avoiding single-officer decisions, staff rotation and effective audit and oversight,[66] and could also offer an opportunity to reward innovation. This is an emerging area in terms of policy dialogue and policy formation, and it is to be hoped that data analysis from framework agreements may assist in its development.

In addition, framework agreements procedures can and do operate as drivers of *procedural* and related innovations – an important consideration

---

[61] Green Paper on the modernisation of EU public procurement policy, towards a more efficient European Procurement Market, Synthesis of replies, at p. 12, available at http://ec.europa.eu/internal_market/consultations/docs/2011/public_procurement/synthesis_document_en.pdf.

[62] UNCITRAL followed this approach in a rare example of reducing discretion available under the 2011 Model Law as compared with its 1994 predecessor, in deleting 'reputation' as a permissible qualification criterion for similar reasons. UN Document A/CN.9/687, at paragraph 47.

[63] J. A. Rueda-Benavides and D. D. Gransberg, 'Indefinite Delivery-Indefinite Quantity Contracting', *Transportation Research Record: Journal of the Transportation Research Board*, N. 2408 (2014): 17–25.

[64] Ibid., citing Thomsen, C. 'Project delivery processes', April 2006, available at http://isites.harvard.edu/fs/docs/icb.topic1043613.files/7-2_Thomsen_Project%20Delivery%20Processes.pdf.

[65] Indefinite Delivery-Indefinite Quantity Contracting, 2014, note 63, supra.

[66] P. Arden, 'Legal Regulation of Multi-Provider Framework Agreements and the Potential for Bid Rigging: A Perspective from the UK Local Government Construction Sector', *Public Procurement Law Review*, No. 5 (2013): 165–182, at p. 175.

given the desired outcome of reducing the administrative burden of procurement procedures.[67] It has been observed that 'commercial purchasing' – a phrase often heard in connection with framework agreements procedures – involves two related but distinct concepts. The first is purchasing items in the commercial market – that is, items not designed to the particular specification of the procuring entity and that are available in an established market,[68] which the US federal procurement system terms 'commercial-off-the-shelf (COTS)' items. The second is the use of commercial procurement practices – such as framework agreements – so that the procuring entity operates more like a commercial purchaser.[69] As has been noted, the drive in the US market towards commercial procurement was motivated in part by attempts 'to break [government's] longstanding habit of demanding that firms create government-unique versions of goods and services available in the commercial marketplace',[70] a practice that involves simulations of the private sector under procurement laws and regulation, which are designed to set a fair price through competition.

Framework agreements offer an opportunity to encourage the greater use of COTS products and services where the government's needs are not different from those of commercial consumers of those products and services. The effect can be marked in framework agreements operated by centralised purchasing agencies, which we consider in Chapter 11, as such framework agreements make standard products and services available to procuring entities at a reduced administrative burden, can discourage gold-plating for these items and can secure economies of scale and value benefits. A related benefit is that the potential supply market can be broadened (as compared with a market defined by a procuring entity's specification), which was a major driving force behind the US reforms.[71] From a procedural perspective, some of the complex planning requirements for setting up framework agreements (considered in Chapters 2 and 3) can be reduced

---

[67] On process innovation, see J. Yeow and J. Edler, 'Innovation Procurement as Projects', *Journal of Public Procurement*, 12, No. 4 (2012), at p. 477.
[68] For which UNCITRAL, for example, permits the use of request-for-quotations (see Model Law, Article 29(2), note 18, supra, which also imposes an upper-value threshold for the use of this procurement method).
[69] For an in-depth consideration of these questions, see Steven L. Schooner, 'Commercial Purchasing: The Chasm between the United States Government's Evolving Policy and Practice', chapter 8 in *Public Procurement: The Continuing Revolution*, Arrowsmith & Trybus, eds., 2003; GWU Law School, Public Law Research Paper No. 25. Available at SSRN: http://ssrn.com/abstract=285536 or http://dx.doi.org/10.2139/ssrn.285536.
[70] Ibid., at p. 6.   [71] Ibid., at pp. 12–17.

*Promoting effective competition* 177

where COTS products or services are appropriate, and the competition requirements can be streamlined and price-focused.

Thus framework agreements procedures offer the potential for procedural innovation – both in terms of reducing administrative burdens and in encouraging the use of COTS products – though, as has been observed, the change in procurement practices that commercial purchasing involves should not be under-estimated. As was reported back in 1998, the first of four necessary pillars for procurement reform is political endorsement and commitment to change,[72] a point that is particularly apposite given that the change in this case is cultural rather than technical.

### 7.6 Chapter summary

- Assessing the degree of competition in framework agreements needs to take into account the concrete design of the two-stage purchasing arrangement. Focusing on the first ('entry') stage of a framework agreement might be misleading as firms would generally be willing to compete fiercely to enter an agreement if they anticipate that there is enough room for recouping additional profits at the call-off stage.
- Framework agreements that allow bundling a stream of procurement contracts of different values will favour both participation and entry of large enterprises as well as SMEs, and so are instrumental to spur competition including at the second stage of the procedure (when a mini-competition is foreseen).
- Full disclosure of the 'rules of the game' of a framework agreement and, specifically, of the rules at *both* stages of the game is vital to promoting healthy competition.
- A clear and objective definition of the subject matter (preferably outcome-based) of the procurement together with a description of the range of flexibility for contract tailoring, avoiding the use of trademarks, standardisation of documents and terminology are the main tools to favour competition at the first stage of the procedure.
- Model 2 framework agreements raise the most serious concerns about the effective level of competition at the call-off stage of the procedure. Competition may be flawed, for instance, by lack of transparency/advertisement of contract opportunities to all framework awardees or

---

[72] See Report of the Proceedings of the Conference on Public Procurement Reform in Africa – 20 November–4 December 1998 – Abidjan, Cote d'Ivoire, discussed in W. Wittig, 'Building value through public procurement: a focus on Africa', 1999, International Trade Centre, available at http://9iacc.org/papers/day2/ws2/dnld/d2ws2_wwittig.pdf.

by abuse of discretion (say, by an unwise use of past performance) by procuring entities in inviting awardees to participate in mini-competitions. The new model of framework agreements recently introduced by Directive 2014/24/EU, which mixes the features of Model 1 and 2, deserves close scrutiny as to the rationale(s) used by procuring entities to have a second round of competition at the call-off stage.

CHAPTER 8

# *Integrity concerns in framework agreements*

## 8.1 Introduction

The preceding chapter considered promoting competition in framework agreements on the assumption that the market operates normally, that is, without distortion, so that competition in fact can be presumed if the appropriate conditions are present. However, as the European Court of Justice has remarked, '[if] the tenders submitted by those taking part are not the result of individual economic calculation, but of knowledge of the tenders by other participants or of communication with them, competition is prevented, or at least distorted and restricted'.[1] This is not a new notion – as a well-known comment by the moral philosopher Adam Smith in *The Wealth of Nations* (1776) reminds us: 'People of the same trade seldom meet together, even for merriment and diversion, but the conversation ends in a conspiracy against the public, or in some contrivance to raise prices'.[2]

A feature of framework agreements is that the closed varieties in particular can limit the market for the subject matter of the framework agreement at issue to a select few suppliers, and so create – albeit on a temporary basis – a potentially cartelised market for the products, services or construction concerned. Bidders in such a market may dislike cut-throat competition, and so prefer to 'coordinate their actions to soften price competition and raise joint profit'.[3]

In such circumstances, competition is absent and so, too, is the value for money that competition is designed to promote. Thus, the integrity of the

---

[1] The European Sugar Cartel [1973] OJ L140/07, and Judgment of the Court of 16 December 1975, *Coöperatieve Vereniging 'Suiker Unie' UA and others v. Commission of the European Communities*. Joined cases 40 to 48, 50, 54 to 56, 111, 113 and pp. 114–73. European Court Reports 1975–01663.
[2] *The Wealth of Nations*, Book IV Chapter VIII, p. 145, para. c27.
[3] G. L. Albano, P. Buccirossi, G. Spagnolo and M. Zanza, 'Preventing collusion in public procurement', chapter 14 in *Handbook of Public Procurement*, N. Dimitri, G. Piga and G Spagnolo, eds. (Cambridge University Press, 2006).

process is compromised.[4] While integrity in public procurement is generally considered as the avoidance of corruption and abuse, ensuring that the personnel involved in procurement act ethically and fairly, avoiding conflicts of interest,[5] it also requires procurement officials to seek best value through ensuring effective competition.

Collusion involves two or more bidders seeking to distort the competition for a procurement contract and need not involve the procuring entity at all. Corruption involves one or more officials in the procurement process as well as bidders or suppliers, and it hinges on an exchange of unlawful benefits.[6] However, corruption and collusion in public procurement should be viewed 'as concomitant threats to the integrity of public procurement',[7] and may be more closely intertwined than many procurement specialists would suspect.[8] For example, a corrupt procurement official might ask for bribes from colluding bidders, in amounts that may exceed bribes demanded in a non-collusive environment – perhaps as a reward for turning a blind eye to collusive practices –[9] and/or might impose distorted qualification requirements to ensure only the colluding bidders are qualified to participate in the procedure.

This chapter will consider distortion of competition in framework agreements procedures. While collusion normally takes place during bidding for procurement contracts (and, conceivably, when bidding at the first stage of framework agreements procedures), corruption is a

---

[4] Thus, the OECD defines integrity as the 'use of funds, resources, assets and authority, according to the intended official purposes and in line with public interest', Draft Recommendation of the Council on Public Procurement, GOV/PGC/ETH(2014)7/REV2, available at www.oecd.org/gov/ethics/draft-recommendation-on-public-procurement.pdf.

[5] See Guide to Enactment of the UNCITRAL Model Law on Public Procurement (2012), Official Records of the General Assembly, Sixty-seventh Session, Supplement No. 17 (para 46, UN document A/67/17). The text of the Guide to Enactment is available at www.uncitral.org/uncitral/uncitral_texts/procurement_infrastructure.html. Hereafter, Guide to Enactment. For a discussion of conflicts of interest, see the commentary on the Preamble, Promoting the integrity of, and fairness and public confidence in, the procurement process, paras 28–29 on p. 41.

[6] That is, the abuse of office (public or private) for private gain, such as through eliciting bribes.

[7] Executive Summary of the OECD Global Forum on Competition debate on Collusion and Corruption in Public Procurement in February 2010, available at www.oecd.org/competition/cartels/46235884.pdf; UNODC: Implementing procurement-related aspects, note submitted by UNCITRAL to Conference of the States Parties to the UNCAC, 2008, available at www.unodc.org/documents/treaties/UNCAC/COSP/session2/V0850164e.pdf.

[8] For instance, G. Kosenok and A. Lambert-Mogiliansky, 'Fine-tailored for the Cartel – Favoritism in Procurement', *Review of Industrial Organization*, 35, No. 1 (2009): 95–121, show that, in order to decrease the uncertainty inherent in public procurement contracts, cartels may capture public authority representatives. In other words, corruption may increase the rate of return from a collusive agreement.

[9] F. Boehm and J. Olaya, 'Corruption in public contracting auctions: the role of transparency in bidding processes', *Annals of Public and Cooperative Economics*, 77, No. 4 (2006): 431–452, at p. 439.

pathological phenomenon that may arise at any stage of the procurement process, from needs definition until contract execution. Although framework agreements, being relatively long-lasting, can provide the ideal environment for opaque interactions between holders of the agreements and procurement officials,[10] and so can facilitate corruption as well as allowing collusive arrangements to go undetected by oversight bodies, the literature provides little evidence that corruption is a greater threat in framework agreements procedures than in other procurement procedures of similar size and scope. Consequently, and also given the significant discussions on corruption in the literature,[11] we shall focus on collusion in framework agreements procedures, given its significant potential as a threat to the integrity of the process.

In order to render the discussion more digestible, we shall start by considering a single framework agreement, being set up for the first time. We shall also assume that the first stage of the procedure is not tainted by collusion: thus, we shall examine the issue of collusion at the call-off stage of a single, existing, framework agreement. Subsequently, we shall comment on some particular difficulties posed by repeated framework agreements, and those concluded in markets that are not themselves intrinsically competitive. Chapter 9 will address some policy responses and mitigation strategies where collusion is suspected.

## 8.2 Extent and effects of collusion

Collusion among suppliers is a major problem for most types of public procurement: studies indicate that it may add at least 20 per cent to the

---

[10] In spite of the possible drawbacks, however, one should not underestimate that establishing a long-term relationship is often essential for a contractor to have the appropriate incentives to make buyer-specific investment, particularly in the procurement of specialized services. This was arguably one of the milestones of the reform of the US federal procurement regulation when Professor Kelman was the head of the US Office of Management and Budget (OMB). For the role of long-term relationships in procurement and the importance of bidders' reputation, see S. Kelman, 'Remaking Federal Procurement', *Public Contract Law Journal*, 31 (2002). See, further, Chapter 7.

[11] G. M. Racca and C. R. Yukins, eds., *Integrity and Efficiency in Sustainable Public Contracts – Balancing Corruption Concerns in Public Procurement Internationally* (Bruylant, 2014); Y. Lengwiler and E. Wolfstetter, 'Corruption in procurement auctions', chapter 16 in *Handbook of Public Procurement*, N. Dimitri, G. Piga and G Spagnolo, eds. (Cambridge University Press, 2006); R. Burguet and Y.-K. Che, 'Competitive procurement with corruption', *The RAND Journal of Economics*, 35, No. 1 (2004): 50–68; T. Søreide, 'Corruption in public procurement – Causes, consequences and cures', Chr. Michelsen Institute Report (2002), available at www.cmi.no/publications/2002%5Crep%5Cr2002-1.pdf.

price that would otherwise be paid in competitive markets,[12] through preventing competition and consequent loss of value for money. In addition to distorting markets, '[b]y suppressing the natural rivalry among bidders, a cartel reduces the incentive to innovate ... negatively affecting consumer welfare also in the long run'.[13] In other words, collusion's negative effects are not restricted to public procurement markets: by excluding competition generally in the market, prices can be higher, and/or quality and innovation lower, than would otherwise be the case, to the detriment of all consumers.

A few examples will suffice to provide a flavour of the extent of collusive arrangements in procurement markets.[14] In 2003, the Netherlands Competition Authority (NMa) fined twenty-two bidders operating in the construction industry as cartels (contrary to the Dutch Competition Act, 1988). The construction companies were fined for price fixing, market-sharing agreements and bid rigging.[15] In 2002, the Italian Competition Authorities (AGCM) fined eight bidders operating in the food voucher industry for bid rigging in a nationwide framework agreement procedure set up by Consip, the national central purchasing body, on behalf of central and local government bodies.

A third insightful antitrust case in the UK procurement market provides at least a flavour of the level of awareness of procurement managers on anti-competitive issues. In 2009, the UK competition authority sanctioned more than 100 companies that colluded in public and private tenders for the construction of hospitals, schools and universities during the period 2000–2006. These cases were investigated pursuant to a complaint filed by an auditor of the national health system. The Office of Fair Trading (OFT) hired a consultancy bidder to assess public buyers' and entrepreneurs' level of perception of the risk of collusion in the construction industry and the perception of the effectiveness of the OFT's fight against cartels. Two rounds of surveys were carried out: the first one in 2008 just before the OFT issued the statement of objections against 112 bidders for alleged bid rigging in 199 tenders; the second one in 2010 after the OFT had fined (in September 2009) 103 out of the 112 bidders a total £129.2 million.

---

[12] See R. D. Anderson and W. E. Kovacic, 'Competition Policy and International Trade Liberalization: Essential Complements to Ensure Good Performance in Public Procurement Markets', *Public Procurement Law Review*, 18 (2009): 67.

[13] A. Heimler, 'Cartels in Public Procurement', *Journal of Competition Law and Economics*, 8, No. 4 (2012): 849–862.

[14] The reader will bear in mind that academic research on collusion in framework agreements is very limited, so we shall be applying more general conclusions on collusion in public procurement.

[15] Described in Section 8.3 below.

The results of the first round of survey were almost shocking: more than 50 per cent of the respondents declared that the most typically observed collusive practices among bidders – such as, agreeing to fix prices, to sit out of a bid or to avoid competing in a particular region – were very infrequent or inexistent; more than 40 per cent did not have any idea that these practices were pervasive.[16]

Collusion is not confined within *public* procurement markets. As recently as 31 March 2015, the US Department of Justice (DOJ) announced that Robert Bosch GmbH, the world's largest independent parts supplier to the automotive industry, based in Germany, had agreed to plead guilty and to pay a $57.8 million criminal fine for its role in a conspiracy to fix prices and rig bids for spark plugs, oxygen sensors and starter motors sold to automobile and internal combustion engine manufacturers in the United States and elsewhere. According to the charge, Bosch and others participating in the scheme conspired through meetings and conversations in which they discussed and agreed upon bids and price quotations on bids to be submitted to certain automobile and internal combustion engine manufacturers and to allocate the supply of the products to those manufacturers.[17] Appendix B to this chapter sets out some additional collusion cases in public procurement to illustrate what may be suspicious behaviour that procurement officials should be on guard against (detection approaches are further discussed in Chapter 9).

In spite of this pervasiveness of collusion in public and private procurement markets, indications are that most procurement officials appear still not to be fully aware of collusion risks, and consequently do not possess the necessary skills to mitigate the risks concerned.[18] This evidence of lack of awareness of the risk of collusion in public procurement markets is particularly worrisome in the framework agreements context, as in some circumstances framework agreements may be *more* at risk of the problem of

---

[16] The OFT report(s) can be accessed through http://webarchive.nationalarchives.gov.uk/20140402142426/http://www.oft.gov.uk/OFTwork/competition-act-and-cartels/ca98/decisions/bid_rigging_construction. For a summary of the report, see A. Georgopoulos, 'Office of Fair Trading Report: The Impact of Public Procurement on Competition', *Public Procurement Law Review*, 14, No. 2 (2005): 48–50.

[17] News taken from the webpage of the US DOJ's Office of Public Affairs: www.justice.gov/opa/pr/robert-bosch-gmbh-agrees-plead-guilty-price-fixing-and-bid-rigging-automobile-parts-installed (last accessed on 21 April 2015).

[18] Collusion detection requires different skills and competences from those needed for successfully organising and running a bidding procedure, and training and/or coordination with competition authorities may be required. See OECD, *Recommendation of the OECD Council on Fighting Bid Rigging in Public Procurement*, 2012, available at www.oecd.org/daf/competition/RecommendationOnFightingBidRigging2012.pdf; 'Cartels in Public Procurement', 2012, note 13, supra.

collusion than other types of public procurement.[19] On the other hand, many markets in which the use of framework agreements procedures are appropriate – those for simple, off-the-shelf, relatively low-value, repeat purchases – may be highly competitive, so that the theoretical risk of collusion may not arise in practice.

Drawing on the demand and market analysis of Chapter 3, we shall proceed to indicate how these risks of collusion may arise in the context of public procurement generally and in framework agreements procedures in particular.

## 8.3 Market structure and demand factors that may facilitate collusion

Although we may have an intuitive idea of what collusion in procurement markets means, it is worth adopting a practical description for the purpose of the current chapter. Collusion in procurement markets can be thought of as any conduct adopted by a group of bidders that aims at reproducing or approximating the market outcome induced by single, dominant bidder. In layman's language, at collusion's core is an agreement not to submit independent, competitive bids, but to deviate from this behaviour and agree that one of the colluding bidders will win the contract. A further objective may be to increase the price (or reduce the quality) of the winning bid so that greater-than-normal profits are realised, and the public purchaser overpays for the products or services purchased.

Various mechanisms are available to this end: bidders can engage in 'cover bidding', 'bid suppression', 'bid rotation' and 'market allocation agreements'.[20] Collusive behaviour in the public procurement context can be referred to as 'bid rigging', which will be our area of focus, though other cartel activities may be in existence in some markets.[21] To achieve this

---

[19] As discussed further below, in that the first stage identifies players in what becomes a limited market, so that coordination among them is facilitated. The analysis carried out in this chapter draws on 'Preventing Collusion in Public Procurement', note 3, supra.

[20] 'Cover bidding' (also called complementary, courtesy, token or symbolic bidding) is designed to give the appearance of genuine competition, whereby bidders agree to submit higher-priced bids than the bid of the designated winner or to submit a bid that is known to be too high to be accepted or to have unacceptable terms; 'bid suppression' consists in one or more bidders agreeing to refrain from bidding or to withdraw a previously submitted bid so that the designated winner's bid will be accepted; in 'bid-rotation' schemes bidders agree to take turns being the winning bidder; in 'market-allocation' schemes bidders agree not to compete for certain contracts or in certain geographic areas. Definitions adapted from OECD, *Guidelines for Fighting Bid Rigging in Public Procurement*, DAF/COMP, 2009.

[21] Including market allocation and sharing. See, for instance, R. C. Marshall and L. M. Marx, *The Economics of Collusion* (MIT Press, 2012), for a thorough and enlightening (non-technical) analysis of the economic forces of collusion.

objective, according to Stigler's (1964) seminal contribution,[22] suppliers need to:

- coordinate their strategies (either tacitly or explicitly);
- determine how to share the collusive profit among themselves; and
- detect and punish deviant behaviour; that is, retaliate against those breaching the collusive agreement ('cheats').

Since the mechanisms for bid coordination are discussed in more depth in other specialised works,[23] here we shall limit ourselves to summarising that public procurement markets possess intrinsic features that make cartels more stable and/or make cartel formation more likely than in other oligopolistic markets.[24]

In general, cartels suffer from an inherent instability as cartel members have an incentive to cheat on the agreed prices and/or quantities; for example, by selling below the agreed price or outside their assigned territory. (In the short term, until they are detected, cheats will make super-profits at the expense of other cartel members.)

It is a well-known tenet of modern economic theory[25] that when deciding whether to adhere to a collusive strategy, each bidder needs to evaluate the net benefits from current deviations – namely, short-run profit minus the expected cost arising from other bidders' punishing strategies, such as price wars involving all cartel members – against the present value of benefits from cooperation. Many features of market interactions exert an effect on each colluding bidder's net value of 'co-operation'. For instance, finding an easy solution to share profits, monitoring each other's actions and reacting quickly to deviant behaviour of one or more cartel cheats help cartel stability.

In public procurement markets, the stability of a collusive agreement is greatly affected by the cartel's ability to prevent new bidders from entering the market. New entrants – perhaps enticed by higher prices in the procurement sector than the commercial market for the same goods and services – might undercut the cartel and yet still generate profits higher than would be obtained in the commercial sector (depending, of course, on the relative costs of participation in each sector).

---

[22] G. J. Stigler, 'A Theory of Oligopoly', *Journal of Political Economy*, 72 (1964): 44–61.
[23] See, for instance, *The Economics of Collusion*, note 21, supra.
[24] On the nature and stability of public procurement cartels, see, also, 'Cartels in Public Procurement', note 13, supra.
[25] See, further, the explanation in note 20, supra.

Framework agreements – particularly the 'closed' models – raise collusion concerns beyond those in public procurement generally as the logic of the two-stage process is to create a new market for the subject matter of the framework agreement with (i) a limited number of players (lower than full-market) who will be known to each other, assuming normal transparency mechanisms apply,[26] and (ii) those suppliers knowing that they will be competing over time for the envisaged purchase orders. In a less-than-full market, suppliers can be tempted to make additional profits through coordination rather than full competition, as coordination becomes feasible. Where the framework is one of the closed models, the new market will generally be more limited than in open framework agreements, and may be to some degree an oligopolistic market; if so, the collusion risk is elevated.

In the remainder of this section, we shall discuss some of the main pro-collusive features of public procurement markets that are likely to be heightened when framework agreements are in place.

### 8.3.1 Barriers to entry and concentrated markets

A first question is whether it is feasible to coordinate and collude, which is largely an issue of whether there are sufficiently few suppliers to allow an effective collusive arrangement to be made among them. In basic economic terminology, how concentrated is the existing market, and are new players able to compete?

The nature of some public procurement markets (energy, specialised construction and so on) is that they are oligopolistic, so the participants will be known to each other and able to share information even outside the procurement processes. In other markets, the existence of a large number of suppliers and a competitive market makes collusion more difficult from both the coordination and the enforcement perspectives.[27] Framework agreements procedures may be appropriate in both types of market: their

---

[26] Most systems require, for example, an award notice when the framework agreement is concluded, identifying the suppliers that have been admitted to the framework agreement, and including pricing information where possible. See, for example, the UNCITRAL Model Law on Public Procurement (2011), *Official Records of the General Assembly, Sixty-sixth Session, Supplement No. 17* (UN document A/66/17). The text of the Model Law is available at www.uncitral.org/uncitral/un citral_texts/procurement_infrastructure.html. Hereafter, Model Law, at Article 23, and Article 50 of Directive 2014/24/EU of the European Parliament and of the Council of 26 February 2014 on public procurement and repealing Directive 2004/18/EC Text with EEA relevance, OJ L 94, 28 March 2014, pp. 65–242, available at http://eur-lex.europa.eu/legal-content/EN/TXT/?uri=celex:32014 L0024. Hereafter, the EU Directive.

[27] Although, interestingly, the cartel in the UK construction case discussed in Section 8.2 comprised more than 100 bidders.

use for repeat purchases of off-the-shelf items in competitive markets is well known, but repeat procurement of fuel, maintenance services, airline or car rental services may also be undertaken in a relatively concentrated market.

Consequently, where a market is relatively competitive before a framework agreement procedure is instituted, collusive behaviour need not be presumed, and a competitive first stage of the procedure can be anticipated. However, closed framework agreements procedures in effect can *create* a mini quasi-oligopolistic market once the first stage is completed, and the aggregate restrictive effects of framework agreements include opportunity costs of excluding suppliers from the market (though, it should be conceded, a large-scale traditional procurement contract with one supplier may have the same effect).[28] Markets may also be *de facto* divided by geography where procuring entities operate locally and so exhibit similar features.

It is self-evident, too, that closed framework agreements operate as a complete barrier to entry to the procurement markets concerned that lasts for the duration of the agreement: by definition, no new suppliers can be admitted to the framework agreement during its period of operation.[29] In the case of open framework agreements, there may still be a temporary or partial barrier – in that new joiners are permitted at any time, but an incumbency advantage may effectively preclude new entry in some markets. By 'incumbency advantage', we mean the incumbent supplier's or suppliers' (potential) informational advantage when bidding for call-offs at the second stage. Such an advantage may arise through developing a better understanding of the procuring entity's requirements or as a result of specific investments made by the successful bidder that give it a cost advantage: in addition to discouraging new entrants, an incumbency advantage may weaken competition during the operation of the (open) framework agreement.[30]

Allied to the barriers to entry to a framework agreement market, a procurement system more generally may include features that can prevent new joiners from expanding the number of bidders in a public

---

[28] A. Sanchez-Graells, *Public Procurement and the EU Competition Rules*, 2nd ed. (Oxford: Hart, 2015), at pp. 298–299.
[29] Absent the exceptional circumstances in which replacement suppliers are permitted, discussed in Chapter 5.
[30] Paras 1.26–1.27, 'Assessing the impact of public sector procurement on competition Volume 1: main report', September 2004 Prepared for the Office of Fair Trading by DotEcon, available at www.dotecon.com/assets/images/oftmain.pdf.

procurement market. These barriers to entry may arise from different sources. Economic and technical requirements imposed by the procuring entity (whether they are excessive qualification requirements or restrictive technical specifications)[31] can exclude potential bidders and may disproportionately dissuade smaller bidders or bidders with alternative technical solutions from participating. In addition, submitting a bid *per se* requires specialised (mainly administrative) expertise, requiring dedicated personnel that only larger suppliers are likely to possess. These (and other participation costs) are fixed rather than varying with the value of the procurement concerned, and so affect smaller bidders proportionately more than larger bidders. Accordingly, where framework agreements procedures are used in markets in which SMEs play a significant part, it may be unexpectedly easy to create barriers to entry, whether intentionally or unwittingly.[32]

### 8.3.2 *Predictability and stability in the market*

The second set of pro-collusive market characteristics relates to the extent to which there is security in the market concerned. Cartels require that the likely extent of procurement opportunities can be predicted with sufficient certainty over a period of time, so that members can be sure of receiving 'their' allocation. This phenomenon is sometimes referred to as 'sharing the pie', and it is axiomatic that the size of the pie needs to be known in order to be able to share it out in a stable way (i.e. in a way that does not threaten the stability of the collusive ring). There are various factors that will contribute to the dimensions of the pie. The main such factors are summarised below.

#### 8.3.2.1 *Demand predictability*

Many procurement contracts are instrumental to the daily functioning of public organisations (e.g. telephone services, IT and medical equipment, building and road maintenance), and so demand is stable and regular. Although downturns in the business cycle also affect public spending, public demand remains more stable and, consequently, more predictable than private demand. Consequently, all else being equal, public procurement processes make it easier for cartels to implement 'bid-rotation' or

---

[31] Addressed, for example, in Articles 9 and 10 of the Model Law (note 26, supra).
[32] For a more detailed discussion of barriers to entry in the framework agreements context, see Chapter 7.

'pie-sharing' mechanisms that would not be enforceable if demand were unstable and/or unpredictable over time, and this effect is enhanced in the case of framework agreements procedures for commonly needed, repeat purchases, particularly where the needs are standardised so that the individual call-offs are identical in terms of design, and perhaps quantity.

### 8.3.2.2 Fixed quantities

Where public authorities announce that they will contract out a fixed number of units through the framework agreement or advertise defined call-off quantities, the certainty of total demand or elements of demand under the framework agreement will leave participating bidders to focus mainly on the technical and financial dimensions of the procuring entity's needs at the call-off stage. As a result, the coordination problem will be easier in that fewer variables need to be accommodated. Moreover, monitoring cartel members' behaviour and detecting cheating are also made easier.

### 8.3.2.3 Few substitutes

Where there are few alternatives for the public purchaser's needs, the cartel's stability is enhanced (as new entrants are less likely). As a general rule, where markets are stable and there is little or no innovation or technical change, so that the products or services at issue are similar and stable, the cartel can also operate more securely; the procuring entity will also have fewer incentives to purchase outside the framework agreement (and possibly further enhancing demand predictability). In addition, the use of unnecessarily detailed or restrictive technical requirements (using technical specifications where more flexible output-based descriptions would allow the needs to be met) can create a situation in which there are few, if any, substitutes for those needs (another way in which to create barriers to entry to the market concerned).

### 8.3.2.4 Demand fragmentation

A fourth question is the overall size of the pie: many small pies can each be shared among different suppliers: this can be referred to as demand fragmentation.

Similar, albeit nonidentical, contracts are awarded every year by a large number of public authorities. For example, in 2013, the Italian National Authority for Public Contracts (now merged with the National Anticorruption Authority) served more than 15,000 contracting authorities; that is, public organisations that can carry out procurement procedures.

Were these to buy similar products or services independently of each other, public demand would in fact be split into thousands of separate lots, which would make market-sharing agreements quite feasible. Thus, for any given value of aggregated public demand, the higher the level of demand fragmentation – that is, the higher the number of procurement processes – the easier the risk of collusion among bidders. However, a potentially counterbalancing effect is triggered by public demand being divided among a higher number of contracts. As the average contract value declines, more (smaller) bidders are in a position to participate – due to less stringent economic requirements – thus enlarging the set of potential bidders.

### 8.3.2.5 *Procedural aspects – public procurement rules and transparency*
A fifth element is whether the potential pie-sharers can be identified, and any cheats on an existing collusive scheme detected and punished. There are both general and specific dimensions to this question.

Public procurement markets possess specific characteristics that ease this task. As the OECD has observed, '[t]ransparency can result in unnecessary dissemination of commercially sensitive information, allowing bidders to align their bidding strategies and thereby facilitating the formation and monitoring of bid rigging cartels'.[33] 'The more information the [procuring entity] conveys about bidder identities, the bids submitted, and [procurement procedure] outcomes, the easier it is for a ring to be effective in its work of suppressing rivalry among members'.[34]

Once a bid-rigging scheme is in place, a mechanism to detect (and punish) cheating is needed to perpetuate it. In the ordinary commercial market, cartels may be required to spend substantial resources to monitor members' behaviour to this end. Here, too, transparency obligations in public procurement make cheating quicker and easier to detect. Stigler originally noted that '[t]he system of sealed bids, publicly opened with full identification of each bidder's price and specifications, is the ideal instrument for the detection of price-cutting'. Transferred to the framework agreements context, the fact that details of bids are revealed at the first stage (including the identities of the awardees) creates a significant opportunity

---

[33] From OECD Global Forum on Competition, Collusion and Corruption in Public Procurement – Executive Summary, 18–19 February 2010, available at www.oecd.org/officialdocuments/publicdisplaydocumentpdf/?cote=DAF/COMP/GF(2010)7/ANN2/FINAL&docLanguage=En.
[34] A. Sanchez Graells, 'The difficult balance between transparency and competition in public procurement: Some recent trends in the case law of the European Courts and a look at the new Directives', citing R. C. Marshall and L. M. Marx, *The Economics of Collusion. Cartels and Bidding Rings* (Cambridge, MIT Press, 2012), available at https://lra.le.ac.uk/bitstream/2381/29334/2/SSRN-id2353005.pdf.

for the awardees to collude and distort competition throughout the second stage.

The unfortunate consequence for the public purse is that transparency can make cheating less likely, particularly in markets in which the procuring entity purchases similar products or services in a relatively short time period so that cheating is deterred through the risk of early detection. As a consequence, punishing behaviour (such as short-term predatory pricing to the detriment of the cheat) is also facilitated, and procurement cartels thus tend to be more stable in public procurement markets than in other commercial markets.

While recommendations to limit transparency in public procurement as an anti-collusion measure merit closer examination (to which we will return in Chapter 9), it is nonetheless instructive to record how little information is needed by cartels in order to enforce a collusive agreement: many other features of public procurement markets tend to facilitate cartels' success. Suppose, for instance, that a procurement contract has been split into different lots and that an active cartel aims at implementing a collusive scheme by selecting for each lot the prospective winner and the winning bid while other cartel members have to submit higher bids (the so-called 'cover bidding' scheme). Any deviation from the collusive scheme generates a different-than-agreed bidder in at least one lot. As soon as that lot is awarded and the prospective winner does not receive an official award notification, it becomes instantaneously clear that a deviation from the collusive agreement has taken place. 'Not-winning' is enough for detecting cheating. So only this tiny piece of information is needed for the cartel's monitoring purposes.

In many markets, in addition, participating bidders may know each other through 'social connections, trade associations, legitimate business contacts, or shifting employment from one company to another'.[35] This knowledge enables market-players to coordinate their strategies. Although this coordination could take place at any stage of a procurement procedure or independent of it and in advance of a framework agreement procedure,[36] it should be noted that awardees can meet in advance of the deadline for submission of bids in a call-off to finalise arrangements. Adam Smith also commented "But though the law cannot hinder people of the same trade

---

[35] Competition Policy and International Trade Liberalization: Essential Complements to Ensure Good Performance in Public Procurement Markets, note 12, supra.
[36] For example, in a procurement cartel in Brazil – for Security Guard Services – regular meetings took place at trade association headquarters, in restaurants and even barbeque parties, as reported by the OECD. See OECD Competition Committee, 'Annual Report on Competition Policy Developments in Brazil', 2007, DAF/COMP (2008) 10, 30 May 2008, page 15, available at www.cade.gov.br/upload/AnnualReport2007[1].pdf.

from sometimes assembling together, it ought to do nothing to facilitate such assemblies, much less to render them necessary". Souce, again, *The Wealth of Nations*, Book IV Chapter VIII, p. 145, para. c27.

The ability to meet for bid-rigging purposes is particularly troubling in the context of framework agreements: partial bid-rigging agreements, which do not completely eliminate price competition, still reduce rivalry between competitors, sometimes substantially, and require limited interaction to conclude. For example, partial agreements can involve the use of a standard formula or ratio to compute prices, and/or a geographical splitting of the market. Significant features of these partial agreements include that the collusive arrangement is made at the outset, does not require any further contact between cartel members for it to be implemented or renewed and need not be recorded.[37] Detection is consequently difficult, and it is clear that this type of arrangement could be relatively straightforward to conclude in the framework agreements context, both within one framework agreement and in a series of repeat framework agreements, especially where demand is highly predicable.

### 8.4 Framework agreements procedures and risk of a pro-collusive market

In this section, we shall explore the most relevant pro-collusive features of the procedures used to conclude framework agreements, and we shall start from the perspective of the structure of the first stage of the procedure; in the following section, we shall further investigate some pro-collusive features that may specifically arise at the second ('call-off') stage, particularly in 'closed' framework agreements, which arguably raise the most urgent anti-competitive concerns. Key issues, derived from the notion of demand predictability, revolve around the extent to which there is symmetry between the bidders admitted to the framework agreement at the first stage of the procedure ('awardees') and the procurement contracts, or call-offs, awarded at the second stage. It can be seen that sharing the pie will be much easier where the numbers of both are certain and one is divisible into the other.

#### 8.4.1 First stage of the procedure

The planning process prior to commencing a framework agreement procedure will generally include market research, which may reveal

---

[37] Cartels in Public Procurement, note 13, supra, citing J. Harrington, 'Posted pricing as a plus factor', *Journal of Competition Law and Economics*, 7, No. 1 (2011): 1–35.

*Integrity concerns in framework agreements* 193

whether or not the market concerned is competitive or has historically been regarded as cartelised. Assessing the market characteristics and the extent of demand predictability will assist in appropriate mitigation strategies, where necessary.

### 8.4.1.1 *The number of awardees and the sequence of procurement contracts*

The number of awardees in a framework agreement affects collusion for two main reasons. First, as we have seen, the higher the number of awardees, the more difficult the coordination among them to split procurement contracts: reaching an agreement on market shares and on prices or quality becomes more complex as the number of bidders, potentially parties to a collusive agreement, increases. Second, the higher the number of colluding awardees, the smaller the share of the overall collusive profit each of them receives, on the basis of any particular estimated value of the procurement contracts to be awarded at the second stage. Consequently, the lower the share of procurement profit, the higher the potential gains from deviating from an all-inclusive collusive agreement. As we have seen for barriers to entry, 'closed' framework agreements in this situation possess an intrinsically more pro-collusive potential than 'open' framework agreements, as call-offs or awards of procurement contracts under the framework agreement cannot be challenged at the second stage by any outsider.

In an 'open' framework agreement, however, a prospective cartel has to face the risk of new entrants entering the system to compete for a specific procurement contract. The varying size of the set of competing bidders for each procurement contract may then act as a potentially effective anti-collusive device. It is therefore precisely this absence of such a 'window for entry' that makes 'closed' framework agreements more exposed to collusion among the selected awardees.

If the collusive agreement is limited to the duration of a single framework agreement, then the total value of potential collusive profit is limited by the sum of all procurement contracts that are awarded at the second stage. The sequence of call-offs could, in principle, be assimilated with a public contract split into several lots, the difference being that lots are awarded at different points in time. Thus, for a given number of awardees and for a given total value of all procurement contracts under the framework agreement, the higher the number of call-offs, the higher the risk of collusion since there will be a higher number of 'pie-sharing' arrangements that allow a more accurate division of the spoils. Put differently, smaller shares of the collusive 'pie' make the allocation of collusive profit among bidders easier, which will provide the necessary incentive for a cartel to be sustainable (i.e. it can stand alone within the framework agreement, without resorting to side payment and/or using market-sharing agreements elsewhere).

Moreover, for a given duration of the framework agreement, a higher number of call-offs gives rise to a higher frequency of interaction among the framework's awardees. A higher number of call-offs is an aspect of demand predictability in that both repeated and more frequent procurement procedures enhance predictability. In the framework agreements procedures, the second-stage competitions, or call-offs, can give rise to two elevations in the risks of collusion. First, where framework agreements involve repeat purchases of regularly needed products and services (perhaps the most commonly encountered version), the average frequency of similar or identical procedures is likely to be higher than traditional contracts for these supplies (a consequence of their administrative convenience). Together with regular call-offs, they may further enable the swifter and more effective detection and punishment of cheats. Finally, the predictability of the stream of call-off contracts allows either a prospective or an already-active cartel to be more confident on 'how much collusion is worth' thus strengthening cartel stability.

To sum up, a limited number of awardees facing a long stream of possibly low-value procurement contracts (which might be generated by few contracting authorities buying frequently as well as by a large number of contracting authorities awarding procurement contracts with longer duration) would find themselves in the ideal environment to tune up collusive agreements.

### 8.4.1.2 *Joint bidding*

Larger-scale contracts, which many framework agreements involve, may adversely affect the participation of small businesses, which will not have the capacity to fulfil the entire requirements contracted for, even when the scheduling of anticipated purchase orders is taken into account. One possible solution for SMEs is to participate in temporary joint ventures. In fact, casual observation in public procurement practices reveals a common instance of joint bidding, that is, the practice of two or more bidders combining to submit a single bid.

There are two categories of joint bid – of which the first is the situation in which the bidders concerned combine to be able to fulfil the requirements in the solicitation documents (which may be a question of capacity in terms of quantity, or in order that all qualification and capacity requirements are satisfied – such as may be the case where the framework agreement combines products and/or services). While this type of joint bidding may enlarge participation and competition, it remains nonetheless true that a second type of joint bid – 'horizontal' bidding consortia – may raise anti-competitive issues. These involve similar bidders that are normally competing with each other, but combine to submit a single bid, and therefore act to reduce the competitive pool. Whether joint bidding raises concerns in individual cases may be difficult to predict, and policy and operational considerations are discussed in Chapter 12.

### 8.4.2 Second stage of the procedure: call-offs or award of procurement contracts under framework agreements

#### 8.4.2.1 The relevance of the number-of-awardees-to-number-of-contracts ratio

While both the number of awardees and the anticipated frequency or number of procurement contracts exert an impact on the risk of collusion in framework agreements, as we have seen, one should not look at them as separate dimensions of the problem: it is the symmetry between them that raises or reduces the collusion risk. In other terms, it is the number of awardees *relative to* the number of procurement contracts that provides a potential insight on the risk of collusion.

Absent any information on the sequence of call-offs, there is no inherent reason why a three-awardee framework agreement is riskier than a five-awardee one. That is, all other things being equal, a five-awardee framework agreement during which twenty-five procurement contracts have to be awarded may turn out to raise more concrete collusion concerns than a three-awardee framework agreement that comprises only three call-offs.

In fact one should also look at the relative values of procurement contracts to each awardee, as this ratio will determine to what extent colluding bidders will be able to allocate profits (i.e. via call-offs or procurement contracts). In essence, each member's bargaining power will influence how profits are shared among the members of the collusive ring. To take the example above with three awardees and three call-offs, if the cartel members have different market shares but the three procurement contracts are of similar value, the situation may not be favourable to collusion. Indeed, any market-sharing agreement giving each supplier one contract is likely to leave the strongest member unsatisfied, whereas allocating unequal shares will inevitably force the cartel to resort to side payments as one cartel member will not be allocated any procurement contract. If, instead, five symmetric bidders – that is, with similar market shares – were to face a stream of twenty-five procurement contracts, it would be easier to find an allocation of contracts among the five-bidder cartel so as to allocate fairly similar shares of the 'collusive pie'.

### 8.4.2.2 The degree of heterogeneity of procurement contracts and the nature of competition at the call-off stage

Recalling the general comments about similarity and predictability of the procurement contracts for products or services under a framework agreement, the degree of homogeneity among procurement contracts will be captured by the extent to which the framework agreement itself already contains the contractual clauses governing the procurement contracts to be awarded at the second or call-off stage. If, for instance, a framework agreement contains most of the contractual conditions – that is, the framework agreement is characterised by a low degree of incompleteness – then procurement contracts will vary little from each other. Consequently, the subject matter of procurement contacts will be fairly homogeneous, which, in turn, makes market-sharing agreements easier. This effect is stronger the lower the number of quality dimensions that can be further specified or completed by purchasing authorities at the call-off stage.

When quality characteristics remain stable over the sequence of procurement contracts and it is also possible to describe them in the framework agreement, then competition is often price-driven. This is the case, for instance, of 'rate contracts' which are customary in Asia.[38] Rate contracts usually aim at providing procuring entities with products at similar, if not identical, value-for-money conditions while ensuring a certain degree of supply differentiation. These objectives are achieved by using an award criterion that is basically the lowest-price technically acceptable criterion. Moreover, bidders that had not submitted the lowest price are offered the possibility of joining the agreement by matching the lowest submitted price. Thus, while offering the same price to all procuring entities, the rate is intrinsically characterised by a degree of uncertainty as to the number of the agreement's awardees. From a competitive viewpoint, though, rate contracts may raise substantial concerns as, intuitively, a cartel which is already active in the market may implement a potentially simple collusive

---

[38] The case of rate contracts in India is described in more detail in Chapter 6.

agreement whereby (i) one of the cartel members is selected to submit as high as possible 'lowest price'; and (ii) all other cartel members submit bids strictly higher than the winning bid and then declare to be willing to match the lowest bid. As a consequence, all the cartel members become holders of the rate contract, which is offered to procuring entities at the same non-competitive price.[39]

When the design of a framework agreement foresees a second stage of competition for awarding procurement contracts, bidders may find themselves in an asymmetric environment when competing on prices but with products or services of different quality. Price competition with different qualities could be easily reinterpreted as price competition among bidders with different costs. There are three main reasons why cost asymmetry is thought to hinder collusion. First, coordination problems are obviously more complex when bidders have divergent preferences concerning collusive prices and there are no natural focal points. Second, it may be difficult to convince an efficient bidder to join a cartel, since it may earn relatively high profits even under competition. Third, cost asymmetry may also hinder the sustainability of collusion, since (i) it may be more difficult to retaliate against an efficient bidder in case it deviates from the cartel agreement, and (ii) a more efficient bidder may gain relatively more from deviating in the short term.

### 8.4.2.3 Symmetric versus asymmetric competition at the call-off stage

Asymmetry among bidders may be a consequence of tender evaluation at the first stage of competition. When the framework agreement is concluded by using the most economically advantageous tender (MEAT) criterion, bidders may be allowed to 'carry forward' a fraction of the awarded technical score. This case may arise[40] when participating bidders' technical proposals refer to aspects that are common to all subsequent call-offs. Thus, upon competing for each single call-off, bidders may become asymmetric if they have inherited a fraction of the initial technical score that was awarded at the first stage. Let us see this with a stylised example in which the maximum technical and financial scores are 60 and 40, respectively. Table 8.1 lists both the awarded technical and financial score of the three highest-ranked bidders.

---

[39] Appendix A at the end of the chapter contains a more formal analysis of collusive-like outcomes in a stylised rate contract with two bidders.
[40] 'Inherited' technical score was one of the features of the two framework agreements designed by Consip in Italy for acquiring IT services on behalf of the Department of Treasury of the Ministry of Economy and Finance in 2008 and 2011. The case study is discussed in Chapter 6.

Table 8.1 *First-stage competition for entering a multi-award Model 2 framework agreement*

|  | Technical score | Financial score | Total score |
| --- | --- | --- | --- |
| Bidder A | 46 | 8 | 54 |
| Bidder B | 40 | 10 | 50 |
| Bidder C | 30 | 15 | 45 |

The framework agreement is concluded with bidders A, B and C. Assume also that when bidding for the sequence of call-offs, each bidder inherits 50 per cent of the technical score awarded at the first stage; that is, bidder A starts with 23 points, bidder B with 20 and bidder C with 15.

How will such an asymmetric scenario affect the risk of collusion among bidders? Let us assume that the evaluation method of the financial dimension of the tender at the first stage was such that the lower the submitted price, the higher the financial score. Then we can safely maintain that bidders B and C had submitted higher discounts than bidder A. If the design of the framework agreement forbids bidders from raising their prices at the call-off stage above those submitted at the first stage,[41] any symmetric 'pie-sharing' collusive agreement (i.e. bidders rotate in winning call-offs by awarding bidder A the first contract, bidder B the second, bidder C the third and so on) would leave bidder A with higher collusive profit than its competitors. Thus, if bidders are alike with respect to other economic dimensions such as market shares/sizes/production costs, incentive-compatibility constraints require the cartel to allocate a higher number of contracts to bidder C than to bidder B, and a higher number to the latter than to bidder A. Thus, for a given value of the framework agreement and for a given stream of call-offs, score-heterogeneous bidders are likely to find it more difficult to agree on a collusive scheme than bidders competing for call-offs on a 'level' playing field.

More generally, quality-price competition both at the first and at the second stage are likely to exacerbate the asymmetries among bidders, thus making collusion, all else being equal, more difficult than in those environments in which competition is driven only by price considerations.

---

[41] The Italian regulation of framework agreements, for instance, goes in that direction.

*8.4.2.4 Using electronic reverse auctions to award procurement contracts*
Any second-stage competition in a framework agreement is suited for electronic bids submission, particularly when competition is only on financial dimensions. There exist, in principle, two major solutions for designing electronic submission of bids at the call-off stage: one-round format (*e-bids*) and multi-round format (*e-reverse auctions*).

Casual observation in many countries shows that there seems to exist a clear preference of public procurement organisations for e-reverse auctions, whereby, typically, bidding takes place during a fixed and publicly announced period of time and the awardee is determined by the lowest bid when the deadline expires. In spite of different versions of e-reverse auctions being in use, the features above constitute the core set of bidding rules.

The main question of the current section can be phrased as follows: Why does the dynamic or reverse format seem to be preferred over the one-shot (single-round) format whereby bidders submit electronic bids just once? Is there any intrinsic advantage in having a multi-round rather than a single-round competition? Do the two formats raise different collusion-related concerns? As we shall see in the following subsections, there are circumstances in which bidders may overcome, at least partially, the uncertainty about the cost of the procurement contract and thus become more aggressive when they are able to observe the process of price formation. This is possible in most configurations of e-reverse auctions. However, prices can be used as messages to coordinate their strategies and thus e-reverse auctions may facilitate collusion. Single-round formats, instead, while useless to provide additional information to bidders, cannot be easily manipulated to coordinate bidders strategies and thus constitute an anti-cartel device.

*8.4.2.4.1 Private versus common components in the production cost for procurement contracts* In order to flesh out under what set of circumstances one format might be preferable to the other, we need to cast light on the logic that competing bidders adopt to formulate bids. In Chapter 3 we discussed that, upon estimating the cost of performing the contract, each tenderer has to consider two main dimensions in the cost function: the private and the common dimension.

Uncertainty about the common component of the cost of serving a contract matters since the contractor may find that the 'true' cost of performing the contract differs from its initial estimate. This may happen if the contractor submitted a bid on the basis of an overly optimistic forecast. More generally, if a supplier does not take this possibility into account at the time of bidding for the contract, it may suffer from the 'Winner's Curse'; that is, it may realise that actual production costs are higher than estimated ones. On the one hand, the danger of running losses *ex post* may induce tenderers to bid too cautiously for the contract, which implies potentially high awarding prices for the buyer. On the other hand, the tenderers' inability to recognise the Winner's Curse may generate too-an-aggressive bidding that results in low awarding prices for the buyer, but may induce the contractor to cut productions costs by lowering the quality of the performance in order to recoup losses or to raise profit. Although in most circumstances, bidders' production costs display both common and private components, it is reasonable to expect one of the two dimensions to exert a relatively higher impact on the bid formulation. When the common component prevails, each bidder could work out a better estimate of its actual production costs if it could have access also to other bidders' pieces of information about the same component. Suppose, for instance, that a procuring entity wishes to purchase janitorial and day-to-day maintenance services for several buildings scattered over a certain area. After carrying out inspections of a subset of those buildings, each tenderer is in a position to formulate at least a ballpark figure of the average size or characteristics of the premises to be cleaned which, in turn, has an impact on estimated costs. If all tenderers could share the inspections' results, then each of them would certainly rely on more precise information about the average characteristics. More reliable estimates about the common value component of the cost function generally translate into a lower risk of suffering from the Winner's Curse.

*8.4.2.4.2 Information production in e-reverse auctions* When each bidder's estimate has to be built on its own set of information, an appropriate design of the competitive mechanism may help bidders infer, at least to some extent, competitors' information about costs and pricing strategies, for example. That is, an e-auction can be designed so as to allow bidders to learn from each other. By allowing bidders to revise bids, e-reverse auctions can generate additional information that was not available to competitors before the bidding activity started.

There exist, however, two sources of concern for a procuring entity when opting for a e-reverse auctions. All else being equal, some information revelation or circulation may increase the risk of collusion. Clearly, in most circumstances, it will not be possible to preserve the anonymity of the bidders: this was the justification for permitting e-reverse auctions in the

EU Directive and Model Law in a framework agreement procedure: the identities are likely to be disclosed at the first stage of the proceedings. The risk is also higher as multiple contracts will normally be awarded under the framework agreement. Indeed, bidders can exploit the openness and the multi-round feature of an auction format to send signals (through prices) to each other in order to coordinate. Moreover, e-reverse auctions may allow members of a bidding ring to detect deviation from a collusive scheme and punish deviating bidders in a very short time frame.

Unlike e-reverse auctions, e-bidding does not generate any additional information to that available to competing bidders before bidding starts. This format is then ineffective in generating information about the common value component of the cost function. Thus, a single round of bidding auction does help reduce the risk of collusion among bidders as any deviation from a collusive strategy cannot be detected and punished during the same auction.

### 8.4.2.5 *Awarding call-offs – average bid and other methods*

As a general rule, the criteria for awarding a public procurement contract are based on best-value (or an equivalent notion, such as most economically advantageous tender) or lowest-price (responsive) bid. Overall, observations of procurement indicate that lowest-price is the most frequently used award criterion generally, though other possibilities have been suggested. These include a 'cascade' approach in which the first-ranked awardee receives all contracts until its capacity is exhausted (a non-competitive call-off), rotation between awardees, percentage allocation and random selection, all of which could also operate as anti-collusive methods.[42] While these methods appear to be used in framework agreements practice, it is not clear that they are in fact permitted in either the EU Directive or UNCITRAL Model Law.[43]

In addition, procuring entities may use 'average bid methods' that select the winner by considering the distance of each bid from the (simple or geometric) average of all bids. Such a mechanism may further protect a cartel from deviations by raising the cost of deviation to any prospective deviant cartel member.

---

[42] S. Arrowsmith and C. Nicholas, 'Regulating Framework agreements under the UNCITRAL Model Law', chapter 2, in *Public Procurement Regulation in the 21st Century* (Eagan, MN: West, 2009); Procurement Lawyers' Association 'The use of Framework Agreements in Public Procurement', 2012, p. 35, available at www.procurementlawyers.org/pdf/PLA%20paper%20on%20Frameworks%20PDF%20Mar%2012.pdf.

[43] See UNCITRAL Guide to Enactment (footnote, commentary to Article 59, para 14 on p. 280.

Table 8.2 *Unit prices resulting from the first stage of competition in a multi-award Model 2 framework agreement*

| Bidder | Stage 1 price (€) |
|--------|-------------------|
| A | 1,150 |
| B | 1,100 |
| C | 1,080 |
| D | 1,050 |
| E | 900 |

When the framework agreement is relatively complete; that is, it specifies all technical dimensions of the product or service and the only remaining variable is the quantities to be purchased at the call-off stage, it would be not unsurprising that price-only competition is used at both stages of the framework agreement. International experiences and specialised literature[44] point out that price competition may take different formats, differing from each other in terms of the extent to which they may facilitate collusion among bidders. In particular, the class of average-bid (AB) awarding criteria may increase the risk of collusion relative to the lowest-price (LP) criterion.

Consider a multi-award incomplete framework agreement for LCD projectors to be concluded with, say, five bidders who have submitted the (five) lowest prices subject to a set of minimal quality standards (e.g. resolution, lumen rating, contrast ratio and physical dimension). At the call-off stage, the procuring entity, after specifying the exact number of projectors needed, carries out the second round of price-only competition. Suppose that the selected bidders have submitted the unit prices listed in Table 8.2.

How would the cartel, including all five awardees, behave at the call-off stage? If a procurement contract is to be awarded by using the LP criterion, the cartel needs to coordinate on the (most profitable) collusive price and to select one bidder as the designated winner. As each bidder's submitted price at the call-off stage cannot be higher than the one resulting from the first stage of competition, the highest possible collusive price for the five-bidder cartel is €900. Suppose the cartel has designated bidder E to be the

[44] See, for instance, the cases reported by G. L. Albano, M. Bianchi and G. Spagnolo, 'Average-Bid Methods in Procurement', *Rivista di Politica Economica*, No. I–II (2006): 41–64; and Ministerio de Industria y Comercio – República de Colombia, 2007.

winner. A simple collusion scheme would then work as follows: bidders A to D submit a (unit) price equal to €900 while bidder E submits €899.[45] If any bidder different from E, say A, were to deviate, it would have to submit a price lower than or equal to €898.[46]

Consider now a particular class of AB awarding criteria, namely the one hinging on the simple (mathematical) average of all submitted bids. One variant of the simple-average criterion determines the winner by selecting the bid closest to and strictly lower than the simple average of all bids. In this case, the collusive scheme would work exactly in the same fashion. Given that cartel members A to D bid €900 while E bids €899, the simple average is €899.9; thus bidder E is awarded the contract. In order to assess whether or not this specific AB criterion favours collusion relatively to the LP criterion, we need to answer the following question: How much should a deviating bidder bid in order to win the contract, and does such a deviation guarantee a higher or lower profit than the one needed under the LP criterion? Bidder A, the deviating member, needs to place a bid such that all other bids remain above the (new) average. It is easy to see that €898 is no longer sufficient for the purpose. Indeed, conditional on the deviation taking place, the new average becomes €899.4, the winner being always bidder E. Bidder A needs to formulate the most profitable price that brings the simple average below €899. Then it needs to bid the highest possible $x$ such that $(x+899+3\cdot(900))/5 \leq 899$, which implies $x = €896$. Since the most profitable deviation under the AB criterion yields lower profit than under the LP criterion, the former displays a stronger pro-collusive feature than the latter.

The pro-collusive feature of the class of AB criteria would be strengthened if the geometric average (GA)[47] were to replace the simple average. In Latin America, for instance, the GA criterion is implemented by awarding the contract to the bidder whose bid is closest (whether from above or from below)[48] to the geometric average of all submitted bids. Notice that under the GA criterion the collusive scheme is slightly different with respect to

---

[45] Assuming, for the sake of simplicity, that prices have to be formulated as multiple of €1. Here we do not worry about the specific profit-sharing scheme adopted by the cartel. A simple one might consist in each bidder taking turns in being designated as the winner throughout the sequence of procurement contacts.
[46] Notice that this is a more profitable deviation than submitting a price equal to €899 resulting in a tie between bidders A and E, which would be resolved by a fair random mechanism. That is, with a price of €899 bidder A would have only a 50 per cent chance of being awarded the contract.
[47] The geometric average (or mean) of $N$ numbers $(x_1, x_2 \ldots, x_N)$ is simply the $N$-th root of the product of the $N$ numbers, that is $(x_1 \cdot x_2 \cdot \ldots \cdot x_N)^{1/N}$.
[48] More formally, the winner is selected by considering the absolute value of the distance of each bid from the geometric average of all bids. Then the contract is awarded to the competing bidder whose bid minimises the computed absolute distance.

the AB criterion: bidders A to C bid €899, bidder D bids €898, while bidder E – the designated winner – bids €899. Since the value of the geometric average of these bids is equal to €899.4, bidder E is awarded the contract. It is easy to replicate the same exercise carried out above in order to compute the most profitable deviation from the collusive agreement. In this case, the deviating bidder needs to bid the highest possible $y$ such that it minimises the absolute difference between itself and the new geometric average. A simple computation shows that $y$ = €33! This is a remarkable lower price than the deviation under the AB criterion, considering the strong pro-collusive feature of the GA criterion.

### 8.5 Repeated and parallel framework agreements

The introduction to this chapter noted that the substantive analysis would focus on the main concerns about collusion in single framework agreements. The nature of the types of procurement for which framework agreements are most suitable, however, is likely to lead to repeated framework agreements and, perhaps, the existence of parallel framework agreements (i.e. the existence of several framework agreements covering the same goods or services).[49]

In the case of parallel framework agreements, an additional form of collusion may arise – across the various agreements – so that the pie to be shared is not the single framework agreement, but a series of agreements in which the collusive ring is operating (such a ring is likely to comprise relatively large-scale bidders, which can operate in more than one market contemporaneously). While these cross-framework arrangements may be more complex to coordinate, and the collusive bidders may be less able to rig each individual bidding opportunity, alternative forms of collusive behaviour such as periodic sharing of profits from within one framework agreement, or other transfers, may also arise. Also cartel enforcement in one agreement is strengthened by the opportunity of punishing cheaters on the other agreement.[50]

In the case of repeated framework agreements procedures, the risk is that the very use of the framework agreement promotes a concentration or even cartelisation of the market. Smaller competitors may leave the market as a

---

[49] The use of Framework Agreements in Public Procurement, note 42, supra.
[50] This pro-collusive effect is driven by multimarket contracts and was first formally analysed by B. D. Berheim and M. D. Whinston, 'Multimarket contact and collusive behavior', *The RAND Journal of Economics*, 21, No. 1 (1990): 1–26.

result of bundling of requirements, and remaining competitors acquire an incumbency advantage for the next framework agreement.

We noted at the beginning of the chapter that demand fragmentation – that is, a large number of procuring entities carrying out their own procurement processes for similar goods or services and facing a smaller set of competing suppliers – may favour collusive agreements. However, an active cartel may still bear the uncertainty of facing a competing fringe of possibly small suppliers, especially for low-value procurement contracts. If, say, the same set of procuring entities were to regroup their needs under a few framework agreements, then an active cartel would benefit from all the advantages discussed above, thus becoming stronger and stronger over time.

## 8.6 Chapter summary

- Public procurement markets possess pro-collusive features that might ease cartel formation and strengthen the stability of those cartels already active. Repeated and relatively stable purchasing patterns, the presence of multiple buyers purchasing similar products/services/works, barriers to entry generated by excessively stringent participation requirements and too narrow technical specifications are among the most pro-collusive traits of public procurement markets. While some dimensions of 'transparency' of public procurement processes may play a role in facilitating enforcement of collusive agreement, cartel members need in fact very little information to monitor each other, thus the impact of transparency in cartel formation and stability is often overestimated.
- 'Closed' framework agreements may be affected by even more pro-collusive features as they allow a potentially restricted subset of firms to operate under the shelter of no competition from outside competitors for the whole duration of a framework agreement.
- Both the absolute number of framework awardees and the number or value of procurement contracts to be awarded at the call-off stage play a role in determining the risk of collusion. More important, though, is the ratio between the two dimensions.
- Procurement contracts in a framework agreement may be assimilated to different lots that are awarded at different points in time. Cartel members with very different (similar, respectively) bargaining power will prefer a stream of differently valued (similarly valued, respectively) procurement contracts.
- Parallel framework agreements for similar products/services/works are likely to strengthen a collusive agreement as cartel members will have a

higher number of opportunities to punish deviant behaviour, which is akin to collusion driven by multi-market contacts.
- Awarding procurement contracts by using average-bid methods is customary especially in the construction industry for non-complex works. The AB method awards a contract to the bidder submitting the bid that minimises the distance from the simple (or even geometric) average of all (valid) bids. The AB method possesses an intrinsically more pro-collusive feature than the lowest-price criterion as it increases the cost of deviating from a collusive agreement.
- The call-off stage of framework agreements lends itself quite naturally to the use of e-auctions, which might speed up the award of procurement contracts. The two main families of e-auctions, namely e-bidding and e-reverse auctions, are generally recognised to have a different impact on the risk of collusion among bidders. Reverse (i.e. multi-round) e-auction is more vulnerable to collusion than e-bidding (i.e. single-round e-auction) as it allows cartel members to detect and punish a cheating firm during the same bidding process.

## APPENDIX A    COLLUSION IN 'RATE CONTRACTS'

Consider the following stylised rate contract and two competing bidders. Bidder 1 bears a production cost which is normalised to naught, while Bidder 2 bears a production cost $c > 0$. The rate contract works as follows. Bidders submit simultaneously bids. Once bids are ranked, the high-bid bidder is asked to match the competitor's (lower) bid. If the high bid accepts, then the low-bid bidder gets a share $k$, $0 < k < 1$, of the rate contract, while the other bidder gets $1 - k$. If it does not accept, the low-bid bidder gets the whole contract. If bidders submit identical bids, then the $(k, 1 - k)$ split is carried out by a flip of a (fair) coin. The value of $k$ is publicly announced before bidders submit their bids. Bidders are long-run competitors in the same market so that they know each other's production cost. Finally, assume that the awarding authority rejects any bid above 1.

### 'Standard' competition *à la* Bertrand

The (seemingly) most intuitive prediction about the outcome of competition for the rate contract is the Bertrand prediction, whereby Bidder 1 bids marginally below its competitor's cost, $c$, while Bidder 2 bids exactly its cost. Then the low bid is equal to a price marginally below $c$ so Bidder 2 will not be willing to match as it would run losses. Consequently, Bidder 1 gets the whole contract, reaping net profit (marginally below) $c$.

## Any collusion-like outcome?

Is it possible that the rate contract is split between the two bidders at a price different from $c$? Notice first that such a price, $p^*$, has to be strictly greater than $c$; otherwise Bidder 2 would not be willing to either submit or match it. Let us consider the following bidding pattern whereby both bidders submit the same bid $p^*$, where $c < p^* < 1$. According to the rate contract's rules, both bidders have equal probability of being offered a share $k$ of the contract. Obviously, regardless of which bidder is offered a share $k$ the other is offered the share $1 - k$ at the same price $p^*$. Given this bidding pattern, Bidder 1's (expected) payoff is equal to $1/2 \cdot k \cdot p^* + 1/2 \cdot (1 - k) \cdot p^* = 1/2 \cdot p^*$, while Bidder 2's (expected) payoff is equal to $1/2 \cdot k \cdot (p^* - c) + 1/2 \cdot (1 - k) \cdot (p^* - c) = 1/2 \cdot (p^* - c)$. We have, however, to check whether such a bidding pattern is rational for both bidders. Rationality means that each bidder has to weakly prefer this outcome over being either the low-bid or the high-bid bidder given that its competitors bid $p^*$. Consider the problem from Bidder 2's viewpoint. Being the high-bid bidder means that Bidder 2 considers bidding any price $p > p^*$, which yields a profit equal to $(1 - k) \cdot (p^* - c)$. If, instead, Bidder 2 considers being the low-bid bidder, then it would just slightly undercut its competitor so that its profit becomes $k \cdot (p^* - c)$. Thus, the above 'equal-bid' strategy is rational for Bidder 2 provided that

$$1/2 \cdot (p^* - c) \geq (1 - k) \cdot (p^* - c) \text{ and } 1/2 \cdot (p^* - c) \geq k \cdot (p^* - c).$$

A similar reasoning would apply to Bidder 1, whose rationality constraints would then become

$$1/2 \cdot p^* \geq (1 - k) \cdot p^* \text{ and } 1/2 \cdot p^* \geq k \cdot p^*.$$

It is quite immediate that the four constraints above can only be fulfilled if $k = 1/2$. Finally, Bidder 1 has to (weakly) prefer to get half of the contract at a price $p^*$ rather than the whole contract at a price (marginally below) $c$ that Bidder 2 would not be willing to match. That is,

$$1/2 \cdot p^* \geq c,$$

which implies that $p^* \geq 2c$, with $p^* \leq 1$. Since bidders' profits are increasing in $p^*$, they have a clear incentive in 'coordinating' on $p^* = 1$. Thus condition

$p^* \geq 2\,c$ can be rewritten as $c \leq 1/2$, which means that the two competitors do not have to be too far away from each other in terms of efficiency.

This stylised environment delivers both good news and bad news. The good news is that the collusion-like prediction can emerge only when the contract is equally split between competing bidders. Therefore the awarding authority would only need to set different shares to destroy bidders' incentives to coordinate on $p^* = 1$, which is the worst possible outcome from the awarding authority's viewpoint. The bad news, though, is that, unless the rate contract is split equally and bidders are not too asymmetric in terms of production costs, the standard Bertrand outcome would prevail, implying a sole-sourcing solution. In other terms, the rate contract would fail to provide final users with supply diversification. The Bertrand prediction seems particularly sharp as the low-cost bidder knows exactly its competitor's cost so it can slightly undercut the latter, thus grabbing the whole contract. In many circumstances, though, bidders are completely informed about competitors' costs. In this case, it might be the case that the lowest submitted bid turns out to be higher than the second-ranked bidder's production cost. Hence, the latter would be willing to match the highest-ranked bidder's price and get a positive share of the rate contract.

## APPENDIX B   ADDITIONAL COLLUSION CASES

### OECD findings

The OECD published a series of examples of cases involving collusion and corruption in 2012:[51]

Canada – On 12 June 2012, the Canadian Competition Bureau announced that, together with the Unité Permanente Anticorruption in Quebec, it had brought 77 charges against 11 individuals and 9 companies in relation to a broad range of allegations that included corruption in municipal affairs. According to the Bureau, the case was the result of a two-year joint investigation. It uncovered evidence of a sophisticated collusion scheme giving preferential treatment to a group of contractors in the awarding of municipal contracts to provide infrastructure projects. The scheme reduced competition and led to a significant increase in costs for the affected cities. The consortium was able to inflate the cost of contracts

---

[51] From OECD Directorate for Financial and Enterprise Affairs Competition Committee, Latin American Competition Forum, Session III – Improving Effective Public Procurement: Fighting Collusion and Corruption, Background Note by the OECD Secretariat, DAF/COMP/LACF(2012) 15, 17 September 2012.

by between 25 and 30 per cent, and the fraud against taxpayers was valued at CAD 1 million. The scheme favoured a small number of contractors to the detriment of new bidders. Municipal officials facilitated bid rigging in exchange for gifts, tickets for shows and home improvements, while others accepted cash bribes for awarding contracts. Numerous criminal charges were brought for the corrupt conduct, and bid rigging charges were also brought under the Federal Competition Act.

United States and Mexico – On 10 July 2012, the United States Securities Exchange Commission (SEC) charged Texas-based medical device company Orthofix International with violating the Foreign Corrupt Practices Act (FCPA) when a subsidiary (Promeca) paid routine bribes, referred to as 'chocolates', to Mexican officials in order to obtain lucrative sales contracts with Mexico's government-owned Institute of Social Security (IMSS). From 2009 to 2011, contracts to Promeca were awarded by IMSS officials under exceptions to the public tenders procedures. The use of these exceptions is permitted, for example, when there is only one supplier in the market. Promeca, however, paid bribes to IMSS officials in order to avoid international public tenders. The bribery scheme lasted from 2003 to 2010 and generated nearly USD 5 million in illegal profits for the Orthofix subsidiary. Orthophix agreed a USD 5.2 million settlement with the SEC and entered into undertakings, including monitoring its FCPA compliance programme and reporting back to SEC for a two-year period. As a result of the US SEC's investigation, Mexico's Secretary of Public Administration (SFP) and the Federal Attorney Office (PGR) in Mexico commenced an investigation into IMSS's corrupt practices on 13 July 2012.

United States – From 2010 to 2012, the US Department of Justice's Antitrust Division, with the assistance of the FBI and the Internal Revenue Service, carried out an investigation related to re-insulation services contracts at the New York Presbyterian Hospital (NYPH). In 2010, a NYPH purchasing official pleaded guilty to conspiring to rig bids. Between October 2000 and March 2005, the official had conspired with others to create the appearance that contracts at the NYPH were awarded in accordance with NYPH's competitive bid policy. The official admitted that he designated which company would submit the lowest bid on a contract, and which company or companies would submit higher bids, to ensure that his designated company would be awarded the contract, thereby creating the illusion of a competitive bidding process. In exchange for awarding the contracts to the designated bidder, the official received cash kickbacks from his co-conspirators.

United States – On 15 September 2011, the US Department of Justice announced that Bridgestone Corporation, a Tokyo-headquartered manufacturer of marine hose and other industrial products, agreed to plead guilty and to pay a $28 million criminal fine for its role in conspiracies to rig bids and to make corrupt payments to foreign government officials in Latin America related to the sale of marine hose and other industrial products manufactured by the company and sold throughout the world. During the bid rigging conspiracy (from 1999 to May 2007) the cartel affected prices for hundreds of millions of dollars worth of marine hose (and related products sold worldwide). Bridgestone and its co-conspirators agreed to allocate shares of the marine hose market and to use a price list for marine hose in order to implement the conspiracy. Bridgestone and its co-conspirators agreed not to compete for one another's customers either by not submitting prices or bids, or by submitting intentionally high prices or bids to certain customers. In addition to the bid rigging conspiracy, and in order to secure sales of marine hose in Latin America, Bridgestone authorised and approved corrupt payments to foreign government officials employed at state-owned entities. As a result of the investigation, nine individuals were convicted and sentenced to a total of 4,557 days in prison for their involvement in the marine hose conspiracy. Bridgestone Corporation was charged with conspiring to violate both the Sherman Act and the FCPA.

*OECD summary of 'Fraud, corruption, and collusion in the roads sector: Findings from the 2011 World Bank Report'*

## Evidence from World-Bank projects

'In Bangladesh, evidence showed that companies paid project officials up to 15 per cent of the contract value in exchange for contract awards. In Cambodia, INT investigators concluded that there were strong indicators that a "well established cartel", aided by government officials, controlled the award of road contracts. In the Philippines, numerous witnesses independently informed ITN investigators that a well-organised cartel, managed by contractors with support from government officials, improperly influenced the Department of Public Works and Highways contracts awards and set inflated prices on projects funded by the Bank and others. In Indonesia, one Indonesian respondent explained that the Indonesian collusive system had been operating for 32 years, and many viewed the free market system as counter to the cultural norm of consensus and co-operation, a statement consistent with reports by Indonesia's competition law authority'.

## Evidence from other projects

'Staff of the UK's Overseas Development Institute reported evidence on an industry-wide cartel to fix prices on roads contracts in Uganda. In Tanzania, a review by a former Prime Minister disclosed an industry-wide cartel in the road sector. In India, a deputy Government Secretary told participants at an international conference that cartels in the road sector operated in various Indian states. A joint study by the Government of Nepal, the Asian Development Bank, the UK's Department for International Development and the World Bank concluded that in recent years no tender in the Nepalese construction industry had been free of collusion. A statistical analysis of bids in road tenders by the Lithuanian competition agency strongly suggested collusion among bidders there. A 2009 World Bank study of public procurement in Armenia noted widespread reports of collusion in tendering'.

CHAPTER 9

# Addressing risks of collusion in framework agreements

## 9.1 Introduction

Chapter 3 considered aspects of how framework agreements function on the assumption that there is an absence of anticompetitive behaviour and of distortion of competition in the markets concerned. The implications for design of framework agreements and the procedures to conclude them are based on analyses of the procuring entity's needs themselves (demand analysis) and the market concerned.

As regards demand analysis and how it is used to design a framework agreement appropriately, a key conclusion in Chapter 3 was that the extent to which the procuring entity's needs and terms of the procurement could and should be specified at the beginning of the framework agreement procedure, and consequently how complete the framework will be, will also feed into the competition model to be used.

The overall design conclusions in Chapter 3 are themselves based on an assumption that 'perfect information is a condition leading to efficiency in competitive markets'.[1] The best available information encourages honest firms to participate,[2] and submit their best offers while, where information is hard to find, it may be 'distributed among firms who have some agreements with the procurer'.[3] Disclosing information on demand-related and contract-related characteristics helps bidders prepare and plan their bids, and formulate more precise and more responsive offers, thus reducing the risk of discovering during the call-off or contract execution stage that estimates were not correct (see, further, the 'Winner's Curse' discussion in Section 8.4.2.4.1). Withholding information may also increase corruption risks and discourage honest firms from participation. It may not be

---

[1] F. Jenny, 'Competition and Anti-Corruption Considerations in Public Procurement', in 'Fighting Corruption and Promoting Integrity in Public Procurement', OECD, 2005.
[2] A. Balsevich, S. Pivovarova and E. Podkolzina, 'Information Transparency in Public Procurement: How It Works in Russian Regions', Series: Economics, WP BRP 1, 2011.
[3] Ibid.

surprising that a recent study showed that greater transparency in terms of 'information disclosure' to the market increased the average number of bidders.[4]

As can probably be sensed by the reader, there is a 'but' to come. The quotation at the beginning of the previous paragraph, in full, reads, 'It is well known that if perfect information is a condition leading to efficiency in competitive markets, it is also true that in oligopolistic markets (and the number of bidders on most public procurement market is limited) transparency can facilitate tacit collusion'.[5] As a result, many commentators recommend that some requirements for transparency in public procurement procedures should be relaxed where collusion is a possibility, sometimes referring to excessive and unnecessary transparency.[6]

This chapter will consider the implications of this recommendation, which, although expressed as a transparency consideration, has implications for other design issues. Transparency is generally understood as requiring the disclosure of the terms of the procurement in advance, a process that limits the flexibility that the procuring entity can apply during the procurement process. In other words, transparency tends to involve the maximum possible completeness of the framework agreement, as we have described in earlier chapters. If transparency obligations are reduced, therefore, the procuring entity may consider that greater flexibility in operation of a framework agreement is possible – whether or not he or she is motivated by anti-collusion or seeks flexibility for other commercial or procedural reasons. Design considerations should also, therefore, focus on whether such flexibility may operate to reduce effective competition because the best available information is not provided to bidders.

There are two main elements to identifying and mitigating the risks of collusion: preventive mechanisms at the planning stage (reflecting the market and the items to be procured), and measures to address collusion where it is suspected to occur.

---

[4] Hiroshi Ohashi, 'Effects of transparency in procurement practices on government expenditure: A case study of municipal public works', *Review of Industrial Organization*, 34, No. 3 (2009): 267–285.
[5] 'Competition and Anti-Corruption Considerations in Public Procurement', note 1, supra. Full transparency may allow competitors to detect deviations from a collusive agreement, punish those firms and better coordinate future tenders.
[6] Albert Sánchez-Graells, 'The difficult balance between transparency and competition in public procurement: Some recent trends in the case law of the European Courts and a look at the new Directives', University of Leicester School of Law Research Paper 13-11, 2013.

The OECD's Recommendation on Fighting Bid Rigging in Public Procurement[7] sets out a series of steps that will be the focus of this analysis. We can take these recommendations and group them into four main steps, as follows:

1. An identification of whether the market for a particular framework agreement is one of those in which collusion is likely (i.e. whether the market indicates that the first stage may be at risk, and/or whether a limited group of suppliers in that market might be expected to collude). As the OECD Guidelines for Fighting Bid Rigging in Public Procurement note (see Item 1 on p. 4), '[b]e informed before designing the tender process',[8] and the Recommendation above notes the importance of cooperation with sector regulators. Market research (into prices and features of what the market can offer, the number of potential suppliers, their geographical dispersion) and data-gathering on recent procurements will be necessary. An important aspect of this research is to define the market appropriately: the literature on competition policy has long since considered market definition as a prerequisite to assess whether or not there may be a threat to competition;[9] but the application to public procurement generally and the framework agreements context in particular is less commonly addressed. Recalling that the description of what the procuring entity will procure creates a mini-market for the products or services concerned,[10] the Model Law, for example, emphasises that descriptions, in the frameworks context, must provide an appropriate level of detail *at the first stage* to frame all call-offs at the second stage, including where

---

[7] Recommendation of the OECD Council on Fighting Bid Rigging in Public Procurement, as approved by Council on 17 July 2012 [C(2012)115 – C(2012)115/CORR1 – C/M(2012)9], available at http://www.oecd.org/daf/competition/RecommendationOnFightingBidRigging2012.pdf.
[8] Guidelines for Fighting bid rigging in Public Procurement, OECD, 2009, available at www.oecd.org/competition/cartels/42851044.pdf.
[9] For example, Articles 82 and 82 of the Consolidated version of the Treaty on the Functioning of the European Union, OJ C 326, 26 October 2012, pp. 47–390, are based on the concept of a definition of a relevant market to evaluate and assess market dominance. The relevant market characteristics, set out in Chapter 8, which may indicate a relatively higher risk of collusion include the presence of barriers to entry, concentrated markets, a predictable and stable market, fragmented demand and where there are few substitutes. These issues may be exacerbated where there are repeat or parallel framework agreements.
[10] For a more detailed consideration of these issues, see Chapter 10. The description includes both quality and quantity aspects – so the mini-market comprises suppliers capable of supplying the products or services in the quantity demanded. It is often assumed that the mini-market is a temporary market, but the effects may not turn out to be 'temporary' if the government is a dominant purchaser and its decisions alter the shape of the market.

second-stage competition is envisaged.[11] While such a description will define the market for the framework agreement procedure concerned, it should not be overlooked that a series of mini-markets can be grouped together. For example, a number of framework agreements for similar products may be concluded by neighbouring local authorities – which may also complicate the relevant market definition in any particular case;[12]

2. An identification of mitigation strategies to address collusion risks through procedure design. The Recommendation above focuses on maximising potential participation and competition,[13] limiting opportunities for coordination including through the use of e-procurement and taking appropriate action with bidders such as requiring internal compliance mechanisms. These steps are explained in a checklist accompanying the Recommendation;

3. An assessment of bids for evidence of collusion (e.g. suspicious pricing of bids); and

4. Undertaking enforcement action where appropriate.

Part A of this chapter will therefore consider preventive measures (Steps 1 and 2). As regards public procurement generally, there is a wealth of regulatory and policy guidance with detailed expositions on transparency and promoting competition in public procurement, and it is consequently not repeated here.

Our focus here will be on the appropriate balance between the application of transparency measures designed to promote competition and avoid corruption, on the one hand, and limitations designed to prevent collusion in the context of framework agreements procedures, on the other. While the literature contains references to tensions in this regard, it has been

---

[11] Guide to Enactment of the UNCITRAL Model Law on Public Procurement (2012), Official Records of the General Assembly, Sixty-seventh Session, Supplement No. 17 (para 46, UN document A/67/17). The text of the Guide to Enactment is available at www.uncitral.org/uncitral_texts/procurement_infrastructure.html. Hereafter, Guide to Enactment. See commentary to Article 10, Rules concerning description of the subject matter of the procurement and the terms and conditions of the procurement contract or framework agreement, para 2.

[12] This simple example also highlights the need for extensive communications among procuring entities and centralised purchasing agencies – a point discussed in Chapter 11.

[13] That is, consider whether the following issues are appropriate: pre-disclosed, fixed quantities; the use of lowest-price or average-bid award criteria, rather than most advantageous or best value tender, whether symmetry between the procurement and suppliers can be avoided (considering the number of awardees and the sequence of procurement contracts, joint bidding, the relevance of the number-of-awardees-to-number-of-contracts ratio, degree of heterogeneity of procurement contracts and the nature of competition at the call-off stage, symmetric competition at the call-off stage and the use of electronic reverse auctions at that stage).

observed that finding the right balance confers benefits: measures to avoid corruption and collusion should then be 'likely to be strongly mutually reinforcing',[14] and they should promote competition in addition.

Part B of this chapter will consider the question of detection and enforcement measures where collusion is suspected.

## 9.2 The transparency paradox – transparency operating to compromise procurement objectives

There are two main groups of information generally disclosed in procurement procedures. The first is information issued prior to the procedure, designed to elicit best offers in the sense described above, and the second is information issued at the conclusion of the procedure – including public bid openings and contract award notices – designed to demonstrate that the relevant procurement procedure was conducted according to the prescribed rules and procedures, and to allow breaches to be corrected and sanctioned as necessary.[15] Issuing *ex-post* information, including in debriefing arrangements, can also operate to encourage participation and best offers in subsequent procurement.

The concern expressed by the OECD and others is that these measures can also facilitate collusion, as the information disclosure increases predictability and stability in the procurement market concerned. In addition, if bidders do not have access to information, collusion will be difficult to sustain.[16] In this chapter, we will consider what has been described as a transparency paradox: pre-bidding and post-bidding transparency measures designed to prevent corruption and promote competition may in practice increase the risk of collusion, and we will consider how to mitigate this risk.

The risk is particularly acute in the conclusion of a closed framework agreement, as it is the fact that limited numbers of awardees are parties to

---

[14] R. D. Anderson and W. E. Kovacic, 'Competition Policy and International Trade Liberalization: Essential Complements to Ensure Good Performance in Public Procurement Markets', *18* Public Procurement Law Review, No. 2 (2009): 67–101. The trade-off between transparency and collusion leads to recommendations to limit transparency, both pre-bid and post-bid. See, further, 'The difficult balance between transparency and competition in public procurement: Some recent trends in the case law of the European Courts and a look at the new Directives', note 6, supra.

[15] This approach is legally required: the United Nations Convention against Corruption, for example, requires '[t]he use of objective and pre-determined criteria for public procurement decisions, in order to facilitate the subsequent verification of the correct application of the rules or procedures'. UN General Assembly, United Nations Convention Against Corruption (hereafter, UNCAC), 31 October 2003, A/58/422, available at: www.refworld.org/docid/4374b9524.html, Article 9(1)(c).

[16] M. Amaral, S. Saussier and A. Yvrande, 'Corruption, Collusion, and Other Strategic Behaviors: The Case of Local Transport in London and France', *Utilities Policy*, 17 (2009): 166–175, at p. 167.

these types of framework agreement that can *create* an oligopolistic market for the procurement concerned. The oligopolistic market is possible even as it is likely that the overall market for the types of goods and services concerned is itself competitive.[17] In other words, what would otherwise be a competitive market may be replaced by collusive arrangements for the call-off stage so that second-stage competition may be compromised. The analysis in this chapter will focus on closed framework agreements, though collusion at the second stage of open framework agreements should not be completely discounted.

Collusive arrangements can be facilitated through pre-bidding disclosure of some types of information, but the following elements need particular attention: the number of parties to be admitted to the framework agreement (awardees – which may be a maximum or an identified number), the anticipated or determined scale and frequency of call-offs, the number-of-awardees-to-number-of-call-offs ratio and the terms of complete or near-complete framework agreements, as the discussion of the second set of pro-collusive factors described in Chapter 8 sets out in more detail. Where this pre-bidding information – which will also include the description of the procuring entity's needs and the participation requirements – is combined with disclosure of the results of the first-stage bidding, such as bidder identities and of the key terms of their bids, the risk may be further elevated.

As they are most commonly used for repeat purchases of relatively straightforward items and services, framework agreements are less commonly found in markets that are concentrated, though exceptions can be found – such as fuel and some types of services (regional janitorial, consulting or advisory services, for example). Where the market concerned can be characterised as oligopolistic, collusion at the first stage (when bidding for the framework agreement) may also be facilitated by pre-bidding transparency.

This effects of disclosing pre-bidding information as a whole – which, to recap, can facilitate collusion as it allows demand to be predicted – may pose elevated risks where that demand need is regular and stable (i.e. expressed in regular purchases of fixed or definable quantities). The effect may be further compounded where the subject matter of the framework agreement comprises standardised products or services so that there are few

---

[17] As has been noted, '[a]t their worst, [ID/IQ contracts – the US term for framework agreements] establish false, if temporary, oligopolies, sheltering just a few select suppliers from ongoing competition'. Christopher R. Yukins, 'Are ID/IQs Inefficient? Sharing Lessons With European Framework Contracting', *Public Contract Law Journal*, 37, No. 3 (2008): 546–566, at p. 555.

or no variations in design, and few substitutes. While information disclosed prior to each framework agreement procedure may raise concerns for that procedure, the combination of such information and information from previous similar framework agreements or where a series of framework agreements is anticipated should also not be overlooked.

As commentators have noted,[18] the appropriate extent of transparency in a particular procurement process will depend on balancing transparency measures designed to promote competition and avoid corruption, on the one hand, and those designed to identify and mitigate the risks of collusion, on the other, *in the circumstances of each framework agreement procedure*.[19] The risk of collusion cannot be assumed to materialise in every case: there are examples of highly concentrated markets, with predictable demand and suppliers known to each other that remain highly competitive (branded soft drinks, mobile phones, tablets and so forth).

An additional point to consider is the regulatory framework. While an appropriate compromise in transparency measures should both avoid opacity (which may impede high-quality, competitive bidding and/or may facilitate corruption) and a level of transparency that may facilitate collusion,[20] many systems impose requirements for transparency throughout the process that limit the degree of flexibility that is available in practice. For example, the requirements of UNCAC on transparency in public procurement, while expressed at the level of principle rather than in terms of regulatory rules, appear to contemplate a fully transparent approach, by providing that public procurement systems should be based on transparency (as well as competition and objective criteria in decision-making), so as to be 'effective, inter alia, in preventing corruption'.[21] Applying the same principles, the WTO GPA allows limited tendering

---

[18] 'Competition Policy and International Trade Liberalization: Essential Complements to Ensure Good Performance in Public Procurement Markets', note 14, supra.

[19] OECD, 'Competition and Procurement: Key Findings' 19 (OECD Policy Roundtables, 2011) www.oecd.org/regreform/liberalisationandcompetitioninterventioninregulatedsectors/48315205 .pdf, 5 November 2013.

[20] See, further, P. Arden, 'Legal regulation of multi-provider framework agreements and the potential for bid rigging: a perspective from the UK local government construction sector', *Public Procurement Law Review*, No. 5 (2013): 165–182.

[21] Chapeau to UNCAC article 9(1), note 15, supra. As of the date of writing, 145 countries have signed and ratified the Convention, so the requirements can be regarded as universally applicable. The UNCAC provisions are considered to mean, for example, that all pertinent information that bidders would need to participate in the procedure, to be provided when their participation is first solicited, should be disclosed. See, for example, Guidebook on anti-corruption in public procurement and the management of public finances, Good practices in ensuring compliance with article 9 of the United Nations Convention against Corruption, United Nations Office on Drugs and Crime, 2013,

*Addressing risks of collusion in framework agreements* 219

to be used where earlier bids have been collusive (Article XIII), and EU Directive 2014/24/EU permits a competitive procedure with negotiation or a competitive dialogue to be used in this situation (Article 26). Further, bids suspected of being tainted by collusion in electronic reverse auctions are to be treated as irregular and will therefore be rejected.[22] The UNCITRAL Model Law[23] does not mention collusion *per se*, though it contains provisions designed to ensure effective competition and allows, for example, certain information to be withheld if there is a risk to fair competition were it to be disclosed. Collusion prevention is similarly afforded little detailed provision in much procurement legislation at the national level; however, reflecting the Model Law's provisions, there are measures to take where collusion is suspected or apparent including withholding information from disclosure. The degree of flexibility available to mitigate risks of collusion and to address collusion itself may therefore vary from system to system, and striking the right balance is in any event more of an art than a science.

PART A   THE DESIGN OF FRAMEWORK AGREEMENTS PROCEDURES AS A MECHANISM TO IDENTIFY AND MITIGATE THE RISKS OF COLLUSION

### 9.3   Transparency-related considerations

Steps 1 and 2 above provide further support for the proposition that planning in framework agreements is critical – addressing collusion once it arises is unlikely to lead to positive results within the framework agreement procedure concerned, even if future procurements can be structured so as to promote effective competition.

Issuing the best available information is a practice designed not only to encourage potential competition and prevent discriminatory practices and

---

available at www.unodc.org/documents/corruption/Publications/2013/Guidebook_on_anti-corruption_in_public_procurement_and_the_management_of_public_finances.pdf.

[22] The World Trade Organisation Revised Agreement on Government Procurement available at www.wto.org/english/docs_e/legal_e/rev-gpr-94_01_e.htm (hereafter, WTO GPA); Directive 2014/24/EU of the European Parliament and of the Council of 26 February 2014 on public procurement and repealing Directive 2004/18/EC Text with EEA relevance, OJ L 94, 28 March 2014, pp. 65–242, available at http://eur-lex.europa.eu/legal-content/EN/TXT/?uri=celex:32014L0024 (hereafter, the EU Directive).

[23] The UNCITRAL Model Law (UNCITRAL Model Law on Public Procurement (2011), *Official Records of the General Assembly, Sixty-sixth Session, Supplement No. 17* (UN document A/66/17). The text of the Model Law is available at www.uncitral.org/uncitral/uncitral_texts/procurement_infrastructure.html. Hereafter, the Model Law.

corruption but also to allow bidders to enforce their procedural rights through review or challenge mechanisms.[24] Unsurprisingly, therefore, robust requirements to this end are found in most regulatory systems: the main international texts on public procurement (which have been updated since UNCAC came into force) also reflect its requirements.[25]

The emphasis in legislative and regulatory systems is on the disclosure of relevant information as pro-competitive and anti-corruption measures. The specific transparency requirements in UNCAC are as follows:

- '[t]he public distribution of information relating to procurement procedures and contracts, including information on invitations to tender and relevant or pertinent information on the award of contracts';
- '[t]he establishment, in advance, of conditions for participation, including selection and award criteria and tendering rules, and their publication'; and
- '[t]he public distribution of information . . . on the award of contracts'.

An initial (and legal) question is whether these legal requirements, as they are reflected in other systems and national rules, impose complete transparency in the sense that all information known to the procuring entity at the outset of the procedure must be disclosed, or whether any pertinent and available information can be withheld without infringing mandatory rules – where the objective is, for example, to prevent collusion. Only if this flexibility is available can the procuring entity consider whether any information *should* be withheld; that is, where it considers that a collusion risk should be mitigated in this fashion.

We will start with an assessment of the main categories of information that must be published; that is, (a) the public procurement law and other rules that apply to procurement procedures, (b) prior announcements of procurement opportunities, (c) descriptions of what is to be procured and how bids are to be assessed and compared and (d) results of bidding and award notices. It should be noted, in particular, that while UNCAC does not address the level of detail at which this information must be provided, the other international texts referred to above and many national systems do so.

---

[24] 'The difficult balance between transparency and competition in public procurement: Some recent trends in the case law of the European Courts and a look at the new Directives', note 6, supra
[25] The WTO GPA, the EU Directive, note 22, supra. The Model Law, note 23, supra. Examples in the analysis will draw on appropriate provisions in these texts, particularly the provisions of the Model Law and accompanying Guide to Enactment, as together they provide the most comprehensive examination of policy issues in this area. Similar provisions are also found in the US federal system.

*Addressing risks of collusion in framework agreements* 221

### 9.3.1 *Disclosure of public procurement law and related legal information*

It is difficult to foresee any circumstances in which the applicable law, procurement regulations, other legal information that guides the procurement system, the standard procedures for the conduct of each procurement procedure[26] and information on how contracts come into force[27] could be exempted from publication requirements to mitigate a risk of collusion, and the authors are unaware of any such cases in practice. Awareness of these regulatory rules and associated procedural information is less likely to facilitate collusion than information about specific procedures, as well as being necessary to set out the framework for the entire procurement system. This provides an example of where the balance must be in favour of full disclosure of the relevant rules and procedures.

### 9.3.2 *Prior announcements and contract notices for each procurement procedure*

The initial information published about future procurement includes procurement plans, notices of forthcoming procurement and prior contract notices.[28] Most systems impose considerably lower requirements about the extent of information that is required in pre-procurement announcements (long-term general plans as well as soon-to-be-initiated procurement opportunities) as compared with initial advertisements and other contract notices (such as invitations to bid and solicitation documents).

Much of the information disclosed in pre-procurement announcements is facilitative, rather than mandatory, and is encouraged for a variety of policy reasons, including discipline in procurement planning; reducing cases of non-competitive 'ad hoc' and 'emergency' procurements; enhancing competition through allowing potential bidders to assess their interest

---

[26] See, for example, Articles 4 and 5 of the Model Law, ibid., and commentary in the Guide to Enactment, note 11, supra. These items also include any requirements imposed by the procuring entity on the form and means of communication and submission of bids, the language of documents for the procurement and so on. For example, mandatory channels of communications with bidders (e.g. on the terms of participation) may not be in a form that may impede access to the procurement – for example, the use of particular software or mobile technology that is not commonly in use (Article 7).

[27] Constitutional law generally requires the publication ('promulgation') of laws before they take effect; UNCITRAL's provisions go further and require all legal texts governing public procurement be published. Article 5, Model Law, note 23, supra.

[28] Articles 33–35, Model Law, note 23, supra.

in participation and plan accordingly; and contributing to the broader governance context, opening up procurement to general public review and civil society and local community participation.[29]

Whether information at such a general level alone can facilitate collusive agreements in most markets has been questioned,[30] in that the information may facilitate 'pie-sharing'. For example, in a consideration of the construction sector in the United Kingdom, recommendations to enhance transparency and forward visibility through publishing a 'pipeline' of forthcoming contracts were considered to risk precisely this result. The extent of information disclosed in the UK situation reviewed was extensive – even including proposed procurement models and suggesting the publication of an 'affordability envelope' – which, as the author reported, would be very useful to cartels seeking to manage their own risk.[31]

Furthermore, publishing information well ahead of the commencement of framework agreements procedures, and concluding framework agreements with a long period between the end of this first stage and the commencement of call-offs, can provide sufficient time for collusive arrangements based on the information disclosed to be concluded.[32] In addition, the collation of centralised data from basic prior information could also facilitate collusive arrangements for future bidding beyond a single procurement or framework agreement procedure – that is, allowing geographical or other splitting of markets involving a group of procedures taken together.

As an example of balancing the competing transparency considerations where collusion is a realistic possibility, a difference can be made between regular, simple and repeat needs – where the market is likely to have enough information, based on previous conduct, to allow for appropriate planning – and new and more complex markets. It is in the latter situation that disclosure of sufficient prior information to allow bidders to plan for the commencement of procedures is likely to yield more significant participation and competition benefits, whereas in others, the legal minimum of information may be a more appropriate mitigation strategy. However,

---

[29] See, for example, Article 6, Model Law, note 23, supra, and the commentary thereto in the Guide to Enactment, note 11, supra.
[30] 'Legal regulation of multi-provider framework agreements and the potential for bid rigging: a perspective from the UK local government construction sector', note 20, supra.
[31] Ibid.
[32] On the other hand, shorter time periods between call-offs can frustrate collusion by enabling swift detection of cheating at the call-off stage.

where these markets are already concentrated – as a general market characteristic and/or because of previous procurement – the benefits of better planning may be outweighed by the disadvantages of possible collusive arrangements.

### 9.3.3 Disclosure of all terms of participation in the solicitation or bidding documents

The main information that must be published at this stage comprises the criteria that will determine whether or not bidders are qualified to participate in a particular framework agreement procedure,[33] the description of the subject matter, the criteria that will determine whether bids are responsive and which bidder will win the contract),[34] the terms of the framework agreement itself and of second-stage awards of procurement contracts (call-offs) and the deadline(s) for bid submission.[35] The information extends to the procedures to award both the framework agreement and call-offs under the framework agreement. We saw in Chapter 5 that the UNCITRAL Model Law and the EU Directive require comprehensive information to be disclosed on the terms of participation – essentially, as more fully explained in that chapter – the principle is that all information available at the first stage, both regarding the terms of participation in the competition to be admitted to the framework agreement *and* regarding the award of procurement contracts at the call-off stage, must be disclosed in the solicitation or bidding documents.

The UNCITRAL Model Law requires the solicitation documents to disclose the terms and duration of the framework agreement, the description of the subject matter of the procurement (including technical specifications), all terms and conditions of the entire framework agreement procedure that are known at the first stage (including all qualification and evaluation criteria for both stages of the procedure), any terms and conditions of the procurement that may be refined through second-stage competition and the procedures and criteria for and the anticipated frequency of second-stage competition. A discussion of how these requirements apply to framework agreements procedures is found in Chapter 5.

---

[33] Articles 9 and 18, Model Law, note 23, supra.
[34] Articles 10 and 11, Model Law, note 23, supra.
[35] Article 9(1)(a) of UNCAC, note 15, supra, requires bid submission deadlines to be sufficiently long to afford bidders a reasonable time to prepare their bids. While it applies to both stages of framework agreements procedures, it should be appreciated that in some circumstances and where systems are run online, the second-stage submission deadline can appropriately be short.

In explaining the policy approach behind the provisions in the Model Law, it is noted that exceptions from the general requirement to provide exhaustive information about the terms and conditions of the procurement at the time of solicitation 'are permitted only so far as needed to accommodate the procurement concerned'.[36] Although there is no strict requirement under the Model Law's provisions for a complete description,[37] it is explained, for example, in the commentary on descriptions in framework agreements procedures that all known terms should be disclosed at the first stage. In other words, only those terms that *cannot* be established at the first stage can be left for finalisation through competition at the call-off stage, and there is a requirement for estimates of all the terms and conditions that will be set only at the call-off stage[38] (which may include the timing, frequency and quantities of purchases, and price). There is also a requirement to disclose whether there will be one or more than one awardee.

Similarly, in the European Union, transparency in these matters is a long-established principle,[39] and generally requires the information disclosed to enable both bidders to understand what is required of them and contracting authorities to award the contract.[40] In our context, a call-off is to be awarded 'on the basis of the award criteria set out in the procurement documents for the framework agreement'. The European Court of Justice (ECJ) has stated that award criteria should be formulated so that 'reasonably well-informed and normally diligent tenderers [can] interpret them in the same way',[41] which as a general description of the relevant requirements implies a certain level of detail about the call-off stage being issued at the first stage. Article 33 of the EU Directive, in addition, clarifies that a framework agreement should set out all terms and conditions for the call-off stage, though the article permits more

---

[36] Guide to Enactment, commentary to Article 58, para 7, note 11, supra.
[37] See the provisions of Article 10, Model Law, note 23, supra, which refer to a 'detailed' description, and (to the extent practicable) that requirements be expressed in terms that are 'objective, functional and generic'. Nonetheless, the commentary to this article in the Guide to Enactment, note 11, supra, refers to 'the importance of the principle of clarity, sufficient precision, completeness and objectivity' in the description.
[38] Estimates must be disclosed '[t]o the extent that they are known, estimates of the terms ... that cannot be established with sufficient precision when the framework agreement is concluded' (Article 59(2)(c), Model Law, note 23, supra).
[39] See, e.g. Case C-120/78, Rewe-Zentral AG ('Cassis de Dijon') [1979] ECR 649 and Case 302/86, *Commission v. Denmark ('Danish bottles')* [1988] ECR 4607.
[40] See, for example, Article 42(3)(a) Model Law, note 23, supra.
[41] Case C-19/00 SIAC *Construction v. County Council of Mayo* [2001] ECR I-7725, paragraph 42. This case was decided on the earlier 2004 Directive, but, it is submitted, the ratio continues to apply.

'precisely-formulated' terms to be applied at the call-off stage and, 'where appropriate, other terms referred to in the procurement documents for the framework agreement'.

An example may assist in understanding the types of disclosure and flexibility envisaged. A framework agreement may record that, at the call-off stage, weighting of the award criteria will be between 50 per cent and 70 per cent for quality, and the remaining 30–50 per cent will be for price. The quality criteria are then split into three main sub-criteria, elements A, B and C, with the application of these elements being determined at the second stage. Supposing class A relates to some performance dimensions of a photocopier, a certain procuring entity may have a preference for extra printing speed and multicolour printing with very low level of noise as it is going to be used in an open space; it may then set out these requirements when inviting bids at the call-off stage.

Along the same lines, in the US federal system, a statement of work, specifications or other description that 'reasonably describes the general scope, nature, complexity and purpose of the supplies or services to be acquired under the contract in a manner that will enable a prospective offeror to decide whether to submit an offer' is required.[42]

While it may initially appear that the regulatory provisions are relatively and perhaps excessively prescriptive in the framework agreements context, it is important to note that the requirements do *not* mean that all permutations and combinations for the call-off stage must be disclosed, even on their most restrictive reading. The objective is to limit the ability of the procuring entity, when designing a framework agreement procedure, by issuing excessively broad descriptions and statements of the terms of the procurement that can be significantly altered during the procedure, perhaps to favour a particular supplier. In other words, descriptions should frame the call-off stage, including in setting the terms of any second-stage competition, but do not require in all cases that the entire set of parameters that will be applied to award a procurement contract at the call-off stage to be settled (and consequently disclosed) at the first stage.

There is a key distinguishing feature between Model 1 framework agreements (which have no competition at the call-off stage) and Models 2 and 3 (which involve competition to identify the winner at the call-off stage) in this regard. To return to the notion of 'perfect information',

---

[42] For Indefinite Delivery contracts, Federal Acquisition Regulation, Code of Federal Regulations (CFR) Title 48, Subpart FAR 16.504(a)(4)(iii). FAR 2005-83/07-02-2015, available at www.acquisition.gov/?q=browsefar.

where all terms of the call-offs are fixed at the first stage (as is the case for Model 1 framework agreements), how the winner will be determined at the call-off stage will already be clear. Under normal transparency rules, this information can and should be set out in the framework agreement. Consequently, the agreement will be, practically speaking, 'complete'. A pragmatic approach to 'completeness', in addition, allows that delivery locations, timing and quantities to be delivered, and even price may remain outstanding, but the key point is that there will be no additional competition to finalise these elements. A Model 1 framework agreement involves competition for the totality of the items or services to be procured under the framework agreement at the first stage, and so the transparency requirements we are considering mean, in practice, that all relevant information both to allow bidders to participate and to enable the terms of the call-offs to be awarded must be disclosed at that first stage. This being the case, collusive practices arranged at the conclusion of the first stage to manipulate competition at the call-off stage can be largely discounted, and concerns about collusion should not in most cases justify the withholding of relevant information in these types of framework agreements.

There is a caveat to this general conclusion: where the Model 1 framework agreement is a multi-supplier framework, there may be concerns about facilitating collusion at the *first* stage where the method of awarding contracts at the call-off stage is disclosed. One possible method is known as the rotation-with-fixed-shares method, whereby, given a decision to select the top three bidders as awardees for the framework agreement, the highest-ranked bidder is awarded 60 per cent of the call-off awards, the second-highest 30 per cent and the third-highest 10 per cent. Obviously, these proportions are a crucial piece of information as they determine the incentive to fight for the highest rank *provided* that firms do not collude. However, this is exactly the most important piece of information a cartel needs to know prior to bidding at the first stage, as it will determine the fraction of collusive profit each cartel member can obtain.[43] This example also provides insight into the transparency paradox as it arises in practice, though it may be considered that systems requiring the procurement contract (the award at the call-off stage in these circumstances) to be awarded to the lowest evaluated bid or the most (economically) advantageous bid do not permit this type of rotation method.

---

[43] In this case, the question of collusion at the first stage is little different from that in any other procurement procedure, though the question of repeated procurements may raise the concern that information released during the operation of framework agreement A may be used to enable collusive arrangements in framework agreement B.

Where demand is heterogeneous and/or the market may fluctuate, second-stage competition (involving a Model 2 or a Model 3 framework agreement) will identify the best offer at the call-off stage for each purchase under the framework agreement.[44] In this situation, the available information is in fact imperfect at the first stage and the framework agreement consequently will be incomplete. We have seen that there is a general rule in the Model Law for full disclosure to the extent possible at the first stage (designed to enable the best offers), but clearly the rules concerned cannot require the impossible – that is, perfect information and a complete contract at the first stage. The concern about possible collusion in Models 2 and 3 framework agreements therefore arises in the context of the *information made available at the first stage regarding the call-off stage* that may affect competition at the call-off stage and so will be considered in this context.

Some helpful guidance in the EU context is found in a discussion of award criteria in framework agreements procedures. The European Commission's Classic Directive Explanatory Note on framework agreements provides that 'the contracting authorities must ensure that the award criteria – not only for the award of the framework agreement itself, but also for the award of individual contracts based on the agreement – and their weightings appear in the specifications of the framework agreement'.[45] The Model Law too, expressly requires the relative weight of the evaluation criteria and the manner in which they will be applied to be disclosed.[46] By using the phrase 'on the basis of the award criteria', the EU provisions may be more flexible than the UNCITRAL equivalent: the Model Law's Article 62(ii) and 63, taken together, state that any variation in the evaluation criteria at the call-off stage must be predisclosed in the framework agreement itself.[47]

---

[44] For an in-depth consideration of this aspect of framework agreements design, see Chapter 10.
[45] European Commission, Directorate General Internal Market and Services, Explanatory Note – Framework Agreements – Classic Directive (2005), CC2005/03_rev/ of 14 July 2005, at p. 6, available at http://ec.europa.eu/internal_market/publicprocurement/docs/explan-notes/classic-dir-framework_en.pdf. While this note addresses the earlier provisions on framework agreements in Directive 2004/EC/18, the provisions themselves remain unchanged in the (2014) EU Directive.
[46] Adapted from Model Law, Articles 59 and 61, Model Law, note 23, supra.
[47] Article 62(4)(ii), Model Law, note 23, supra: 'A *restatement* of the procedures and criteria for the award of the anticipated procurement contract, including their relative weight and the manner of their application'; and Article 63: 'Changes to other terms and conditions of the procurement, including to the criteria (and their relative weight and the manner of their application) and procedures for the award of the anticipated procurement contract, *may occur only to the extent expressly permitted in the framework agreement*' (emphasis added).

These requirements are considered in public procurement generally to mean that evaluation criteria, any sub-criteria and weightings must be disclosed in the initial contract notice and/or in the solicitation documents. Although one decision of the ECJ might be taken to imply that the weightings of sub-criteria need not be fully disclosed (provided that they are predetermined), the main ECJ decision in this area (on criteria in procurement generally, not in the framework agreements context) held that this level of detail can be withheld only where the weightings

- do not alter the criteria for the award of the contract set out in the contract documents or the contract notice;
- do not contain elements which, if they had been known at the time the bids were prepared, could have affected that preparation; and
- are not influenced by discrimination among bidders.[48]

It should be assumed, therefore, that the rules effectively require all elements of the award criteria – down to sub-criteria and weightings, relating to both stages of the framework agreements procedure – to be disclosed at the first stage. This poses some difficulty given the need to accommodate variations in needs (and even more so where there is aggregation of purchasing by diverse procuring entities). The European Commission has advised that 'It should be emphasised that the award criteria do not have to be the same as those used for the conclusion of the framework agreement itself', but it continues that call-offs must be based on the criteria 'set out in the specifications of the framework agreement'.[49]

UNCITRAL's Model Law follows the same principle, but has a practical solution to the difficulty. Flexibility is given to permit relative weights of the evaluation criteria to be varied at the call-off stage, provided that the framework agreement specifies the range of permissible variation, using a matrix or similar approach.[50] This flexibility neither compromises the transparency rules, nor does it provide complete predictability in call-offs and how they will be assessed in advance (which could otherwise facilitate collusion). The disclosure of the permissible range allows bidders to identify the parameters of second-stage competition and so to decide whether to participate, without unnecessarily restricting the procuring entity's freedom at the call-off stage.

---

[48] See Case C-331/04 ATI EAC *Srl e Viaggi di Maio Snc and Others v. ACTV Venezia SpA and Others* [2005] ECR I-10109, pt para 32.
[49] Explanatory Note – Framework Agreements – Classic Directive, note 45, supra.
[50] Articles 59(1)(d)(iii) (closed framework agreements) and 61(2)(f) (open framework agreements), Model Law, note 23, supra.

*Addressing risks of collusion in framework agreements* 229

Clearly a similar approach may be of assistance as regards other terms and conditions of the call-off stage elements that enhance predictability, such as the schedule of or intervals between call-offs (particularly where they are symmetrical with the number of participating suppliers, and where quantities are also set out). Including elements of asymmetry in second-stage or call-off profiles will avoid complete predictability and make it less easy for collusive arrangements to be concluded. In these circumstances, too, a matrix approach may be the most practicable route to issuing the best available information on these elements of the design of the framework agreement, or, alternatively, to issue information about the aggregate value of anticipated call-offs during a particular period without full precision about the individual call-offs themselves. These approaches also serve to balance the pro-competition and anti-corruption objective, on the one hand, and the anti-collusion objective, on the other. From a theoretical perspective, the pro-competitive and collusion-avoiding recommendations operate in tandem here. Where there is no real asymmetry or variation in demand or market, there is likely to be little advantage in concluding a Model 2 framework agreement rather than a Model 1 framework agreement in which there can be full competition at the first stage. In other words, a second round of competition at the call-off stage on the same terms as the first round of bidding, though with fewer participants, is in most markets not likely to yield significant benefits (unless the first round of competition was flawed).

It can also be noted that these transparency requirements also reflect a key safeguard in framework agreements procedures – the prohibition on material change during the operation of the agreements themselves.[51] As a general rule, in addition, bidders are to be notified of any amendments to the initial information provided about any and all terms of participation, which might involve re-advertisement if the amendments make the initial information materially inaccurate.[52]

### 9.3.4 *Results of bidding and award notices*

While pre-bidding information can create an information flow that allows collusive arrangements to be made, many commentators have expressed the view that it is information given about bids themselves that poses the highest risk so far as collusion is concerned, because it allows a collusive

---

[51] Model Law, Article 63, note 23, supra; EU Directive, Article 33(2), note 22, supra.
[52] Model Law Article 15(3), note 23, supra.

ring to detect and punish any cheats: '[A]s a general rule, the more information the [contracting authority] conveys about bidder identities, the bids submitted, and auction outcomes, the easier it is for a ring to be effective in its work of suppressing rivalry among members.'[53]

This risk is recognised as being elevated where bids are opened in a public forum, as many systems require for open and competitive procurement methods, and where standstill notices are given,[54] because detection is instantaneous and any punishment for cheating will be swift. In fact the post-bidding information poses a broader risk: award information disclosed at the first stage of a framework agreement procedure (to all bidders or via a public opening) can complement pre-bidding information, and so facilitate a collusive arrangement to distort the call-off stage, as well as allowing cheating on a collusive arrangement for the framework agreement itself to be detected. In addition, award information disclosed at the call-off stage allows detection of cheating at that stage.

In order for the information that could be disclosed to facilitate collusion or to detect cheating, it has to link bids and bidders. It has been therefore suggested that procurement officials should consider keeping the identities of the bidders confidential, perhaps referring only to bidder numbers in published information.[55]

Public bid submission and opening will reveal identities: allowing bids to be submitted electronically or without personal presentation[56] and replacing public bid opening with monitored bid opening[57] are suggested as ways of preserving anonymity without compromising governance. Public bid opening is often required in open tendering and similar procedures (as it is in the UNCITRAL Model Law and World Bank procurement system), but it is not under the EU Directive, and is generally not a requirement in procurement methods in which participation is restricted through pre-qualification, short-listing, direct solicitation and

---

[53] R. C. Marshall and L. M. Marx, *The Economics of Collusion. Cartels and Bidding Rings* (Cambridge, MA: MIT Press, 2012) at 200, as cited in 'The difficult balance between transparency and competition in public procurement: Some recent trends in the case law of the European Courts and a look at the new Directives', note 6, supra.

[54] Under the Model Law Article 10(2), note 23, supra, for example, the procuring entity must provide a notice containing the name and address of the winning bidder(s) and 'the contract price or, where [quality factors are also relevant] the contract price and a summary of other characteristics and relative advantages' of the successful bid.

[55] Fighting Cartels in Public Procurement, OECD Policy Brief, OECD 2008 n 5, available at www.oecd.org/competition/cartels/41505296.pdf.

[56] Ibid.

[57] 'Competition Policy and International Trade Liberalization: Essential Complements to Ensure Good Performance in Public Procurement Markets', note 14, supra.

so forth. Although some systems requiring public bid opening may be flexible enough to allow for limited disclosure of information, in others there are immutable requirements to disclose the identities of winning bidder(s), unless there is a previously identified risk of collusion. Moreover, an application of the general rules on choice of procurement method that are designed to promote participation and competition to the framework agreements context indicates that open and competitive methods are likely to be mandatory for that first stage.

Further, whether either of these suggested ways to preserve anonymity will be successful depends on the market concerned – guessing identities is more difficult in broad, competitive markets rather than markets with a stable and limited pool of suppliers, where the framework agreement procedure is not one of a series, and will in any event depend on how second-stage competition is conducted. For example, e-bidding and e-reverse auction systems can ascribe identification tags to each bid that do not compromise anonymity.

More generally, the risk remains that bidders are also likely to be identified through communications and observations outside the procurement process in a longer-term arrangement with repeat call-offs. Thus, reliance on preserving anonymity may not be realistic, and consideration of whether or not to limit the information disclosed about the terms of the submitted bids in addition to or as an alternative to releasing the identities of the bidders may also be necessary.

Information on bids themselves is generally required to be disclosed, whether as part of mandatory rules for contract notices or in debriefings. This is a reflection of the premium on transparency generally in public procurement: the Guide to Enactment explains that disclosure of information submitted in bids – even where commercially sensitive information is concerned, and whether to competing suppliers or contractors or to the public in general – is important for a variety of policy reasons. These include the need to ensure transparency and integrity in the procurement proceedings, to allow for meaningful challenge by suppliers or contractors and to facilitate proper public oversight. In this context, the critical elements to be disclosed include (in addition to the identity of the winning bidder) key terms at public bid openings, in standstill notices, in public notices of awards of framework agreements and in procurement contracts. The procuring entity may also be required to disclose parts of the procurement record on request (disclosure that may also take place in the context of challenge proceedings).[58]

---

[58] See Guide to Enactment, note 11, supra, commentary to Article 24(2), para 5.

Debriefings, in addition, are designed to reduce the potential for challenges, and to enhance accountability and the quality of future bids. The Guide to Enactment states that the following information, at a minimum, should be included in debriefings:

(a) evaluation of the significant weaknesses or deficiencies in a bid and/or the qualifications of the requesting bidder, and a summary of the rationale for qualification decisions and award of the procurement contract or framework agreement; and

(b) a comparative assessment of the constituent elements of the successful bid, and of qualifications, overall evaluated price and technical rating of the successful and requesting bidders and bids.[59]

In a similar vein, Article 55(2)(c) of the EU Directive requires procuring entities to provide to '(c) any tenderer that has made an admissible tender of the characteristics and relative advantages of the tender selected as well as the name of the successful tenderer or the parties to the framework agreement'. It has been noted that the ECJ has 'reinforced very strict debriefing standards that require contracting authorities to provide substantial information concerning other tenderers' offers (notably, at least, the winning tenderer's) to all participating tenderers'.[60] One ECJ ruling states that while the full evaluation report need not be disclosed, 'tables relating, in particular, to the technical evaluation of the tenders ... and indicating, for each award criterion, the number of points obtained by [the disappointed tenderer] in comparison with the successful tenderer, broken down each time into sub-criteria, as well as the maximum number of points attainable per sub-criterion and the weighting of each of those sub-criteria in the overall evaluation' were to be provided.[61]

It is hardly necessary to add commentary on the potential of this information to support an existing collusive ring and/or to allow a new collusive arrangement to be concluded. As has been added to such a general view, the risk is of 'strategic use of review mechanisms in order to try to obtain confidential information or business secrets from competitors'.[62]

---

[59] Guide to Enactment, note 11, supra, commentary to Article 22, para 25.
[60] 'The difficult balance between transparency and competition in public procurement: Some recent trends in the case law of the European Courts and a look at the new Directives', note 6, supra.
[61] Case C-629/11 P Evropaiki Dynamiki v. European Commission (ESP-ISEP) [2012]. For a more detailed evaluation of this point, see 'The difficult balance between transparency and competition in public procurement: Some recent trends in the case law of the European Courts and a look at the new Directives', note 6, supra.
[62] Ibid.

As a result, the very extensive disclosure of information on bids submitted that appears to be imposed through case law in the European Union raises a considerable risk in terms of facilitating collusive arrangements and enforcement. The same level of disclosure is not required, for example, under the UNCITRAL system, which prohibits the release of more than a summary of the comparative evaluation of bids, including their price and key elements (see Article 25(4)(b) of the Model Law),[63] though participating bidders are entitled to ask for a copy of any written procurement contract or framework agreement (Article 25(1)(r) of the Model Law). This approach reflects an understanding that the policy goal is less directed at allowing suppliers to enforce rights against procuring entities than it is at protecting the integrity of the system. The procurement official's decisions and conduct will stand unless they breach the relevant rules and procedures, or are demonstrably tainted by prejudice. In other words, the UNCITRAL system is not designed to allow a comprehensive re-consideration of the exercise of commercial judgement.

In addition, distinctions can perhaps be drawn between the types of information that are disclosed or published and when that disclosure or publication takes place – such as between the type of information that is disclosed to the public to ensure the accountability of the procuring entity and procurement officials and information that is disclosed to bidders only to, among other things allow them to challenge decisions of the procuring entity. The latter information must be disclosed in a prompt fashion in order to fulfil the purposes of disclosure in the first place. The appropriate timing of disclosure of other information to the public can be more flexibly assessed. Information on the conduct of the procedure – such as why a procurement method was chosen, the name of the successful bidder and winning price and information on any challenge proceedings – is made available upon request to any person under the Model Law, but only after the procurement procedure itself has been completed. Clearly there will be a risk that disclosing either type of information may facilitate collusion (even if it is the bidder-specific information that raises a higher risk), so, as we shall see, the disclosure is without prejudice to an overall flexibility as regards risks of collusion and prejudicing future competition discussed below.

---

[63] The price requirement generally does apply to framework agreements themselves, as is further explained below.

## 9.4 Possible extent of non-disclosure

The above concerns bring us back to the need to balance anti-corruption and pro-competition disclosure and to withhold information to inhibit collusion. It can be seen that a key issue is the award notice, because it may contain information about both bids and bidders.

There are two limitations on transparency in the UNCITRAL regime that in effect allow for a more flexible approach that may in practice help avoid the 'excessive transparency' problem, though it is evident that they were not conceived as anti-collusion measures.

The first is that the Model Law does not require the price to be included in the notice of award of a framework agreement – the requirement for price disclosure applies only at the call-off stage.[64] Where bidders' prices are disclosed,[65] those prices will both operate as a ceiling or reserve price for second-stage competition and can encourage collusive agreements. The Model Law's provisions therefore exclude the requirement to disclose prices in award notices for framework agreements. The policy reason behind this limitation is that any price given at this stage may not be sufficiently indicative to be useful for governance purposes (at least in framework agreements procedures with second-stage competition), but a perhaps unintended side effect is that the procuring entity is not required to disclose the bidders' identities and their prices at the first stage – information that, together, might facilitate collusion.

A second limitation, conceived as an administrative efficiency measure, is that while contract award notices for procurement contracts and framework agreements are mandatory, those below a particular threshold can be grouped and published together, with the caveat that publication must be at least once annually.[66] This flexibility – which is evidently unlikely to apply to framework agreements themselves given the threshold requirement – may assist in disrupting the information flow that would allow collusive arrangements at the call-off stage to be monitored by the cartel and cheats punished. The information itself does eventually become public and so provides a further example of the type of 'balancing' we discussed at the beginning of this chapter.

More generally, and as a way of addressing the excessive transparency concerns, both the Model Law and the EU Directive contemplate

---

[64] Model Law, Article 23(1), note 23, supra.
[65] Price disclosure may not be possible in all types of framework agreement, or may not be meaningful, in any event.
[66] Model Law Article 23(2), note 23, supra.

exemptions to transparency rules to protect competition. The Model Law *requires* a procuring entity to withhold information that 'would impede fair competition', and notes that the 'phrase should be interpreted broadly, referring not only to current but also to subsequent procurement'.[67] Article 53(3) of the EU Directive provides that

> [c]ontracting authorities *may* decide to withhold certain information ... regarding the contract award, the conclusion of framework agreements or admittance to a dynamic purchasing system, where the release of such information would impede law enforcement or would otherwise be contrary to the public interest, would prejudice the legitimate commercial interests of a particular economic operator, whether public or private, or might prejudice fair competition between economic operators.[68] [emphasis added]

However, identifying a risk of collusion should not automatically allow unrestricted withholding of information. Indeed, the policy direction of most regulatory systems is to encourage the broadest possible information disclosure about future procurement as a spur to competition and improving bids – so withholding information will remain an exceptional measure.[69] Consequently, individual items need to be assessed separately for their pro-collusive potential, and a consideration of the interaction and usability of all information pertaining to the framework agreement concerned is also required.

In this regard, we saw in Chapter 7 that information has to be useable to facilitate collusion: as has been noted in the financial services context, 'transparency does not mean simply more reporting: what matters is the usefulness, clarity and comparability of disclosures',[70] and there is some uncertainty as to what information can in fact facilitate collusion.[71]

---

[67] Model Law 24(1), note 23, supra, and commentary thereto in the Guide to Enactment, note 11, supra.

[68] It is considered that the better interpretation of the UNCITRAL provisions in practice is that they allow the procuring entity to withhold information: determining information that 'would' impede effective competition involves an assessment that is more of a probability risk than one that can be said to be 'right or wrong'.

[69] Procuring entities in the construction sector in the United Kingdom are encouraged to facilitate meetings between bidders to explore benefits and best practice that might be shared, and to issue information about forthcoming pipelines of construction procurement. See, further, 'Legal regulation of multi-provider framework agreements and the potential for bid rigging: a perspective from the UK local government construction sector', note 20, supra.

[70] M. Čihák, A. Demirgüç-Kunt and R. B. Johnston, 'Good Regulation Needs to Fix the Broken Incentives', World Bank, 2012, available at www8.gsb.columbia.edu/sites/richman/files/files/Demirguc-Kunt%20Abstracts.pdf.

[71] Directorate for Financial And Enterprise Affairs, Competition Committee, Global Forum on Competition, Roundtable on Collusion and Corruption in public procurement, DAF/COMP/GF(2010)6, 15 October 2010, p. 11.

Procurement officials will be required to assess the threshold requirement for potential distortions of competition when assessing whether or not to withhold information from disclosure. The OECD has recommended that procuring entities be afforded some flexibility in this regard, such as adapting procedural requirements.[72] As will be evident from the discussion in this chapter, the threshold is more likely to be met regarding *ex-post* information on bids and bidders than prior information on the terms of the procedure, for which flexibility is built into the system. As the Guide to Enactment recommends, additional rules and policy guidance on the scope of this exemption from transparency will be required given the potential for abuse where there are flexible exemptions that would permit the procurement official to protect himself or herself from scrutiny,[73] and given the potential to harm future competitions.

Moreover, a cost–benefit analysis of whether or not to withhold information will be complex: as has been noted elsewhere, whether or not action to prevent and detect collusion can be considered as a responsibility of procurement officials on a par with seeking to meet the procuring entity's needs and achieve value for money is open to doubt.[74] As procurement officials have a fiduciary duty to safeguard public funds and avoid corruption, the likelihood is that – taking their cue from the tone as well as the provisions of the regulatory system and the decisions of the ECJ, among others – they will prefer to avoid censure for withholding information, to err on the side of caution, and so disclose all relevant information. Policy guidance and any rules on the issue will need to tackle this extremely difficult issue: realigning procurement officials' incentives may be a challenging and long-term task, and this may be an area where cooperation between procurement and competition authorities would be fruitful. The OECD recommends that there should be ongoing relationships between competition and procurement authorities, so that procuring entities can report suspected collusion to competition or other relevant authorities, with confidence that they will help investigate and prosecute any potential anticompetitive conduct.[75] Although the emphasis in that recommendation is on detection and punishment, it is suggested that the experience of the competition authorities could

---

[72] A. Heimler, 'Fighting Cartels in Public Procurement', *Journal of Competition Law and Economics*, 8, No. 4 (2012): 849–862.
[73] Commentary to Model Law Article 25, Guide to Enactment, note 11, supra. See, also, the discussion of disclosure about bids themselves, below.
[74] Cartels in Public Procurement, note 72, supra.
[75] See 'Recommendation of the OECD Council on Fighting Bid Rigging in Public Procurement', note 7 supra, – recognising, however, that market definition in the framework agreements context may require additional consideration, as we noted in the introduction to this chapter.

be beneficial to the prevention of collusive mechanisms through providing input and guidance at the design stage.

In addition, some recent commentary indicates that the role of transparency in facilitating collusion may be overstated, at least in the context of framework agreements: one view is that higher transparency enables effective control that might outweigh the higher risk of collusion.[76] Furthermore, information transparency decreases monitoring costs,[77] and allows for the participation of different parties in monitoring (raising the possibility of detection).

From this perspective, informal information flow – or tacit collusion, as described in Chapter 8 – has been suggested as a possibility in collusive or concentrated markets – which could include closed framework agreements. Consequently, 'procurement opacity may prevent only third parties from monitoring collusion rather than the collusive players themselves [from communicating]'.[78] In other words, very little additional information from the procurement process may in fact be needed to enforce anticompetitive agreements. The nature of framework agreement markets tends to facilitate the success of cartels, as we have seen – and where bidders' identities are known, cartel members may be required to disclose bids submitted as part of bid-rigging arrangements, irrespective of regulatory requirements for disclosure of identities and key terms.[79] Consequently, it has been suggested that any doubt about whether to disclose or withhold information should be resolved in favour of disclosure, because the risks of limiting transparency may outweigh the possible benefits in terms of collusion prevention.

## 9.5 Design issues that may affect the possibility of collusion

We outlined common design issues in framework agreements procedures in Chapter 3, which coalesce around both market conditions and the

---

[76] F. Boehm and J. Olaya, 'Corruption in Public Contracting Auctions: The Role of Transparency in Bidding Processes', *Annals of Public and Cooperative Economics*, 77, (No. 4 (2006): 432–452, at p. 442.
[77] Ibid.; I. Kolstad and A. WiigKolstad, 'Is Transparency the Key to Reducing Corruption in Resource-Rich Countries?', *World Development*, 37, No. 3 (2009): 521–532.
[78] Publishing Government Contracts, Addressing Concerns and Easing Implementation, A Report of the Center for Global Development Working Group on Contract Publication, citing Hendricks, McAfee and Williams, available at www.cgdev.org/publication/ft/publishing-government-con tracts-addressing-concerns-and-easing-implementation.
[79] 'Legal regulation of multi-provider framework agreements and the potential for bid rigging: a perspective from the UK local government construction sector', note 20, supra.

nature of the procuring entity's needs (demand considerations). In Chapter 8, we identified a series of pro-collusive factors that may arise in framework agreements procedures. Akin to the decisions on the required and appropriate disclosure of information to potential bidders discussed above, balancing these possibly competing considerations is a necessary part of the planning process prior to commencing a framework agreements procedure.

As regards market conditions, we saw in Chapter 8 that public procurement operates to create a market for defined quantities of a product or service, operating as a subset of the overall market concerned. Consequently, when planning for a framework agreement procedure, the procuring entity should consider not only general market definition but also the impact of the procurement in question. Furthermore, as we have also seen, framework agreements (in common with some types of long-term traditional procurement contracts) have the potential to create an oligopolistic market, which may facilitate bid-rigging and other collusive behaviour – not just within the framework agreement itself, but also in the broader market if the result is the long-term exclusion of suppliers,[80] especially where the procuring entity is a dominant purchaser and/or with mandatory use of framework.

The way that the procuring entity's needs are expressed can exacerbate this potential by limiting the market beyond what is strictly necessary: where the terms of the framework agreement as advertised at the first stage are vague or diverse so that the framework agreement will be substantially incomplete, for example, potentially responsive bidders might decide not to participate or may be excluded because their offers are too specific, limiting the scope of the potential market. From a governance perspective, too, there may be a risk of substantial modifications to the framework agreement during its duration, which most regulatory and policy systems seek to discourage.)[81]

A similar situation may arise if quantities needed by the procuring entity are mismatched with the remainder of the market and capacity of its players or if qualification or technical specifications (as discussed above) effectively limit the market. It has therefore been suggested that frameworks whose size or diversity automatically excludes a significant part of the market should be avoided, unless consortia or joint bids to allow – for

---

[80] Imposing a maximum duration on framework agreements is considered a key governance mechanism in the light of competition concerns, and is discussed in Chapter 12.
[81] See, further, Chapter 5.

example – smaller suppliers to meet larger quantity needs – are envisaged.[82] Some aspects of unnecessary market limitation can be mitigated through appropriate design (avoiding excessive quantity estimates through an indication of relatively small-scale individual purchases, for example), but a danger that framework agreements 'may favour larger firms that are able to stock or import quickly the required goods, works of services to meet the requirement response time',[83] has been noted, particularly in the developing country context.

As regards demand considerations, relevant design decisions range in the collusion context from seeking to broaden access to the relevant market to avoiding predictability and structuring second-stage competition, as we have seen. Demand predictability, in particular and when combined with knowledge of the terms of first-stage bids, poses a significant risk to the integrity of second-stage competition. Reducing predictability can involve creating a degree of asymmetry between suppliers and call-offs – the more the one category is symmetrical, the greater the appropriate degree of symmetry in the other category. A summary of these issues is set out below.

*Market access issues*

- Whether the framework is to be 'closed' in the sense that new suppliers are not permitted to join the framework agreement or supply goods or services under it after the framework agreement is concluded, or whether it is 'open' to new suppliers throughout its term[84]
- Whether replacement bidders will be permitted to join the framework agreement if awardees leave it[85]
- Whether the procuring entity's needs are to be expressed in technical or functional terms, recalling that functional statements of needs may enhance market access
- The related issue of how narrowly-defined or diverse the products or services to be supplied will be, recalling that either type of statement of needs may exclude some bidders

---

[82] 'The difficult balance between transparency and competition in public procurement: Some recent trends in the case law of the European Courts and a look at the new Directives', note 6, supra.
[83] S. Karangizi, 'The Use of Framework Agreements in Africa', chapter 6 in S. Arrowsmith (ed.), *Public Procurement Regulation in the 21st Century: Reform of the UNCITRAL Model Law on Procurement* ((Eagan, MN: West, 2009), at pp. 258–260.
[84] Most systems permit either variety, as explained in Chapter 5.
[85] Whether this is permitted will depend on the regulatory framework – see, further, Chapter 12.

- The number of awardees – minimum, maximum or defined number (generally relevant only in closed framework agreements),[86] recalling that a higher number of awardees may reduce the potential collusive profit
- The aggregate value of the framework agreement – high or excessive indications of value may exclude some bidders – and the anticipated size of call-offs, which may do likewise
- The duration of the framework agreement – the longer the duration, the longer the awardees are protected from full competition,[87] noting that if framework agreements are re-let on the same terms after the maximum duration has been reached, the practical effect may be to perpetuate the earlier framework agreement in terms of scope and awardees.[88]

*Predictability-related decisions*

- Whether or not the use of the framework agreement is optional or mandatory for procuring entities that are entitled to use it – mandatory or effectively universal use of the framework agreement will enhance demand predictability. Similarly, if the framework does not contain a binding or minimum purchase obligation, predictability will be lessened
- Whether or not the framework agreement is a unique procurement tool for the needs concerned, or whether there are other parallel framework agreements or procurement procedures, so that fragmented demand across a series of procurements can be aggregated and a collusive scheme agreed among bidders for all of them
- The number and frequency of envisaged call-offs – a higher number and more frequent call-offs provide greater opportunity to interact and rig bids

---

[86] A minimum number may be required to ensure security of supply and there may need to be sufficient awardees to ensure effective competition. On the other hand, limiting the number of awardees may be necessary (as is the case in a Model 2 framework agreement) to ensure that each has a realistic chance of being awarded a contract under the framework agreement, and to encourage it to participate. See, further, Chapter 10.

[87] Issues in identifying the appropriate duration are discussed in Chapter 12: it is generally considered that a maximum duration for closed models is appropriate to mitigate the anti-competitive potential.

[88] For a discussion on the possibility of an effective extension or repeated effective extensions of the term that may have a similar impact, such as through large call-offs awarded near the end-date, see Chapter 12.

- Whether the ratio of awardees to call-offs is defined and whether the call-offs exceed the awardees and/or are divisible into the number of awardees, each of which may facilitate a bid-rigging agreement
- The relative value of each call-off to likely bidders, recalling that a collusive ring will need to satisfy each awardee in a manner commensurate with its bargaining power
- Whether partial offers or joint ventures will be permitted, recalling that allowing partial bids may increase the competitive pool[89] and allowing joint ventures may broaden or reduce it, depending on the nature of the joint ventures[90]
- The extent to which the framework agreement is complete and so call-offs more predicable – that is, the extent of terms that remain to be settled at the second or call-off stage, and the extent to which variations in purchases are permitted. Not only do more complex call-off competitions reduce predictability, but they also make bid rigging a considerably more complex undertaking. Relevant indications include

  - whether or not the framework agreement contains minimum, defined or maximum quantities and/or aggregate values;
  - the complexity of second-stage competition – whether different quality and quality/price considerations are envisaged, whether other key terms (delivery times, locations, warranty periods, etc.) vary and whether certain combinations of products or services may vary or be 'locked-in';
  - whether the award criteria for call-offs at the second stage will be based on lowest-price responsive bid, or most economically advantageous bid, and how they will vary between the two stages (if at all);[91]

---

[89] Permitting these may broaden the potential supply market by allowing access to smaller operators that cannot meet the entire need of the procuring entity. This flexibility is envisaged in the UNCITRAL Model Law generally and as regards framework agreements in Articles 58 and 60 (note 23, supra).

[90] Joint ventures may allow bidders that otherwise cannot meet the entire requirement or qualify for the procedure to participate, or they may operate to restrict the number of bidders – conceivably as part of a collusive scheme.

[91] Where longer-term and centralised purchasing are concerned, there may be benefits in terms of value for money and administrative efficiency in permitting the procuring entity to set the relative weights and their precise needs only at the second stage – to avoid, in extreme cases, that there be only one responsive awardee at the second stage. On the other hand, governance considerations indicate that limitations on variations are appropriate so as to avoid abuse.

- how regular or diverse the call-offs will be (in terms of timing and quantities);
- whether the call-offs will all be competitive, or whether some may be made through application of the terms of the framework agreement;[92] and
- whether the call-offs will be handled through one-stage bidding, or an e-reverse auction, recalling that auctions add a further level of collusive potential.[93] A subsidiary issue is how to reduce the collusive potential of the auction format, which is considered separately below.

While a common feature of these latter design elements is that they define the relative predictability of demand under the framework agreement, and we have seen that the potential for bid rigging is reduced where there is an element of unpredictability in that demand,[94] avoiding collusion is only part of ensuring effective competition. We have also considered, in Chapter 7, the importance of design and transparency issues in creating the conditions in which effective competition can take place – for example, issuing the best available information and reducing uncertainty allows bidders to submit their best offers. Consequently, these potentially competing considerations need to be balanced in the circumstances of the market and procurement at hand and, where an appropriate balance is not achievable in some types of framework agreement or framework agreements as a whole, alternative tools are necessary.

For example, where there is second-stage competition, bidders have a two-stage opportunity to submit their offers. The relevance of the first stage in Model 2 framework agreements is that the lower-quality or least responsive bidders will be excluded, so that second-stage competition takes place among a more limited pool. Simply repeating the terms of an earlier competition in that situation is likely not to generate effective competition unless the market itself is highly unstable and is also inefficient in terms of administrative burden. Limiting the second-stage competition to the variable elements that will identify the most responsive and best-value bidder for the procuring entity's needs at that time, when combined with other design features – for example, if the competition is on price only for a

---

[92] 'Mixed' Models 1 and 2 framework agreements, which are now permitted in the EU system but not currently under the Model Law (note 23, supra).
[93] See Section 8.4.2.4.
[94] In that the collusive players cannot plan how to 'share the pie' with certainty.

defined quantity, and if the number of call-offs is fixed and higher than the awardees – may be too predictable.

A relatively straightforward response may appear to be to increase the number of bidders and awardees using some of the mechanisms noted above without moving to an open framework agreement, but this may require the procuring entity to soften its requirements. There are two main possible impacts of doing so. First, competition may be reduced at the first stage – in extreme cases, bidders may not in reality be bidding to fulfil a single need but a range of them (significant asymmetry in scheduling, bidders or in their bids alone or in combination may generate ineffective competition). The second is that the scope and administrative burden of competition for call-offs is increased (not least because many systems, such as those based on the UNCITRAL Model Law or EU Directive, require all or all capable awardees to be invited to bid on call-offs), which may compromise the administrative justification for using a closed framework agreement procedure at all. In some circumstances, alternatively, a straightforward first-stage competition leading to an open framework agreement in which all competition takes place at the second stage may offer a more acceptable compromise. In others, if the conclusion is that second-stage competition is likely to prove illusory, a Model 1 framework agreement without second-stage competition at all may be the most appropriate alternative.

It can be seen, therefore, that designing framework agreements procedures both to be effective in creating the conditions in which competition can take place and to avoid facilitating collusion is a complex task, and one to which there will not be a right answer. The governance and capacity issues involved are further considered in Chapter 12.

*Second-stage competition – seeking to reduce the collusive potential of an e-reverse auction*
There are three commonly encountered ways of holding a multi-round e-reverse auction, differing in the way that the auction closes. The auction may close (i) at a predetermined time; (ii) when the procuring entity, within a specified period of time, receives no further valid bids outbidding the previous top-ranked bid; or (iii) after a predetermined number of rounds of bidding. Clearly, type (i) is the most likely to facilitate a collusive scheme, because of its greater certainty and predictability, followed by type (iii), whereas type (ii) is the least predictable.

There are ways of reducing the information flow during a multi-round auction that might reduce the potential for detection of deviations from a previously agreed collusive scheme or tacit collusion to be undertaken, while still encouraging competition. The rules governing an e-reverse auction are likely to require the system promptly or instantaneously to communicate relevant information to facilitate revised rounds of bidding to the bidders, so that each bidder can determine the standing of its bid vis-à-vis other bids. There are various ways of doing this: (a) disclosing – to each bidder – only whether or not it is leading the auction (i.e. has the leading price); (b) disclosing the leading price, so that each bidder can work out how much it has to improve its bid; (c) disclosing each bidder's standing to that bidder, but only as compared with the (anonymised) leading bid, without information on other bids;[95] and (d) disclosing the spread of all bids to all bidders. It is evident that there is a balance in selecting among these options between giving the information that should encourage the most competitive bidding and allowing the detection of possible deviations from a collusive strategy.[96]

## PART B   DETECTING COLLUSION, ENFORCEMENT ACTION AND SANCTIONS

Certain findings on fraud, corruption and collusion in the roads sector found in a 2011 World Bank report[97] are summarised in a 2012 OECD publication,[98] which also provides some insight into behaviour that may indicate possible collusion.

---

[95] Evidence from some systems is that disclosing only information about the leading price tends to encourage very small reductions in that leading price.

[96] See, further, Guide to Enactment, note 11, supra, Commentary to Article 56, para 3. Whatever information is disclosed to bidders, the procuring entity can have access to all relevant information. If there is a risk that the procurement official may be involved in the collusion, additional steps to reduce the information flow may again be required.

[97] World Bank (2011), Curbing Fraud, Corruption and Collusion in the Roads Sector, World Bank Group, Washington DC, Available at http://siteresources.worldbank.org/INTDOII/Resources/Roads_Paper_Final.pdf. It was noted that 'road projects around the globe are plagued by fraud, corruption, and collusion. The Bribe Payers Index 2011, a Transparency International poll, ranked construction as the industry most prone to corruption, while a survey of international firms revealed that companies in the construction industry were more likely than firms in any other sector to have lost a contract because of bribery. World Bank-financed projects are not immune. Roughly one-fourth of the 500 plus projects with a Bank-funded roads component approved over the past decade drew one or more allegation of fraud, corruption, or collusion, according to the Bank's Integrity Vice Presidency'.

[98] OECD Directorate for Financial and Enterprise Affairs Competition Committee, Latin American Competition Forum, Session III – Improving Effective Public Procurement: Fighting Collusion and Corruption, Background Note by the OECD Secretariat, DAF/COMP/LACF(2012)15, 17 September 2012, available at http://www.oecd.org/officialdocuments/publicdisplaydocumentpdf/?cote=DAF/COMP/LACF(2012)15&docLanguage=En.

*Addressing risks of collusion in framework agreements* 245

> OECD summary of *'Fraud, corruption, and collusion in the roads sector: Findings from the 2011 World Bank Report'*
> Evidence from World-Bank projects
> In a project in Eastern Europe a World Bank procurement specialist alerted [the World Bank Integrity Vice-Presidency, INT] to a pattern in the bids on a street rehabilitation contract that suggested bid rigging. The cost figures in the bids submitted by the only two firms competing were virtually identical – down to the same typos in both. The only difference in the two bids was the total price: one was one per cent below the engineering cost estimate, and the other was one per cent higher. While INT could not substantiate collusion in this case, it did find that the high bidder had provided a false bid security.
> In Latin America three firms that submitted low bids on a contract were disqualified for reasons that INT suspected were aimed at keeping new entrants out, a common strategy for preserving a bid rigging scheme.

The OECD has reported a case of collusion among twelve bidders for security guard services in Brazil, from 1990 to 2003, concluded through regular meetings held at trade association headquarters, and informal events in restaurants.[99]

### 9.6 Detecting bid rigging

Despite an apparent regular uncovering of cartels,[100] their existence is not easy to detect. As has been observed, cartel membership may cover the entire industry, and purchasers will generally have no external benchmark price that indicates they are being overcharged.[101] However, in the public procurement context, 'bid rigging requires that the participating firms agree on the bid participation strategy (who wins and at what price, who will participate today and also who wins and who participates to future bids). As a result, bid riggers leave a lot evidence on the strategies pursued that a well-trained public administration official could indeed identify'.[102]

---

[99] The case came to light through a leniency programme (such programmes are described later in this chapter). See OECD Competition Committee, 'Annual Report on Competition Policy Developments in Brazil', 2007, DAF/COMP(2008)10, 30 May 2008, p. 15, available at www.cade.gov.br/upload/AnnualReport2007[1].pdf.

[100] See the examples in 'Roundtable on ex officio cartel investigations and the use of screens to detect cartels– Background Note by the Secretariat', DAF/COMP(2013)14, 4 November 2013, available at www.oecd.org/officialdocuments/publicdisplaydocumentpdf/?cote=DAF/COMP(2013)14&docLanguage=En. Nonetheless, there are indications that the discovered cartels are the tip of the iceberg, at least in the European Union. See M. Maci, 'Bid-rigging in the EU public procurement markets: some history and development', European Competition Law Report (2011), 3298, 406–413.

[101] Cartels in Public Procurement, note 72, supra.   [102] Ibid.

### 9.6.1 Data and bid analysis

There are many sources of guidance for procurement officials explaining how bids and bidding patterns may provide evidence that bid rigging is a possibility, particularly when combined with market research and analysis that may indicate the propensity for collusion or cartel behaviour in the overall market concerned.

At the international level, the OECD Competition Committee has issued a 'Checklist for Detecting Bid Rigging in Public Procurement' as an annex to its Recommendation on Bid-rigging, along with guidance for procurement officials.[103] At the national level, many countries – including Barbados,[104] Canada,[105] Finland[106] and Sweden,[107] among others – have developed similar checklists and guidance, as the OECD has also observed.[108] As these checklists and guidance are publicly available, this chapter will highlight the key factors they indicate may constitute evidence of potentially collusive behaviour.

These warning signs can be collated into three main areas:

**Unusual bidding patterns in bids themselves:** Do bids show signs of coordination among bidders? Are they closely correlated (after adjusting for market conditions)? Do they show the same errors or use the same phraseology? Is only the winning bid carefully drawn up – the others being careless? Do they appear to come from the same source (paper, system)? Are there unexpected bidders – such as those whose geographical location indicates that they would be unable to fulfil the contract profitably – whose participation may indicate 'complementary bids'? Are there suspiciously few bids? Do bidders withdraw inexplicably? Are there unnecessary joint bids?

**Suspicious bidding patterns in repeat procedures – within a framework agreement procedure or across framework agreements:** In suspicious geographical distribution, do some bidders always participate but submit

---

[103] See Recommendation on Fighting Bid Rigging in Public Procurement, 17 July 2012, note 7, supra, and Guidelines for Fighting bid rigging in Public Procurement, note 8, supra.
[104] 'Detecting, mitigating and fighting bid-rigging in Public Procurement, Guidelines and Checklist', available at www.ftc.gov.bb/library/2011-02-07_ftc_guidelines_checklist_procurement.pdf.
[105] 'Bid-Rigging – Awareness and Prevention', available at www.competitionbureau.gc.ca/eic/site/cb-bc.nsf/eng/02646.html.
[106] 'Tips for fighting bid-rigging', available at www.kilpailuvirasto.fi/tiedostot/Vinkkeja-tarjouskartellien-havaitsemiseen-2012-EN.pdf.
[107] Checklist Konkurrensverket (Swedish Competition Authority) – 'Twelve ways to detect bid-rigging cartels', available at www.konkurrensverket.se/en/publications-and-decisions/checklist–twelve-ways-to-detect-bid-rigging-cartels/.
[108] 'Fighting Cartels in Public Procurement', note 72, supra.

very high prices? Is there evidence of rotating among a group of bidders to submit the winning bid? Do winning bidders subcontract to losing bidders? Do prices change inexplicably from procurement to procurement?

**Unusual or unexplained pricing behaviour – the relationship between costs and prices in independent bids should be evident or explicable:** Is there a correlation between them? Is there an unusual difference between the winning and other bids, or is there an unusual spread among bid prices?

It has been observed that bid-rigging agreements are difficult to detect in a single bid because the colluding parties can simulate an artificial environment that looks competitive.[109] Framework agreements procedures, generally involving repeat procedures, therefore offer a relatively novel opportunity to observe suspicious behaviour in a series of bidding procedures. This may be particularly helpful where they are operated by centralised purchasing agencies (which can collect data on different framework agreements procedures) or where procuring entities share data, and this type of cross-procurement analysis can allow the comparison of bidding patterns across different procurements. Suspicious indications can include situations in which correlation patterns differ among those procurements, bids from the same bidder in different procurement procedures or among call-offs vary even where the terms of the procurement are the same or similar and bids vary over time differently from the market. Indeed, these collaborative approaches may provide an element of benchmark pricing that addresses the information gap noted above. The collation of data and subsequent analysis can also be used to predict the probability of bid rigging. Evidence- and data-analysis approaches, also involving economic screening models, have been used successfully to identify bid rigging in a wide range of countries, according to the OECD.[110]

However, it is important to note that suspicious behaviour is not itself evidence of bid rigging or attempted bid rigging, and further appropriate investigation is required. Similar to the situation in which an abnormally low bid is suspected, the procuring entity cannot automatically conclude that there is bid rigging simply on the basis that the bids appear to be suspicious without giving the bidder concerned the opportunity to explain the facts and could lead to abuse. As the Guide to Enactment has explained, in addition, different patterns need not be suspicious, such as

---

[109] Cartels in Public Procurement, note 72, supra.
[110] 'Roundtable on ex officio cartel investigations and the use of screens to detect cartels – Background Note by the Secretariat', note 100, supra. Examples are provided from, for example, the United States, Korea, Mexico, Canada and Australia.

in international procurement.[111] The procedures set out in the Model Law[112] and the EU Directive[113] can be adapted to provide minimum standards for procuring entities to investigate suspicions of collusion. Supporting guidance, as in the OECD recommendations, can helpfully indicate that action at an early stage of the procurement process can enhance any necessary competition enforcement or other appropriate response.

There is evidence that bidders alerted to the existence of a screening or similar programme have taken the countermeasures to avoid detection by altering their behaviour. In the United States, an 'Identical Bid Unit' programme was undermined as bidders started to submit very similar but not identical bids, and the programme was consequently discontinued. Programmes designed to assess warning signs will therefore need to keep step with bidders' activities.

It has also been observed in the United Kingdom that a requirement in the construction sector for project bank accounts from which subcontractors are paid has had an unexpected anti-collusion effect. The administrative process of providing details of the subcontractors for these payment purposes appears to have reduced the scope for last-minute changes of subcontractor – changes that may indicate reward payments for losing a bid.

### 9.6.2 Practical aspects – outreach, coordination with competition authorities and use of anti-collusion clauses in procurement documents

The policy recommendations and guidance summarised above all emphasise the importance of outreach programmes to procurement officials and the need for coordination with competition authorities.

As regards outreach, many observers have noted that procurement officials' main duty is to deliver efficient procurement procedures, not to act as competition law enforcers. Consequently, and while they may be able to raise red flags, they do not necessarily have expertise in the matter, and nor may their incentive structure encourage them to report suspicions to the competition agency. Higher prices via bid rigging are unlikely to be visible, and so active steps to assess bids for the warning signs noted above will be needed. Suspicion that there is a cartel delays the procurement

---

[111] See, further, commentary on Article 20 of the Model Law, Guide to Enactment, note 11, supra.
[112] Model Law, Article 20, on 'Rejection of abnormally low submissions', note 23, supra.
[113] EU Directive, note 22, supra.

process, which may compromise the official's main duty: assessing warning signs may divert scarce time from finalising a procurement, and consequently is unlikely to be a priority – especially in the context and probable time frame of call-offs under a framework agreement. Finally, 'the money that is being saved because of the dismantling of a cartel does usually not remain in the administration that actually discovered or helped discovering the cartel, but is redistributed to the general administration budget'.[114] For all these reasons, outreach needs to extend beyond training and should encourage cooperation with competition authorities, and policymakers will need to address the incentive structure.

Cooperation with competition authorities also has benefits from the sanctions and enforcement perspective, as it may enable the screening of a variety of markets that might otherwise exceed available resources. It has been noted that

> procurement officials are likely to have better information on the functioning of the market and the activity of firms than economists running screens at the competition agency; such information may be crucial for effectively monitoring the market and also for limiting the number of false positives and negatives. In particular, because procurement officials interact with bidders directly, they are able to observe behaviour or notice statements which are not recorded in the documents submitted by the bidders, and may be outside the direct reach of the competition agency.[115]

The OECD Public Governance Committee has issued a toolbox for enhancing integrity in public procurement, which, among other things, suggests that an anti-collusion tender clause may be included in the procurement documents to warn 'bidders that procuring authorities are aware of the risks of bid rigging and will take the necessary actions to prevent such behaviour',[116] and to require certificates of independent bid determination from suppliers (which confirm that a bid has been developed independently and without collusion).[117] While views differ on whether these measures – and indeed, Integrity Pacts and similar measures – will in practice be a sufficient deterrent by themselves, when

---

[114] Cartels in Public Procurement, note 72, supra.
[115] 'Roundtable on ex officio cartel investigations and the use of screens to detect cartels– Background Note by the Secretariat', note 100, supra, Section 3.3.2 National and international guidelines for detecting bid rigging in public procurement, at p. 43.
[116] 'Enhancing integrity in public procurement: a toolbox', p. 41, 15 October 2009, OECD, GOV/PGC (2009)8, available at www.oecd.org/officialdocuments/publicdisplaydocumentpdf/?cote=GOV/PGC%282009%298&docLanguage=En.
[117] Ibid, at p. 44.

combined with an obligation on bidders to declare whether they have been subject to previous proceedings in any jurisdiction regarding collusive practices, the risk of aggregated punishment if collusion is then discovered may increase the deterrent effect.

### 9.6.3 Leniency programmes

Leniency programmes, common in many jurisdictions,[118] are designed to encourage a colluding party to disclose cartels to cooperate with competition enforcement authorities thereafter. They operate to enhance detection of cartels by offering an incentive to the first party to reveal the existence of the cartel – immunity from prosecution or other enforcement action, or reduced penalties – against evidence that will allow action to be taken against the other members. While there are many examples of cartels being discovered through such programmes in commercial markets, their effectiveness may be linked to the stability of cartels,[119] in that the more unstable a cartel may be, the greater the incentive to become a whistle-blower. As we have seen, bid rigging in procurement markets generally leads to cartels that are more stable than those in other commercial markets, so the incentive and deterrent effects may be less persuasive in the public procurement context. Nonetheless, they are a policy tool that should not be disregarded.

## 9.7 Enforcement action and sanctions

Enforcement action for bid rigging or cartels will generally be undertaken by competition authorities and/or through criminal prosecution, topics that fall outside the remit of this book. However, collusion also requires a response within the procurement function: as The Guide to Enactment states, a key feature of an effective procurement system is the existence of mechanisms to monitor that the system's rules are followed and to enforce them if necessary:[120] these mechanisms may involve sanctions on bidders in the case of collusion.[121]

---

[118] Originating in the United States prior to 2000, they are now found in most OECD countries, and several countries in Africa, Asia and Latin America.
[119] M. Alfter and J. Young, 'Economic Analysis of Cartels – Theory and Practice', *European Competition Law Review*, 26, No. 10 (2005): 546–557.
[120] Guide to Enactment, Introduction to Chapter VIII, note 11, supra, at p. 295, referring to reviewing and challenging procurement officials' decisions, audits and investigations.
[121] Model Law, Article 9(f), note 23, supra.

*Addressing risks of collusion in framework agreements* 251

Sanctions can include disqualification or exclusion from an ongoing procedure[122] – which can be a useful tool in, for example, open framework agreements if there would remain sufficient awardees to allow the procurements to continue effectively. More commonly, however, and almost invariably in the case of closed framework agreements, the appropriate sanction will involve both a disqualification from the framework agreement concerned and an exclusion from future procurement (otherwise known as suspension or debarment, which may be temporary or permanent).[123] Policymakers may also be aware that 'effective, proportionate and dissuasive' sanctions where a corruption offence is committed (including collusion) are also a baseline requirement of the United Nations Convention against Corruption (UNCAC).[124] Currently, there is no international model for sanctions procedures, and systems at the national level vary widely[125] – some are 'discretionary', and others 'mandatory' or 'punitive', meaning that the primary objectives range from encouraging appropriate self-cleaning or other remedial action and protecting procuring entities from performance and reputational risk, to the punishment of guilty bidders. Nonetheless, an appropriate sanctions regime is an integral part of the anti-collusion policy toolkit, as the OECD has noted.[126]

### 9.8 Chapter summary

- Preventive measures can go only so far in fighting collusion – the risk is inherent in public procurement markets, as in other markets.
- Closed framework agreements may inevitably create pro-collusive tendencies, no matter how carefully designed.

---

[122] Model Law, Article 21, note 23, supra.
[123] Suspension refers to temporary measures, typically a year or less, whereas debarment refers to restrictions of up to three years or longer. Debarment has serious consequences, potentially taking a company out of the marketplace long enough to lose competitive standing in a field, but systems vary in their use of the terminology. See, also, Guide to Enactment, commentary on Administrative Support, para. 74, note 11, supra.
[124] Article 30 of UNCAC, note 15, supra, requires that each state party 'make the commission of an offence established in accordance with [the] Convention liable to sanctions that take into account the gravity of that offence', and it is noted that suspension and debarment are among the appropriate sanctions. See, further, The United Nations Convention against Corruption, a Resource Guide on State Measures for Strengthening Corporate Integrity, United Nations Office on Drugs and Crime, 2013, available at www.unodc.org/documents/corruption/Publications/2013/Resource_Guide_on_State_Measures_for_Strengthening_Corporate_Integrity.pdf.
[125] As reported at a 2012 event on the topic: 'Colloquium on suspension and debarment: towards an integrative approach?' http://globalforumljd.org/events/2012/100912_suspension.htm.
[126] 'Fighting Cartels in Public Procurement', note 72, supra.

- Data-gathering and an evaluation of the operation of framework agreements to detect possible instances of collusion, and appropriate sanctions and enforcement measures where collusion is detected, will be important elements of effective use of framework agreements procedures.
- Preventing collusion is only one of a series of policy objectives in designing and using framework agreements procedures, one requiring a careful planning and design process.

PART III

*The design of framework agreements*

CHAPTER 10

# Essential issues in framework agreements for the individual buyer

## 10.1 Introduction

The analysis carried out in previous chapters depicted how economic forces may interact with each other in the different families of framework agreements. Given the multitude of forces at play, it would be unwise to attempt at precisely predicting the outcomes resulting from a two-stage interaction among competing firms. Designing the appropriate framework agreement solution(s) then requires the procuring entity's ability to assess its needs and to understand supply markets dynamics as well as the humility to accept that learning often stems from coupling a sound economic approach with a systematic trials-and-errors approach.

This chapter will lay down the pillars of a sound methodology for designing framework agreements. We shall borrow the point of view of a procuring entity concluding a framework agreement for its own use. In Chapter 11, we shall enlarge the picture to cover additional aspects that are specific to centralised procurement; that is, to the case where a third party – generally a centralised procurement agency – awards framework agreements on behalf of other public organisations.

While providing a comprehensive toolbox, we shall nonetheless refrain from making clear-cut prescriptions. Our main conclusions need to be adapted to different local circumstances, which also evolve over time. We shall adopt a rather intuitive approach, moving from the potentially simplest to the most complex scenario. We shall also concentrate our attention on the potentially most demanding aspects of the design, namely how to choose the appropriate number of awardees and how to balance competition between the first and the second stage of a Model 2 framework agreement concluded with more than one awardee.

## 10.2 Basic design of framework agreements

In this section, we shall combine the essential features of demand and supply to derive simple operational indications for choosing the appropriate model of framework agreements. As always in procurement design, the underlying ambition is to flesh out a sound methodological approach to tackle concrete problems rather than compiling a list of ready-to-use recipes.

### 10.2.1 The main drivers on the two sides of the market

#### 10.2.1.1 Supply side

*Market characteristics: size and degree of competitiveness of the market and number of potential participants* As emphasised throughout this book, the number of potential competitors for a bundle of procurement contracts is very rarely an exogenous variable. While this is a well-known concept in the antitrust world,[1] public procurement experts are generally less familiar with the concept of a 'relevant market'. If, for instance, procuring entities wish to *purchase* four-wheeled motor vehicles, then the relevant supply market is likely to be populated by producers and resellers. If, instead, the procurement strategy hinges on long-term rental of the same vehicles, then the relevant market will be mostly populated by financial intermediaries.[2] In reality, of course, the market is unlikely to be defined this broadly.

In the procurement context, the relevant market is determined by the nature of the envisaged procurement contracts and how the needs to be met are defined. The number of potential participants may be also determined by the aggregate value of the procurement contracts: larger firms may be expected to have some degree of capacity advantage over SMEs. Hence, in the remainder of the discussion in this chapter, the number of potential participants is to be thought of as the highest possible number of firms that would be in a position to participate, given the nature and the distribution of values for the ultimate procurement contracts, as well as the procuring entity's choice of participation requirements.

---

[1] See, for instance, M. Motta, *Competition Policy – Theory and Practice* (Cambridge University Press, 2004).
[2] Sometimes, though, both financial intermediaries and producers belong to the same holding.

## 10.2.1.2 Demand side

*The degree of demand heterogeneity* As discussed in Chapter 3 demand heterogeneity stems from various sources, among which are (i) fluctuating quantities over time, (ii) procuring entity-specific preferences in terms of quality dimensions, (iii) different contractual terms (such as payment terms) for similar products/services/construction and (iv) procuring entities' intrinsic characteristics that are likely to affect competing firms' offers (e.g. payment time frames and delivery location). Heterogeneity is then not necessarily determined by one single cause but also by the simultaneous interaction of different sources. In what follows, we shall assume that demand heterogeneity is economically determined, rather than the result of a 'strategic choice' by a procuring entity seeking to differentiate its circumstances so as, say, to provide a rationale for purchasing outside of an otherwise *mandatory* framework agreement.[3]

*Need for supply diversification: single- or multi-supplier framework agreement?*
The need for supply diversification – meaning a framework agreement with multiple suppliers rather than with a single supplier – may arise in different environments, some of which are as follows:

1. Requirements may or will exceed one supplier's capacity, requiring the diversification of supply among different firms. Examples include procurement in emergency conditions to minimise the risk that supplies are not provided when and where needed, and when seeking to ensure that SMEs can participate;
2. Products or services characterised by some degree of complementarities or (in)compatibilities among different inputs. For example, server racks and server blades or specialised maintenance services for IT equipment;
3. Where demand is heterogeneous, so that the best suppler will be known at the second stage (for example, variations in timing of call-offs – in the services context, are the relevant personnel available?); where the market fluctuates (electricity, commodities, fast-changing technology); and where demand varies in terms of which combination of components will offer best value for money.

Condition 1 was already mentioned in Chapter 3, where we emphasised the importance of having multiple firms ready to supply as soon an emergency strikes. Supply diversification in emergency procurement plays the role of

---
[3] This problem is commonly known as 'maverick buying' and will be dealt with in Chapter 11.

insurance to minimise several risks after an adverse event occurs, among which stands the one of lack of available capacity or inventory when supplies are to be swiftly delivered. In Chapter 3, we also alluded to Condition 2 with reference to maintenance services for IT equipment, whereby each kind of machines requires a dedicated service. Thus, a procuring entity with a stock of different brands will need to have several maintenance firms simultaneously active.[4] Condition 3 arises when purchased products/services display the same basic characteristics, although different combinations of additional features may offer the best value for money according to the procuring entity's need at the call-off stage – for example, where there are different quality-price ratios. Examples would include basic and sophisticated configurations of electronic equipment and maintenance services with different service-level agreements (SLAs).

*The burden of process costs in carrying out each purchase as a separate procurement process*   Process costs comprise human, financial and other resources for awarding a procurement contract, which are incurred from needs definition to contract award.[5] They are part of the broad family of transaction costs, inevitably arising for trade to occur. Arguably, the level of process costs is related to (i) the breadth of the procuring organisation's needs; (ii) the degree of 'complexity' of the procurement contracts reflecting, for instance, whether the subject matter refers to standardised commodities such as petrol, rather than a bundle of different services for the maintenance of buildings or IT systems maintenance – also the presence of some dimensions of lock-in (e.g. inputs complementarities in IT equipment) may affect the complexity of the procurement contract; (iii) whether quality dimensions are easily verifiable, such as the speed of a computer's processor, rather than hard to verify, as in the case of human capital (e.g. consultants); and (iv) the related issue of relative ease of comparing bids, such as whether the award will be based on lowest-price or most economically advantageous bid, whether specifications are input- or output-based[6]

---

[4] An alternative procurement strategy would consist in setting a separate single-award framework agreement for each make. The choice would heavily rely on transaction-cost considerations. All else being equal, it would be fair to say that the higher the number of different makes, the less likely that many co-existing single-award framework agreements are adopted.

[5] While the procurement cycle extends through contract management, the discussion in this chapter will focus on the costs of the prior phases. Process efficiencies in the procurement phase may also extend to the contract management phase.

[6] The difference between the two can be explained thus: an 'Output' specification will state the intended result, for example, a clean hospital ward. This has the advantage of leaving the supplier/provider to determine how to execute the requirement and encourages innovation. An 'Input'

*Essential issues in framework agreements for the individual buyer* 259

and the extent of quality requirements. An efficiency-seeking organisation will wish to avoid duplicating process costs at both stages of the framework agreements procedure, particularly where they are elevated.

## 10.3 The main scenarios

Let us first consider an environment characterised by

1. low level of demand heterogeneity;
2. limited set of potential participants; and
3. significant process costs if carrying out each purchase as a separate procurement process.

Condition 1 points towards a complete, one-size-fits-all master contract that would contain all relevant contractual conditions for future purchases. Thus, competing firms will be able to take into account the potential level of economies of scale generated by demand aggregation at the first stage of the procedure, and there will be no need for contract tailoring at the second stage of the procedure. Moreover, since the relevant market is populated by few competitors, the degree of competition will be maximised if the procedure involves a 'winner-takes-all' feature. This stylised scenario then indicates a Model 1 framework agreement with one supplier.

It is worth underlining that, while demand might be homogeneous in terms of quality specifications and major contractual conditions, a source of heterogeneity is likely to survive in most circumstances; namely, the quantities/values of purchases that will be determined at the call-off stage. Efficiency would then be enhanced if awardees were to compete at the call-off stage on the basis of declared quantities and precise terms for each specific procurement contract.

Consequently, while variable quantities or values of purchases at the call-off stage might in principle call for a second stage of competition, a low number of potential participants (such as would be the case in a closed framework agreement) may reduce the effective level of competition at that stage. In this scenario, collusion may result, as further discussed in

specification will specify what materials/products, labour inputs, timings and so on you must use, for example, three experienced cleaners to use environmentally accredited products to clean a hospital ward from 6.00am to 8.00am, seven days a week. This method reduces freedom to innovate and bring in alternative/better products than those identified in the ITT. From CPC Guidance on undertaking a further/mini competition within an awarded EU tendered framework agreement, available at www.thecpc.ac.uk/help/eudirectives.php.

Chapter 8, and preventing collusion from materialising may need to play a bigger role than designing second-stage competition to maximise efficiency. Hence the procuring entity should provide as precise information as possible about the overall value of purchases and, possibly, about the values of individual purchases at the first stage – for example, using a matrix approach. This will reduce the amount of uncertainty at the first stage, thus allowing competition for the entire market at that stage and spurring competition among competing bidders. Accordingly, a certain level of demand heterogeneity can in fact be accommodated under a Model 1 framework agreement.

A Model 1 framework agreement with a single supplier is, consequently, more commonly used for purchasing

- landline and mobile telephone services
- Internet connectivity services
- petrol, electricity and gas
- basic IT equipment (e.g. desktop PCs and printers)

As discussed in the previous section, and more extensively in Chapters 3 and 4, there are many circumstances in which, while being able to specify precisely from the outset all the terms and conditions for the framework agreement procedure, procuring entities would benefit from supply diversification. Intuitively, though, where there will be multiple bidders admitted to the framework, in order for competition to be meaningful at the first stage of the framework agreement procedure, the elimination of some suppliers at that stage is required. Thus, one crucial decision concerns the appropriate number of firms to be selected as the framework agreement awardees, which we shall deal with in Section 10.4.

Examples of Model 1 framework agreements concluded with more than one awardee would include

- office supplies (e.g. stationery and more specialised IT equipment)
- medical equipment (e.g., x-ray and ultrasound machines)
- essential products/services/construction for emergency situations (e.g. food, water, medical supplies, shelter kits)
- travel services

Consider now a quite different procurement scenario characterised by

1. high level of demand heterogeneity and need for supply diversification;
2. large set of potential participants; and

3. relatively low process costs in carrying out each purchase as a separate procurement process.

Procuring entities may differ from each other not only with respect to quantities or values of purchases but also with respect to the main contractual terms. In other words, Condition 2 indicates that the procuring entity will wish to buy differentiated products/services/construction, which could be thought of as variants of the same subject matter. The relevant supply market, once defined, might reveal that firms seek to differentiate themselves in what they offer so as to soften price competition. Hence the appropriate purchasing arrangement is to be found in the class of Model 2 framework agreements with multiple awardees whereby competition at the first stage is against a statement of needs that is sufficiently flexible and contains only generic contractual terms that allow the best supplier to be identified and appropriate terms for the procurement contract to be set at the call-off stage. Examples would include

- composite maintenance services for buildings (e.g. janitorial, surveillance and gardening services);
- motor vehicles such ambulances and off-road vehicles for which procuring entities might reveal different needs about possible configurations;
- professional services;
- street lighting services (mostly relevant for central purchasing bodies at regional and national level, as will be discussed in Chapter 11); and
- desktop services.

If the terms of the procurement contract as disclosed at the first stage are excessively vague, bidders will not be able to engage in effective competition because it will be difficult to distinguish among offers, and to exclude poorer-quality offers from admittance to the framework agreement. If there are too many awardees at the first stage, the second-stage competition will be both costly and softer than in the full market (because some bidders were excluded), so the worst of all possible worlds results. Accordingly, the procuring entity should set a maximum number of awardees for the framework agreement, and that number should be high enough so that there are sufficient awardees to ensure effective competition in the mini-market at the second stage, but should be low enough to ensure real competition at the first stage, in the context of the relevant market. On the other hand, if the number is set too high, there will be no real competition

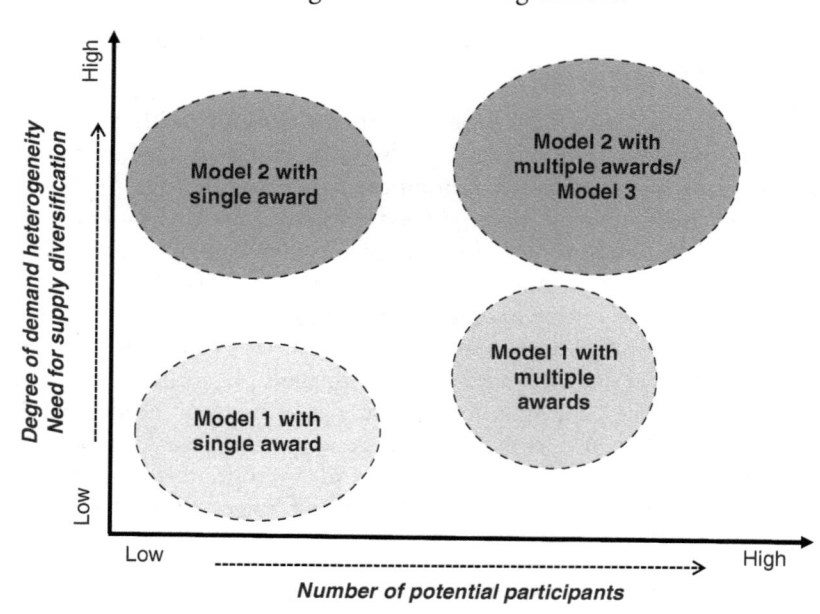

Figure 10.1 The choice of the appropriate family of framework agreements based on the main features of demand and supply.

at the first stage. While it would be hazardous to establish a universally valid threshold for the minimum acceptable number of awardees, a simple rule-of-thumb approach – supported indirectly by international regulations on request-for-quotations and shopping bidding methods, for example – would advise procuring entities not to conclude a Model 2 framework agreement with multiple awardees unless the number of awardees is at least three. Should this not be the case, and still assuming that procuring entities' needs cannot be squeezed into the same contract, a Model 2 framework agreement concluded with one awardee would become an appropriate solution. As discussed in Chapter 4, this class possesses the potential inconvenience of leaving the framework awardee with an excessive bargaining power when the master contract has to be completed according to procuring entities' needs at the call-off stage. In Section 10.8.1, we shall discuss a potential solution that may limit the awardee's bargaining power.

The discussion carried out so far is illustrated in Figure 10.1, showing the appropriate choice of the framework agreement model depending on the most relevant features of the demand and supply sides.

## 10.4 Multi-award framework agreements: choosing the 'right' number of awardees

An appropriate number of awardees strikes the correct balance between competition at the first stage and supply diversification and contract-tailoring at the call-off stage. Indeed a conflict normally arises between the two objectives: a higher number of awardees softens competition at the first stage, but raises the variety of supply sources for procuring entities at the call-off stage. Competition is adversely affected not only because the number of prizes is high relative to the number of competitors but also because, from an *ex-ante* perspective, each awardee will have lower chances of being awarded a procurement contract at the call-off stage, while having to bear the financial costs of remaining party to the agreement.

Which aspect has to play a bigger role depends crucially on the purpose for setting up the agreement. For emergency-driven framework agreements, it seems sensible to have 'supply differentiation/diversification' play a major role. Thus, it would seem reasonable to expect low levels of competition at the first stage, which, in turn, would deliver financial conditions not dissimilar to market prices for similar goods or services. Hence, choosing among a larger number of suppliers at the call-off stage is equivalent to buying insurance: the more complete the insurance, the higher the premium (i.e. the financial conditions resulting from first-stage competition).

When a multi-award framework agreement requires a second round of competition, the 'optimal' number of awardees will also depend upon the degree of incompleteness of the master contract. Intuitively, if procuring entities' needs are very heterogeneous, the first-stage competition will not be very predictive of the results at the call-off stage, and will also not be rigorous, as bidders will have little information to bid meaningfully against. Hence, the number of awardees should be high enough to maximise the chances that the variety of demand is matched by an appropriate variety of supply (i.e. that there are enough awardees capable of meeting the precise need of the procuring entity at the call-off stage to allow for meaningful competition to meet that need).

There exist two main methods for determining the number of awardees. The first consists in *exogenously* fixing the number of awardees, for instance, the four highest-ranked suppliers. Fixing an exact number of awardees raises some significant concerns about whether competition at the first stage will be rigorous. The extent of competition is roughly determined by the ratio between the number of 'prizes' and the number of competing

> **Example 10.1 A simple algorithm for determining the number of awardees**
>
> If the number of valid bids is $N^*$ then the number of awardees $A^*$ is such that
>
> - $A^* = 3$ if $3 \leq N^* \leq 5$;
> - $A^* = 4$ if $6 \leq N^* \leq 8$;
> - $A^* = 5$ if $9 \leq N^* \leq 13$;
> - $A^* = 6$ if $3\ N^* > 13$.

firms, where the latter crucially depends on most aspect of the procurement design such as the contract subject matter and selection criteria. Thus, fixing the number of awardees requires a comprehensive knowledge of supply markets. Also, it may be difficult to distinguish between, say, the top five bidders and the next few bidders, and the procuring entity may risk challenge if it sets a precise number of awardees in advance, and then excludes bidders very closely matched to the awardees. The procuring entity may therefore wish to set a range for the number of awardees – say between three and six – to allow flexibility and mitigate this risk.

The second method consists of determining the number of awardees as dependent on some specific aspect of competition at the first stage; that is, the number is *endogenous* to the competition process. Various aspects of first-stage competition might be envisaged. For instance, it would be possible to determine the number of awardees as those bidders whose tenders have been evaluated above a determined level of value for money (possibly measured by a certain level of the total score assigned to tenders). Another method would consist in setting an algorithm that determines the number of awardees as a function of the number of valid bids. An example of such an algorithm is presented in Example 10.1.

## 10.5 Balancing competition between the two stages of a Model 2 framework agreement with multiple suppliers

For practical purposes, we can think of the 'degree of (price) competition' as the extent to which each firm is willing to submit its best possible offer given its expectations about other competing firms' behaviour and the quantity or quality of information at the bidding stage. One of the most crucial aspects in designing a Model 2

# Essential issues in framework agreements for the individual buyer

framework agreement is precisely against 'what' firms have to bid for at the first and the second stage, which involves two dimensions. The first is the proportion of contractual conditions that are laid down at the stage when the framework agreement is concluded, and the second is the variety of choices available to procuring entities at the call-off stage. The first dimension refers to the degree of (in)completeness of the 'master contract': the lower (or the higher, respectively) the proportion of contractual terms laid down at the first stage, the more (or the less, respectively) incomplete the master contract. The second dimension refers to the degree of freedom the procuring entity enjoys in completing each term left unspecified in the framework agreement. Thus, the degree of heterogeneity of procurement contracts results in fact from the interaction between the two dimensions. Example 10.2 will help clarify this concept.

---

**Example 10.2 Framework agreements with different levels of heterogeneity of procurement contracts**

Consider a simplified Model 2 framework agreement for photocopying machines, whereby bidders compete at the first stage on the price of the equipment (subject to a minimum level of quality standards), while contractual terms regarding additional services are left unspecified and become the object of competition at the call-off stage.

SCENARIO 1

In the framework agreement, two clauses are left unspecified: (i) MRO[7] level: {8h/day, 24h/day}; (ii) disposal service: {Yes, No}. Then four different procurement contracts are generated by four possible combinations of the two contractual terms. For a given number of contractual terms, the degree of heterogeneity of procurement contracts may rise by adding additional values for each term. For instance, the MRO level may foresee three rather than two possible levels, that is {8h/day, 12h/day, 24h/day}. Hence the overall number of combinations becomes six rather than four.

SCENARIO 2

In the framework agreement, three clauses are left unspecified: (i) MRO level: {8h/day, 24h/day}; (ii) disposal service: {Yes, No}; and (iii) post-purchase upgrade: {Yes, No}. One can easily notice how the degree of heterogeneity leaps to eight by adding just one binary term. If the possible MRO levels were to become three rather two, then the overall number of possible procurement contracts would be twelve.

---

[7] Maintenance, repair and operations.

One could interpret the number of terms to be completed at the call-off stage as a *horizontal* dimension of contract heterogeneity, while the number of degrees of freedom for each unspecified contractual term could be thought of as a *vertical* dimension. Having two sources of heterogeneity of procurement contracts does not imply *per se* that they would exert the same impact on competing bidders' bidding strategies. In most cases, the horizontal dimension of contract heterogeneity is likely to have a bigger impact on firms' pricing strategies than the vertical dimension. The reason is that an extra term may require an additional investment, possibly of a different nature. An example is provided by Scenario 2, where the extra term 'post-purchase upgrade' is likely to generate different kinds of costs from those related to 'MRO level' and 'disposal service'.

The degree of incompleteness of the framework agreement affects both the nature and the intensity of competition at the first stage mainly through two channels: (i) the number of awardees, and (ii) the relative weight of price over non-price competition.

### 10.5.1 The number of awardees

In a fragmented and specialised supply market, bidders are likely to behave as 'niche' players. Procurement of this type of supplies is also likely to involve a relatively high degree of heterogeneity in the procuring entity's needs, translating into a higher degree of incompleteness of the framework agreement. Combined with 'niche players', this requires, in turn, a higher number of awardees at the first stage so as to maximise the chances that a procuring entity will be served by the most efficient 'niche' firm at the call-off stage. Thus, for a given number of competing firms at the first stage, where the terms of the procurement include a higher number of awardees, softer competition is likely to result.

Moreover, firms will have to adopt a pricing strategy taking into account all foreseeable 'tailored' prices at the call-off stage, where tailoring refers to the need of setting prices according to the combination of terms made explicit in procurement contracts. Consequently, the more incomplete the framework agreement, the larger the room for manoeuvre awardees will need to have, so as to fine-tune their pricing strategies at the call-off stage. Hence, designing a largely incomplete master contract is coupled, at least in principle, with a higher number of awardees and a softer degree of (price) competition at the first stage. Alternatively put, greater incompleteness translates into greater risk for bidders, which translates into higher prices.

*Essential issues in framework agreements for the individual buyer* 267

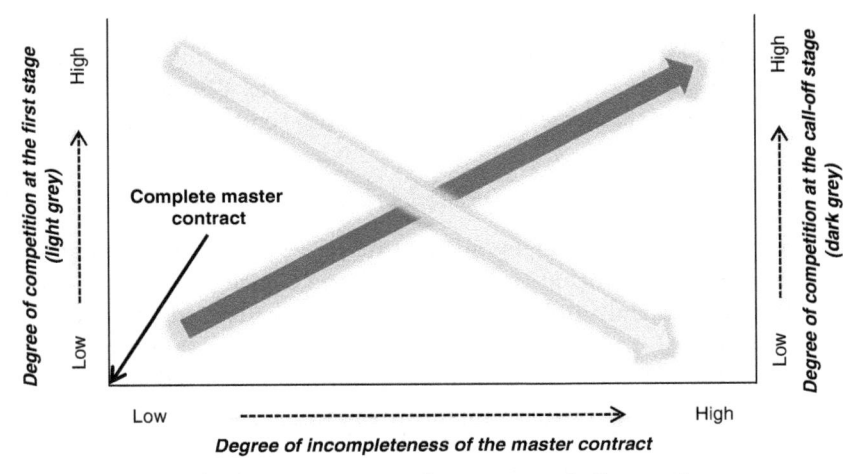

Figure 10.2 Balancing competition at the two stages of a framework agreement.

### 10.5.2 Price versus non-price competition

So far we have assumed that competition at both stages is price-driven only. A framework agreement may also be awarded on the basis of price and non-price criteria. Consider again Scenario 1 in Example 10.2 and amend it by assuming that the procuring entity is willing to reward bidders offering higher-than-minimum quality photocopying machines combined with low(er) emission of polluting chemical agents and/or low(er) electricity consumption. Hence, when the framework agreement is concluded, price competition is also affected by the weight assigned to non-price factors in the award criteria. A crucial decision is then whether and to what extent quality factors will be included in the award criteria at the first rather than at the call-off stage of a framework agreement, which will be discussed in the upcoming section.

The discussion carried out in this section can be summarised by using Figure 10.2.

## 10.6 Award criteria

In competitive procurement, the choice of award methodology between lowest price (LP) and the most economically advantageous tender (MEAT) affects participation and competition similarly to the impact of the variety of 'solutions' from which the awarding authority will select the best-value-for-money offer. In what follows, we shall flesh out the main forces that should guide the choice between LP and MEAT methodologies in Model 1 and Model 2 framework agreements. The choice of the appropriate award methodology is more straightforward in Model 3, so we shall limit ourselves to a few supplementary comments at the end of the section.

### 10.6.1 Award criteria in Model 1 framework agreements

Consider first the case whereby one awardee is selected when the framework agreement is concluded. In this case, the choice between the two award criteria is mainly driven by the extent to which procuring entities are willing to reward quality characteristics in addition to minimum quality standards. For instance, the procuring entity might reward 'renewable sources' when concluding a framework agreement for electricity, thus revealing to the supply market that it is willing to pay a different price for electricity generated by wind or geothermal sources. As Chapter 12 discusses, this decision must be taken prior to issuing the solicitation or bidding documents, and how it will be implemented – that is, how it will factor against price elements – must be disclosed in those document.

In the case of basic IT equipment, using the MEAT criterion seems a more appropriate choice when procuring entities are willing to consider different quality-price combinations and when potential bidders are known to adopt different commercial strategies depending on the nature of the technical specifications. For instance, one bidder may adopt a very aggressive pricing strategy for low-quality PCs and a high-margin one for the high-quality tier, whereas another bidder might decide to limit its business to high-quality PCs and is willing to accept lower margins. The MEAT is thus instrumental in providing incentives to bidders to offer different quality-price combinations, which, in turn, allows the procuring entity to assess a wider set of solutions.

In many cases, though, procuring entities' needs are so precise that competition can be limited to financial dimensions only, subject to predetermined minimum-quality standards. It is worth emphasising that price-only competition might embed life-cycle cost considerations or near-price criteria; that is, the evaluation of financial dimensions might include maintenance and disposal costs.[8]

---

[8] See, for instance, Articles 67 and 68, Directive 2014/24/EU of the European Parliament and of the Council of 26 February 2014 on public procurement and repealing Directive 2004/18/EC Text with EEA relevance, OJ L 94, 28 March 2014, pp. 65–242, available at http://eur-lex.europa.eu/legal-content/EN/TXT/?uri=celex:32014L0024. Hereafter, the EU Directive.

The choice of the award criterion in Model 1 framework agreements with more than one awardee will depend mainly upon the specific reason for adopting such a solution, as investigated in the remainder of this section.

*Supply diversification for homogeneous needs* An example related to the emergency procurement given above may arise in health-care procurement, where the health authority is a procuring entity for several hospitals with needs for life-saving medicines or chemical reagents. Assuming that a main objective is to select more than one awardee to reduce the risk of supply disruption to a minimum, and to have a single framework agreement containing the essential terms and conditions for the procurement (e.g. input specifications such as the chemical composition of the product, and delivery conditions), then the LP methodology, combined with other terms of the procurement to keep the award process as simple as possible, will be appropriate. The hybrid model of 'rate contracts' described in Chapter 4 might also provide an alternative procurement strategy.

Supply diversification and swift contract award are quintessential features of effective emergency procurement. Although the range of basic emergency needs may vary depending on the nature of the adverse event, it remains nonetheless true that it is possible to describe in advance the main characteristics of most of the products and services that will be required by procuring entities.[9] Thus the lowest-price criterion seems the easiest option. In order to avoid price heterogeneity due to multiple awardees, one could also consider the adoption of the 'rate contract' model. Individual hospitals' potential need for different quality levels might be tackled by splitting each family of products or services into lots, using a matrix approach.

*Supply diversification driven by different preferences over procurement solutions* Specialised (and often high-value) medical equipment (e.g. ultrasound and x-ray machines, PET and CT scanners, dialysis machines) is characterised by a core of similar functionalities and a set of additional attributes with different quality levels. Thus, for each group of similar products, prices normally vary according to the combination of additional attributes. Since producers are often specialised – that is, they produce only a few if not a single combination of quality

---

[9] See J. I. Schwartz, 'Katrina's Lessons for Ongoing U.S. Procurement Reform Efforts', *Public Procurement Law Review* 15 (2006): 362–373.

characteristics – bundling the needs of individual hospitals falling under one procuring entity with different preferences over combinations of attributes would require the MEAT criterion, so that the relative weight of the quality dimensions can appropriately reflect the importance of additional attributes[10] over the core or basic elements. As discussed in Chapter 4, the potentially thorniest issue in this context is to award contracts when framework agreement awardees have committed to different levels of value for money. We shall revisit this issue in Section 10.8.1.

*Supply diversification driven by technological complementarities*  Considering technical needs and, more broadly speaking, complementarities between two inputs implies that using one raises the productivity of the other. In some cases, complementarities can take rather extreme forms so that one is essential for the other to function properly. In the case of IT equipment, for example, high levels of complementarities characterise a particular make of photocopying machines and computer servers, and the necessary maintenance services for their components (chassis, blades, etc.). Regardless of the nature of the complementarities, the outcome is virtually always that the consumer suffers from a 'lock-in' effect. Thus, when procuring entities have purchased, over time, different makes of photocopiers or servers, a framework agreement to cover service requirements for all makes simultaneously may be considered appropriate. If so, the framework agreement will have to be concluded with a sufficiently high number of firms so as to fulfil all different needs (whether in terms of types of maintenance or of types of server blades).

If the procuring entity seeks to guarantee standard maintenance terms for all kinds of photocopiers and/or servers, then the LP criterion would provide the easiest solution. The MEAT criterion, instead, would be likely to produce uneven quality of maintenance services among makes of photocopiers. However, this solution might be appropriate when the equipment concerned comprises machines operating at different parts of their life cycle (e.g. recently purchased machines working with others close to decommission).

### 10.6.2  Award criteria in Model 2 framework agreements

The choice of the award criteria in Model 2 framework agreements might raise a different set of problems, particularly when a second round of

---

[10] The weight assigned to each quality dimension should in fact stem from a weighted average of the absolute weights that each procuring entity would attach to the same dimension, where the weighting coefficients would reflect the relative values of foreseeable purchases to be carried out by each procuring entity.

# Essential issues in framework agreements for the individual buyer 271

competition is necessary for awarding procurement contracts. While in Chapter 4 we argued that certain combinations of awarding criteria at the two stages might produce undesirable outcomes from the procuring entities' viewpoint, in what follows we shall focus on those choices of award criteria that are most coherent with the logic of this class of framework agreements.

At its simplest, Model 2 framework agreements with a second round of competition are to be used when the relevant market is populated by a sufficiently large number of potential bidders and procuring entities are differentiated with respect to their specific needs. When, for instance, final quantities may vary to a large extent across procuring entities and also play a major role in determining the level of economies of scale (through, say, transportation costs), having a second round of competition may help firms better 'tailor' their pricing strategies. Thus when the subject matter of the master contract foresees the supply of a fairly standardised commodity such as petrol, electricity and gas, two rounds of lowest-price competition would be the best option.

A caveat is in order here. When a framework agreement for petrol is concluded by a relatively small-sized public organisation, say, a local authority, it is reasonable to expect the relevant market to be populated by (possibly numerous) local distributors or retailers, as large producers might not find it profitable to compete for small-scale procurements. Being that local distributors are price-sensitive to capacity constraints at the delivery stage and to the geographical distance of procuring entities from the location of storage tanks, a second round of price competition goes exactly in the direction of matching the procuring entity with the most 'efficient' firm.

As the estimated value of the framework agreement rises because the same commodity is needed by a much larger and dispersed public organisation (e.g. a highly populated and geographically stretched municipality or a region), the most immediate relevant market would comprise fewer and bigger producers. Thus, if smaller distributors are unlikely to form joint ventures and/or the awarding organisation is not inclined to split the framework into geographical lots to favour the participation of smaller firms as solo bidders, then competition at the second stage might become meaningless (or, bluntly, pro-collusive), which would indicate a Model 1 framework agreement with more than one awardee.

When demand heterogeneity is not limited to differences among values of procurement contracts but also touches on some quality characteristics of the good/services/construction using the MEAT criterion at the first stage would appear a sensible solution. At the call-off stage, competition will always take place on a value-for-money basis even if procuring entities are not willing (or entitled) to reward additional technical aspects that had not been evaluated at the first stage. Hence, two slightly different scenarios may emerge, as illustrated in Example 10.3.

---

**Example 10.3 Using the MEAT criterion in a Model 2 framework agreement with a second round of competition**

Consider a stylised framework agreement for building maintenance services whereby all procuring entities need, say, basic janitorial services, repair of electrical systems and air-conditioning maintenance, possibly with different service-level agreements. Moreover, they may or may not need additional services such as preventive maintenance and gardening.

SCENARIO 1

Procuring entities differ only with respect to the level of quality of the basic maintenance services (say, the number of times per day spaces are to be cleaned), but they need neither preventive maintenance nor gardening. Suppose that basic maintenance consists in one shift of cleaning per day and that procuring entities are willing to consider offers for two and three daily shifts of cleaning. The awarding authority wishes also to assess (i) how and to what extent maintenance activities, particularly when carried out more than once per day, may affect its employees' working activity and (ii) the environmental impact of cleaning products (e.g. the content of potentially aggressive chemicals).

Then competition at the first stage might take place according to the MEAT criterion whereby

- Technical score (TS): up to 35 points. More specifically,
  - A maximum of 15 points is awarded to the 'organizational model' of the maintenance activities;
  - A maximum of 20 points is awarded according to the content of substances 'X', 'Y' and 'Z' in cleaning detergents.

- Financial score (FS): a maximum of 65 points. More specifically, the financial score is inversely proportional to the submitted weighted rebate $r_w = \alpha_1 \cdot r_1 + \alpha_2 \cdot r_2 + \alpha_3 \cdot r_3$, where $r_i = \{1, 2, 3\}$ is the percentage rebate with respect to the highest acceptable price per square meter when the service is carried out once ($r_1$), twice ($r_2$) or three times per day ($r_3$); and $\alpha_1 + \alpha_2 + \alpha_3 = 1$.

# Essential issues in framework agreements for the individual buyer 273

### Example 10.3 (cont.)

Suppose that three awardees are selected according to the following ranking:

|            | TS  | FS  | Total score |
|------------|-----|-----|-------------|
| Awardee 1  | 30  | 45  | 75          |
| Awardee 2  | 20  | 50  | 70          |
| Awardee 3  | 10  | 55  | 65          |

What options are available to procuring entities at the call-off stage? Notice that the nature of technical points does reveal a common feature of all downstream procurement contracts; thus, Stage 1 technical points will logically carry over all procurement contracts. However, it is possible that each procuring entity might wish to vary the weight of this 'inherited' technical score on tenders' evaluation. Moreover, firms will be asked to submit new triplets of rebates to be evaluated by means of a vector of coefficients, say $(\beta_1, \beta_2, \beta_3)$, that may or may not coincide with the one used at the first stage, thus leaving enough room to procuring entities to solicit 'tailored' prices. As a result, procurement contracts will be awarded by using the MEAT criterion whereby (i) the weight of the (inherited) technical score might be different from 35 per cent;[11] and (ii) rebates will be evaluated according to a possibly different vector of weights.

### SCENARIO 2

The stylised framework analysed above can be enriched by introducing two additional dimensions of heterogeneity among procuring entities: let us assume that some but not all of them need 'preventive maintenance' and 'gardening', which need to be included in the set of evaluation criteria, although tenders are not necessarily ranked according to these dimensions at the first stage.

Competition at the call-off stage may look similar to that described in Scenario 1 if a procuring entity is not interested in evaluating tenders by adding either 'preventive maintenance' or 'gardening'. If, instead, a procuring entity is interested in evaluating technically a project of preventive maintenance and in soliciting a fourth financial dimension concerning

---

[11] Suppose that, when designing its own mini-competition, a procuring entity wishes to lower the weight of the *inherited* technical score to spur price competition among the three awardees. It may, for instance, decide to set the weight of the technical aspects equal to 20 per cent rather than 35 per cent. Consequently, the awardees' inherited technical scores will be proportionally scaled down so that awardee 1's TS becomes $(30/35)\cdot 20 = 17.14$; awardee 2's TS = $(20/35) 20 = 11.43$; and awardee 3's TS = $(10/35)\cdot 20 = 5.71$.

> **Example 10.3 (cont.)**
>
> gardening (expressed also as price/square meter given a predetermined frequency of the service), then it will have to
>
> - set the overall weight of technical score whereby a fraction is inherited from Stage 1, while the remaining part will be allocated to the evaluation of the 'preventive maintenance' projects; and
> - introduce an additional dimension to the rebates list ($r_4$) and set the corresponding vector of coefficients/weights ($\sigma_1, \sigma_2, \sigma_3, \sigma_4$).

## 10.7 Participation and competition: division into lots

In Chapter 8, we investigated why public procurement markets generally, and framework agreements specifically, may contain elements that inhibit full competition. In most cases, obstacles to competition are due to a lower-than-desirable level of participation, especially where SMEs are concerned.[12]

Generally, splitting a procurement contract into lots favours participation via less stringent economic requirements that apply to each single lot, which becomes a separate procurement contract. Sometimes lots have similar if not identical subject matter (e.g. geographical lots), and other times the subject matter is different (e.g. product/service lots). In both cases, dividing the entire intended procurement into a greater number of lots aims at promoting the entry of smaller but possibly more specialised bidders. These bidders, by virtue of their specialisation, may be more efficient and so may submit better-value-for-money proposals than bigger competitors. Multiple lots also raise the chances that more than one awardee is selected today, thus contributing to the creation of a set of incumbent suppliers, which promotes competition tomorrow.

Let us see how the logic underlying the choice of a specific model of framework agreement intersects with the above rationales on design of lots. In Section 2.2, we derived the conclusion that a procuring entity's choice of a single-award Model 1 framework agreement is mainly justified on the ground of relatively homogenous needs arising at different points in time. If delivery points are not scattered over a sufficiently large territory – where the latter should be measured by the ratio between the area where needs arise and each competing bidder's geographical reach – then geographical lots would only reduce the level of competition, which, to recall, is a single round of competition at the first stage, for each lot.

---

[12] Promoting participation, especially of SMEs, in framework agreements is dealt with in Chapter 7.

## Essential issues in framework agreements for the individual buyer 275

Hence splitting into different lots would be a sensible choice if each lot is related to a different product/service whether the differentiation arises in technical characteristics or delivery characteristics. A simple example is provided by medical equipment for clinical imaging (e.g. ultrasound, X-ray machines), produced in most cases by few big suppliers that often display some degree of specialisation. Thus, a procuring entity may decide not to award one single contract for many different machines for fear of not receiving offers from all market-players: rather, it would maximise potential participation by having a limited number of products, perhaps one product only, in each separate lot.

The same logic for the design of lots is replicable in a Model 2 or Model 3 framework agreement provided that the number of awardees is high enough to generate effective competition at the call-off stage (where the Model 3 case raises by far lesser concerns given that new suppliers can enter the system at any stage and bid for a procurement contract).

Example 10.4 illustrates the nature of the decision facing a procuring entity.

---

**Example 10.4 Lots design: participation and competition**

A procuring entity wishes to award a single-award Model 1 framework agreement for six different products. According to market analyses, five major producers are active with the following specialisation pattern:

|        | Product 1 | Product 2 | Product 3 | Product 4 | Product 5 | Product 6 |
|--------|-----------|-----------|-----------|-----------|-----------|-----------|
| Firm A | x         | x         | x         |           |           |           |
| Firm B | x         |           | x         |           | x         |           |
| Firm C | x         | x         | x         | x         | x         | X         |
| Firm D | x         |           |           | x         |           | X         |
| Firm E |           |           |           | x         | x         | X         |

Suppose that the procuring entity is envisaging regrouping products into lots since it believes that bidders can exploit some form of synergies (e.g. economies of scale/scope at the production and/or distribution stage). If bidders were to have a preference for bidding as solo players (i.e. if some reason they were unwilling to form joint ventures), then the procuring entity would be expecting the following participation patterns for each specific lots design (numbers in brackets indicate the products in each lot on the left-hand sides and firms that are able to bid on the right-hand side):

a. {1, 2, 3, 4, 5, 6} = {C};
b. {1, 2} = {A, C}, {3, 4} = {C}, {5, 6} = {C, E};
c. {1, 5} = {A, B, C, D}, {2, 3} = {A, C}, {4, 6} = {C, D, E};

> **Example 10.4 (cont.)**
> d. {1, 2, 3} = {A, C}, {4, 5, 6} = {C, E};
> e. {1} = {A, B, C, D}, {2} = {A, C}, {3} = {A, B, C}, {4} = {C, D, E}, {5} = {B, C, E}, {6} = {C, D, E}.
>
> Different options are easy to interpret. In option (a), for instance, all six products are grouped into one lot for which only bidder C can submit a tender. In option (d), Products 1, 2 and 3 are grouped into one lot for which only bidders A and C can submit a tender, while Products 4, 5 and 6 are grouped into another lot for which only bidders C and E can compete.
>
> Some stark conclusions can be derived from this picture. Bundling all products into one big lot would make participation collapse to one bidder only, thus raising serious competition concerns. Although there exist fifteen ways of bundling products in pairs (here for sake of brevity, we are considering only 2 out 15), they are not equivalent in terms of participation and competition. Take, for instance, configuration (b) and (c), where the latter clearly dominates the former in terms of expected number of bids per lot. In the first case, participation varies for 1 to 2 (potential) bids per lot, while in the second case it varies from 2 to 4 (potential) bids per lot. Notice that the number of (potential) bids also varies from 2 to 4 when each product represents a separate lot. So the procuring entity may prefer design (c) over (e) as, given a similar (potential) participation pattern, in case (c) bidders may compete more intensely because of synergies among products bundled in the same lot.

## 10.8 Awarding contracts: some practical hints

Awarding procurement contracts is a relatively straightforward activity in Model 1 framework agreements with one supplier because all the terms are hardwired in the master contract and procuring entities are always bound to trade with the same party. In all other cases, the interplay between international regulation and sound economic principles does not necessarily pin down a straightforward and clear-cut method of awarding procurement contracts. In what follows, we shall briefly point towards some simple 'tricks of the trade', which are particularly addressed to practitioners in to public procurement.

### 10.8.1 Model 1 framework agreements with more than one awardee

As discussed in Chapter 4, international regulations foresee two main criteria for awarding procurement contracts at the second stage; namely, the 'cascade' and the 'rotation' criteria. While the rotation concept may be less easily interpreted than the cascade concept, both have potentially adverse effects, especially on the degree of participation and competition at the first stage.

The 'cascade' criterion seems to be preferable when procuring entities are willing to choose goods/services/construction from an array of different solutions, although the latter are not so heterogeneous to justify splitting the contracts into lots. Furthermore, it is advisable that the number of awardees be low enough so as to (i) make competition intense at the first stage, and (ii) minimise the risk that only a few awardees will be eventually awarded procurement contracts. Since in most regulatory systems awardees will bear financial costs for being part of an agreement, the event of not getting any of the procurement contracts will have dramatic effects in terms of participation in and competition for *future* frameworks. This does imply necessarily coupling the cascade criterion with fixed quotas of contracts to awardees[13] to make sure that each of them gets a slice of the framework agreement 'pie'. If the overall value of procurement contracts is such that each awardee, and particularly the highest-ranked one, is unlikely to have always spare capacity to serve all procurement contracts, then contracts will also be awarded to lower-ranked suppliers.

'Rotating' awardees is arguably a trickier criterion to implement mainly for two reasons. First, rotating awardees does not have a unique interpretation. Second, each of the most sensible interpretation seems to be affected by serious drawbacks, as described at length in Chapter 4. Broadly speaking, the logic of rotating awardees seems appropriate when the supplier–buyer 'matching' at the call-off stage need not be exclusively determined by the level of value for money; otherwise, the cascade logic would immediately apply. Thus, there ought to exist sensible reasons for a procuring entity to prefer the third-ranked supplier over the highest-ranked one. Indeed, we have emphasised that presence of some forms of input complementarities (e.g. specialised maintenance services for IT equipment of different makes or servers chassis and blades) will induce a rotation among awardees, which will be determined by, say, which make of IT equipment needs maintenance at each point in time over the duration of the framework.

---

[13] In fact, it would be easy to argue that 'cascade plus quotas' is virtually identical to rotating awardees according to fixed fractions of contracts, starting from the highest-ranked supplier.

A slightly different form of complementarity may arise between some pieces of equipment and human capital. This is the case of medical equipment whereby specialist medical practitioners may be better acquainted with a certain kind of, say, ultrasound machines. Long-time acquaintance translates normally into a better accuracy for visiting patients and/or more confident training of younger practitioners, but may also be caused by mere 'personal' preferences. So it is a rather fragile complementarity effect that needs proper safeguards in order to minimise the risk of abuse.

In emergency procurement, where supply diversification is one of the main goals, as delay in delivery is a crucial variable in the aftermath of catastrophe, supplier–buyer matching may take place by using an objective and non-discriminatory criterion such as the distance between the place where the procuring entity needs the products/services/construction and the awardees' warehouses.

### 10.8.2  Model 2 framework agreements with one awardee

Awarding procurement contracts to a 'monopolistic' awardee raises in principle concerns to the potentially excessive bargaining power that the selected supplier may enjoy when some of the terms have to be defined at the call-off stage. In simple words, replacing a many(-supplier)-to-many(-procuring-entity) situation with a one-to-many situation may reduce the demand side's ability to reap the best possible terms of trade when awarding procurement contracts. The following are two major practical hints to put a bridle on the awardee's bargaining power:

- It is advisable to limit the range of variations of those contractual terms that have to be further specified at the call-off stage. If possible, the number of contractual terms that are not laid down in the master contract should also be limited to a bare minimum (subject to the degree of heterogeneity of procurement contracts). The use of reserve price(s) – that is, of maximum acceptable prices – for those unspecified terms may also provide an additional insurance.
- If all terms of future procurement contracts can be fully described at the first stage, although there is uncertainty as to which terms will become relevant in each procurement contract, it would be advisable to require competing firms to submit offers for all possible terms so that the procurement contracts' financial conditions cannot be the object of further (re)negotiation at the call-off stage.

*Essential issues in framework agreements for the individual buyer* 279

## 10.9 Chapter summary

- A thorough analysis of demand and supply characteristics is a prerequisite for defining the most appropriate class of framework agreements. However, the two sides of the market are more interdependent than usually believed. Procuring entities' needs may be differently expressed in the framework's subject matter, and this, in turn, will have a consequence on the relevant market and on the potential degree of competition.
- The degree of demand heterogeneity – that is, the extent to which procuring entities need products/services/construction with different technical specifications and/or contractual conditions – is the driving dimension for choosing the appropriate family of framework agreements.
- Model 1 framework agreements with one awardee constitute arguably the most manageable solution for a procuring entity that wishes to undertake a learning process on how to rationalise repeat purchases over time. Consequently, the procuring entity should consider targeting first all types of purchases that would be best handled with that family of framework agreements. After acquiring some experience, the procuring entity might consider experimenting multi-award Model 2 framework agreements, including the adoption of the most economically advantageous tender criterion at both stages of the procedure.
- The choice of the appropriate number of awardees in multi-award Model 1 and 2 framework agreements is one of the procuring entity's crucial decisions. Fixing exogenously the number of awardees requires a profound knowledge of the relevant supply market. A decision rule that would depend, for instance, on the number of valid bids (i.e. endogenous number of awardees) will be more adequate to a less knowledgeable procuring entity, but vulnerable to manipulations by firms.
- In multi-award Model 2 framework agreements, the higher the degree of incompleteness of the master contract, the higher the uncertainty competing firms have to bear on the degree of heterogeneity of procurement contracts while bidding at the first stage. This situation requires a higher number of awardees and lower weight on price competition at the first stage.

CHAPTER 11

# Framework agreements for centralised procurement

## 11.1 Introduction

This chapter will be devoted to the distinguishing features of framework agreements designed for aggregating, either partially or completely, the demand for goods, services and construction for different public organisations, possibly on behalf of different levels of government. In such cases, the aggregation is almost always carried out through a specialised centralised purchasing agency (CPA) operating on behalf of a group of procuring entities (i.e. final users) and most commonly operating in the fields of standardised goods and services, particularly in the ICT, office supplies, telecommunications and energy sectors. We shall refer to the framework agreements concluded by CPAs as centralised framework agreements.

As we saw in Chapter 6, there are many examples of CPAs operating at the national and federal levels outside the European Union – including, Australia, Brazil, Chile, Colombia, Ethiopia, India and the United States. In addition, the centralisation process has been quite marked in Europe, especially during the past decade, where many CPAs have been established and operate at different levels (central, regional and sectorial).

Unlike the case of a public organisation designing a framework agreement for its own use, operating centralised framework agreements through a CPA raises additional difficulties, among which are the presence of a third entity matching demand and supply (the CPA) and the potentially higher heterogeneity of procuring entities which may differ in terms of institutional mission, location and budgeting rules. This process takes place against a policy preference over the past two decades for *decentralisation* of procurement – that is, delegating authority for public procurement away from central tender boards, and the like and towards the end user. It therefore raises the issue of whether aggregation of demand is incompatible with decentralisation of procurement. In this regard, we should distinguish centralised purchasing from centralised

*Framework agreements for centralised procurement* 281

procurement. Centralised *purchasing* offers optional tools to final users that can leverage government spending power to achieve economies of scale (via the voluntary use of centralised framework agreements), whereas centralised *procurement* involves limiting certain goods and services available to final users to those selected by the CPA (via the mandatory use of centralised framework agreements).

In this chapter, we shall touch on the most relevant aspects of design for centralised framework agreements, both voluntary and mandatory, using some stylised examples, and we shall attempt to provide some practical hints for 'quick wins'.

## 11.2 The main challenges of demand aggregation through a centralised procurement agency

Managing the demand for goods, services and construction from several public bodies through centralised framework agreements operated by a CPA raises specific concerns that may affect the choice of the appropriate class of framework agreements and may require specific ad hoc solutions. In what follows, we shall explore the most immediate sources of complexity generated by centralised framework agreements.

### *11.2.1 Separation of roles and tasks specialisation*

In most cases, the CPA's task is confined to concluding framework agreements under which final users procure through call-offs by contracting directly with suppliers. A clear separation of roles then arises between the first and the second stage of any framework agreement procedure, in that the CPA conducts the first stage to award the framework agreement and final users conduct the second, or call-off, stage.

This separation may bring about tangible benefits through specialisation. For instance, it creates the conditions necessary for CPA personnel to focus on market intelligence and acquire technical knowledge and expertise in each class of goods and services (becoming what can be described as 'product-oriented procurement specialists'), as well as developing horizontal know-how concerning legal, economic and managerial aspects of the procurement process. Thus, procuring entities are in the favourable position of potentially being able to free up their human resources, traditionally employed from end to end of the procurement process, to focus on contract enforcement. It also facilitates the provision of information and data to the CPA before a framework agreement is concluded (enabling demand analysis) and when the framework itself expires (*ex-post* assessment of outcomes in procurement contracts awarded, which is an essential input for effective design framework agreements over time).

These potential benefits may go, however, hand in hand with some specific problems. Because of their specialised skills and of their physical separation from final users, CPA personnel may become more attentive to technical inputs coming from the supply side (i.e. from awardees and potential bidders) rather than to the requests from the demand side (i.e. from the final users). If final users become progressively 'unheard', they may be tempted to resort to alternative procurement vehicles even when the use of the CPA's framework agreements is, in theory, mandatory (through creative use of exemptions, as further discussed below). Moreover, as final users become contract managers they may play a relatively minor role in the procurement process, which may, in turn, cause low enforcement effort at the contract execution stage.[1]

### 11.2.2   *Process costs*

Demand analysis is likely to be a time-consuming and possibly an imprecise process in centralised framework agreements as compared with the case of a procuring entity awarding a framework agreement for its own use. Information-gathering costs about final users' preferred purchasing solutions will depend on many factors, including whether final users (i) belong to the same level of government (e.g. local or central), (ii) share similar missions (e.g. educational, purely administrative or health-care providing bodies), and (iii) are physically located in a restricted area or scattered over a wider territory. This situation will be exacerbated when the final users are a relatively undefined class of procuring entities – either because the CPA is not needed to identify final users at all (as in the US federal system) or because the final users are generically described by reference to a class (e.g. 'local authorities in region X').[2]

---

[1] For a real-life case of procurement contracts mismanagement in centralised procurement, the reader is referred to Chapter 4.

[2] Marta Andrecka, 'Framework Agreements', *EU Procurement Law and the Practice*, No. 2 (2015), p. 127, Upphandlingsrättslig Tidskrift, available at www.urt.cc/?q=oa_papers, at page 142. Recital 63 to Directive 2014/24/EU of the European Parliament and of the Council of 26 February 2014 on public procurement and repealing Directive 2004/18/EC Text with EEA relevance, OJ L 94, 28 March 2014, pp. 65–242, available at http://eur-lex.europa.eu/legal-content/EN/TXT/?uri=celex:32014L0024 (hereafter, the EU Directive) explains that it must be possible to identify any procuring entity, so that future users cannot be included, which may limit some uncertainty.

Furthermore, where the CPA structure permits suppliers to update their offers outside second-stage competition (as the US federal system permits), regular changes to keep pace with technology (or earlier final user preferences) will compound the complexity of the task facing the CPA.

The same factors will play a major role throughout the duration of the framework agreement when the CPA attempts to collect as precise information as possible about the outcomes of the procurement contracts awarded at the call-off stage. Here, too, where the final users have considerable freedom to select from the goods and services offered by the CPA – again, a feature of the US GSA and MAS schedules in particular, assessing performance in a meaningful way is made considerably more difficult.[3]

### 11.2.3 Funding the CPA

The 'business model' of a CPA may have a dramatic impact on the effectiveness of the framework agreements system. As illustrated in specialised research,[4] different funding solutions have been put in place in the European Union and also elsewhere. Two extreme models seem to emerge: (a) funding through general taxation, (b) funding through fees paid by framework agreements holders, which are generally computed as a percentage of the actual purchases. Various hybrid models mixing the two extremes are also in place.

The challenge in model (a) arises, essentially, in aligning the CPA's primary function – to centralise the purchasing of goods and services – with that of the final users – to maximise outcomes determined locally. The challenge is far from being easily met, as final users, even when providing as detailed information as possible to the CPA, are not given any assurance that the CPA will adopt a framework agreement solution that best reflects their needs. The problem is exacerbated where the use of the framework agreement is mandatory, so that final users are, at least in principle, forbidden from finding or using their own purchasing solutions. To make the system work, an additional (public) party is then necessary,

---

[3] For a discussion of the lack of meaningful control over final users and marketing by suppliers in the context of the US federal system, see Daniel I. Gordon and Jonathan L. Kang, 'Task-Order Contracting in the U.S. Federal System: The Current System and Its Historical Context', chapter 5, S. Arrowsmith (ed.), *Public Procurement Regulation in the 21st Century: Reform of the UNCITRAL Model Law on Procurement* (Eagan, MN: West), at pp. 232–233.

[4] OECD, 'Centralised Purchasing Systems in the European Union', SIGMA Paper N. 47, 2011, downloadable from www.oecd-ilibrary.org/governance/centralised-purchasing-systems-in-the-european-union_5kgkgqv703xw-en.

such as a department/ministry that oversees and/or directly funds the CPA (in many countries, the Ministry of Finance would be such a party). Consequently, a potentially complex three-tier hierarchy needs to be articulated, involving setting targets for the CPAs and measuring their performance as well as monitoring the final users' purchasing behaviour and their level of satisfaction about the CPA's framework agreement solutions.[5]

The most striking challenge related to model (b) is that, while the CPA may perform well in terms of streamlining the final users' acquisition processes, it may have a (perverse) incentive not to foster competition among suppliers at either stage of the framework agreement procedure. All else being equal, if prices inside the framework agreements decline over time, a CPA funded on a percentage of sales basis will suffer from declining revenues. Somewhat paradoxically, the CPA might therefore be tempted to inflate its budget by reducing price competition among suppliers (so as to be able to hire high-quality procurement specialists and to improve the quality of framework agreements, at least on paper). There is no immediate solution to this potential problem, as prices inside a framework agreement might still be lower than those in the marketplace. Hence, those arguing that there would have been further room for competition may be met by the counter-arguments that the CPA preferred to provide final users with better-than-necessary quality (generally positively correlated with higher prices) or adopted design solutions without focusing on the risk of anti-competitive practices among awardees at the call-off stage (which may explain higher prices and may fall outside the CPA's remit in any event).

Also as regards model (b), the fees may give encouragement to CPAs to market goods and services offered directly to final users and, in some cases, encourage suppliers to sell aggressively to those final users, risking distortions in the efficiency of the system. This situation may be exacerbated where percentage fees are subject to a minimum value, so that more smaller call-offs become desirable from the CPA/suppliers' perspective,[6] and again may be notionally explained through maximising customer service.

---

[5] For an insightful analysis of public procurement based on a principal-supervisor-agent (i.e. a three-tier hierarchical) model, see Christopher R. Yukins, 'A Versatile Prism: Assessing Procurement Law through the Principal-Agent Model', *Public Contract Law Journal*, 40, No. 1 (2010): 63–86.

[6] This concern has arisen in the US federal system, citing the experience of large advertising campaigns. See 'Task-Order Contracting in the U.S. Federal System: The current System and Its Historical Context', note 3, supra.

## 11.3 Where and how to start?

Setting up a centralised framework agreement is a challenge, particularly where use is mandatory and in those environments historically characterised by decentralised procurement, and in which cultural resistance is to be expected. However, both the nature and the magnitude of risks may vary depending on different factors such as the level of government where centralisation is to be implemented, whether the latter aims at aggregating a large set of heterogeneous goods and services rather than at targeting a well-defined category (say, health-care supplies) and, importantly, the percentage of final users' demand that is managed through the CPA's purchasing arrangements. In what follows, we shall again provide a few hints that may increase the likelihood of obtaining 'quick wins'.

### 11.3.1 Demand side

CPA-driven demand aggregation is more likely to succeed the better that final users' needs can be accommodated in similar contractual terms. This obviously depends upon the degree of differentiation in the marketplace for the goods and services concerned (discussed below) as well as the intrinsic characteristics of the final users. The latter include the nature of the entity concerned (e.g. purely administrative, educational, health), the level of government entities (e.g. local versus central government) and their share of the overall public procurement expenditure, and geographical location.

The interaction of these aspects may give rise to several scenarios that need to be carefully evaluated before taking the first step towards centralisation. For instance, central government bodies tend to be concentrated in and around the capital city, although their needs may still vary. For example, the ministry in charge of the police force is likely to have a different pattern of needs for vehicles than, say, the Ministry of Education. In the education sector, on the other hand, state-operated primary schools, while scattered over the national territory, tend to have similar patterns of need for basic goods and services.

Budgeting rules for different levels of government also mean that suppliers may perceive final users differently depending on where they sit in the government system. Central government entities, for instance, depend entirely on direct transfers from the state budget to conduct their procurement, whereas local government entities in some cases enjoy a higher degree of flexibility (where they are largely funded through local taxation – noting that, in some countries such as the United Kingdom, local government remains largely centrally funded). Local government entities could then use any financial room for manoeuvre to broaden their set of purchasing options, whereas central government entities might be directed towards more narrow – that is, standardised – bundles of solutions.

Setting the relative priority of the dimensions characterising the demand side is arguably the national policymakers' most significant strategic choice. If the decision to implement some form of centralisation is motivated by the need to tighten control of public procurement spending, then it might appear sensible to focus on the level of government with the higher share of overall spending. Where this means central government, effective control may be strengthened given that central government entities operate under similar budgetary rules and are less dispersed over the territory than local government entities.

### 11.3.2 Markets

The characteristics of the various categories of procurement – goods, services and construction – differ as regards the degree of (product) differentiation among suppliers, the speed of obsolescence, the presence of technological lock-in and the relative share of fixed costs in total production costs. Measures of seller concentration[7] also provide crucial information about the supply side.

Product homogeneity will generally not sit alongside a high degree of flexibility in contractual terms and conditions, thus fulfilling one necessary condition for implementing a process of centralisation. Goods such as petrol, gas and electricity, and services such as basic Internet connections, data exchange and, to some extent, telephone services, are therefore amenable to centralisation and unsurprisingly feature commonly in CPAs. Economies of scale often characterise these markets either at the production stage or at the distribution stage, and also raise barriers to entry for new suppliers in consequence. It also comes as no surprise, therefore, that in many countries CPAs have started aggregating central government demand (and sometimes that of local government entities,

---

[7] 'Seller concentration' refers to the number and distribution of firms. Two measures of seller concentration are commonly used in (industrial) economics: the Herfindahl-Hirschman Index and the Concentration Ratios. For a formal definition, see, for instance, J. Church and R. Ware, *Industrial Organisation – A Strategic Approach* (McGraw-Hill, 2000).

in addition)[8] by awarding Model 1 framework agreements with one supplier for these items (notably, petrol, electricity and telephone services).

The world of 'services' is normally populated by both big players and SMEs. In the market for maintenance services for IT equipment, buildings, and urban open spaces as well as the supply of foodstuffs and raw food components, large suppliers compete alongside small, and even micro, competitors. These markets are in general the most sensitive to the degree of centralisation as high-value procurement contracts, and represent one potentially major barrier to entry for SMEs.

## 11.4 The impact of commitment in centralised procurement

Commitment in a framework agreement can be simply described as a guarantee that the framework agreement will lead to trade between the parties. This applies both to the framework agreement awardees and to the procuring entities. When commitment is 'strong' on the demand side (e.g. where the framework agreement contains guaranteed quantities or use of it is mandatory), some procuring entities will purchase a certain good or service through the framework agreement alone. When commitment is 'weak', procuring entities may or may not purchase through the framework agreement. A similar reasoning applies to the supply side. When commitment is strong – that is, where the framework agreement contains binding commitments – suppliers must fulfil orders from any procuring entity that is allowed to use the framework agreement, whereas it is weak when any supplier may refuse to accept an order.

The degree of commitment on both sides affects the level of uncertainty between parties, and thus has a potentially significant impact on the overall effectiveness of the purchasing arrangement. In what follows, we shall examine the main consequences of different degrees of commitment by each side of the market on efficiency, competition and value for money. It should also be noted that an equivalent to strong commitment can arise in practice where the framework agreement in fact offers good terms and value for money (on the positive side), or where its procedural advantages are such that other procurement vehicles may be

---

[8] Italy and Austria are two major examples in which the national CPAs (Consip and BBG, respectively) aggregate demand of both levels of government, although the mandatory constraint to use the CPA's framework agreements holds only for central government.

ignored (the less positive side), so the notion of commitment should be considered a dynamic rather than a static one.

### 11.4.1  Demand side commitment

Demand uncertainty dramatically affects the financial terms that bidders offer. In Chapter 4, we argued that, from the competing bidders' viewpoint, uncertainty comprises two main dimensions, particularly at the first stage of the process: the aggregate value of anticipated demand (and how this value will be distributed across the sequence of procurement contracts) and, second, the individual characteristics of identified final users, or in some cases a lack of knowledge about who potential users may be. The former determines the extent to which suppliers are able to respond to anticipated economies of scale, while the latter feeds into the likely degree of customisation of the procurement contracts at the call-off stage – the greater the possibility and degree of customisation, the greater the uncertainty.

Making the use of framework agreements mandatory (i.e. mandating a 'strong' commitment), at least for a certain group of procuring entities, is a potentially effective tool to create a commitment to a certain level of purchases, which reduces the level of uncertainty as regards the first dimension. For instance, in many systems, framework agreements awarded by CPAs at the national level are mandatory for central government bodies. This is the case of national CPBs in Italy, Austria and Finland in the European Union, as well as Ethiopia in Africa and Colombia in South America.

The policy reasons for making the use of framework agreements mandatory are clear: they avoid the all-too-common situation of different prices paid for the same goods and services across government departments, they facilitate economies of scale and they allow greater commercial flexibility in allowing a range of solutions that (for the suppliers) can be amortised over a range of users, to name but a few.

When centralisation is carried out through Model 1 framework agreements with one supplier, policymakers may need to address the likelihood that the solution provided may not be well suited to all procuring entities that will use the framework agreement. Consequently, they may be inclined to add a requirement to the effect that the use of the framework agreement is mandatory, unless the procuring entity can justify why the solution is unsuited to its specific needs. The possibility of such exceptions means a lower-than-strong commitment. Mandatory use of framework agreements is, in principle, a pro-efficiency provision in that it recognises that a wide variety of needs cannot be squeezed into the same one-size-fits-all contract. In fact, the greater the extent of (enforced) centralisation, the more likely that this scenario arises. Unfortunately, mandatory purchasing solutions together with an 'exit' option for procuring entities may trigger the so-called 'maverick buying'[9] phenomenon, whereby some users for which the framework agreement is mandatory seek to evade the framework by asserting that the terms do not suit their needs, for example, to suit personal preferences.

There is, once again, no immediate solution to this phenomenon. One potentially drastic approach would be to implement a 'full obligation' provision so that procuring entities are forbidden to buy outside the framework agreement unless the estimated value of the framework agreement cannot accommodate the actual demand. A less drastic approach would be for the CPA to seek to minimise the risk of maverick buying by (i) widening the variety of lots of the goods concerned and/or, in the case of services, (ii) adopting a Model 2 framework agreement with one supplier, in which the awardee offers a list of negotiated variants of the available services that should, in principle, better meet different needs.

An alternative approach is to focus on the reasons why centralisation has not previously taken place. An initial and relatively simple starting point is to encourage better understanding of the benefits of centralised framework agreements, focusing on the overall advantages that we examined in Chapter 4. More strategic elements include tackling some cultural elements: that many government departments guard their independence jealously, that effective incentives for efficiency are often absent (expenditure savings may simply translate into reduced budgets in the future) and, insufficiently linked to a cooperative agenda, that there is insufficient ability to challenge budgets at the departmental level and to harmonise approaches, there is a lack of procurement data and sufficient oversight of spending and efficiency and that skills and experience among final users vary widely.[10] It was reported in the United Kingdom that centralisation of 75 per cent of the central government gas and electricity need over a four-year period resulted in cumulative savings that exceeded GBP 500 million,

---

[9] K. Karjalainen and E. M. van Raaij, 'An Empirical Test of Contributing Factors to Different Forms of Maverick Buying', *Journal of Purchasing & Supply Management*, 17, No. 3 (2011): 185–197.

[10] See, for example, Efficiency Review, Key findings and recommendations, Sir Philip Green, available at www.gov.uk/government/uploads/system/uploads/attachment_data/file/61014/sirphilipgreenreview.pdf.

though other sectors remained decentralised.[11] Inadvertent obstacles to centralisation arising from practice – including varied specifications for standard commercial items,[12] variety in terms and conditions, different local interpretations of the regulatory framework, multiplicity of approaches to contracting and managing the supply chain – are all issues that, as we saw in Chapter 6, can also be viewed as legitimate expressions of heterogeneity.

Given these sensitivities, centralisation may take the form of voluntary framework agreements. Unlike the mandatory case, a voluntary framework agreement represents a weak form of commitment, whereby procuring entities can purchase through the agreement if they find it in their interest. That is, under normal circumstances, the framework agreement will be used where the value for money guaranteed by the standing quality-price combinations inside the framework agreement are (perceived to be) better than in the marketplace or than alternative purchasing solutions. While solving the 'maverick buying' phenomenon, weak commitment emphasises the role of expectations of either side of the market on the behaviour of the other side. To put it in simple terms, if economies of scale are potentially significant, then the higher the *expected use* of the framework agreement, the more competing firms will be willing to submit lower prices at the first stage. However, the extent to which procuring entities will be willing to purchase through the framework agreement will depend on the *expected terms* of trade relatively to other purchasing solutions, which in turn depend upon the *expected level* of competition.

This chicken-and-egg or Catch-22 problem is quite commonly encountered in the business development of platforms for e-commerce. The message coming from the specialised literature[13] is that some mechanism favouring participation of both sides of the market does help strengthen the beliefs that transactions on the e-marketplace will grow over time. In other words, guaranteeing a minimum level of demand makes firms more willing to join the market, thus promoting competition. This in turn makes the demand side even more willing to trade on the e-marketplace.

A relatively strong prescription emerges from the above discussion. If policymakers are determined to undertake the transformation of the public procurement system at any level of government through some form of

---

[11] Ibid.  [12] See Section 6.3 for a discussion of this issue in the US context.
[13] See, for instance, A. Hagiu and J. Wright, 'Multi-Sided Platforms', Harvard Business Scholl Working Paper 12-024, 2011, and references therein. The paper can be downloaded from http://faculty.chicagobooth.edu/workshops/marketing/past/pdf/MultiSidedPlatformsHagiu.pdf.

centralisation, they need to show to all relevant stakeholders that immediate or short-term benefits can be achieved. Thus, they need to make sure that purchases through framework agreements awarded by a CPA (be it at a regional or national level) take off as quickly as possible. This result becomes more likely if the use of framework agreements is made mandatory, although not necessarily for the procuring entities' entire needs but for the goods, services and construction in question.[14]

### 11.4.2 Supply-side commitment

Commitment on the supply side may include a legally binding commitment by framework awardee(s) to *supply* any procuring entity (Model 1 and Model 2 framework agreements). An absence of such a commitment may generate undesirable outcomes especially in Model 1 framework agreements with one supplier, particularly when procuring entities are obliged to purchase through the framework agreement. We shall flesh out the main arguments by borrowing the scenario depicted in Example 4.1.

Example 11.1 emphasises the risk that weak commitment on the supply side may induce firms (i) to adopt a 'cherry-picking' strategy at the call-off stage and (ii) to compete more fiercely on the financial dimensions at the first stage of the framework agreement. Weak commitment on the supply side is also inconsistent with a provision of mandatory framework agreements since some procuring entities would be left without any security of supply or any other available purchasing arrangements. Consequently, mandatory framework agreements seem to require also a relatively strong commitment on the suppliers' side.

As an example of the dynamic nature of the effect of commitments in practice, if a CPA regularly issues unreliable estimates of the anticipated extent of purchases, suppliers may leave the framework agreement where their commitments to supply are not legally binding; they may choose not to participate in future framework agreements otherwise. Thus, the link between expectations and outcomes noted above will have a significant impact on commitments in reality.

---

[14] Less-than-full centralisation might also be a strategy to accommodate for a certain degree of demand heterogeneity as some procuring entities will not be able to purchase through standing framework agreements. Obviously, it is far from being clear that procuring entities will self-select according to their actual needs rather than merely trying to avoid using the standing purchasing arrangements. In other words, less-than-full centralisation inevitably raises additional 'maverick buyer' concerns.

> **Example 11.1 Mandatory framework agreements with no commitment on the supply side**
>
> A CPA is to award a Model 1 framework agreement with one supplier for car insurance contracts on behalf of two types of central government bodies: high risk (H) and low risk (L). Suppose that bidding firms know the share of demand stemming from high-risk procuring entities (say, 60%) and from those with low risk (40%). Suppose that if firms could bid for separate contracts, then the resulting competitive insurance premia would be $p_H > p_L$. However, since the nature of the framework agreement requires only one price, $p_{FA}$, for all procuring entities competition will be such that $p_{FA} = 0.6 \cdot p_H + 0.4 \cdot p_L$.
>
> This outcome hinges, however, on a strong commitment by both sides of the market. More precisely, only if the shares of procurement contracts between the two groups of procuring entities coincide with the composition of potential demand will the competitive price for the bundle of contracts will be the weighted average of the 'tailored' prices for the two groups of procuring entities (demand-side commitment). At the same time, because the awardee cannot refuse to trade with any procuring entity, then $p_{FA} = 0.6 \cdot p_H + 0.4 \cdot p_L$ is the highest possible competitive price.
>
> The prediction would change dramatically if we were to assume that, once selected at the first stage, the awardee was allowed to supply those procuring entities it finds of its interest. The consequence is that at the first stage *all* competing firms will realise that they have a chance to be selected by submitting a price below the value of $p_{FA}$ and trading at the call-off stage only with low-risk procuring entities (thanks to the weak commitment assumption). Consequently, competition at the first stage will drive the price down to $p'_{FA} = p_L$ and the awardee will accept to trade only with low-risk users.

## 11.5 Centralised public procurement and participation of SMEs: sound design at the service of competition and participation

The potential conflict between centralisation and participation of SMEs in the public procurement markets is one of the most pressing policy issues particularly in those regulatory environments where 'positive discrimination' towards SMEs is not permitted.[15] In the European Union, for

---

[15] China, South Africa and the United States are among the most noticeable examples where, instead, various kinds of 'positive discrimination' towards well-defined classes of potential bidders are permitted and implemented.

instance, the animated debate over the past decade has led to the adoption of a European 'Small Business Act',[16] providing public organisations with an array of best practices that are supposed to encourage the participation of SMEs in public procurement.

A closer look at the centralisation practices around the world reveals that, in many cases, SMEs-related concerns are not necessarily well grounded. For instance, centralised strategies for purchasing petrol, gas, electricity, telephone and data connection services, vehicles and insurance services would reveal no SME in the relevant markets. In these cases, centralisation does not hurt any SME as no SME is active. One major field investigation on CPBs in the EU reports that SMEs are in general well represented in the CPBs framework agreements in most member states covered by the study.[17] Further, recent statistics in Sweden provided by local CPBs show that SMEs are awarded 85 per cent of the tenders and take 50 per cent of the total contract value. Similar figures are disclosed by a recent Swedish study of the total procurement market. SMEs are awarded 50 per cent of the total procurement value for public sector contracts,[18] and the European Commission has found that micro and small enterprises rather than medium-sized enterprises are under-represented in public procurement in the European Union.[19] Moreover, the majority of contracts below the EU thresholds using simplified tendering procedures are awarded to SMEs.

The above observations are not meant to dismiss the potential problem of SMEs' experiencing barriers to entry in the public procurement market when centralisation strategies are being adopted. Rather, the *main* concerns are essentially those caused by centralisation strategies that cut SMEs off from competing for procurement contracts, whereas more considered strategies could facilitate SMEs participation (as we have seen in Chapter 4).

As emphasised earlier in this chapter, the markets for maintenance services (buildings, open urban areas, IT equipment), foodstuffs and raw

---

[16] Available at http://eur-lex.europa.eu/LexUriServ/LexUriServ.do?uri=COM:2008:0394:FIN:EN: PDF.
[17] OECD, 'Centralised Purchasing Systems in the European Union', note 4, supra.
[18] Figures based on interviews carried out in Sweden by P. Blomberg with SKL Kommentus (CPB for local authorities) and Kammarkollegiet (CPB for central government). Figures on the overall procurement market in Sweden are also contained by a recent report by the Swedish Competition Authority available at www.konkurrensverket.se/globalassets/publikationer/uppdragsforskning/forsk_rap_2015-4.pdf.
[19] European Union (2014) 'Small and Medium-Sized Enterprises', available at http://epp.eurostat .ec.europa.eu/portal/page/portal/european_business/special_sbs_topics/small_medium_size d_enterprises_ SMEs.

food as well as specialised IT services are fragmented, with firms of different sizes participating. Depending on how the CPA's main function is defined, demand aggregation in these markets might most appropriately be carried out by Model 1 or Model 2 framework agreements with multiple suppliers. In both cases, a CPA should consider three main aspects of procurement design, which might favour the participation of SMEs:

- division of goods and services into lots,
- geographical lots, and
- minimum turnover requirements.

### 11.5.1 Division of goods and services into lots

In Chapters 4 and 10, we discussed the main economic dimensions that a procuring entity should consider when deciding to bundle or to unbundle different goods and services. When goods and services are heterogeneous, then bundling might be driven by economies of scope[20] rather than economies of scale. As a consequence, particularly in case of services, the procuring entity may ultimately contract with a group of suppliers (through a joint venture) with one supplier acting as a lead or general contractor and that coordinates other (possibly smaller) specialised suppliers.

When the anticipated value of the framework agreement increases through implementing a centralisation strategy without division into lots, then this 'general contractor' solution is likely to be encouraged by the fact that only larger firms can compete for the framework agreement. Thus, it is more likely that smaller and specialised firms will lose some of their bargaining power inside the joint venture. To tackle this risk, a CPA might adopt an 'unbundling' strategy, thus slicing up a framework agreement into multiple lots, where each lot corresponds to a different product/service as illustrated by Figure 11.1.

From a practical perspective, the bidding documents may allow individual bidders to respond to part of the framework agreement rather than to the entire framework agreement (as UNCITRAL's Model Law envisages) or to allow (temporary) joint ventures to be formed before or after the framework agreement has been awarded. It should, however, be borne in mind that any unbundling strategy inevitably raises final users' transaction

[20] For instance, carrying out ordinary maintenance services in a building makes further inspections for, say, roof insulation interventions easier and/or cheaper.

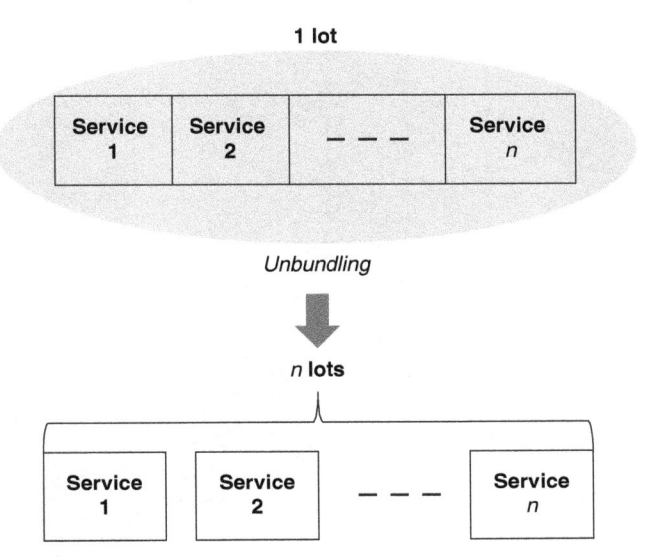

Figure 11.1 Unbundling *n* different services in a framework agreement.

costs as they will have to sign and administer multiple procurement contracts with multiple suppliers.

### 11.5.2 Geographical lots

When final users of a CPA-concluded framework agreement are scattered over a large territory, SMEs may be disadvantaged from the CPA's perspective; that is, they are likely to have a smaller business area than the geographic span of the framework agreements. In this case, splitting the framework agreement in geographical lots (possibly in conjunction with division into lots of goods and services) may be necessary so as to promote the *direct* participation of SMEs either as solo bidders or in (temporary) joint ventures.

Splitting a framework agreement into geographical lots requires a thorough understanding of the business model in the relevant market, that is, to what extent any single supplier is able to carry out the tasks foreseen in the framework agreement, without necessarily relying on some form of outsourcing. In general, the smaller the geographical lots (and thus, ceteris paribus, the lower the estimated value of each lot), the higher the number of potential participants. However, reducing the size of each lot adversely affects the perceived magnitude of economies

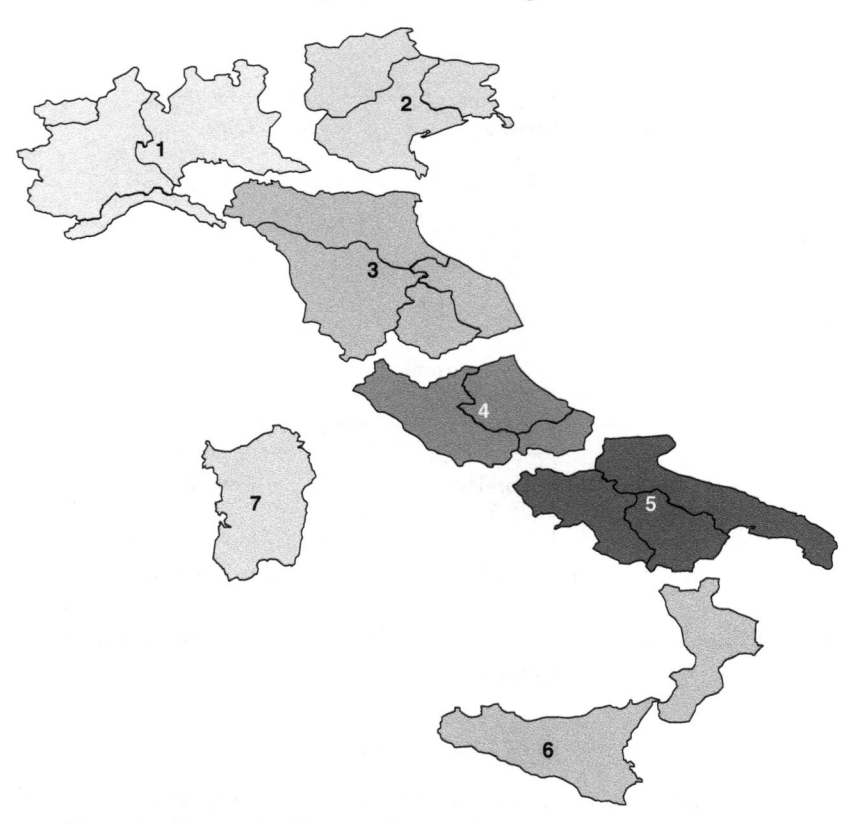

Figure 11.2 Geographical lots in a framework agreement for petrol and oil for heating.

of scale that participating bidders will factor in when preparing their bids. As a consequence, the appropriate number of geographical lots needs to strike a balance between these competing considerations and can rarely be the result of a clear-cut algorithm. Accurate market intelligence and ability to learn over time from past experience are essential ingredients for the effective design of lots.

Figure 11.2 shows a real-world example of a nationwide framework agreement for petrol and heating oil awarded by Consip (Italy) in 2014. The national territory was divided into seven geographical lots (aka macro-regions), and for each geographical lot, two 'product' lots were foreseen; namely, petrol and oil for heating.

### 11.5.3 Turnover requirements

Firms' turnover is generally used as one of the proxies for their capacity to carry out a procurement contract. While raising turnover requirements reduces the risk that a contractor will not be able to fulfil the contract task, a disproportionately large requirement constitutes a concrete barrier to entry for smaller-sized firms.[21] In the EU Directive, for instance, the European policymaker has explicitly set out an upper limit to the minimal turnover requirement as a mitigating measure:

> contracting authorities should not be allowed to require economic operators to have a minimum turnover that would be disproportionate to the subject-matter of the contract; the requirement should normally not exceed at the most twice the estimated contract value.[22]

In spite of its simplicity, the provision seems to be tailored to the case of a single procurement contract, and arguably not to a framework agreement under which many, possibly very differently valued, contracts are to be awarded. On the other hand, the reference to 'contract' may indicate flexibility where the awards will be divided into lots. Therefore setting appropriate turnover requirements for awarding a framework agreement should take into account the estimated composition of procurement contracts to be awarded. To see this, let us consider the following stylised example (Example 11.2).

---

**Example 11.2 Leveraging turnover requirements to favour the participation of SMEs**

Consider two framework agreements with a similar estimated value equal to euro 10 million to be concluded by a CPA. The fundamental difference between the two framework agreements arises in the (expected) sequence of procurement contracts to be awarded. In the first case, five contracts of euro 2 million each are to be awarded. In the second case, two contracts of € 2 million each, five contracts of € 500,000 each and ten contracts of € 400,000 each are to be awarded.

---

[21] The potential impact of this and other barriers in practice, and mitigating measures, are considered in Chapter 4.
[22] EU Directive note 2, supra, Recital 83.

> **Example 11.2 (cont.)**
> In the first scenario, given the unvarying contract value, turnover requirements ought to be related to the representative contract value of €2 million. In the second case, however, if the CPA were to determine turnover requirements on the basis of the two most-valued contracts, the requirements themselves would turn out to be disproportionately large for all other contracts. Thus, a more sensible approach would consist in taking the fifteen lower-valued contracts as the 'target' contracts. As a consequence, smaller firms would be able to compete at the first stage alongside bigger firms. At the call-off stage, then smaller firms would be able to compete for low-value contracts, while bigger firms would be to compete for all of them.

## 11.6 A simulated case study[23]

We shall consider that the Ministry of Defence wishes to implement a centralised procurement strategy to supply the army with raw foodstuffs. The supply includes fresh food (e.g. meat, fish, vegetable etc.) as well as non-perishable food (e.g. pasta, rice) and beverages to be prepared in the army barracks, each of which has its own kitchen facilities and cooking personnel. Each barracks is to be allowed to place periodic orders (yearly, monthly or weekly, depending on the kind of food and stocking capacities) for varying quantities of different goods.

### 11.6.1 Demand side's main features

All barracks are required to purchase at least 80 per cent of their annual food supply using the framework agreement. Hence, the framework estimated value approximates total demand, which is estimated on the basis of the number of soldiers and historical data.

There are 200 barracks in the country. About 70 per cent of them are located in the North and 30 per cent are located in the South of the country. The North is flat with good road connection, while the South territory is mountainous and with shabby and insecure infrastructures. Barracks also differ in number of quartered soldiers: in 10 barracks the number of soldiers is more than 1,000 units, in 100 barracks it is less than 100 soldiers, while in the other 90 barracks the number of housed ranges in

---

[23] We are very grateful to M. Sparro for having developed most of the material contained in this section.

between 100 and 1,000. The barracks are also heterogeneous with respect to delivery schedules, stocking capacities, kitchen facilities – before accommodating issues of location and size.

### 11.6.2  Supply side's main features

Production is mostly carried out by micro, small and medium-sized enterprises operating at a very local level (say regional, provincial and even municipal level). Distribution firms are generally of larger size. More specifically,

- Three large suppliers with well-organised logistic networks are able to deliver any type of food anywhere in the country. Moreover, two large suppliers in the North would be able to serve the whole northern part of the country.
- Six local suppliers in the North and three local firms in the South would be able efficiently to serve large parts of the regions, but neither the whole North nor the whole South.

### 11.6.3  The main objectives of the centralised strategy

The main goals of the ministry are (i) to achieve savings from demand aggregation and tighter control on barracks' spending; (ii) to standardise and streamline barracks' purchasing procedures, allowing each of them to contract with one supplier for all types of food categories; and (iii) to implement sustainability-oriented policies at the central level, mainly aimed at ensuring opportunities to local producers, encouraging local and organic food consumption and reducing $CO_2$ emissions from transportation.

### 11.6.4  Procurement strategy and framework agreement design

The ministry opts for a multi-award hybrid model of (closed) framework agreement[24] whereby the framework agreement contains all the terms governing procurement contracts to be issued, and thus barracks can make purchases orders to the highest-ranked awardee; if, instead, procuring entities wish to amend some of the framework agreement's conditions,

---

[24] For example, as permitted by EU Directive, Article 33(4)(b), note 2, supra.

then a second round of competition among all selected awardees is necessary. The framework agreement is also split in two geographical lots, North and South, in order to reduce heterogeneity arising from different transport or logistics costs and to promote participation of firms not operating at the country level.

The framework agreement is concluded, per lot, with 3 suppliers if the number of (valid) tenders is at most 4, with 4 suppliers if valid tenders number at most 6, and with 5 firms if the number of valid tenders is greater than 6. Given our market analysis, this rule is set so as to trade off savings from first-stage competition and more streamlined procedures against the benefits from higher participation, particularly by smaller and local firms.

Spitting the framework agreement into two fairly wide geographical lots reveals procurement strategies aiming at favouring the participation of distributors (i.e. the relevant market) rather than producers, which operate at a more local level.

### 11.6.5 First- and second-stage competition design

At the first stage, the framework agreement is concluded by means of the most economically advantageous (MEAT) criterion whereby

- the financial score (FS) is assigned to a weighted average of unit prices submitted on a wide and detailed list of items;
- the technical score (TS) in attributes to quality features which the ministry deems relevant for *all* the call-off contracts such as quality of the ICT application to manage and monitor periodic orders, delivery schedules and reports on total spending; percentage (in terms of quantity) of both local and organic food guaranteed in each order of specific food categories; reduction and recyclability of packaging materials; and improved frequency of delivery schedules for fresh food.

At the second stage, procurement contracts can be awarded by means of two alternative mechanisms, both based on the MEAT criterion:

*Direct award*
Those procuring entities (barracks) whose estimated annual demand falls below a certain predetermined threshold value may make direct awards applying the terms of the framework agreement. That is, the procurement contract is awarded on the basis of the same award

criteria as the first stage but, while the TS remains unchanged, the FS is recalculated by multiplying the unit prices resulting from the first stage by a vector of weights based on the actual demand of the final user. Suppliers are committed to serve any such contract as to ensure that even low-demand barracks are served.

*Mini-competition*
All other procuring entities whose estimated annual demand is above the predetermined threshold can hold a second-stage mini competition, if they so wish. In the mini-competition process, the TS score of the first stage remains unchanged.[25] However, an additional fraction of the TS is to be assigned based on procuring entities' specific needs (say, improved delivery schedules, shares of local/organic food, specific packaging specifications, possibility to expand the range of products offered). To do so, procuring entities are then allowed to vary the quality-price weights within predetermined limits.

### 11.6.6 Any alternative procurement strategy?

The stylised procurement strategy depicted so far hinges on the ministry's decision to target mainly the market for foodstuffs distributors rather than producers. When distributors are larger sized than producers – and thus can operate over a wider geographical area – the appropriate centralisation strategy will depend above all on the quality of market intelligence regarding the two markets concerned. A CPA may be in a better position to interact with larger and fewer firms, rather than with smaller producers with perhaps little ambition to form joint ventures for targeting high-value contracts. Another declared objective of the ministry was also to standardise procurement contracts at least for all procuring entities with relatively lower-value needs. Indeed, contract tailoring was permitted only to procuring entities with higher-value demand (say, barracks with more than 1,000 soldiers).

Promoting the participation of producers themselves may, however, be instrumental in favouring the emergence of a local procurement market centred on the location of procuring entities, which would

---

[25] In Chapter 4, we defined 'inherited' technical score as the fraction of technical score assigned at the first stage that is carried forward to the second stage.

support the proposition that final users should consume local products (and so reduce long-haul delivery-induced pollution externalities, which may be part of the government's environmental policy goals).

An alternative strategy would be to set up an open (i.e. Model 3) framework agreement,[26] whereby suppliers are selected if they are qualified and responsive (i.e. capable of supplying a variety of foodstuff categories, and they fulfil minimum quality standards). The awardees are then allowed to bid for procurement contracts of different values, where their annual turnover meets the qualification requirements for relevant lots. At the call-off stage, each procuring entity would be in a position to design a round of competition, which could range from a simple price-only to a more sophisticated value-for-money process.

### 11.6.7 *Centralisation: an appropriate strategy?*

In this chapter, we have considered practical measures that can facilitate the achievement of the benefits of centralisation, and some of the challenges approaches to centralisation can pose. In particular, we have noted that effective data-gathering and information transfer (reflecting market, design and supplier characteristics) present practical challenges to the efficient operation of centralised framework agreements. Similarly, the design characteristics can operate to encourage or discourage their use. In addition, imposing centralised procurement (through, for example, mandatory use of centralised framework agreements) may encounter both additional cultural challenges and an element of resistance from final users, which, if unaddressed, has the potential to undermine the effectiveness of those agreements.

From this perspective, ensuring that centralisation sits within an appropriate organisational structure is critical. As has been observed, this structure should respond to the circumstances at hand – there is no one-size-fits-all design. Further, a 'blended or tight/loose model' has been proposed. This model recognises that whether centralised framework agreements are appropriate for goods and services *a* and *b* for procuring entities *x* and *y* will vary – some may yield better outcomes in tight (centralised) structures, and others in loose (decentralised)

---

[26] Defined as a dynamic purchasing system (DPS) as defined by the EU Directive, Article 34 (note 2, supra).

ones.[27] Framework agreements – including hybrid models – offer an opportunity to define the key elements (qualification requirements, specifications, key contractual terms and conditions) while allowing final users to refine their needs as they undertake call-offs, as our stylised example indicates. Thus, the process efficiencies can be achieved through standardising the elements that final users are likely not to resist, including that the use of ICT systems can reduce the administrative complexities of permitting options, while allowing the fine-tuning that final users will probably seek. Nonetheless, one final user's view of available goods and services that it can fine-tune to suit its needs may be another's opinion that a centralised framework agreement is an unacceptable interference with its operational procurement independence. Consequently, a phased approach to centralisation may be necessary to allow the benefits to be appreciated before wading into these turbulent waters.

## 11.7 Chapter summary

- Demand aggregation through centralised procurement agencies – called central purchasing bodies in the European Union – represents one of the most striking features of many public procurement systems in OECD countries. The establishment of CPAs has been historically motivated by the opportunity of raising government's bargaining power to achieve better value for money, the standardisation of contractual conditions for common-use items and professionalisation of the procurement workforce, but its introduction needs to take account of the pre-existing structure and characteristics of the procurement function among procuring entities.
- Centralisation through a CPA creates a separation of responsibilities between the pre-award and post-award phase of any framework agreement. This might lead to better specialisation of the procurement workforce, but might also generate divergent objectives between the CPA and the procuring entities. An appropriate funding solution for CPAs is of paramount importance for a centralised procurement system to achieve the policymakers' desired goals.

---

[27] P. Smith, 'Centralise or devolve procurement? Why not both. How technology is enabling new operating models', Spend Matters, Briefing Paper, 2014, available at http://spendmatters.com/research-library/papers/centralise-or-devolve-procurement/.

- For a centralised model to deliver 'quick wins', some degree of commitment on both sides of the market is needed.
- Splitting a framework contract into several (product and geographical) lots is potentially the most effective solution to promote the participation of SMEs in centralised procurement.
- In order to promote such participation of SMEs, economic participation requirements should be set by taking into account the distribution of values of procurement contracts rather than the estimated value of purchases under the agreement itself.

CHAPTER 12

# Legal and regulatory issues in framework agreements procedures

## 12.1 Introduction

As we saw in Chapter 5, there are some uncertainties in the main systems regulating framework agreements in the EU, US and even in the UNCITRAL Model Law (which regulates framework agreements procedures in considerably more detail) – including which rules apply and how they apply. When drafting the regulatory and guidance framework for framework agreements procedures, it may therefore be tempting to try to eliminate all ambiguities. However, as we shall see, this may prove to be an impossible task, and, indeed, it may not be helpful to attempt to do so.

The regulatory and guidance framework will generally comprise the primary law, secondary regulations or decrees, internal rules and guidance, drawing on the policy choices made for the system overall.[1] A significant question, therefore, is how best to reflect the various policy and design issues we have examined throughout this book among these elements of the system. After an initial discussion of the need for formal rules, and what policy statements, laws, rules and guidance are designed to achieve, we will apply the findings to some practical examples, with a view to assist policymakers in designing or reforming their systems.

---

[1] Directive 2014/24/EU of the European Parliament and of the Council of 26 February 2014 on public procurement and repealing Directive 2004/18/EC Text with EEA relevance, OJ L 94, 28 March 2014, pp. 65–242, available at http://eur-lex.europa.eu/legal-content/EN/TXT/?uri=celex:32014L0024 (hereafter, the EU Directive); UNCITRAL Model Law (UNCITRAL Model Law on Public Procurement (2011), *Official Records of the General Assembly, Sixty-sixth Session, Supplement No. 17* (UN document A/66/17). The text of the Model Law is available at www.uncitral.org/uncitral/uncitral_texts/procurement_infrastructure.html (hereafter, Model Law). See Article 4, and commentary thereto in the Guide to Enactment of the UNCITRAL Model Law on Public Procurement (2012), *Official Records of the General Assembly, Sixty-seventh Session, Supplement No. 17* (para 46, UN document A/67/17). The text of the Guide to Enactment is available at www.uncitral.org/uncitral/uncitral_texts/procurement_infrastructure.html (hereafter, Guide to Enactment).

## 12.2 Need for a dedicated regulatory framework – obstacles to the use of framework agreements without express legal provision

We saw in Chapter 5 that some countries had used framework agreements without express legal provision. That situation is increasingly less common, but more 'traditional' public procurement laws, or systems still operating without a formal public procurement law, may need to address the following potential obstacles to the use of framework agreements procedures:

- The application of thresholds: If there are thresholds for a procurement procedure, how will they apply to framework agreements procedures in the absence of aggregation requirements?
- Can a procurement contract be concluded with more than one supplier? The definition of a procurement contract in a procurement law or internal rules may state that only one supplier can be awarded the contract, effectively ruling out multi-supplier framework agreements.
- Is more than one round of bidding during a procurement procedure permitted? If not, which will be the case in many sealed tendering-based systems, second-stage offers may not be possible.
- Requirements for information on specifications and fixed quantities in the bidding or solicitation documents may not permit necessary flexibility in the context of framework agreements procedures.
- There may be no provisions permitting awardees be selected if there is no determination of price at the first stage – for example, if the evaluation criteria are based on 'lowest-price bid'.
- How any standstill period and rules on contract notices apply to framework agreements procedures may be unclear.

It is clear, in the light of these potential obstacles and the uncertainties we saw in Chapter 5, that effective use of framework agreements procedures will be enhanced where there are dedicated provisions regulating their use.

## 12.3 Elements of the regulatory framework

It has long been acknowledged that the primary law, the main normative text, has to comply with a double constraint: it must 'simultaneously be both general and specific enough'.[2] In other words, laws must be very

---

[2] R. Hiltunen, Chapters on Legal English, Suomalainen Tiedeakatemia, Helsinki (1990).

precise in defining the obligations they are meant to impose and the rights they confer, so prohibitions and permissions need to be clear and unambiguous. On the other hand, they need to be adaptable to a wide variety of applications,[3] not all predictable. This need is generally considered to imply all-inclusiveness in scope, which itself is incompatible with clarity and precision – elements of vagueness will be inevitable.

An Australian author explained two main different legal styles and their impact some twenty years ago: one style of legislative drafting favours openness and generality (sometimes referred to as 'fuzzy' law, and largely drawing from a civil law tradition), while another favours precision and particularity (which may be called 'fussy' law, largely in the common law tradition). Fussy law concentrates on detailed distinctions thrown up by a focus on specific circumstances. Fuzzy law, on the other hand, provides general principles in the context of broad legislative purposes.[4] Fuzzy law may be insufficiently clear and unambiguous; fussy law may be insufficiently adaptable. The legal and administrative tradition in a country will also have significant bearing on drafting style, as will the manner in which overall policy objectives are to be expressed: should the system be rules-based, principles-based, outcome-based or a combination of some or all of these approaches?[5]

The advantages of the fussy approach include greater certainty in many situations, though the law becomes more complex to follow. It avoids the fuzzy law's abstract set of principles, which permit a multitude of different interpretations and, probably, markedly different outcomes in particular cases, increased need for legal advice and delegation of much power to the judiciary. On the other hand, no matter how detailed the provisions, comprehensiveness is not possible – attempting to be comprehensive is likely to leave something out, and not every eventuality can be foreseen. As the author points out, this in itself generates uncertainty: Did the drafters intend to omit the circumstance, or not? The discussion of framework agreements and framework contracts, and whether or not they are procurement (public) contracts in Chapter 5, is a clear case in point.

---

[3] Maurizio Gotti, 'Vagueness in the Model Law on International Commercial Arbitration', in M. Gotti, D. Heller, J. Engberg and V. K. Bhatia (eds.), *Vagueness in Normative Texts* (Peter Lang 2005): 227, also citing V. K. Bhatia, *Analysing Genre: Language Use in Professional Settings* (London: Longman, 1993).
[4] Lisbeth Campbell, 'Legal Drafting Styles: Fuzzy or Fussy?', *Murdoch University Electronic Journal of Law*, 3, No. 2 (1996).
[5] Steven L. Schooner, 'Desiderata: Objectives for a System of Government Contract Law', *Public Procurement Law Review*, 11 (2002): 103–110.

In the light of all these circumstances, as a general rule, it is suggested that a principles-based approach will function best in the context of clearly established practice and consensus on appropriate standards of conduct, whereas in more challenging or novel circumstances, in which there may be attempts to manipulate the law and its restrictions, a more detailed and rules-based approach is recommended (tax laws being an easy-to-follow example of the latter). Absent systematic problems of corruption, for the purposes of public procurement in general, and framework agreements procedures in particular, it is evident that most systems will fall somewhere in between. Further, as experience is gained with new procedures, the need for detailed rules may lessen.

UNCITRAL has addressed these issues when drafting the Model Law. The Guide to Enactment of the explains how the Model Law is drafted in the light of these constraints, as follows:

> The Model Law is intended to provide all the *essential procedures and principles* for conducting procurement proceedings in the various types of circumstances likely to be encountered by procuring entities. In this regard, the Model Law is a 'framework' law *that does not itself set out all the rules and regulations that may be necessary to implement those procedures in an enacting State* [emphasis added].[6]

The Model Law is designed, therefore, generally towards the fuzzy end of the spectrum (its longer length and detail compared with other international public procurement texts reflects that it is a template for national procurement legislation, rather than an international agreement).[7] To address the concerns that a purely fuzzy approach would indicate, however, the above guidance continues that

> legislation based on the Model Law should form part of a coherent and cohesive procurement system that includes regulations, other supporting legal infrastructure, and guidance and other capacity-building tools. Addressing the procurement system in such a holistic manner will assist in developing the capacity to operate it, an important issue as the Model Law envisages that procurement officials will exercise limited discretion throughout the procurement process, such as in designing qualification, responsiveness and evaluation criteria and in selecting the procurement method (and manner of solicitation in relevant cases).[8]

---

[6] Guide to Enactment, note 1, supra, Part one, General remarks, para 58 at p. 17.
[7] Caroline Nicholas, 'A Critical Evaluation of the Revised UNCITRAL Model Law Provisions on Regulating Framework Agreements', *Public Procurement Law Review* 2 (2012): 19–46.
[8] Guide to Enactment, note 1, supra, Part one, General remarks, paras 58–59 at p. 17.

Nonetheless, the provisions on framework agreements are far more detailed than those found in, for example, the European Union and the United States and, by comparison with some procurement methods in the Model Law, are relatively fussy. This approach can be explained, perhaps, because of the relative novelty of the technique – the different approaches in the two main systems informing UNCITRAL when deciding on the manner in which the Model Law would address framework agreements procedures indicating that there was neither clear consensus on how the system should operate, nor clearly established practice.

More detailed rules that can avoid uncertainty and ambiguity in how the primary law may operate in practice can be set out in supporting regulations, internal rules and guidance, which have the significant advantage of possible amendment as experience is gained without requiring new parliamentary approvals as amendments to primary laws require. This flexibility, however, is appropriate provided that the main principles and procedures are set out in the primary law, so that they cannot themselves be amended without public scrutiny. This is the approach that the UN member states took when producing the Model Law – and clearly it is an art, rather than a science.

The Guide to Enactment also notes that, to fill in the details of procedures in the Model Law and to take account of the specific circumstances in enacting states, some of which may be evolving (such as the real value of thresholds and technical standards), regulations should be issued and published (on whose contents UNCITRAL has also issued guidance).[9] For example, the regulations should address where to publish award notices and details of what they should contain; provide technical standards on identity management and security of data in open framework agreements and e-reverse auctions, including at the call-off stage of framework agreements procedures; regulate how to use price preferences or other policies to promote SMEs or other socio-economic policies where available; require an estimate the value of the entire framework agreement; set out rules on the application of standstill periods in framework agreements procedures; provide rules on the record of the procurement in the framework agreements context and so on. Regulations are of general application; at a more detailed level, internal rules within procuring entities may also be needed.

---

[9] Guidance on Procurement Regulations (2013), available at www.uncitral.org/uncitral/en/uncitral_texts/procurement_infrastructure.html. Regulations, in addition, enable an enacting state to tailor the Model Law to its own particular needs and circumstances.

Furthermore, as the design considerations we have examined indicate, not all – in all likelihood the minority of – questions arising in framework agreements procedures are legal issues. Effective use and implementation of laws and rules at all levels will require guidance notes and manuals. These documents can also operate to standardise procedures, specifications and terms and conditions of participation in procedures and resultant contracts, which can encourage participation (perhaps more so in the case of SMEs, as we saw in Chapter 7) and build capacity. They will, in turn, be supported by standard forms and sample documents. The salient difference between laws and rules, on the one hand, and guidance, on the other, is that laws and rules set out what – in our context – a procurement official may and may not do, but guidance advises him on what it is *appropriate* to do. Policies are quite different – they set out the objectives that the rules and guidance are intended to achieve. An effective system will include all these elements.

The more the law tends towards the fuzzy end of the spectrum, the more important case law or other administrative rulings – as well as other guidance – will be in interpreting the provisions, and to provide guidance for future procurements. The decisions of the ECJ have in practice been significant in setting standards in the European Union, for example; in the United Kingdom, case law from Northern Ireland has been particularly instructive; in the United States, the audit and bid protest reports of the General Accountability Office (GAO) have provided much-needed clarification and guidance.[10] In common law systems in particular, case law may offer legally binding precedents; in others, judicial rulings may not be binding but can offer good practice. For this reason, UNCITRAL recommends that reports of rulings that offer precedent should be centralised and published,[11] and extending this to reports into good and not-so-good practice, as GAO does, is also to be recommended.

## 12.4 Policy, law, regulations, rules and guidance – where are the dividing lines?

The aim of the recommendations set out above, therefore, is to ensure that a comprehensive set of rules and guidance, preferably collated in a user-friendly format, is available. This begs the question, however, of where among these elements particular issues should be addressed.

---

[10] Available at www.gao.gov.
[11] Guide to Enactment, note 1, supra, commentary to Article 5, para 7 on p. 65.

*Legal and regulatory issues in framework agreements procedures* 311

### 12.4.1 Policy statements

Many systems include a declaration of the policy objectives for their public procurement system in a preamble or other statement of purpose in the primary law.[12] While a statement might give procurement officials a yardstick or general guidance on motivations to which they may refer in making decisions under the law,[13] it is unlikely to give clear direction as to the use of framework agreements in practice. A statement of objectives may give some general guidance as part of the package of tools to support the use of framework agreements – emphasising the importance of administrative efficiency, for example – but it does not give rights to or place obligations on procuring entities or suppliers, which are the backbone of a public procurement system.[14]

### 12.4.2 Formal and other legal rules versus guidance

Rights and obligations expressed in rules – whether in formal rules, that is, in the primary law and regulations, or in internal rules within a procuring entity – will support transparency and accountability where they are publicly available, as the Model Law requires for generally applicable legal texts.[15] Whether drafted in a fuzzy or fussy manner, formal legal rules will make framework agreements procedures available and set out mandatory procedures for concluding and using them (and they will prohibit some actions).

We will consider, using the example of decisions on whether to set up a framework agreement, how appropriate standards could be reflected in formal rules and/or in internal rules and guidance. As we saw in Chapters 10 and 11 of this book, a robust analysis will be necessary to assess whether the benefits of framework agreements are likely to materialise in practice, and whether the potential disadvantages of using framework agreements may arise, involving 'strategic planning, adequate process

---

[12] Such a statement 'illuminates the principles on which the statute is based and facilitates its interpretation, particularly when a provision of the statute is ambiguous or unclear . . . and is not a substantive component of a statute, but an interpretative one [citing R. Sullivan [2008], on the Construction of Statutes [5 ed.]. LexisNexis Canada: Markham, Ontario, p. 388]'. See Duncan Berry, 'Purpose Sections: Why They are a Good Idea for Drafters and Users', 2011, available at www.opc.gov.au/calc/docs/Loophole_papers/Berry_May2011.pdf.
[13] See, also, ibid., in which it is recalled that a purpose statement is not a substantive component of a statute, but an interpretative one.
[14] Guide to Enactment, note 1, supra, commentary to Preamble, Section A, Introduction, para 2.
[15] Article 5, Model Law, note 1, supra.

design and management, and anticipation of market and competition conditions',[16] particularly to close the 'gap between the potential benefits ... and obtaining the benefits in practice'.[17] The analysis will also need to consider whether the benefits are likely to be sufficient to justify any compromise of other procurement objectives – the potential for which was discussed in Chapter 5. Ultimately, is a framework agreement procedure likely to be a *more* effective solution than other available procurement methods?[18]

The decisions involved go well beyond the rather mechanical application of thresholds used to select procurement methods in some more traditional procurement systems, and involve essentially subjective assessments on the part of the procurement officials concerned. These decisions are difficult to oversee and particularly to challenge. In addition, the decisions are likely to reflect the capacity of the individuals concerned, and the extent of information available to them, rather than the presence or absence of defined circumstances.

A formal legal requirement to consider and justify the use of framework agreements procedures can be imposed through prescribing 'conditions for use' of the technique, as the Model Law does. Unless the conditions are present, a framework agreement procedure cannot be used. The conditions for use are that framework agreements may be used where the procuring entity determines that '(a) the need for the subject-matter of the procurement is expected to arise on an indefinite or repeated basis during a given period of time, or (b) by virtue of the nature of the subject-matter of the procurement, the need for that subject-matter may arise on an urgent basis during a given period of time'.[19] The Model Law also requires a justification of the type of framework agreement chosen, by reference to the relevant circumstances, further requiring a consideration of the main planning issues. (This requirement might in fact have been accidental.)[20]

---

[16] Serban Filipon, 'The Winding Road from Policy Objectives and Procedural Rules to Practical Reality – An Overview of Framework Agreements and Electronic Procurement under the New UNCITRAL Model Law', in *Public Procurement: Global Revolution VI Conference*, Nottingham, UK, 24–25 June 2013, at pp. 4–5.
[17] Desiderata, note 5, supra.
[18] Will the additional costs of a two-stage procedure will be recouped, and will an appropriate balance of administrative costs and value for money is likely to result?
[19] Article 32(1), Model Law, note 1, supra.
[20] It was initially suggested to exempt the provision from challenge (UN document A/CN.9/648, para 58, available at www.uncitral.org/uncitral/en/commission/working_groups/1Procurement.html), but, subsequently, UNCITRAL decided not to exempt any procurement decision from review (UN document A/CN.9/664, para 26, available as above).

# Legal and regulatory issues in framework agreements procedures 313

These conditions are self-evidently fuzzy, rather than fussy. As has been observed, an 'expectation' is undefined and is so subjective that the result may be little more than a box-ticking exercise[21] and to that extent may add an unnecessary administrative step (which would be particularly unwelcome in a technique founded on the notion of *reducing* administrative burdens, which is also not mentioned). In addition, the uncertainty means that legal enforcement would be difficult.

There are no equivalent restrictions in the European Union: Article 33(1) of the EU Directive states simply that 'Contracting authorities may conclude framework agreements' (provided certain procedural rules are met). In the United States, the Federal Acquisition Regulations (FAR) state that GSA and MAS contracts provide '[f]ederal agencies ... with a simplified process for obtaining commercial supplies and services at prices associated with volume buying'.[22] A similar approach is taken in some systems in Asia and Africa.[23]

It has been suggested that conditions of use can 'force a proper consideration of [the] issues',[24] but if the conditions are effectively unenforceable, they will have little impact. An alternative approach could be to follow the United States in setting out the main circumstances in which framework agreements can be used, as in Uganda,[25] and as the

---

[21] Guide to Enactment, note 1, supra, Commentary to Chapter VII of the Model Law, Introduction to Framework Agreements, para 17, p. 203. Procurement methods are listed under Article 27(1) of the Model Law, with the conditions in following articles, and explained in the Guide to Enactment's commentary to those articles.

[22] Federal Acquisition Regulation (FAR), Code of Federal Regulations (CFR) Title 48, 8.402. FAR 2005-83/07-02-2015, available at www.acquisition.gov/?q=browsefar.

[23] S. Karangizi, 'The use of framework agreements in Africa', Chapter 6 in S. Arrowsmith (ed.), *Public Procurement Regulation in the 21st Century: Reform of the UNCITRAL Model Law on Procurement* (Eagan, MN: West, 2009), at pp. 248–250.

[24] The Winding Road from Policy Objectives and Procedural Rules to Practical Reality – An Overview of Framework Agreements and Electronic Procurement under the New UNCITRAL Model Law, supra, note 16, at p. 3.

[25] The use of framework agreements in Africa, note 23, supra, at p. 247, referring to Article 58(c) of the Uganda Public Procurement and Disposal of Public Assets Act 2003, which provides that a procuring entity shall 'make use of framework contracts wherever appropriate to provide an efficient, cost effective and flexible means to procure works, services or supplies that are required continuously or repeatedly over a set period of time'. Regulations implementing the primary legislation allow the use of framework agreements (a) where a requirement is needed 'on call', but where the quantity and timing of the requirement cannot be defined in advance; or (b) to reduce procurement costs or lead times for a requirement which is needed repeatedly or continuously over a period of time by having them available on a 'call off' basis. Regulation 237. (1) of the PPDA Regulations, available at www.ppda.go.ug/dmdocuments/Regulations.pdf. Similar approaches are found elsewhere in Africa, and, indeed, in France before it adopted the EU Directives: single-supplier framework agreements ('split contracts') were 'exceptional' procedures available only when the rate of ordering or scope of requirements could not be completely defined for economic, technical or financial reasons and multi-supplier framework agreements were 'exceptional'

Model Law recommends for open framework agreements (which are intended to provide for commonly used, off-the-shelf goods or straightforward, recurring services that are normally purchased on the basis of the lowest price). This approach would also reduce the complexity of the decision-making process and make oversight mechanisms more likely to be effective.

The difficulties encountered in the United States in seeking to define 'commercial items' available for purchase under ID/IQs and in trying to keep up-to-date listed or defined products or services for which framework agreements are suitable, also indicate that *describing* circumstances rather than *defining* circumstances may be a more effective approach.[26] They can be combined with explanations of when framework agreements are clearly unsuitable. As UNCITRAL provides these circumstances include complex procurement, and highly technical or specialised items, for which the terms and conditions will vary for each purchase.[27] There is insufficient repetition in these procurements, and so administrative efficiencies are unlikely to arise. This approach recognises the reality that clear and unambiguous conditions for use are unlikely to be feasible in the framework agreements context.

Consequently, internal rules and guidance that set out the planning process may prove more effective accountability measures in practice. UNCITRAL's Model Law also requires the procuring entity to record 'a statement of the reasons and circumstances upon which it relied to justify the use of a framework agreement procedure',[28] which can form the basis of how the planning process is to be documented.

On the other hand, the procedures for awarding the framework agreement and issuing call-offs under it need to be clear and unambiguous, given that they will determine a contractual relationship between the procuring entity and suppliers. We saw in Chapter 5, for example, the EU and US provisions are relatively fuzzy as regards the call-off stage (though less so as regards the first stage). The Model Law, however, has

---

procedures in that their use was allowed only when further conditions were met – for example, certain types could be used only when no single supplier could fulfil the order; for reasons of security of supply; for reasons of volatility of prices or the rapid obsolescence of the requirement; and for reasons of urgency. See, also, L. Folliot-Lalliot, 'The French Approach to Regulating Frameworks under the New EC Directives', Chapter 4, in *Public Procurement Regulation in the 21st Century: Reform of the UNCITRAL Model Law on Procurement*, note 23, supra.

[26] See, further, Chapter 5.
[27] 'A Critical Evaluation of the Revised UNCITRAL Model Law Provisions on Regulating Framework Agreements', note 7, supra.
[28] Article 32(2), Model Law, note 1, supra.

*Legal and regulatory issues in framework agreements procedures* 315

more detail regarding the second-stage procedures: it sets out in detail the procedural steps to be followed, which suppliers can participate and on what terms and the contents of the solicitation (or procurement) documents.[29] A fuzzy element is that suppliers capable of fulfilling the needs of the procuring entity must be invited to participate in the call-off stage, unless all suppliers are so invited. Here, the Model Law addresses the uncertainty by requiring notice to all participating suppliers (and a public notice in the case of open framework agreements) announcing the call-off, so that excluded suppliers can request participation – an example of a middle way between fuzzy and fussy drafting. Nonetheless, supporting rules or guidance to ensure that the provision functions as intended will be needed – for example, that the restriction should be interpreted in a very narrow sense, taking into account the terms and conditions of the framework agreement and first-stage offers.

### 12.4.3 Regulation of and guidance on detailed aspects of framework agreements procedures

Elements of the regulatory system that require further regulation or guidance as compared with the provisions in the Model Law, and equally for other systems, include questions relating to the status of the framework agreement as a matter of contract law in enacting states. We saw in Chapter 5 that, whether or not the framework agreement may be a binding *contract* (a matter of locally applicable law), it may or may not be a *procurement contract* under the relevant law. If it is not, the procurement contract itself is issued *under* the framework agreement (even if it takes the form of a purchase order). Clarity on this aspect is vital, as we saw in Chapter 5, not least because it may determine which procedures and rules are applicable.

In addition, the enforceability of the framework agreement and whether it is 'binding' in the legal sense needs to be clear, as do any circumstances indicating that separate framework agreements are needed with different awardees. Separate agreements might be needed, for example, to accommodate intellectual property rights or where different licensing terms or where suppliers have submitted partial offers. Further, is the procuring entity (or procuring entities where the framework agreement is operated by a lead procuring entity or a centralised purchasing agency) bound to use it; and, if the framework is an open one, how will new joiners

---

[29] Articles 58–62, ibid.

become bound by its terms? As regards a centralised purchasing agency, is it a principal, or an agent, and how are contractual liabilities provided for among them?[30]

A second area is planning. Rules or guidance will need to address how to choose among the three models of framework agreements (if all three are available, as further discussed below), given the different ways in which competition operates in each type; and how narrowly the procurement need can and should be defined at the first stage (which will dictate the extent of competition that is possible and appropriate at the second stage).[31] The greater the extent of second-stage competition, the more administratively complex and lengthy the second-stage competition will be (and, by comparison, the simpler the first stage should be – such as is provided for in an open framework agreement), the less predictable the first-stage offers will be of the final result; this can make effective budgeting more difficult. Similarly, the advantages and disadvantages of single-supplier or multi-supplier and single-user and multi-user framework agreements should be considered in the circumstances at hand. Should the Model Law's conditions for use be enacted, additional regulations and guidance on how to interpret the term 'expectation' and how to assess in an objective manner the extent of likelihood of the anticipated need are required.

### 12.4.4 *Detailed design, planning and operational issues*

As we saw above, the main issues are addressed in the primary law, whether it is fussy or fuzzy. If the latter, more detail in regulations may be needed; in either case, additional issues will need rules and/or guidance. These issues include:

- For multi-supplier closed framework agreements, understanding whether setting either a minimum or a maximum number of awardees or both would be appropriate and, if so, what to consider in doing so.

---

[30] See, further, Chapter 11.
[31] As we have seen, if the needs can be precisely expressed and they will not vary during the life of the framework agreement, a framework agreement without second-stage competition will generally produce the best offers. However, this approach is inflexible and requires precise planning: precise specification and rigid standardisation may be difficult or inappropriate, especially in the context of centralised purchasing where the needs of individual purchasing entities may differ, and where the needs will probably vary over time such as in uncertain markets. If the procuring entity's needs may not vary, but the market is dynamic or volatile, second-stage competition will be appropriate unless the volatility is addressed in the framework agreement (such as through a price adjustment mechanism).

*Legal and regulatory issues in framework agreements procedures* 317

For example, a minimum number may be required to ensure security of supply; a sufficient number will be needed to ensure effective competition in a competitive call-off (and which can be included in the solicitation documents and framework agreement); but a maximum limit may be necessary to ensure that each awardee has a realistic chance of being awarded a contract under the framework agreement, and to encourage it to price its offer and to offer the best possible quality accordingly, as well as to avoid the need for the procurement official to evaluate large numbers of second-stage offers. Rules should address what should happen if the stated minimum is not achieved (e.g. the procuring entity can specify in the solicitation documents that it might cancel the procedure).

- Whether framework agreements will be operated centrally and/or electronically, and if e-reverse auctions are to be used at the call-off stage, whether to require that the entire framework be administered and operated through a central agency and/location (noting that doing so should also enhance transparency, efficiency and monitoring).
- How to address who may appropriately be included as potential users, require them to be notified of the existence of the framework agreement and consider whether there should be any requirements regarding the extent to which permitted users may or must in fact use existing framework agreements (to avoid over- or under-use).
- Assuming that a statutory maximum duration of the framework agreement is in place, how to decide on the appropriate duration on a case-by-case basis, and how to prevent abuse in extensions and exceptions to the initially-established duration, such as the award of a lengthy or sizeable contract towards the end of the validity of the framework agreement to avoid conducting a new procedure.
- How to address pricing in the framework agreement – prices at the first stage may not be realistic (if the goods or services are subject to price or currency fluctuations, the combination of service providers may vary); on the other hand, closed framework agreements with prices at hourly rates are generally relatively expensive, and task-based or project-based pricing may be more appropriate.
- Recalling that a major concern is how to balance issuing the best information that may elicit the best offers from suppliers, and the potential for collusion as we discussed in Chapters 8 and 9, lessons are likely to emerge – indicating that the primary law should be sufficiently flexible to allow for more dedicated rules and their amendment. That being so, the primary law should set out clearly the

transparency principles and that any exceptions to prevent collusion must be publicly stated.
- The EU Directive and Model Law establish limits to the permissible range of changes to terms and conditions of a framework agreement, and rules or guidance will be required to ensure that permissible changes are made in a transparent and predictable manner, and also to oversee flexible and varying evaluation or award criteria between the first and second stages. The design considerations include that functional or output-based specifications, with minimum technical requirements, will more easily allow subject matter modifications or technical substitutions, but raises the risk that the framework agreement may be used for administrative convenience beyond its intended scope, allowing non-transparent and non-competitive awards of procurement contracts.
- Ensuring that all operational and technical information for joining an open framework agreement is available on the website of the procuring entity, to allow prompt applications to participate. Call-off invitations should be in writing, issued simultaneously and automatically by the system to each awardee (or 'capable' awardee). Although there is no requirement to issue a general notice of the second-stage competition, placing a notice on the website would have the same effect, and may usefully support the general transparency provisions.
- Addressing time periods – deadlines for presenting second-stage offers, which in open framework agreements may be appropriate as hours or a couple of days, but in paper-based closed agreements may need considerably longer, standstill periods likewise.
- Many systems limit users of framework agreements to the 'original parties'; while the EU Directive, for example, has limited rules on replacements, other issues such as whether joint ventures formed at the call-off stage are permitted should be addressed – including the fact that some joint ventures may be set up to *avoid* competition.

Finally, a robust system for gathering and analysing data on the operation of framework agreements, particularly where centrally operated, is unlikely to be addressed in the formal legal rules but, as we have seen, is a central plank for assessing whether the potential benefits are materialising in practice, as well as allowing for over- or under-use to be identified.

There is self-evidently no clear dividing line between what should be contained in rules or guidance on the above issues. As in the procurement system as a whole, the extent of discretion and rule-bound stages will need to reflect the capacity of the users and overall robustness of the system. As can be seen, there are many detailed issues that are clearly unsuitable for formal rules and where the appropriate discretion/control balance may lie may differ between procuring entities in one system, indicating that internal rules and guidance may be appropriate.

## 12.5 Avoiding over- and under-use of framework agreements

We saw in Chapter 5 that over-use of framework agreements reflecting their administrative convenience is a real risk in practice, and also that over-use is unlikely to be challenged.[32] Rules or guidance limiting the use of existing framework agreements, by reference to the terms and conditions of the agreements themselves – such as requiring a certain level of specificity in descriptions as the Model Law does, commitment levels and on interpretation of requirements that are drafted in relatively broad terms can be helpful, particularly to prevent out-of-scope orders being placed under framework agreements. An additional example is the risk of distorting competition in the market by placing large call-offs shortly before the end of the term of a framework agreement, which is not regulated in detail in the EU Directive and not regulated in the Model Law. The rules or guidance will need to be sufficiently flexible to allow for necessary extensions – for example, where they might offer better value than conducting a new procurement procedure – and could draw on the EU Directive's approach to review clauses in framework agreements.[33]

On the other hand, there is some emerging indication of under-use of concluded framework agreements, particularly in the United Kingdom, as a result of a proliferation of overlapping framework agreements without binding commitments. In essence, under-use may reflect procuring entities' ability to shop around various framework agreements providing the same or similar products or services. As a result, suppliers appear to be incurring significant costs in responding to invitations to participate at the first stage of framework agreements procedures, without then receiving a level of call-offs to recoup those costs; these suppliers are then are

---

[32] Daniel I. Gordon and Jonathan L. Kang, 'Task-Order Contracting in the U.S. Federal System: The current System and Its Historical Context', chapter 5, in *Public Procurement Regulation in the 21st Century: Reform of the UNCITRAL Model Law on Procurement*, note 23, supra.
[33] Article 33, EU Directive, note 1, supra.

disinclined to participate in subsequent invitations for framework agreements.[34] The situation also indicates less-than-optimal administrative efficiency: procuring entities may be setting up more framework agreements than necessary, and wasting administrative time and costs for themselves and suppliers.

Thus, from a policy perspective, there is a need to encourage the appropriate level of use of a framework agreement procedure – enough to amortise the costs of setting up the two-stage procedure and to yield economies of scale, but not at a level that indicates inappropriate use or probable underuse, or a level that may negatively affect longer-term competition (if suppliers are excluded from a significant section of the market). Consequently, periodic review of the extent and scope of use should be undertaken.[35]

## 12.6 Avoiding excessive complexity in decision taking

On this question, the first and second stages of a framework agreement procedure require separate but related treatment. The first stage, at which major planning and design decisions to set the terms for the entire duration of the framework agreement are required, is a complex one as the previous section indicates, and it should also form part of the decision as to whether to set up a framework agreement at all.[36]

Good design at the first stage is also critical to mitigate the operational risks at the second, as we have seen in Chapter 10. The planning process, and setting the terms and call-offs at the second stage, should be designed to secure competition and transparency throughout the procedure, as we saw in Chapter 9.

However, this process should exempt the users of framework agreements – the procurement officials – from needing to design procedures at the second stage. In other words, care is needed to avoid the 'accretion of ... options [making] the ... system as a whole incredibly complex',[37] a risk that is all too

---

[34] Procurement Lawyers Association, 'The use of framework agreements in public procurement', March 2012, available at www.procurementlawyers.org/pdf/PLA%20paper%20on%20Frameworks%20PDF%20Mar%2012.pdf, at p. 13.

[35] 'Task-Order Contracting in the U.S. Federal System: The Current System and Its Historical Context', note 32, supra.

[36] A. Sanchez-Graells, *Public Procurement and the EU Competition Rules*, 2nd ed. (Oxford, Hart, 2015), at pp. 294–296; 'Regulating Framework Agreements under the UNCITRAL Model Law', ch. 2, in *Public Procurement Regulation in the 21st Century: Reform of the UNCITRAL Model Law on Procurement*, note 23, supra; 'A Critical Evaluation of the Revised UNCITRAL Model Law Provisions on Regulating Framework Agreements', note 7, supra.

[37] J. I. Schwartz, 'Katrina's Lessons for Ongoing US Procurement Reform Efforts', *Public Procurement Law Review*, 15 (2006): 362–373, at p. 373.

evident should users of framework agreements be required to assess all the variables described above at the second stage. If the planning process is effective, implementing appropriate levels of competition and transparency at the second stage need not be administratively cumbersome.

This reflects a key requirement for the second stage of the procedure – that is, using a framework agreement once established should involve a simple, rapid and efficient process. Users will be focussing on meeting their needs with as little procedural formality as possible. Thus, for example, the design variables that are fixed and those that can be competed at the second stage should be determined at the first stage, so that the information needed to be submitted and evaluated at that stage is limited. Consequently, the time frame for submitting bids and other procedural steps in competitive call-offs can and should be reduced significantly compared with a traditional bidding procedure. A simple and efficient second stage may be most effectively achieved using a simple lowest-price approach or one involving simple, quality criteria that are easily monetised, rather than on more complex quality criteria.

Most systems envisage the use of all models of framework agreements that we have considered, but there are some systems that offer a more restricted approach – for example, where only multi-supplier frameworks are provided for[38] – perhaps because the potential benefits of single-supplier frameworks are considered not to justify the additional complexity that the system requires to accommodate them.[39] In addition, some systems have included a statutory preference in favour of framework agreements for selected types of procurement.[40]

In this regard, care is needed to avoid over-burdening the procurement official with choices. Reforms in the US system (which we described in Chapter 5), while designed to offer a simplified contracting mechanism optimised for different procurement circumstances (by carving out 'specific areas in which a less rigidly structured system of competitive procurement may be desirable'),[41] in aggregate appear to offer too many

---

[38] Examples include Regulating Framework Agreements under the UNCITRAL Model Law, note 27, supra.
[39] 'A Critical Evaluation of the Revised UNCITRAL Model Law Provisions on Regulating Framework Agreements', note 7, supra.
[40] According to 'Task-Order Contracting in the U.S. Federal System: The current System and Its historical context', note 32, supra, at p. 226, 'Under the FAR provisions that implement FASA, a contracting officer must, to the maximum extent practicable, give preference during acquisition planning to multiple awards of ID/IQ contracts under a single solicitation for the same or similar supplier or services [footnote omitted]'.
[41] 'Katrina's Lessons for Ongoing US Procurement Reform Efforts'. note 37, supra.

overlapping options to procurement officials.[42] This may have practical consequences: If they are required to justify using existing framework agreements rather than other simple and low-value procurement methods, or choosing among framework agreements, the administrative efficiency may be compromised. On the other hand, a lack of justification and control may encourage over-use of less suitable framework agreements for administrative convenience.

For policymakers, therefore, the options available for purchasing the simple, low-value and relatively straightforward types of goods and services that a framework agreement is most suited to need to be considered as a whole (including procurement methods such as request-for-quotations, single-source procurement, e-catalogues and e-reverse auctions) to ensure that there are as few overlapping methods as possible. This may indicate a phased approach to the introduction of framework agreements procedures (starting with only one model, for example), and expanding the options as experience is accumulated if it is considered warranted. An element of the ongoing revisions may be to remove some procurement methods – request-for-quotations, for example, and restricted tendering where it is permitted on the basis that the time and cost required to examine and evaluate a large number of tenders would be disproportionate to the value of the procurement.[43] In addition, the use of illustrative lists can make certain elements of the decision-making process easier.

Balancing the design of a complex procurement tool at the first (i.e. planning) stage with ease of use at the second (i.e. implementation and use) stage is a key distinction in framework agreements procedures, and one that is not regularly encountered elsewhere in procurement practice. Effective user manuals addressing the issues set out in this chapter can collate all levels of regulation and guidance thematically, further allowing the procurement official to focus on the decisions to be taken rather than identifying various sources of these elements of the framework.

## 12.7 Chapter summary

- We have seen that ensuring effective competition is a key concern in framework agreements procedures, especially at the second stage. Requirements for practical measures to promote competition, in almost all cases, need to be strengthened through including requirements applicable to other procurement tools and techniques.

[42] Ibid., at p. 373.   [43] Model Law Article 20(1)(b), note 1, supra.

## Legal and regulatory issues in framework agreements procedures 323

- Transparency requirements, which are in many cases largely absent from the second stage, are a case in point.
- Framework agreements need to be a flexible tool, and easy to use at the second stage. The key to ensuring these qualities is detailed planning at the first stage – involving design and market considerations – reflecting that demand is being aggregated, so that the overall value of the contracts is significant.
- To assist in these areas, the regulatory system needs to provide rules and guidance to supplement primary law and regulations, in more detail than many systems currently do.
- The entire regulatory framework needs to be clear and accessible – whether the rules themselves are expressed in fuzzy or fussy language.
- There may be benefits in using fuzzy language in the primary law to set out the main principles and procedures and using more fussy (i.e. detailed) language in lower orders of rules.
- Policymakers should take into consideration that the decision-making process for individual procurements of relatively simple and low-value goods and services should itself be simple and straightforward.

# Conclusions

Public procurement policy and practice have undergone profound changes over the past two decades – moving from a clerical, box-ticking, tightly regulated activity to developing the function of procurement professionals, charged with achieving a variety of strategic goals. While commentators differ about the relative priority of some of the goals themselves, there is a broad acceptance of the importance of the economic goals – allocating public resources efficiently and delivering value to the taxpayer. There is also an international consensus about the importance of avoiding abuse and corruption. More recently, there is an emerging view (though not a consensus) that public procurement systems provide an effective tool for pursuing a heterogeneous array of socially relevant objectives. Often, unfortunately, policy debates tend to focus on how to expand the list of objectives rather than on how to assess to what extent these agreed objectives might be compatible with each other.

In light of such a multifaceted and evolving environment, we are left wondering what features would define a *sound* procurement system. Without pretending to paint a comprehensive picture, we can assert that two principal conditions need to be fulfilled: 'a) the system comprises decision centres setting possibly multiple and non-contradictory objectives, and periodically assessing whether the system works coherently with those objectives; b) the system works according to a set of processes that maximize the likelihood of reaching the system's objectives while minimising the use of resources'.[1]

Clearly this methodological approach is apposite for framework agreements: what are the underlying objectives for using these purchasing arrangements? How are the overarching regulatory rules defined? What

---

[1] The two conditions are borrowed from G. L. Albano, 'Public Procurement Performance Measurement', discussion paper prepared for the *OECD Meeting of Leading Practitioners on Public Procurement*, 2012, available at http://search.oecd.org/officialdocuments/publicdisplaydocumentpdf/?cote=GOV/PGC/ETH(2013)1&docLanguage=En.

would characterise good design of framework agreements? It would be both inappropriate and risky to provide a complex set of purchasing solutions – which framework agreements clearly are – to procuring entities without providing them with the necessary tools to implement and use them successfully.

We have sought to provide a toolbox to this end in this book. Throughout our journey, while setting out possible solutions to concrete problems, new questions have emerged, proving that the complexity of real-world cases often overcomes the theoretical concepts. At the same time, though, we have arrived at a set of conceptual milestones and practical guidelines that we shall attempt to encapsulate in these final considerations.

### Why framework agreements?

Public procurement, with limited exceptions, involves repeated purchases of similar items. While the time between repetitions may vary – compare basic IT equipment with the redesign of an IT system – it is clear that there will be administrative gains from aggregating the purchases, so that some of the procedural steps can be carried out once for the entire series. This is the main justification for framework agreements – and they have the potential to confer benefits not only to procuring entities but also to suppliers.

A significant implication is that the planning process needs to address the entire series of purchases, and therefore will be much more complex than that required for – to take a simple example – a dozen laptops. Nonetheless, with effective planning, the benefits are not merely administrative – economies of scale will (or should) be reflected in lower prices and/or a better price-quality ratio. However, before procurement officials are tempted to use framework agreements for nearly all procurements, a caveat is in order. Their needs will be similar, but not identical (if only because delivery quantities and locations vary). Here, there is a significant challenge for our procurement official – a sort of reverse inductive reasoning process is required, in that he or she needs to foresee all relevant and reasonably predictable scenarios well in advance if the potential benefits are to materialise. Our analysis in Part I of the book identified some of the economic forces at play when analysing needs and markets and how they may be accommodated in different types of framework agreements.

We examined, too, the important reality that there are many types of framework agreements. Framework agreements are not just useful for enhancing administrative efficiency and – with appropriate planning – yielding better value for money, but procuring entities also can use them to insure, in effect, against adverse events such as disruptions of supply or natural disasters, where some essential supplies – such as medicines – might otherwise be available only at exorbitant prices. Here, the goal is to secure a ready supply – perhaps through source diversification. A further scenario is that simple and low-value procurement is often undertaken 'below the radar' using unstructured and non-transparent procurement methods, whose results are regularly questioned. While the individual case may have limited economic impact, the aggregate value may be significant. Framework agreements can aggregate these purchases so that the benefits of open, transparent competition can be obtained without the disproportionate administrative burden that the procedures involved would impose on each purchase. Thus, there are different types of framework agreements suitable for different circumstances. We have classified the main variants as 'models' (of which there are three), and, within those models, there are many other variables.

Clearly in these different cases, the primary motivator is different – and so may be the extent of competition, reflected in price and quality outcomes, that can be expected. Seeking supply diversification and readiness is akin to *buying* an insurance: a certain class of risks is transferred from the procuring entity to suppliers. Where the primary motivator is aggregation, the procuring entity is basically *selling* to a possibly restricted subset of competing firms the right to be the sole contender or limited group of contenders for a stream of contracts, who will then be able to sell to the procuring entity without being threatened by outside competitors. All other things being equal, price competition should be more intense in this latter case.

We started these conclusions by recalling the now-common use of public procurement for strategic ends. Bundling low-value procurement contracts together should lead to many immediate benefits to the procuring entity, but may run headlong into other government policy objectives. Bundling involves larger contracts, which by definition are less accessible to SMEs. We identified some approaches that can mitigate the effect – such as dividing the purchases under a framework agreement into smaller lots – but these approaches are generally more administratively time-consuming and complex, with potentially lower economies of scale, than larger contracts.

### The nature of competition in 'framework agreement' markets

The question of market access is likely to be thrown into stark relief where centralised purchasing agencies take over the procurement of commonly used goods and services. The international experience we have surveyed indicates that many such agencies use framework agreements in which a single supplier is awarded the contract to fulfil the entire need over a defined period, on preset terms and conditions (which we have classified as a single-supplier Model 1 framework agreement). The effect is that all the competition is concentrated into one single process that will favour larger suppliers to an even greater extent. While this is not a new procurement issue – large-scale contracts of this type have existed for decades – the centralisation process means that the scale of the potential problem is greater. In addition, the process introduces inefficiencies in terms of knowledge transfer and has the potential to reduce the extent to which procuring entities' precise needs are met.

The effect is that competition concerns are becoming more of an issue. The centralisation strategy may involve a 'winner-takes-all' result, with the consequence that some suppliers that do not win contracts leave the market. Concentration in the market may result in more anti-competitive behaviour and make the behaviour more likely to be successful, so that the interaction between procurement and competition policymakers and enforcement agencies becomes an important resource for mitigating the risks concerned.

Our analysis in Part II of the book demonstrated that framework agreements may give rise to new forms of competition. From the supplier perspective, it is often assumed that suppliers in fact compete for the opportunity to sell as much as possible to the government purchaser. As with many economic assumptions, it bears closer examination. Where there will be a fixed number of suppliers admitted to the framework agreement – determined in advance by the procuring entity – some suppliers may price their offers at a level that they hope will admit them to the framework agreement but yield few relatively profitable contracts. Others may price their offers more competitively, with the hope that they will win more contracts with a lower profit margin. The design of the procedure – how many 'prizes' or places on the framework agreement, the evaluation criteria and the number of potential suppliers – will all affect bidding strategies, which indicates just how sensitive an understanding of the underlying market and economic forces needs to be.

Furthermore, the potential for anti-competitive behaviour should also be borne in mind. Such behaviour is a known structural weakness in public procurement markets, but some types of framework agreements – which we have classified as 'closed' in that the awardees are selected at one point and from that point on are fixed – may allow suppliers to implement a market-sharing agreement. As we have seen, within those closed framework agreements, one simple award mechanism (procurement contracts being awarded according to a predetermined rotation mechanism) is the most at-risk variant.

Nonetheless, in models of framework agreement that are concluded with a limited sector of the market – say three out of twenty suppliers – there may be fierce competition to be admitted to the framework agreement, but thereafter, the competitive impetus may completely disappear. So an innocent reader may see a competitive process but overlook the awardees' incentive to coordinate their strategies thereafter. Our survey of international experience also indicates that procurement and competition authorities may not undertake the comprehensive analysis of both stages of the process that tackling this problem requires.

## The challenge of framework agreements design

The above summary highlights that framework agreements raise almost the entire gamut of procurement challenges, and, as ever in the public procurement world, competing considerations are at play. Despite the reports of cartels constantly lurking over framework agreements, the picture is not as gloomy as it may appear. In Part III of the book, we strive to provide guidance to both policymakers and procurement practitioners seeking to overcome the myriad challenges. The former need to provide clear and flexible regulatory architectures to allow procuring entities to adopt a trial-and-error approach, experiment with solutions and adapt them to outcomes and evolving circumstances. The latter are always looking for a down-to-earth methodology to follow the complexity and the subtleties of framework agreements design. As always in procurement design, there is no right answer, and the devil is in the details.

We also addressed a special 'class' of procurement practitioners in our comments; namely, those working for centralised procurement agencies. Centralisation is gaining ground in many regulatory environments. While there exist sensible reasons for establishing a separate entity in charge of aggregating public demand for goods and services, the potential benefits might be dwarfed by the emergence of countervailing disadvantages. Most important among them are the potentially diverging objectives between the centralised purchasing agency itself and the procuring entities it serves, and a low degree of commitment on both sides of the procurement market to trade inside rather than outside framework agreements.

Effective centralised procurement strategies will require an increasingly specialised workforce as well as specialisation in tasks between different parts of the public sector. Much information needs to be gathered, organised and analysed. In particular, data about demand and market characteristics, the terms of tenders and contractors' prior performance have to be collected and interpreted so as to undertake the more challenging step forward in the construction of modern procurement systems: performance measurement.

## The road ahead: measuring performance of framework agreement solutions

We return to the starting point of these final considerations: How do we measure whether a public procurement system is sound? The importance of the task has recently been confirmed by the OECD Recommendation of the Council on Public Procurement, particularly where it recommends:

> that Adherents drive performance improvements through evaluation of the effectiveness of the public procurement system from individual procurements to the system as a whole, at all levels of government where feasible and appropriate.[2]

Interestingly, the recommendation points towards measuring the performance of the whole system as well as that of the individual procuring entities operating within it. Hence, we can rephrase the above question at the level of the procuring entity: How do we measure the performance of *framework agreements solutions*?

There are at least three main dimensions that may be relevant for any measurement endeavour: process efficiency, value for money and the effectiveness of any secondary or horizontal objectives being pursued.

The first dimension requires us to ask ourselves whether the overall amount of organisational and human resources engaged is reduced when bundling several procurement contracts into one framework agreement. This is far from being a trivial exercise even in the case of a single procuring entity. It becomes challenging when a centralised purchasing agency is set up and generates all new costs for the system as a whole.

The second dimension – enhancing value for money – is often considered to be the primary objective of public procurement systems. Even adopting a

---

[2] The recommendation can be downloaded from www.oecd.org/gov/ethics/Recommendation-on-Public-Procurement.pdf.

narrow stance towards the concept of value for money and thus limiting our attention to savings, how can we measure savings from, say, centralised public procurement? Centralised procurement agencies at the national level in many countries report positive savings, although it is far from being clear what methodologies are adopted and whether they are similar to or compatible with each other.

Finally, how to measure the performance of framework agreements with respect to horizontal or secondary considerations, particularly pro-SME policies, may be the most difficult challenge of all. Not all policymakers consider that the public procurement system should be used in this manner (though it is a declared objective in both the EU and US federal systems), and the divergence of views is reflected in suggestions about how to measure performance. What would a benchmark of the SMEs' production share in the economy as a whole tell us?

## Policy and regulatory implications

In the final chapter, we have outlined some thoughts about how regulation of framework agreements might be undertaken (and, in some cases, improved) in light of the varied and complex issues of policy and practice that framework agreements pose. It may not be an exaggeration to say that they are among the most challenging aspects in the public procurement of the twenty-first century – framework agreements may account for more than a third of expenditure in public procurement in some systems (meaning, in very broad terms, we may be discussing 5 per cent of GDP in those systems). The need to 'get it right', as the US reforms in the mid-2000s were termed, not only gives us some insightful food for thought but, we hope, will spur policymakers, practitioners and, possibly, academics, into action on one of the most internationally relevant issues in public procurement.

# Glossary of commonly used terms that vary among systems

| Terms used in this book | Common synonyms |
| --- | --- |
| Bid | Tender, offer |
| Centralised purchasing agency | Centralised purchasing body |
| Closed framework agreement (see Chapter 2) | Framework agreement |
| Construction | Works |
| Evaluation criteria | Award criteria |
| Framework agreement | Indefinite-delivery, indefinite-quantity contract |
|  | Task-and-order contract |
| Goods | Supplies, products |
| Most economically advantageous tender (MEAT) | Most advantageous tender, lowest evaluated tender, best-value bid/offer |
| Open framework agreement (see Chapter 2) | Dynamic purchasing system |
| Procurement contract | Contract, public contract |
| Procuring entity | Contracting authority |
|  | Agencies |
| Qualification (identifying which suppliers are eligible and suitably qualified to sell to the procuring entity) | Selection |
| Request-for-quotations | Shopping |
| Second-stage (of a framework agreement procedure) | Call-off, task order |
| Selection (identifying the winning supplier) | Award |
| Single-source procurement | Direct contracting, direct award |
| Supplier | Bidder, economic operator, vendor |
| List of suppliers | Approved list, Preferred suppliers' list, Shortlist |

# Index

Africa, framework agreements in, 313–314
    in Ethiopia, 60, 144–147
        defined, 144
        federal PPPDS, 146
        Oromiya PPPDS, 144–145
aggregation rules
    CPAs and, 281–284, 285–286
    in EU Directive, 93–94
    in framework agreement procedures, 29–30
    in framework agreements, 5
    under UNCITRAL Model Law, 115, 116
all-purpose frame contracts (APFCs), 130–132
asymmetric competition, 197–198
auctions, 37
    electronic reverse, 199–201, 243–244
Australia
    panel arrangements in, 12
    panel contracts in, 44, 151–154
        establishment of, 151–152
        MULs compared to, 152–154
        open/closed, 152
average bid methods, 201–204
award criteria, 267–272
    for closed complete framework agreements, 268–270
    for closed incomplete framework agreements, 270–272
    item-by-item, 65
award notices, 229–233
awarding of contracts, 276–278. *See also* multi-award framework agreements; single-award framework agreements
    for closed complete framework agreements, 276–278
    for closed incomplete framework agreements, 278
    collusion issues and, 193–194, 195–196

bid rotation, 184–185
bid suppression, 184–185
bidders, 35, 38–40

bidding. *See also* bid-rigging schemes
    cover, 184–185
    joint, 194–195
bidding documents, 223–229
bidding notices, 229–233
bid-rigging schemes
    collusion through, 190–192, 245–250
    detection of, 245–250
    enforcement actions against, 250–251
    leniency programmes and, 250
    OECD strategies for, 214–215
    practical aspects of, 248–250
    pricing behaviours in, 247
    sanctions for, 250–251
    suspension measures, 251
    suspicious patterns in, 246–247
    through bid analysis, 246–248
    through data analysis, 246–248
    under UNCITRAL Model Law, 247–248
    unusual patterns in, 246
blanket purchase agreements (BPAs), 107
Brazil
    CPAs in, 135–138
    framework agreements in, 135–138
    PR system in, 135–138
        benefits of, 137–138
        inefficiencies of, 137–138
        institutions and assignments in, 136–137
bundling, 38
    in cascade method, 65
    in single-award agreements, 52–53
buying clubs, 7

call-offs, 195–204
Canada
    collusion cases in, 208–209
    standing offers in, 12, 14
cartels, collusion through, 185
cascade method, in closed complete framework agreements, 62–66, 276–277
    allocative efficiency, 63–64

## Index

applications of, 63–64
bundling in, 65
call-off stage, 63
item-by-item award criterion, 65
LP criterion, 65
catalogue contracts, 12
central procurement agencies, 40
centralised purchasing agencies (CPAs)
   APFCs and, 130–132
   closed incomplete framework agreements and, 129–132
   collusion with, 241
   commitment in, 287–291
     demand side, 288–291
     supply side, 291
   demand aggregation challenges for, 281–284, 285–286
   design of, 280–281
   in EU, 128–132
   funding of, 283–284
   GSA, 132–135
   in Italy, 128–129
   in Latin America, 135–143
     in Brazil, 135–138
     in Colombia, 142–143
   in OECD countries, 125–126, 127–128
   process costs for, 282–283
   procurement markets and, 286–287
   purpose of, 124
   role of centralisation in, 281–282
   simulated case study, 298–303
     centralisation strategies, 302–303
     demand side features, 298–299
     first-stage competition design, 300–301
     objectives of, 299
     procurement strategies, 299–300, 301–302
     second-stage competition design, 300–301
     supply side features, 299
   SMEs and, 292–297
     divisions of goods and services, 294–295
     geographical lots, 295–296
     turnover requirements, 297
   task specialisation in, 281–282
   in U.S., 132–135
Chile, CPAs in, 138–142
CICA. *See* Competition in Contracting Act
Clinger-Cohen Act, 103–104, 112–113
closed complete framework agreements (Model 1 framework agreements), 16–17, 52–69
   cascade method in, 62–66, 276–277
     allocative efficiency, 63–64
     applications of, 63–64
     bundling in, 65
     call-off stage, 63
     item-by-item award criterion, 65
     LP criterion, 65
   design of, 260–262
     award criteria, 268–270
     supply diversification in, 269–270
   as framework contract, 17
   multi-award agreements, 58–61
     economic rationale for, 59–60
     LP criterion, 59–60
     MEAT criterion, 59–60
     second-stage contracts, 60–61
   procuring entity needs in, 43
   random allocation in, 68–69
   regulatory systems for, 89
   rotation method, 66–67
     fixed shares, 67
     queuing, 66
   single-award agreements, 52–57
     adverse selection of users, 57
     bundling in, 52–53
     contract enforcement, 53–55
     degree of competition in, 55–56
     flexibility of, 57
     in Italy, 52, 54
     NFCs Monitoring System, 53–54
     standardisation of, 55
     transaction costs in, 52–55
   transparency requirements for, 225–227
closed incomplete framework agreements (Model 2 framework agreements), 17–19, 69–77
   accommodation in procuring entity needs, 44–49
   collusion with, 186
   CPAs and, 129–132
   design of, 264–267
     award criteria for, 270–272
     awarding of contracts in, 278
     heterogeneity levels in, 264–266
     MEAT criterion in, 272–274
     non-price competition in, 267
     number of awardees, 266
     price competition in, 267
   effective competition for, 168–172
   flexibility of, 170
   in India, 151
   in Italy, 129–132
   multi-award agreements, 69–70
     award criteria, 72–76
     competition in, 72–76
     evaluation criteria, 72–76
     MEAT criterion, 75
     standardisation of, 70
     two-stage competition, 70–71
     under UNCITRAL Model Law, 72

closed incomplete (cont.)
  regulatory systems for, 89
  single-award agreements, 76–77
    for chemical reagents, 77
    standardisation of, 77
  transparency requirements for, 170–172, 225–227
  under UNCITRAL Model Law, 170–172
  UNCITRAL recommendations, 19
closed panel contracts, 152
collusion, 180
  through barriers to entry, 186–188
  bid rotation, 184–185
  bid suppression, 184–185
  through bid-rigging schemes, 190–192, 245–250
  in Canadian cases, 208–209
  through cartels, 185
  with closed incomplete framework agreements, 186
  in concentrated markets, 186–188
  corruption through, 180
  cover bidding, 184–185
  with CPAs, 241
  demand factors for, 184–192
  through demand fragmentation, 189–190
  through demand predictability, 188–189
  through design issues, 237–245
    electronic reverse auctions, 243–244
    market access, 239–240
    predictability-related decisions, 240–243
  in EU cases, 182
  extant and effects of, 181–184
  through fixed quantities, 189
  framework agreement procedures and, 192–204
    asymmetric competition and, 197–198
    average bid methods, 201–204
    call-offs and, 195–204
    common components, 199–200
    degree of heterogeneity and, 196–197
    electronic reverse auctions, 199–201
    first stage of, 192–195
    information production, 200–201
    through joint bidding, 194–195
    number of awardees as factor in, 193–194, 195–196
    private components, 199–200
    rate contracts and, 196–197
    second stage of, 195–204
    sequence of contracts as factor in, 193–194
    symmetric competition and, 197–198
  through joint ventures, 241
  through lack of substitutes, 189
  in market allocation agreements, 184–185

  market predictability and, 188–192
  market stability and, 188–192
  markets structures for, 184–192
  in Mexico cases, 209
  through pre-bidding information, 217–218
  in private procurement markets, 183
  through procedural aspects, 190–192
  public procurement policy and, 181–183, 190–192, 221
  in rate contracts, 196–197, 206–208
  in repeated framework agreements, 204–205
  among suppliers, 181–184
  transparency paradox and, 216–219
  transparency requirements for, 190–192, 219–233
    through award notices, 229–233
    in bidding documents, 223–229
    through bidding notices, 229–233
    contract notices and, 221–223
    disclosure of public procurement law, 221
    in EU, 224–225, 227–228
    legal information for, 221
    non-disclosure issues, 234–237
    prior announcements and, 221–223
    in solicitation documents, 223–229
    under UNCITRAL Model Law, 223–224, 227–228, 229–233, 234–237
    in U.S., 225
  in U.K. cases, 182–183, 235
  under UNCITRAL Model Law, 219, 229–233
  in U.S. cases, 209–210
  in World Bank projects, 210
Colombia, CPAs in, 142–143
commercial-off-the-shelf (COTS) items, 103–104, 175–177
commitment
  in CPAs, 287–291
    demand side, 288–291
    supply side, 291
  in mandatory framework agreements, 292
competition, in framework agreement procedures, 32–34, 326–328. *See also* effective competition
  asymmetric, 197–198
  economic benefits of, 157–158
  in hybrid models, 80
  for ID/IQ contracts, 108–112, 159–160
  incentivisation of, 32
  information and, 38–40, 41
    for bidders, 38–40
    contract (in)completeness, 40
    about demand characteristics, 38–40
    Winner's Curse, 39
  innovation through, 158
  in MAS contracts, 108

# Index

in multi-award agreements, 72–76, 198, 202
for open and incomplete agreements, 77–79
in procurement markets, 32
product improvement through, 158
public procurement policy and, 32, 33–34
in rate contracts, 80
in single-award agreements, 55–56
symmetric, 197–198
threats to, 158–161
transaction costs, 40–41
transparency requirements, 33
under UNCITRAL Model Law, 32–33, 121–123
Competition in Contracting Act (CICA), 100–101
concentrated markets, collusion in, 186–188
Consip. *See* Italy
contract (in)completeness, 40
contract notices, 221–223
contract tasks, 36
contractor team arrangements (CTAs), 107
corruption, 180
through collusion, 180
COTS items. *See* commercial-off-the-shelf items
cover bidding, 184–185
CPAs. *See* centralised purchasing agencies
CTAs. *See* contractor team arrangements

delivery-order contracts, 15
demand and market analysis, 34–49
defined, 34
heterogeneity in, 39–40
of procurement markets, 34–49
accommodation of needs, 44–49
bidders, 35
bundling in, 38
in closed complete framework agreements, 43
in closed incomplete framework agreements, 44–49
contract tasks in, 36
efficiency in, 35–36
framing entity needs, 41–44
information in, 38–40, 41
in Italy, 47
KONEPS e-shopping mall, 43
under Model Law, 43
NHS Estate Procure 21, 43
of price, 37–38
product differentiation in, 37–38
production costs, 36
of quality, 37–38
requirements contract, 42
demand fragmentation, 189–190
demand predictability, 188–189
demand side commitment, 288–291

Denmark, term contracts in, 92
design, of framework agreements
for alternative procurement strategy, 258
award criteria, 267–272
for closed complete framework agreements, 268–270
for closed incomplete framework agreements, 270–272
awarding of contracts, 276–278
for closed complete framework agreements, 276–278
for closed incomplete framework agreements, 278
basic aspects of, 256–259
challenges of, 328–329
for closed complete framework agreements, 260–262
award criteria, 268–270
awarding of contracts in, 276–278
supply diversification in, 269–270
of closed incomplete framework agreements, 264–267
award criteria for, 270–272
awarding of contracts for, 278
heterogeneity levels in, 264–266
MEAT criterion in, 272–274
non-price competition in, 267
number of awardees, 266
price competition in, 267
collusion through, 237–245
electronic reverse auctions, 243–244
market access, 239–240
predictability-related decisions, 240–243
for CPAs, 280–281
demand heterogeneity, 257
demand side, 257–259
legal and regulatory systems in, 316–319
main drivers of, 256–259
for multi-award agreements, 263–264
process costs, 258–259
procurement cycle, 258
of SLAs, 258
splitting of procurement lots, 274–275
supply diversification, 257–258
supply side, 256
Directorate General of Supplies and Disposal (DGS&D), 148–149
Dynamic Purchasing System (DPS), 47
in EU Directive, 98–100

effective competition
barriers to entry, 161–165
for closed incomplete framework agreements, 168–172
contracting authorities and, 168–169

effective competition (cont.)
  defined, 157
  disclosure of terms and conditions for, 165–168
  under EU Directive, 161–162
  flexibility in, 166
  under GPA, 161–162
  GSA and, 171
  for ID/IQ contracts, 171
  MAS contracts, 171
  for open incomplete framework agreements, 168–172
  risk aversion for, 173–174
  for SMEs, 162–164
  statutory preferences for, 168
  threats to, 158–161
  transparency requirements for, 170–172
  under UNCITRAL Model Law, 161–162, 165–166
  wide participation as prerequisite for, 161–168
efficiency
  in cascade method, 63–64
  defined, 23
  of PR system, 137–138
  in procurement systems, 5, 22–24
efficiency, of procurement markets, 35–36
electronic reverse auctions, 199–201, 243–244
Ethiopia, framework contracts in, 60, 144–147
  defined, 144
  federal PPPDS, 146
  Oromiya PPPDS, 144–145
EU. *See* European Union
EU Directive
  aggregation rules in, 93–94
  DPS in, 98–100
  effective competition under, 161–162
  framework agreements under, 78
  hybrid models under, 80–81
  main procedures of, 93–97
    first stage, 95–96
    second stage, 96–97
  regulatory systems under, 86, 87–89, 91, 93–97
EU Remedies Directive, 91
European Commission, 90–91, 160–161
European Union (EU). *See also specific countries*
  classification of framework agreements in, 50
  collusion in, 182
    transparency requirements, 224–225, 227–228
  CPAs in, 128–132
  framework agreements in, 12–13
  multi-award framework agreements in, 58–61
    economic rationale for, 59–60
    LP criterion, 59–60
    MEAT criterion, 59–60
    second-stage contracts, 60–61

regulatory systems in
  in closed complete agreements, 89
  in closed incomplete agreements, 89
  defined, 91
  development of, 86–121
  DPS and, 98–100
  dynamic purchasing systems, 87–100
  early use of, 86–87
  under EU Directives, 86, 87–89, 91, 93–97
  under EU Remedies Directive, 91
  under European Commission, 90–91
  experience in use of, 97–100
  in open incomplete agreements, 89
  scope of provisions for, 90–93
  for term contracts, 92–93
  under UNCITRAL Model Law, 87, 92
single-award agreements in, 52–57
  adverse selection of users, 57
  bundling in, 52–53
  contract enforcement, 53–55
  degree of competition in, 55–56
  flexibility of, 57
  in Italy, 52, 54
  NFCs Monitoring System, 53–54
  standardisation of, 55
  transaction costs in, 52–55
under UNCITRAL Model Law, 114–121
  competition requirements, 121–123
  first stage of, 117–119
  second stage of, 119–121
  transparency requirements, 121–123

FAR. *See* Federal Acquisition Regulation
FASA. *See* Federal Acquisition Streamlining Act
Federal Acquisition Regulation (FAR), 42, 101
  reforms of, 112
Federal Acquisition Streamlining Act (FASA), 101
  reforms of, 112
Federal Supply Schedules (FSS) contracts, 104–108
  GSA and, 133
fixed shares, 67
flexibility
  of closed incomplete framework agreements, 170
  in effective competition, 166
  of framework agreements, 6–7
  of open incomplete framework agreements, 170
  in single-award agreements, 57
  of UNCITRAL Model Law, 118–119
framework agreement procedures. *See also* competition, in framework agreement procedures
  administrative efficiency, 22–24
  aggregation of procurement in, 29–30

# Index

collusion and, 192–204
  asymmetric competition and, 197–198
  average bid methods, 201–204
  call-offs and, 195–204
  common components, 199–200
  degree of heterogeneity and, 196–197
  electronic auctions, 199–201
  first stage of, 192–195
  information production, 200–201
  through joint bidding, 194–195
  number of awardees as factor in, 193–194, 195–196
  private components, 199–200
  rate contracts and, 196–197
  second stage of, 195–204
  sequence of contracts as factor in, 193–194
  symmetric competition and, 197–198
commercial purchasing, 175–176
common variables in, 21–22
COTS items, 175–176
enhancing outcomes in, 172–177
guidance on, 315–316
low-value procurement, 26–27
motivations for use of, 22–30
parallel, 204–205
process efficiencies of, 25
public procurement methods, 4–5, 26–27
regulation of, 315–316
repeated, 204–205
risk aversion for, 173–174
risk management in, 174–175
security of supply, 28–29
standardisation of, 25
urgent procurement methods, 25–26, 28
framework agreements, 12. *See also* closed complete framework agreements; closed incomplete framework agreements; design, of framework agreements; legal and regulatory systems, for framework agreements; multi-award framework agreements; open incomplete framework agreements; single-award framework agreements
  in Africa, 313–314
  aggregation of purchases in, 5
  in Brazil, 135–138
  buying clubs and, 7
  characteristics of, 12–16
  common criticisms of, 94–95
  common variables in, 20–22
  consensus on, 6
  demand and market analysis of, 34–49
  design issues for, 6
  in European Union, 12–13
  Federal Acquisition Regulation and, 15
  flexibility of, 6–7
  hybrid models, 79–81
    competition in, 80
    complete-but-amendable agreements, 80–81, 82
    EU Directive, 80–81
    rate contracts, 79–80
  identification stage in, 4
  incompleteness of, 50
  mandatory, 292
  multi-supplier, 29
  panel arrangements, 12
  performance measures for, 329–330
  procedural costs of, 4–5
  procuring entities in, 7, 20
  as public contracts, 91
  public officials and, 4–5
  in public procurement policy, 4–5, 26–27
  purpose of, 325–326
  single-supplier, 28–29
  SME participation, 29
  standing offers, 12, 14
  subject-matter of, 4
  suppliers and, 13–14
  taxonomy for, 16–20
  under UNCITRAL Model Law, 14
  in U.S., 15
framework contracts. *See also* multi-award framework agreements; single-award framework agreements
  in Ethiopia, 60, 144–147
  defined, 144
  federal PPPDS, 146
  Oromiya PPPDS, 144–145
FSS contracts. *See* Federal Supply Schedules contracts

General Services Administration (GSA), 70, 132–135
  effective competition and, 171
  FSS programme, 133
Government Wide Acquisition Contracts (GWACS), 104–108
GSA. *See* General Services Administration
GWACS. *See* Government Wide Acquisition Contracts

heterogeneity, in demand and market analysis, 39–40
hybrid models, 79–81
  competition in, 80
  complete-but-amendable agreements, 80–81
    for laptops, 82
    for photocopying machines, 81
  EU Directive, 80–81
  rate contracts, 79–80

ID/IQ contracts. *See* indefinite delivery/
	indefinite quantity contracts
IFFs. *See* industrial funding fees
indefinite delivery/indefinite quantity (ID/IQ)
		contracts, 12–13, 100–114
	under Clinger-Cohen Act, 103–104, 112–113
	commercial items in, 103
	competition for, 108–112, 159–160
	COTS items in, 103–104
	defined, 101
	effective competition for, 171
	FSS contracts, 104–108
	GSA and, 132–135
	GWACS contracts, 104–108
	incumbency issues, 110–111
	MAS contracts, 104–108
	minimum quantity in, 102
	misuse of, 111–112
	under NDAA, 113–114
	in practice, 108–112
	reforms for, 102–103, 112–114
	regulatory systems for, 100–114
	restrictions in, 102
	second-stage competition for, 171
	under Small Business Jobs Act, 114
	transparency requirements, 108–112
India, rate contracts in, 60, 147–151
	closed incomplete framework agreements, 151
	of DGS&D, 148–149
	open incomplete framework agreements, 151
	retail prices compared to, 150
	at state-level, 149–150
	under World Bank Procurement Guidelines, 150–151
industrial funding fees (IFFs), 135
information, competition in framework
		agreement procedures, 38–40, 41
	for bidders, 38–40
	contract (in)completeness, 40
	about demand characteristics, 38–40
	Winner's Curse, 39
innovation, through competition, 158
integrity
	collusion and, 180
	compromise of, 179–180
	corruption and, 180
Italy
	APFCs in, 130–132
	closed incomplete framework agreements in, 129–132
	collusion cases in, 182
	CPAs in, 128–129
	procurement markets in, 47
	single-award agreements in, 52, 54
item-by-item award criterion, 65

joint bidding, 194–195

Kelman, Steven, 112
KONEPS e-shopping mall, 43

Latin America
	CPAs in, 135–143
		in Brazil, 135–138
		in Chile, 138–142
		in Colombia, 142–143
	Mexico, collusion cases in, 209
legal and regulatory systems, for framework
		agreements
	avoidance of excessive complexity in, 320–322
	dedicated, necessity of, 306
	design of, 316–319
	elements of, 306–310
	in EU
		in closed complete agreements, 89
		in closed incomplete agreements, 89
		defined, 91
		development of, 86–121
		DPS and, 98–100
		dynamic purchasing systems, 87–100
		early use of, 86–87
		under EU Directives, 86, 87–89, 91, 93–97
		under EU Remedies Directive, 91
		under European Commission, 90–91
		experience in use of, 97–100
		in open incomplete agreements, 89
		scope of provisions for, 90–93
		for term contracts, 92–93
		under UNCITRAL Model Law, 87, 92
	formal rules in, 311–315
	guidance in, 311–315
	long-term implications for, 330
	operational issues in, 316–319
	for overuse of, 319–320
	policy statements, 311
	under UNCITRAL Model Law, 308–310
	for underuse of, 319–320
	in U.S.
		evolution of, 100–104
		ID/IQ contracts, 100–114
leniency programmes, 250
lowest price (LP) criterion, 59–60, 65
low-value procurement methods, 26–27
LP criterion. *See* lowest price criterion

mandatory framework agreements, 292
market access, collusion through, 239–240
market allocation agreements, 184–185
market analysis. *See* demand and market analysis
MAS contracts. *See* Multiple Award Schedules
		contracts

# Index 339

MEAT criterion. *See* most economically advantageous tender criterion
Mexico, collusion cases in, 209
Model 1 framework agreements. *See* closed complete framework agreements
Model 2 framework agreements. *See* closed incomplete framework agreements
Model 3 framework agreements. *See* open incomplete framework agreements
most economically advantageous tender (MEAT) criterion, 59–60, 75, 272–274
MULs. *See* multi-use lists
multi-award framework agreements
  assignment of awardees in, 263–264
  closed complete, 58–61
    economic rationale for, 59–60
    LP criterion, 59–60
    MEAT criterion, 59–60
    second-stage contracts, 60–61
  closed incomplete, 69–70
    award criteria, 72–76
    competition in, 72–76
    evaluation criteria, 72–76
    MEAT criterion, 75
    standardisation of, 70
    two-stage competition, 70–71
    under UNCITRAL Model Law, 72
  competition for, 72–76, 198, 202
  design of, 263–264
Multiple Award Schedules (MAS) contracts, 78–79
  competition requirements, 108
  CTAs, 107
  effective competition and, 171
  first stage procedures, 105–106
  ID/IQ contracts, 104–108
  IFFs in, 135
  open market items, 108
  second stage procedures, 106–108
  transparency requirements, 108
multi-supplier framework agreements, 29
multi-use lists (MULs), 152–154

National Defense Authorization Act (NDAA), 113–114
National Framework Contracts (NFCs) Monitoring System, 53–54
NDAA. *See* National Defense Authorization Act
the Netherlands, collusion cases in, 182
NFCs Monitoring System. *See* National Framework Contracts Monitoring System
NHS Estate Procure 21, 43

OECD countries. *See* Organisation for Economic Development countries
open incomplete framework agreements (Model 3 framework agreements), 19–20
  competition in, 77–79
  effective competition for, 168–172
  under EU Directive, 78
  flexibility of, 170
  in India, 151
  MAS contracts, 78–79
  regulatory systems for, 89
  transparency requirements for, 170–172, 225–227
  under UNCITRAL Model Law, 78, 170–172
open panel contracts, 152
open-tendering, 26–27
Organisation for Economic Development (OECD) countries
  bid-rigging schemes in, strategies against, 214–215
  CPAs in, 125–126, 127–128
  public procurement policy in, 84–85
Oromiya PPPDS, 144–145

panel arrangements, 12
panel contracts, 44, 151–154
  establishment of, 151–152
  MULs compared to, 152–154
  open/closed, 152
parallel framework agreements, 204–205
periodic requirements arrangements, 12
periodic/recurrent purchase arrangements, 12
PPPDS. *See* Public Procurement and Property Disposal Services
Price Registration (PR) system, 135–138
  benefits of, 137–138
  inefficiencies of, 137–138
  institutions and assignments in, 136–137
pricing
  in bid-rigging schemes, 247
  in closed incomplete framework agreement design, 267
  in India, rate contracts compared to retail prices, 150
  LP criterion, 59–60, 65
  in procurement markets, 37–38
private procurement markets, 183
  collusion in, 183
procedural costs, of framework agreements, 4–5
process costs
  for CPAs, 282–283
  in framework agreement design, 258–259
procurement markets
  competition in, 32
  CPAs and, 286–287

procurement markets (cont.)
  demand and market analysis of, 34–49
    accommodation of needs, 44–49
    bidders, 35
    bundling in, 38
    in closed complete framework agreements, 43
    in closed incomplete framework agreements, 44–49
    contract tasks in, 36
    efficiency in, 35–36
    framing entity needs, 41–44
    information in, 38–40, 41
    in Italy, 47
    KONEPS e-shopping mall, 43
    under Model Law, 43
    NHS Estate Procure 21, 43
    of price, 37–38
    product differentiation in, 37–38
    production costs, 36
    of quality, 37–38
    requirements contract, 42
  in Italy, 47
procuring entities
  in framework agreements, 7, 20
  low-value, 26–27
  urgent, 25–26, 28
public officials, framework agreements and, 4–5
Public Procurement and Property Disposal Services (PPPDS), 145, 146
public procurement policy
  administrative efficiency, 5, 22–24
  closed incomplete framework agreements and, 17–19
  collusion and, 181–183, 190–192, 221
  competition influenced by, 32, 33–34
  framework agreements in, 4–5, 26–27
  IDIQ contracts, 12–13
  long-term implications of, 330
  in OECD countries, 84–85
  open-tendering, 26–27
  purpose of, 3
  SMEs under, 162–164
  task-order contracts, 12–13
  UNCITRAL guidelines, 12–13

queuing, in rotation method, 66

random allocation, in closed complete framework agreements, 68–69
rate contracts. *See also* multi-award framework agreements
  collusion in, 196–197, 206–208
  competition in, 80
  defined, 147–148
  in hybrid models, 79–80

  in India, 60, 147–151
    closed incomplete agreements, 151
    of DGS&D, 148–149
    open incomplete agreements, 151
    retail prices compared to, 150
    at state-level, 149–150
    under World Bank Procurement Guidelines, 150–151
regulatory systems. *See* legal and regulatory systems, for framework agreements
repeated framework agreements, 204–205
requirements contract, 42
rotation method, 66–67
  fixed shares, 67
  queuing, 66

second-stage contracts, 60–61
service level agreements (SLAs), 258
single-award framework agreements, 52–57
  adverse selection of users, 57
  bundling in, 52–53
  in closed incomplete agreements, 76–77
    for chemical reagents, 77
    standardisation of, 77
  contract enforcement, 53–55
  degree of competition in, 55–56
  flexibility of, 57
  in Italy, 52, 54
  NFCs Monitoring System, 53–54
  standardisation, of closed incomplete agreements, 77
  standardisation of, 55
  transaction costs in, 52–55
single-supplier framework agreements, 28–29
SLAs. *See* service level agreements
small and medium enterprises (SMEs)
  CPAs and, 292–297
    divisions of goods and services, 294–295
    geographical lots, 295–296
    turnover requirements, 297
  effective competition for, 162–164
  in framework agreements, 29
Small Business Jobs Act, 114
SMEs. *See* small and medium enterprises
Smith, Adam, 179
solicitation documents, 223–229
standardisation
  of framework agreement procedures, 25
  of multi-award agreements, for closed incomplete framework agreements, 70
  single-award agreements
    for closed complete framework agreements, 55
    for closed incomplete framework agreements, 77

standing offers, 12, 14
suppliers
  collusion among, 181–184
  framework agreements and, 13–14
  multi-supplier, 29
  security of, 28–29
  single-supplier, 28–29
  under UNCITRAL Model Law, 115
supply side commitment, 291
supply vehicles, 12
symmetric competition, 197–198

task-order contracts, 12–13, 15
term contracts, 92–93
transaction costs
  of competition, 40–41
  in single-award agreements, 52–55
transparency paradox, 216–219
transparency requirements, 33
  for closed complete framework agreements, 225–227
  for closed incomplete framework agreements, 170–172, 225–227
  for collusion, 190–192, 219–233
    through award notices, 229–233
    in bidding documents, 223–229
    through bidding notices, 229–233
    contract notices and, 221–223
    disclosure of public procurement law, 221
    in EU, 224–225, 227–228
    legal information for, 221
    non-disclosure issues, 234–237
    prior announcements and, 221–223
    in solicitation documents, 223–229
    under UNCITRAL Model Law, 223–224, 227–228, 229–233, 234–237
    in U.S., 225
  defined, 213
  for effective competition, 170–172
  ID/IQ contracts, 108–112
  MAS contracts, 108
  for open incomplete framework agreements, 170–172, 225–227
  in UNCAC, 218–219, 220, 223
  under UNCITRAL Model Law, 116–117
Treaty on the Functioning of the European Union, 214

U.K. *See* United Kingdom
umbrella contracts, 12
UNCAC. *See* United Nations Convention against Corruption
UNCITRAL Model Law, 32–33
  aggregation rules in, 115, 116
  articles of, 114

bid-rigging schemes under, 247–248
closed incomplete framework agreements, 170–172
in closed incomplete framework agreements, 19, 72
collusion and, 219, 229–233
  transparency requirements, 223–224, 227–228, 234–237
development of, 6
effective competition under, 161–162, 165–166
estimates under, 118
framework agreements defined by, 14
in EU, 114–121
  competition requirements, 121–123
  first stage of, 117–119
  second stage of, 119–121
  transparency requirements, 121–123
flexibility of, 118–119
legal and regulatory systems under, 308–310
open incomplete framework agreements under, 78, 170–172
partial submissions and, 43
on procurement techniques, 12–13
policy objectives of, 115
public procurement policy guidelines, 12–13
regulatory systems under, 92
suppliers under, 115
transparency requirements, 116–117, 121–123
in U.S., 114–121
  competition requirements, 121–123
  first stage of, 117–119
  second stage of, 119–121
  transparency requirements, 121–123
United Kingdom (U.K.)
  collusion cases in, 182–183, 235
  term contracts in, 92
United Nations Convention against Corruption (UNCAC), 218–219, 220, 223
United States (U.S.)
  CICA in, 100–101
  collusion in, 209–210, 225
  COTS items in, 175–177
  CPAs in, 132–135
  FAR in, 15, 42, 101
  FASA in, 101
  framework agreements in, 15
  GSA in, 132–135
  ID/IQ contracts in, 12–13, 100–114
    under Clinger-Cohen Act, 103–104, 112–113
    commercial items in, 103
    competition for, 108–112, 159–160
    COTS items in, 103–104
    defined, 101
    FSS contracts, 104–108
    GWACS contracts, 104–108

United States (U.S.) (cont.)
  incumbency issues, 110–111
  MAS contracts, 104–108
  minimum quantity in, 102
  misuse of, 111–112
  under NDAA, 113–114
  in practice, 108–112
  reforms for, 102–103, 112–114
  regulatory systems for, 100–114
  restrictions in, 102
  under Small Business Jobs Act, 114
  transparency requirements, 108–112
MAS contracts, 78–79
  competition requirements, 108
  CTAs, 107
  first stage procedures, 105–106
  ID/IQ contracts, 104–108
  open market items, 108
  second stage procedures, 106–108
  transparency requirements, 108
regulatory systems in
  evolution of, 100–104
  ID/IQ contracts, 100–114
  under UNCITRAL Model Law, 114–121
    competition requirements, 121–123
    first stage of, 117–119
    second stage of, 119–121
    transparency requirements, 121–123
urgent procurement methods, 25–26
  security of supply in, 28

Wales, term contracts in, 92
*The Wealth of Nations* (Smith), 179
Winner's Curse, 39, 132
World Bank, 210
World Bank Procurement Guidelines, 150–151